BAY OF NAPLES & SOUTHERN ITALY

'Everyone in the empire, from Londinium to Baalbek, had heard of the bay and its prodigies of beauty and luxury...'

CADOGANguides

1 The Tyrrhenian coastline, Basilicata

2 The Duomo Cathedral bell tower (*campanile*), Piazza del Duomo, Amalfi
3 Majolica Cloister, Church of Santa Chiara, Naples, Campania
4 Greek temple ruins at Paestum, Campania
5 The coastal town of Monopoli, Puglia

35 MOSTRA DELLA CERAMICA

6 The Old Town, Piazza del Duomo, Cosenza, Calabria
7 Fresh local produce at a Pugliese market
8 Mussels (*mitili*) from the Mare Grande, Puglia
9 Fresh clams (*vongole*), Puglia
10 Streetside amphorae, Grottaglie, Puglia

11 The splendid glass-roofed arcade of Galleria Umberto I, Naples, Campania
12 The chaotic streets of Naples, Campania

FOTOCOPIE
ELIOGRAFIA
NEL PALAZZO
BAR
TRATTORIA
E. D'ANDREA
DISCHI
DI IMPORTAZIONE

13 The impressive Duomo Cathedral façade, Piazza del Duomo, Amalfi

14 Renaissance, Baroque and whitewashed buildings at Ostuni, Puglia
15 Original frescoes at Santa Maria di Idris, Matera, Puglia
16 The picturesque harbour at Procida, near Ischia

15

16

17

17 Flowers and plants cascading over limestone karsts at Capri, Campania

18 *Trulli* country, south of Bari

About the authors

Dana Facaros and **Michael Pauls** have lived all over Europe and have written over 40 books for Cadogan Guides. They currently live in an old Presbytère near the Lot.

About the updater

James Alexander has edited and contributed to a range of guidebooks for Cadogan. He is also author of Cadogan's forthcoming guide to *Malaysia & Singapore*. Southern Italy is James's favourite corner of Europe and this is the second time he has updated the Bay of Naples guide. When not on the move, he lives in Hastings with his wife and daughter.

Contents

Reference

Maps and Plans

Cadogan Guides
Network House, 1 Ariel Way,
London W12 7SL
info@cadoganguides.co.uk
www.cadoganguides.com

The Globe Pequot Press
246 Goose Lane, PO Box 480, Guilford,
Connecticut 06437–0480

Art direction: Sarah Rianhard-Gardner
Front cover: © Demetrio Carrasco/Jon Arnold
Photo essay: © John Ferro Sims
Maps © Cadogan Guides,
drawn by Map Creation Ltd
Managing Editor: Natalie Pomier
Editor: Anna Amari-Parker
Editorial Assistant: Nicola Jessop
Proofreading: Pat Bulhosen
Indexing: Isobel McLean
Production: Navigator Guides
Printed in Italy by Legoprint

A catalogue record for this book is available
from the British Library
ISBN 1-86011-184-X

Please help us to keep this guide up to date. We have done our best to ensure that the information in this guide is correct at the time of going to press. But places and facilities are constantly changing, and standards and prices in hotels and restaurants fluctuate. We would be delighted to receive any comments concerning existing entries or omissions. Authors of the best letters will receive a copy of the Cadogan Guide of their choice.

Introduction

The Italian south is one of the extremities of Europe, poised in a calm sea between the Balkans and the Sahara. And extremes are what this book is all about. On the one hand, the south is the home of many Italian stereotypes – pizza and pasta, piety and emigration. On the other, its history is so crowded with Greeks, Lombards, Byzantines, Saracens, Normans, Spaniards and such that there hardly seems room for the Italians.

Unlike other parts of Italy, the south is seldom a picture-perfect land of polished country landscapes and serene art towns. Its attractions may be equally compelling, but they always carry a touch of the exotic: the palm trees and whitewashed villages on the long Puglian shore, mirages and bergamots on the straits of Messina, Greek temples, Albanian villages, crusader ports.

A Guide to the Guide

The **History, Art and Architecture** and **Topics** chapters explore the influences that have shaped the area, from Magna Grecia to Mussolini. **Food and Drink** introduces the home of pasta and pizza, with an essential restaurant vocabulary. The **Travel** chapter includes details of getting to and around the region, plus special interest holidays. **Practical A–Z** covers everything else you need, from safety to the weather.

The book then explores southern Italy, starting with **Naples**. Love it or hate it, you can't avoid it, and a whole chapter is devoted to its peculiar madness.

The next three chapters deal with the area around Naples, which contains southern Italy's biggest tourist attractions: the **Bay of Naples**, the **Islands of the Bay** and, for the most memorable settings on Italy's coasts, the **Amalfi coast**. The following three chapters describe less-visited regions: the rest of **Campania**, rugged **Calabria** and the **Basilicata** and **Puglia**, with its medieval art and architecture.

The reference chapters at the end of the book include a **Further Reading** list, a **Glossary** of historical and architectural terms and some **Language** basics.

Highlights of the Region

Coast and Beaches

For classic Mediterranean scenery, the obvious places are the spectacular **Amalfi coast** or **Capri** and the other islands of the Bay of Naples. For coastal scenery, there's also the **Gargano** in Puglia and Campania's **Cilento coast**, while for beaches there's the 'Calabrian Riviera' around **Tropea**. But you'll never have to go far for a cooling swim: southern Italy contains hundreds of kilometres of often deserted beaches and many casual little resorts catering mainly for Italian holiday-makers.

Ancient Greeks and Romans

For ancient sites and museums, Campania is the equal of Sicily and even Rome. Start with **Naples** and its great Archaeological Museum. **Pompeii** and **Herculaneum** each require a day to see them in detail, while another day can be spent exploring the

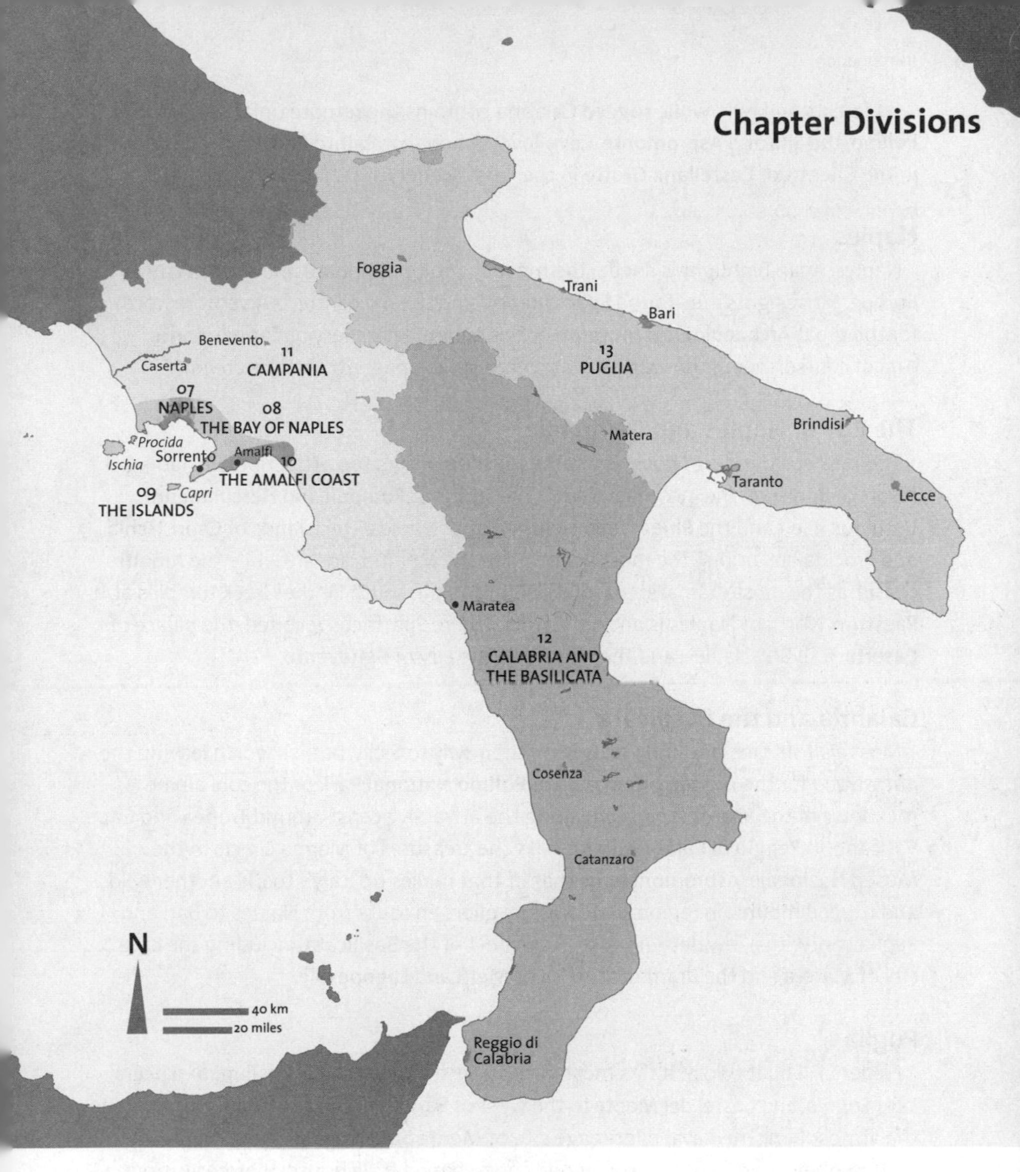

sites west of Naples: **Cumae**, **Baia**, **Solfatara** and so on. South of the Bay of Naples stand mainland Italy's best-preserved Greek temples at **Paestum**, while **Reggio di Calabria** and **Taranto** each have a Museo Nazionale with splendid remnants of Magna Grecia.

Natural Attractions

Despite the crowds, the **Sorrento peninsula**, **Amalfi coast** and **Capri** still boast Italy's finest coastal scenery, plus some lovely walks in the hills above. For a look at what's bubbling under the surface of the Bay of Naples, visit **Vesuvius** or steaming **Solfatara**. The **Gargano** and **Cilento** peninsulas both have national parks in their interiors, with wild forests and hills, while rugged Calabria contains the remote uplands of **Monte Pollino**, the **Sila** and **Aspromonte**. Cave-lovers should drop into **Pertosa** or **Castelcivita** in the Cilento, or **Castellana Grotte** in the karst scenery south of Bari.

Naples

Naples' main highlight is itself – the most chaotic, passionate and vibrant city in Europe. Most sights are around **Spaccanapoli** and the old centre, but venture north for the great **Archaeological Museum** or the palace/art gallery of **Capodimonte**. And of course, there's the world's best coffee, pizza, spaghetti and ice cream.

The Bay of Naples and Campania

The area surrounding Naples contains southern Italy's top attractions, including the resort of **Sorrento**, the incomparable Roman ruins of **Pompeii** and **Herculaneum**, **Vesuvius** itself and the **Phlegraean Fields** west of Naples. The islands of **Capri**, **Ischia** and **Procida** are among the most beautiful in the Mediterranean, while the **Amalfi coast** has the most dramatic coastline in Italy. To the south lie the Greek temples at **Paestum**. North of Naples is ancient **Capua**, where Spartacus revolted; the palace of **Caserta**, Italy's Versailles; and the pleasant little city of **Benevento**.

Calabria and the Basilicata

Most visitors race through Calabria on their way to Sicily, but it's worth leaving the *autostrada* for the rugged mountains of **Pollino National Park** or the cool alpine meadows of the **Sila**, or for a swim along the attractive coast around **Tropea** and Cape Vaticano. In **Reggio di Calabria**, don't miss the treasures of Magna Grecia in the Museo Nazionale. **Aspromonte**, the massif that makes up Italy's toe, is another wild and rugged mountain region. Similarly, travellers en route from Naples to Bari and Puglia can, with a few detours, take in the best of the Basilicata, including the cave city of **Matera** and the dramatic castles of **Melfi** and **Lagopesole**.

Puglia

Frederick II built two of Italy's most impressive medieval castles in Puglia – **Lucera**, near Foggia, and **Castel del Monte** to the west of Bari. The **Gargano** peninsula contains the atmospheric medieval pilgrimage site of **Monte Sant'Angelo**. South of Bari, detour to **Alberobello**, centre of a region of odd cone-shaped *trulli* houses, before visiting Baroque **Lecce**, the architectural gem of southern Italy.

History, Art and Architecture

02

Naples and southern Italy have a long and rich history, but unfortunately for the locals, it has mainly been others who got rich at their expense. The long list of invaders and conquerors includes Greeks, Romans, Goths, Vandals, Normans, French and Spanish. Some of the earlier arrivals created great civilizations. Magna Grecia, for instance, or Roman cities such as Pompeii, Cumae, or even the great castle-builder Frederick II, were glorious. Most of those who came later, such as the Bourbons, were at best vainglorious, building extravagant palaces while the countryside fell into the state of poverty and lawlessness from which it is only now beginning to escape.

History

Prehistory

Some 50,000 years ago, when the Alps were covered by an icecap and the low level of the Mediterranean made Italy a much wider peninsula than it is now, Neanderthal Man was gracing Italy with his low-browed presence. His successors, the more debonair Cro-Magnon Italians, turned up about 18,000 BC. They knew about fishing and keeping animals and, as elsewhere in Europe, they created some genuine art: female statuettes made from bone and other bones carved with tidy geometric patterns. They were fond of shellfish and used the shells for jewellery. The transition from the Palaeolithic (old Stone Age) to the Mesolithic (middle Stone Age) occurred in the 9th millennium BC. The time of nomadic hunters had passed, and an agricultural society came soon after with the Neolithic era, probably reaching Italy around 7,000 BC. The first Neolithic Italians may have come in an invasion or migration from the Balkans. These peoples installed themselves on the plains around Foggia, in Puglia; by 4,000 BC, they had spread across the peninsula. Never great builders (except in Puglia, which has almost all of the dolmens in Italy), these apparently peaceful folk proved easy marks for the Indo-European tribes who arrived about 3,000 BC.

800–358 BC: Magna Grecia

When the first Greek colonists arrived in the 8th century BC, they found the region inhabited by a number of powerful, distinct tribes. Chief among them were the powerful Samnites, who occupied much of inland Campania and the south, while the area around the Bay of Naples was inhabited by the Ausones (or Oscans) and the Opici. Further south were the Daunii in northern Puglia, the dolmen-building Messapians in southern Puglia and the Bruttians in Calabria. The Greeks, whose trading routes had long covered Italy's southern coasts, looked upon that 'underdeveloped' country as a New World for exploration and colonization. All over the south there are archaeological clues that the Greeks had begun settlements even earlier – in the Mycenaean age before the fall of Troy – but little is known about these.

In 775 BC, the Greeks founded a trading settlement at Pithecusa, on the island of Ischia, squarely in the middle of the important trade route that carried Tuscany's iron to the east. The first planned urban colony in Campania was Cumae, in 750 BC. After that, new Greek cities started springing up all over the south and Sicily, including Elea in Campania, Rhegium (Reggio di Calabria) on the straits, and Taras (Taranto), Sybaris, Croton and Metapontum on the Ionian Sea. Another band of Greeks founded a city called Parthenope, on the hill called Pizzofalcone that now divides the old and new quarters of Naples, and on the nearby island where the Castel dell'Ovo is now.

Centuries later, the poet Virgil, who loved this coast and spent much of his life on it, dressed up the city's origins with the story of a siren named Parthenope. According to Virgil, Odysseus visited here, and when he resisted all her attempts to seduce him into remaining with her, Parthenope threw herself off the cliff and drowned.

The city Parthenope didn't fare too well either. Throughout Greek Italy, neighbouring cities tended to fight like cats, and Cumae and Parthenope slugged it out until the latter succumbed. The Cumaeans may have destroyed their rival; in any case, they founded a new city – Neapolis – right next to it. Like most Greek foundations, Neapolis was laid out in a rigid rectangular grid, like Manhattan or Chicago, a pattern that has survived with almost no changes in the Spaccanapoli district today.

The Greeks could never hope to have such a desirable land entirely to themselves. In the 6th century BC, the Etruscans arrived from the north. This powerful and talented nation, then at the height of its culture and expanding in all directions, colonized much of Campania's interior, founding the cities of Capua, Nola and Acerra. Modern historians trace Etruscan expansion by their manic habit of surveying land into 2,300ft squares; besides gladiatorial combats, portrait busts, rampant superstition and many other contributions, the Etruscans also taught their Roman neighbours how to make straight roads. Conflict with the Greeks, their greatest trade rivals, was inevitable. Warfare began in 524 BC with an unsuccessful Etruscan siege of Cumae. The Greeks got the better of it from then on, and finally defeated the Etruscans at sea in the decisive Battle of Cumae (474 BC). Their southern colonies straggled on for a while, but the taking of Capua by the Samnites in 432 BC put an end to Etruscan hopes in the south forever.

Greek Campania by this time was only the northernmost province of a genuine New World – Magna Grecia. It was a land of rich culture and wealthy cities that included Sicily and all of southern Italy's coasts save the Adriatic. Greek Italy's painters and sculptors took their places among the greatest of Greece's golden age, but its most memorable contributions were in philosophy. The Elean School (from the city of Elea, in the Cilento) included some of the most important pre-Socratics: Parmenides, who invented the concept of atoms, and Zeno, with his pesky paradoxes.

In Calabria and Sicily, the Greeks fought constantly; wars between cities and civil wars within them, with the losers usually massacred or sold off as slaves. The Campanian towns avoided most of the unpleasantness while playing an important role in teaching art and culture to their Italian neighbours. The Ausones, Samnites and other nations became more or less Hellenized, until the emergence of a bellicose and rapidly growing little republic up north – Rome.

358 BC–AD 406: The Romans

By the 6th century BC, Rome had chased out its Etruscan rulers and had begun terrorizing the towns and tribes of central Italy. By the 4th century BC, she had gobbled up the lot and the borders of the Roman state extended into Campania. Around 358

BC, the senators were able to turn their attention to the only other power remaining in Italy: the Samnites. These rugged highlanders of the southern Apennines, with their capital at Benevento, had begun to seize parts of coastal Campania from the Greeks. The Romans drove them out in 341 BC, but in the Second Samnite War, the Samnites dealt them a severe defeat (Battle of the Caudine Forks, in 321 BC). In the third war, the Samnites, surrounded by Roman allies, formed an alliance with the northern Etruscans and Celts, leading to a general Italian commotion in which the Romans beat everybody, annexing almost all of Italy by 283 BC.

After the Samnites, it was the turn of the Greeks. The frightened cities of Magna Grecia sent for Pyrrhus of Epirus, a brilliant adventurer with a big army, to help keep the barbarians out. Pyrrhus won a string of inconclusive 'Pyrrhic' victories, but after finally losing a battle in 275 BC at Benevento, he quit and returned home, allowing the Romans to leisurely take over the deserted Greek cities one by one. Now the conquest was complete. All along the Romans had been diabolically clever in managing their new demesne, maintaining most of the tribes and cities as nominally independent states, while planting Latin colonies everywhere in or near the ruins of those cities they had destroyed, such as Paestum, Puteoli (Pozzuoli) and Benevento.

Rome went on to fatten on even bigger prey – the Carthaginians in the 3rd century BC, the rest of the Mediterranean in the 2nd – while the south became thoroughly integrated into the Roman system. Wealthy senators and businessmen lined the Bay of Naples with their villas, while Puteoli grew up as the leading port of Italy, the terminus for the grain ships from Sicily and Africa. Campania was booming, largely from the manufacture of ceramics and luxury goods; its metropolis, Capua, renowned for perfume and fair ladies, was Italy's second city in population and wealth.

But Roman rule had its darker side, especially south of Naples. The conquerors appropriated most of the good land and divided it among themselves, creating vast estates called *latifundia* and a new society where a small class of fantastically rich landowners lorded it over an impoverished peasantry and middle class. Debt and Roman law pushed large numbers of the poor into slavery. In other parts of Italy, the situation was just as bad; the 1st century BC witnessed a continuous political and social crisis, breaking out into a series of civil wars and rebellions that did not end until the accession of Augustus and the end of the Roman Republic. In the year 91 BC, a coordinated revolt, called the Social Wars, broke out among the southern peoples. This constituted a genuine threat to Rome that was finally defeated by the campaigns of Marius and Sulla, and by an offer to extend Roman citizenship to all Italians. Both generals – the former a populist, the latter an archreactionary – later ruled as dictators in Rome. Under the tyrannous Sulla, an effective autocracy was created and opponents either murdered or exiled. Italy careered into anarchy, with many rural districts reverting to bandit-ridden wastelands, the setting for the revolt in 73 BC of Spartacus, an escaped gladiator of Capua who led a motley army of dispossessed farmers and runaway slaves – some 70,000 of them – until the legions finally defeated him in 71 BC.

The later civil wars – Pompey vs. Caesar and Augustus vs. Antony – largely spared the south, though many of the plots were hatched in villas around the Bay of Naples. Under Augustus and his imperial successors, things settled down considerably, while the bay continued its career as the favoured resort of the emperors and the rich. In the economic decline of the late empire, troubles returned. The rural south sank deeper into decline, while even the commerce of Magna Grecia gradually began to fail, ruined by foreign competition, high taxes and bureaucracy. The great eruption of Vesuvius in AD 79 must have increased the economic disarray; three sizeable towns – Pompeii, Herculaneum and Stabiae – completely disappeared, and vast tracts of fertile land withered under volcanic ash. In northern Italy, meanwhile, a sounder, more stable economy led to the growth of new centres – Milan, Padua, Verona, Florence and others. The economic north–south divide, a problem for which no solution is in sight even today, was already beginning.

406–1139: Goths, Greeks, Lombards, Normans

The 5th-century barbarian invaders of Italy, Goths and Vandals, passed through Campania without any notable outrages and, after they passed, the region and the rest of the peninsula got a half-century's breathing space under Theodoric's tolerant, well-run Gothic kingdom of Italy. The real disaster began in 536, with the invasion of Italy by the Eastern empire, part of the relentlessly expansionist policy of the great Justinian. The south, still largely Greek by race and sentiment, welcomed the Greek army from Constantinople, but much of the worst fighting of the Greek-Gothic War took place in the region. Neapolis, or Naples, by now the largest city in the south, was captured and sacked in turn by both sides. Justinian's brilliant generals, Belisarius and Narses, ultimately prevailed over the Goths in 563, but the damage to an already stricken society and economy was incalculable. Italy's total exhaustion was exposed only five years later, when the Lombards, a Germanic tribe who worked hard to earn the title of barbarian, overran northern Italy and parts of the south, establishing a kingdom at Pavia in the north and a separate duchy at Benevento (571). A new pattern of power appeared, with semi-independent Byzantine dukes defending much of the coastal area, and Lombard chiefs ruling the interior. Byzantine control was tenuous at best and cities like Naples and Salerno gradually achieved a *de facto* independence.

No one usually bothered to write down what was going on in the south during the Dark Ages, but even if they had, it would be a confusing story. The Lombard Duchy of Benevento reached its height in the 9th century, while enclaves around the coasts remained in the hands of the Byzantines, and for a short time in the 9th century, much of Puglia was held by Arabs from Sicily as the 'Emirate of Bari'. Some of the coastal cities, at least, weren't doing too badly. Naples, which proclaimed its complete independence in 763 under its dukes, seemed to have been keeping itself afloat and carrying on at least a little trade, as were Sorrento and Salerno. And in this unpromising time a new city rose up to join them and cut a surprising career for itself as a merchant republic: Amalfi. As early as the 7th century, Amalfi had its fleet. In the 900s, the city established its independence from Naples and elected a doge, like Venice's. Its trading stations extended across the eastern Mediterranean and there was a large colony of Amalfitan merchants in Pera, across from Constantinople.

The year 1000 makes a convenient date for the beginning of the Middle Ages and the great economic and cultural upsurge that came with it. In southern Italy, the major event of this time was the arrival of the Normans. The first of them arrived in the 9th century, as mercenaries or pilgrims to Monte Sant'Angelo in the Gargano.

They liked the opportunities they saw for booty and conquest, and from about 1020, the younger sons of Norman feudal families moved into the south, first coming as mercenaries but gradually gaining large tracts of land for themselves in exchange for their services. Often allied with the popes, they soon controlled most of Puglia and Calabria. One of their greatest chiefs, Robert Guiscard, came to control much of the south as Duke of Puglia. In 1084 he descended on Rome for a grisly sack that put the best efforts of the Goths and Vandals to shame. His less destructive brother, Roger de Hauteville, began the conquest of Sicily from the Arabs in 1060, six years before William the Conqueror sailed for England. Naples fell to the Norman armies in 1139.

1139–1494: The Kingdoms of Sicily and Naples

Roger de Hauteville eventually united the south into the 'Kingdom of Sicily' and by the 1140s, under Roger II, this strange Norman-Arab-Jewish-Italian-Greek state, with its glittering, half-oriental capital of Palermo, had become the cultural centre of the Mediterranean, a refuge of religious tolerance and scholarship. Under Roger and his successors (William the Bad, who wasn't bad at all, and William the Good, who was something of a weakling), it was one of the strongest and best-organized states in Europe. The 12th century was a boom time for the south, as it was for most of Europe. Puglia, in particular, enjoyed its greatest age and its trading towns began the Romanesque cathedrals that are among the south's greatest architectural treasures.

In 1194 the Hauteville line became extinct and the Kingdom of Sicily fell to Holy Roman Emperor Henry IV of Hohenstaufen, who brought down an army from Germany to claim it. His son, the legendary Frederick II (1194–1250), was at once emperor and king of Sicily, though he spent most of his time in southern Italy, presiding over a court even more brilliant than that of Roger II. Frederick gave his lands a constitution – the *Constitutio Melfitani* – and founded Naples University, the third in Italy and the first in the south.

Frederick did not have an easy reign, largely thanks to his most dangerous political enemies: the popes. During his reign, they excommunicated him twice. After his death, Pope Urban IV set a disastrous precedent by inviting in the French, in the person of Charles of Anjou, brother of the King of France, to seize the southern kingdom. Charles defeated Frederick's son Manfred (Battle of Benevento, 1266) and foully murdered the last of the Hohenstaufens, Conradin, in 1268. He held unchallenged sway over southern Italy until 1282, when the famous revolt of the Sicilian Vespers chased the hated French from Sicily and inaugurated a period of wars and anarchy throughout the south.

Despite its unity under the Normans and Hohenstaufens, the south was falling behind both politically and economically. The Normans ruled their domains fairly and intelligently, but they also introduced feudalism into a country that had never known it – just as the mercantile states of the north were breaking loose from the feudal arrangements brought down by the Goths and Lombards. Now the 'Kingdom of Naples', as the southern state became known (to distinguish it from the by-now separate Kingdom of Sicily), was a tapestry of battling barons, each busily improving his castle and less inclined to listen to kings or popes. The trading cities – especially Naples, Amalfi and Bari – faced strong competition from the Venetians and Genoese.

Robert the Wise (1309–43), the patron of Giotto, Petrarch and Boccaccio, was succeeded by his granddaughter, Giovanna I, and under her unsteady hand, the barons increased both their power and their contentiousness. Her reign witnessed the Black Death (1347–8), in which Italy lost one third of its population, and also the beginnings of civil war between Angevin factions, something that would continue fitfully through a century of confusing intrigues and insurrections. It ended in the hands of yet another foreigner, Alfonso the Magnanimous, king of Aragon, who conquered Naples and tossed out the last Angevins in 1442. (Alfonso, a student of the classics, had been reading an account of how Belisarius took Naples during the Greek-Gothic Wars by sending men through the channel of a Roman aqueduct that breached the walls. He located the exact spot, with the ruined aqueduct still present, and sent his soldiers in the same way.) Once more the kingdom was reunited with Sicily, part of the Aragonese crown since the Sicilian Vespers. Alfonso and his successor, the cruel King Ferrante, ruled Naples with harshness and skill; both were typical Renaissance princes who, as leaders of the only kingdom in Italy, played major roles in the eternal petty wars and intrigues of the age.

1494–1713: Spanish Rule

The Wars of Italy, that terrible series of conflicts that brought down the curtain on the Renaissance and Italian liberty, began in 1494 with a quarrel over Naples. Charles VIII, King of France, took advantage of Italian disunity to invade the peninsula, seeking to make good the claim to the kingdom he had inherited from the Angevins. The last Aragonese king, the ineffectual Alfonso II, fled the city rather than face him. Spain was at the height of its powers after the union of Aragon and Castile in 1492, under Ferdinand and Isabella, and the Spaniards sent El Gran Capitan, Gonsalvo di Córdoba, with a strong army. He restored Naples to its Spanish king the following year. More fighting between Aragonese factions followed, and when the dust settled in 1502, Naples and its kingdom were directly under the Spanish crown and ruled by a viceroy.

In the decades to come, nearly all of Italy would be beaten or bullied into the Spanish system, either through puppet rulers, alliances or outright control, but nowhere was the Spanish influence stronger than in Naples. The Inquisition snuffed out the city's intellectual life, while the nobles of the realm learned to forsake their wonted gay colours and dress all in black; they came to affect the haughty manners of the grandees, started calling each other Don, and carried rapiers and poignards in the streets – in the atmosphere of the Wars of Italy, it had become an extremely violent age. The greatest of the viceroys, Don Pedro de Toledo, was a benefactor to Naples, and rebuilt much of it; he also built Castel Sant'Elmo on the highest hill to keep watch over the Neapolitans.

Spanish rule lasted over two centuries, and as Spain decayed into senile decadence, its government in southern Italy grew ever more oppressive and useless. Times would have been bad enough in the general Italian economic collapse of the 17th century, but Spanish misrule gradually turned the already poor rural south into a nightmare of anarchic depravity, haunted by legions of bandits and beggars, and controlled ever more tightly by its violent feudal barons. Peasants by the thousand gave up their lands and villages for a marginally safer life in Naples, and the city's population ballooned to an estimated half-million by 1700, making it the largest in Europe. Then, to everyone's surprise, the south rose up and staged an epic rebellion. Beginning in Naples (Masaniello's Revolt, 1647), the disturbances soon spread all over the south and Sicily. For over a year, peasant militias ruled some areas and makeshift revolutionary councils defended the cities. But when the Spanish finally defeated them, they massacred some 18,000 and tightened the screws more than ever.

1713–1860: The Bourbons

In 1713, after the War of the Spanish Succession, the Habsburgs of Austria came to control most of Spain's Italian possessions, including Naples. The Austrians made no impression on anyone, and Naples' hard luck continued when the Austrians were forced to transfer it to a branch of the House of Bourbon (1734); under them, the kingdom was again independent but just as poorly governed as before. For the next century and a quarter, the south enjoyed a colourful era of backwardness, bad art and intellectual torpor, during which the city of Naples perfected the peculiar charms and vices it displays today. An exception was the reign of Charles III (1734–59), who introduced many long-overdue reforms. Charles also built the San Carlo Opera House, the Archaeological Museum and the palaces at Capodimonte and Caserta.

His son, Ferdinand I, has gone down in history as the 'Lazzarone King'. (*Lazzarone*, a key Neapolitan word, refers to the crowds of gainfully unemployed men that lounged on every street corner of old Naples. It does not literally mean 'good-for-nothing', but that would be an accurate translation.) The perfect king for the time, Ferdinand ruled with a light hand and spoke only Neapolitan dialect. State visitors generally found him surrounded by noise, food and children.

The French invasion of 1799, during the Napoleonic Wars, woke Naples up with a start from its Baroque slumbers. Local patriots gaily joined the French cause – even the monks of San Martino, who sewed tricolour flags for the new 'Parthenopean Republic' and invited all the French officers for a banquet. In 1799, however, while Napoleon was off in Egypt, the advance through Italy by an Austro-Russian army, aided by Nelson's fleet, restored the status quo. This was often accompanied by bloody reprisals, as peasant mobs led by clerics (the 'Army of the Holy Faith' or *Sanfedisti*) marched across the south massacring liberals and French sympathizers.

In 1800, after Marengo, Napoleon returned and crowned himself King of Italy; Joseph Bonaparte, and later Joachim Murat, ruled in Naples. For the second time, Admiral Nelson and his fleet had to remove the king and his family to Sicily for safety. Napoleonic rule lasted only until 1814, but in that time ,important public works were begun and laws, education and everything else reformed on the French model; church properties were expropriated and medieval relics everywhere put to rest.

The 1815 Congress of Vienna put the clock back to 1798. Indeed, the Bourbons seemed to think they could pretend the Napoleonic upheavals had never happened, and the political reaction in their territories (which from this time on, incidentally, was officially and confusingly called the 'Kingdom of the Two Sicilies') was fierce. But the experience had given Italians a taste of the opportunities offered by the modern world, as well as a sense of national feeling that had long been suppressed. Almost immediately, revolutionary agitators and secret societies like the famous Carbonari kept Italy convulsed in intrigues. A big revolt in Naples forced King Ferdinand, now a bitter old reactionary after his experiences with the French, to grant a constitution (1821), but when Austrian troops came down to crush the rebels, he took it back.

The next king, Ferdinand II (1830–59), gets a bad press; his subjects nicknamed him Re Bomba (King Bomb) after his army shelled Messina during the popular revolt of 1848–9. On the plus side, Ferdinand exerted himself mightily to bring his kingdom into the modern world, building the first railways and laying the foundations for modern industry and a merchant fleet. (He also built the Amalfi Drive – a great feat of engineering.) But his autocratic and paternalistic rule was out of step with the atmosphere of the Italian Risorgimento, and when the climactic events of national reunification took place in 1859–60, few were left to support the Bourbon monarchy.

In 1860, when the north was in revolt and ready to unite under the Piedmontese King Vittorio Emmanuele, Giuseppe Garibaldi and his red-shirted 'Thousand' sailed from Genoa to Sicily, electrifying Europe by repeatedly beating the Bourbon forces in a quick march across the island. The Thousand became 20,000 as they crossed the straits and marched to the capital, meeting little resistance. Garibaldi entered Naples on 7 September (on Ferdinand's new railway) and the Bourbon kingdom was finished.

1860–1944: Unification to Fascism

The new Italy established a constitutional monarchy under Vittorio Emmanuele, one in which the radical aspirations of Garibaldi and his followers were given little hearing. The new parliament almost immediately split into cliques and political cartels representing powerful interests. Italy's finances started in disorder and stayed that way, while corruption was widespread. There were other problems. Naples' loss of capital status was a heavy blow to the city, both politically and culturally, and the new state's tariff policies, dictated by northern interests, caused a sharp decline, first in the south's small industrial base and then in its agriculture. Thus was the new Italy born with the 'problem of the south' as the biggest item on its agenda – and with a regime doing little or nothing about it.

In the disappointed south, agents of the displaced Bourbons and of the pope contributed to the continuing unrest, though conditions were such that most of the troubles began spontaneously. Throughout the 1860s, over 100,000 troops were tied down pursuing the 'bandits' of the south. The guerrillas concentrated on killing landowners and officials of the new government, raiding town halls to burn the tax and property records. The army responded in kind, with the brutality of an occupying power, and the woes of the south found scant sympathy in the more developed regions of Italy. Ironically, southerners came to hold a disproportionate share of power and positions in the new regime. The *galantuomini* – the ignorant, parasitical class of local bosses and landlords – soon learned the possibilities offered them by Italy's limited democracy, and found it as easy to manipulate as the Bourbon kingdom had been. Their influence has contributed much to Italy's political troubles in all the years since. Meanwhile, southerners were solving the problem in their own way – by packing their suitcases. Some two and a half million Italians emigrated to the Americas and elsewhere between 1880 and 1914, most of them from the south.

For all the south's discontent, Fascism made very little headway in the region in the years after the First World War. Mussolini choreographed his march on Rome in 1922, but even a year after that, his power in the south was negligible. The Fascist takeover only occurred here when it was clear the Duce was dismantling the parliamentary state. Southern Italians realized that they were to have a new master and adjusted accordingly. While the most powerful party, the Socialists, dithered and fiddled uncomprehendingly, the local authorities suddenly began turning a blind eye to the terror tactics of the Fascist *squadri*. Fascist Party groups around the south, usually bankrupt and squabbling among themselves, just as suddenly found themselves swamped with new members and contributions. When the dust settled, everyone who was anyone was in the Party and things went on as before, run by the same faces only in new uniforms.

The Fascist government's 'Battle for Wheat' – a drive to make Italy self-sufficient in food – did more harm than good in the south, destroying valuable pastureland and orchids. But at least Mussolini contributed plenty of impressive public works to the south (the Puglian aqueduct, civic centres for cities like Bari and Taranto), and under Fascism, the region took the first steps on the road to industrialization. The Fascists also promoted the Bay of Naples and its islands as tourist destinations and waged a relatively successful war against the Camorra; a rival gang, after all, was the last thing Mussolini would tolerate.

Southern Italians greeted Italy's entry into the Second World War enthusiastically, but the region suffered heavily during the latter stages of the conflict, with the Allies choosing it as the staging post for their re-invasion of Europe. Many of Naples' monuments were severely damaged in the Allied invasion, including the church of Santa Chiara. After the Salerno landings – the successful short cut that put the Allies on Naples' doorstep – the city surprised everyone by staging the 'Four Days in Naples' – a tremendous spontaneous popular revolt that drove the Germans from the city. Other parts of the south suffered too. Foggia, Bari, Benevento and Reggio di Calabria, in particular, were bombed first by the Allies, and then by the Germans.

1944–the Present

For the south, liberation was a nightmare of destitution and corruption, brilliantly chronicled in Norman Lewis's book, *Naples '44*. The problems of a region with no government or services and an economy in total collapse proved too much for the Allied government. Cholera and malaria were widespread and up to a third of the female population in Naples was forced into prostitution to survive. A third, too, of all the supplies unloaded by the Allies disappeared, fuelling a gigantic black market in everything from flour to armoured vehicles. Bands of robbers appeared once more in the countryside – helped by the Allied policy of emptying the jails wherever they went during the war. The Camorra resurfaced and tightened its grip over Naples, as did the similar 'Ndrangheta in Calabria and smaller gangs elsewhere.

In the 1946 referendum that established the Italian Republic, the south was the only region that said no. In Naples, 80 per cent voted to keep the monarchy. Still, change came quickly in the post-war decades: a wave of building in the cities, much of it *abusivo* or illegal; and new industry, such as the Alfa-Sud plant and Bagnoli steel works around Naples and the huge industrial area at Taranto; all financed by the government's southern reconstruction fund, the *Cassa per il Mezzogiorno*. But it wasn't enough to enable the southern economy to keep even, let alone catch up with northern Italy, and tens of thousands of southerners flocked north to work in the factories of Turin, Milan and Germany. One advance was the reclamation of huge coastal areas from malaria by the use of DDT; regions that had been wastelands since Roman times became populated once more. In Calabria especially, it gave rise to an agricultural revolution that is only just beginning to bear fruit.

Post-war politics in Naples was dominated by 1950s mayor Achille Lauro, a shipping magnate who had been well-connected with the Fascists under Mussolini, although he opposed the war. When the Christian Democrats didn't meet his terms, he founded his own rightist populist movement, *Uomo Qualunque* ('Everyman'). Amidst the usual claims of graft, most of them justified, this eventually fizzled out, to be replaced by a close Christian Democrat-Camorra machine that ran the city until 1993 under 'modern bosses' such as Antonio Gava.

Italy's politics became ever more turbulent in the 1990s. Corruption scandals opened the way for right-wing media baron Silvio Berlusconi to become Prime Minister (despite himself being found guilty of corruption in 1998), and neo-Fascist right-wing parties such as the National Alliance and the Northern League grew in influence. Naples, meanwhile, enjoyed a modest cultural renaissance under Antonio Bassolino, the city's reforming mayor from 1993 to 2000. When Bassolino stepped aside in 2001 to take the post of regional governor, the feisty Rosa Russo Iervolino became Naples' first-ever woman mayor. Her first years in office have seen a slight waning of the optimism instilled during Bassolino's years as mayor.

And as if all that wasn't bad enough...

So far, this history has said little about one of the most prominent features of life in this region – the disasters. But we could mention the Black Death of 1347–8, the plague of 1529 that carried off 50,000, the plague of 1656 that took 200,000 more, a dozen or so volcanic eruptions and as many earthquakes – especially the terrible one of 1688 that wrecked much of Naples, or the 1908 one that destroyed Reggio di Calabria – or the severe cholera epidemics of 1884, 1944 and 1973; or the earthquake of 1980, largely ignored in the press, which caused tremendous damage and suffering in rural Campania. In 2002, yet another earthquake devastated the village of San Giuliano di Puglia, where a number of children died when the local school collapsed.

These events have shaped southern Italy: they help to explain the sombre, fatalistic side of the southern Italian character, its philosophical seriousness – and the other side, too: the frivolous, laugh-in-the-face-of-Vesuvius manner and strong resilience of Neapolitans, inhabitants of a city that has recovered and rebuilt itself so many times.

Lately most of the catastrophes have been man-made: economic stagnation, widespread political corruption, the vampirism of the local mafias and an ever-increasing degradation of public services. The leftist administration in Naples is still grappling with an inherited urban crisis of the first order: hospitals, public transport and sanitation in scandalous condition, chronic traffic gridlock; the list runs depressingly on and on. In the hinterlands, refugees from the 1980 earthquake still live in public buildings; in Benevento, you can see bomb damage from the Second World War.

Art and Architecture

Greek and Roman

With the arrival of the Greeks and Etruscans in the mid-8th century BC, Italy joined the wider Mediterranean world, artistically as well as politically. The wealthy cities of Magna Grecia imported classical Greek art and artists wholesale and, even though many of the cities themselves have disappeared, the superb archaeological museums of **Naples**, **Taranto**, **Bari** and **Reggio di Calabria** have huge stores of sculpture, painted vases, architectural decoration, figurines and lovely terracotta *ex votos*. Native artists also made endless copies of painted Greek ceramics, many of them excellent. For Greek architecture, there is the great Doric temple at **Paestum** (which also has an extremely rare Greek fresco in a tomb), and ruins at **Cumae**, **Velia** and **Metapontum**.

In Campania, the art and architecture of the Roman world is out on display, in Naples' museum and at the matchless sites of **Pompeii** and **Herculaneum**. There are plenty of other ruins of Roman buildings to see: at **Pozzuoli**, **Baia** and other sites around the western bay, including some grandiose survivals of Roman engineering, such as the reservoirs and canals of the great naval base at **Cape Misenum** and, in Naples, the **Fuorigrotta** road tunnel, the longest ever built in antiquity. What's left of the second- and third-largest amphitheatres of the Roman world can be seen at Capua and Pozzuoli; **Capua** also has a remarkable underground Mithraic temple.

Most of these spectacular works came in the confident, self-assured age of the Flavian and Antonine emperors (late 1st–2nd centuries), a time that also saw important progress in sculpture. Until then, Roman work had been closely bound to Hellenistic styles or was expressed in outright copies of classical Greek sculpture. The new vivid style can be seen on the reliefs of Trajan's arch in **Benevento**.

Painting and mosaic work were both present from at least the 1st century BC, though Romans always considered them as little more than decoration, and only rarely entrusted to them any serious subjects. Both are a legacy from the Greeks, and both found their way to Rome by way of talented, half-Greek Campania. Painting, in the days of Caesar and Augustus, usually meant wall frescoes in the homes of the wealthy (*see* p.112), with large scenes of gardens in the form of window views, making small

Roman rooms look brighter and bigger; also mythological scenes, paintings of battles and a few portraits (the best, courtesy of Vesuvius, are at Pompeii and Herculaneum, also in the museum of Naples and in the Mithraeum at Capua).

Mosaics, another import, had their greatest centre at Antioch, in Hellenized Syria, and only became a significant medium in Italy as painting was declining. As with the other arts, mosaics were done better in cultured Campania. If Rome, too, had been buried under volcanic lava, it is unlikely that much would be found to surpass the 2nd- and 1st-century BC paintings and mosaics discovered at Pompeii.

Byzantine and Medieval

So much has been lost to earthquakes and neglect that even the most rudimentary structure from the Dark Ages is a rarity. Two churches that survive are the small 5th-century S. Maria Maggiore near **Nocera Inferiore**, and 8th-century Santa Sofia at **Benevento**, both central-plan temples more in keeping with the contemporary architecture of Byzantium than of Rome. Naples' cathedral retains its 5th-century baptistry. Further south, Byzantine influence predominated until the late Middle Ages, especially in areas that remained Greek in religion and culture. In Calabria, two small Byzantine churches survive at **Stilo**.

In the 10th–12th centuries, cultural revival was made possible by a number of factors. The trade and overseas contacts of Amalfi, Naples and the Puglian cities not only created wealth but brought in influences from Byzantium and the Muslim world. The Normans brought the blessings of political stability and a sophisticated court. Artistically, through the work of Abbot Desiderius at the great Abbey of Montecassino between Naples and Rome, they imported artists and architects from Constantinople, helping to spread their advanced styles and techniques across the south. One good example is finely incised bronze church doors, a Greek speciality. Nearly a score of southern towns have them, beginning with the set made for **Amalfi** (1066). The fashion spread to many other cities, and Italian artists were soon producing their own – notably those of Barisano da Trani at **Trani** and **Ravello**.

Painting, too, in this age was largely a matter of importing styles and artists from Greece, and Byzantine art, so unfairly disparaged by the Renaissance, would continue to influence all of Italy until the fall of Constantinople. Byzantium's own medieval 'renaissance' shows up clearly in the exceptional 11th-century frescoes at S. Angelo in Formis in **Capua**, in the 14th-century S. Maria del Casale in **Brindisi**, and in the cave churches of **Matera** and **Massafra** (along with scores of little-known works in caves all through southern Puglia and the Basilicata).

Because of religious and cultural prejudices, the role of Muslim influence in Italian medieval art has never been satisfactorily examined. In Campania, it is often obvious, in the interlaced arches of Amalfi cathedral and the exotic patterned decoration in its façade, and in the churches of **Salerno** and **Caserta Vecchia**. Another southern speciality to which Muslim art probably contributed is the decoration of pavements, pulpits, candlesticks and tombs with geometric patterns in chips of coloured stone or glass, an art that reached a plateau of excellence at Amalfi, Ravello and Salerno.

Romanesque architecture, so important in northern Italy and the rest of Europe, does not seem to have made much of an impression in Campania. In Puglia, however, one of the most distinctive and sophisticated of all Romanesque styles appeared. Beginning with the construction of San Nicola in **Bari** in 1087, a wave of cathedral building swept over the region. Some of the best are in **Troia**, **Bitonto**, **Trani**, **Molfetta** and **Matera**. These churches draw their inspiration from numerous sources. There are hints of Norman French work, as well as Lombard and Pisan Romanesque. Some of the features of Puglian Romanesque are the profile of the sharp roof-line angle and small rose windows, which combine to create the distinctive Puglian façade, along with blind arcading around cornices, galleries (both interior and exterior), elaborately carved portals and apses and, above all, an emphasis on height that anticipates the Gothic. To match the architects, Puglia developed a talented group of sculptors. Their fantastical beasts make up the cathedrals' most important decoration, along with finely carved pulpits and bishops' thrones, as at Bari. Other medieval monuments of Puglian architecture include the tomb of the crusader knight Bohemund, in **Canosa di Puglia**, and Frederick II's mystical castle, **Castel del Monte**.

One of the most ambitious buildings of the early Middle Ages in southern Italy was Salerno cathedral, begun by Robert Guiscard in 1085 – an idiosyncratic work that shows a faithfulness to early Christian fashions (such as the exterior *quadroporticus*). Gothic churches are more common than in most parts of Italy; the style was brought down by the French under the rule of Charles of Anjou after 1266 (San Domenico Maggiore in Naples is one of the best examples). Late Puglian cathedrals, where Romanesque has evolved into Gothic, are those at **Altamura** and **Ruvo di Puglia**, while Gothic churches also survive at **Cosenza** and **Altomonte** in Calabria.

An Imported Renaissance

In the 15th and 16th centuries, the rest of Italy was the centre of a revolution in Western art and culture. But with the economic decline of the southern cities, there was little opportunity for similar artistic advance in the south. Northern artists still came to **Naples** in the 1400s. Notable visitors to Naples included Donatello, Michelozzo (tomb in S. Angelo a Nilo), Antonio Rossellino (tombs at S. Anna dei Lombardi) and Giuliano da Maiano (the Capua Gate). Many other early Renaissance painters are represented at Naples' **Capodimonte Museum**. Yet the ideas and artistic innovations of the Renaissance failed to penetrate deeply among local artists.

There were a few exceptions. In **Galatina**, a small town near Lecce, the church of Santa Caterina contains a remarkable fresco cycle, an attempt by southern artists to adapt the early Renaissance manner of Tuscany. Giovanni da Nola, a first-rate though little-known sculptor, decorated many churches in Naples. Other noteworthy works in the city include Tommaso Malvito's Cappella Carafa in the **Duomo**, and Romolo Balsimelli's Santa Caterina a Formiello. But the most important Renaissance achievement in Naples was the **Castel Nuovo** (1454–67), and especially its triumphal arch. Built for Alfonso I, this was a Renaissance landmark, a mythological rendering of statesman-like virtue entirely equal to the arches and columns of antiquity.

Baroque and Neoclassicism

If the Baroque began in Rome, it found a warm welcome throughout the south. With its escapism, emotionalism and excess, the new style proved an inspiration to a troubled and long somnolent region, and the concentration of wealth in the hands of the court and the Church ensured a lavish patronage.

In **Naples**, the greatest exponent of the Baroque was a brilliant, tortured soul named Cosimo Fanzago (1591–1678) – the sculptor, architect and decorative artist who designed the great cloister of San Martino, the *guglia* in Piazza San Domenico and a little masterpiece of a church, Santa Maria Egiziaca, at Pizzofalcone. (A *guglia* is a tall, elaborately decorated religious monument for a piazza, a Neapolitan speciality.) Fanzago is known for his love of *pietra dura* work, exquisite floral patterns in brightly coloured marble inlay (as in S. Domenico Maggiore) – an art from late Renaissance Florence that set the trend for the lush interiors of Neapolitan churches over the next century. Another Neapolitan worthy of mention is Ferdinando Sanfelice, a light-hearted pastry chef of churches (such as the Nunziatella) and palaces, famous for his geometrically complex grand staircases (including those in the Palazzi Sanfelice, Bartolomeo di Maio and Serra di Cassano).

For all that, the most distinctive brands of southern Gothic appeared not in the capital, but in provincial centres such as Noto, Catania and Mazara del Vallo in Sicily and, best of all, **Lecce**, near the southern tip of Puglia. It was a remarkable achievement – an obscure little city, only a little more prosperous than its neighbours, and doing its best to uphold a threadbare but ardent heritage of cultural distinction, Lecce created and advanced its own style of architecture for almost two centuries. It began in the 1500s, with the surprisingly sophisticated Renaissance folly called the Sedile, and reached its height with architects Giuseppe and Antonio Zimbalo and sculptor Cesare Penna in the mid-17th century. (All three collaborated on Lecce's masterpiece, Santa Croce.) Exotic, ornate decoration, more than any advances in building forms, is the hallmark of the Leccese style, and upon close examination, this proves to be more influenced by the Renaissance and even Puglian Romanesque than anything from contemporary Naples or Rome. Reflections of the Lecce style can be seen in many towns in southern Puglia, notably **Ostuni**, **Manduria**, **Maglie** and **Nardò**.

In sculpture, the best Neapolitan works are the most eccentric: the spectacular virtuosity of Francesco Queirolo, Antonio Corradini and Giuseppe Sammartino in the Sansevero Chapel. (Art historians hate them – but what do they know?) Almost all the Neapolitan sculptors devoted much effort to figures for *presepi* (Christmas cribs); the San Martino Museum has a delightful collection.

In painting, the south began the Baroque era under the spell of Caravaggio, who arrived in Naples in 1607 (paintings at Capodimonte). Among his followers, adapting the dark and dramatic realism of the master to different ends, were the Spaniard José Ribera (San Martino) and the Calabrian Mattia Preti, one of the most talented southern artists, who did much of his best work for the Knights of Malta. (He also worked at Capodimonte and S. Pietro a Maiella in Naples, and in his home town of **Taverna**.) Another important painter, at his best in highly original landscapes, was the native Neapolitan Salvator Rosa (1615–73).

Later Neapolitan painting was frivolous and colourful, with little to challenge the intellect or imagination. It was just right for the times and enjoyed a widespread influence. Luca Giordano – the mercurial and speedy Luca fa presto (1634–1705) – painted all over Italy and spent 10 years at the court in Madrid, yet still found time to cover acres of Neapolitan ceilings with clouds and *putti*, tumbling horses and pastel-robed floating maidens (as at the Duomo and San Martino). His greatest follower – and in his day perhaps the most popular painter in Italy – was Francesco Solimena (1657–1747; S. Paolo Maggiore, Gesù Nuovo).

A more modern, sober turn in Neapolitan art came with the reforming King Charles III in 1750. That year saw the death of Ferdinando Sanfelice and the arrival of two architects from the north who brought the Neoclassical manner to Naples. Ferdinando Fuga was, for a time, court architect to the Bourbons (his work includes the Albergo dei Poveri on Via Foria, the biggest and fanciest poorhouse in the world). The 18th century, though, belonged to Luigi Vanvitelli (1700–1773), son of the Italianized Dutch painter Gaspar van Wittel and favourite architect of King Charles III, the most assiduous builder among the Bourbon kings. Most of Vanvitelli's energies were expended on the huge Royal Palace at **Caserta**, fully in line with the international Neoclassicism of the time with its tastefully unimaginative façades, grand stairways and axis-planned gardens. Neoclassicism in Naples, a surprising reaction against the city's long-standing love affair with the Baroque and the bizarre, dominated the 1700s and indeed the remainder of the Bourbon period, as seen in such buildings as the Capodimonte Palace and the **San Carlo** Opera House (both by GA Medrano, in the 1730s) and the grandiose, domed San Francesco di Paola (1817).

Topics

On Pleasure's Shore: Rome's California

If they had had postcards in Roman times, your Aunt Vulpecula would have sent you one from Campania – *Having a Wonderful Time in Baiae on the Sinus Puteolanus.* The photo on the front would show gaily painted pleasure boats in the bay, with silken canopies and slaves waving golden fans over the languorous occupants. In the background, there would be a row of delicious villas, each with two or three levels of gleaming marble porticoes perched on the cliffs over the blue Tyrrhenian. This playground of the Roman world is the place where holidays as we know them were invented. The young world had never seen anything like it. Everyone in the empire, from Londinium to Baalbek, had heard of the bay and its prodigies of beauty and luxury; no doubt everyone dreamed of actually going there.

The first mention of a villa on the bay comes from the early 2nd century BC. The Roman state, which had seized all the land in the area after conquering it, was now selling it off to help finance the Second Punic War, the bloody and expensive struggle against Hannibal and the Carthaginians. One of the first buyers was Scipio Africanus, the general who brought that war to a successful conclusion, and who became the richest man in Rome. He built himself a villa near Liternum, overlooking the sea, and other members of the Roman elite soon followed. Over the next two centuries, as Rome spread its rule over the Mediterranean world and the booty rolled in, the dour senators and knights found something they had never had before – *otium* (leisure). Thanks to contact with the cultured Greek world, in Campania and in Greece itself, Rome was growing up, and even becoming civilized in its awkward, bumptious way.

If they hadn't yet acquired many of the accomplishments of culture, at least the Romans knew how to tack up a good façade: the villas housed copies of Greek statues and frescoes, as well as Greek cooks, poets and musicians. The nabobs affected Greek dress, the elegant *chlamys* worn by the locals instead of their impractical togas. Some of them even learned the language, and impressed their friends at dinner parties by extemporizing a few lines of verse. In the 1st century BC, everyone who was anyone in Rome had a villa on the bay, and the Campanian coast entered its golden age of opulence. The populist dictator Marius had one. The reactionary dictator Sulla who followed him built an even bigger model, which he shared with his family, a few hundred of his picked slaves, kept ladies and whichever of his clients and hangers-on were lucky enough to be invited. There was plenty of entertainment, too – among others, 'Roscius the comedian, Sorex the mime and Metrobius the female impersonator', as a historian of the time solemnly recorded. Julius Caesar owned a few villas, and his murderers plotted the deed at Cinna's place just up the coast.

These famous names of history, and the clique of politicians and speculators that went with them, had serious money. When Rome conquered the world, a select few raked in the lion's share of the loot, amassing fortunes that make the greatest private hoards of our day seem like pocket change in comparison. Cicero often wrote disapprovingly of his fellow Romans' ostentatious displays of wealth – but he had three villas on the bay himself, and a string of lodges all the way to Rome so he would always have somewhere cosy to sleep as he travelled back and forth.

The holiday trip was called the *peregrinatio*, and everyone would come down in mid-April. In the heat of summer, they would go back to Rome or retire to a cooler villa up in the mountains. Most would be back on the bay in autumn, and stay as long as there was *otium* left to enjoy. In any season, amusements were never lacking. There were the famous baths of Baiae, the most sumptuous such establishment in the ancient world, and above all, there were dinner parties which would be held nearly every evening. For the afternoon, lazy cruises on the bay were in favour, or rides in slave-borne litters to Puteoli, Neapolis or the countryside. In Caesar's time, pet fish were a craze among the bay set: bearded mullets decorated with jewels, trained to leap up and eat out of their masters' hands. Humbler citizens must have been as fascinated with the doings of the rich as they are today, and even if they had no patron to invite them to stay, they must have come in great numbers to gawk and dream.

The bay, having invented holidays, can also probably take credit for the first secular souvenirs. Archaeologists have dug up plenty of examples: small items of Puteoli's famous glassware decorated with handpainted scenes of the coastline and its villas. Contemporaries describe the entire bay, from Misenum to Sorrentum, as being solidly lined with these palaces, giving the impression of a single, tremendous marble city. It must have been one of the grandest sights of the classical world.

The bay remained in fashion well into the imperial age. Augustus bought Capri from the city of Neapolis and covered it with pavilions and terraced gardens; his villa on the island was decorated with whale bones and other marvels of the sea, as well as relics of classical heroes. All the other early emperors spent much of their time there, notably Tiberius (*see* p.131). Some of the glamour wore off in greyer times, under Vespasian and after, and later emperors would build their own pleasure palaces closer to the necessities of power or military leadership. (Some of these were huge cities in themselves, such as Trajan's near Tivoli, or Diocletian's, which survives today as the city of Split, Croatia.)

By the late 5th century there were no more pleasure boats in the bay – only Vandal pirate craft from Africa. The last mention of any villas was when Romulus Augustulus, last pathetic emperor of the west, was sent to live under close guard in the Villa of Lucullus (now Naples' Castel dell'Ovo) by his Gothic conqueror Odoacer. Many of the villas would have been destroyed during this era. Earthquakes, Vesuvius, time and stone quarriers have done for the rest. Such reminders of the impermanence of all our glories may contribute to the melancholy many visitors to Naples have always felt. But there's no need to be melancholy: the Neapolitans, true heirs of antiquity, hardly ever are.

The Lady and the Dragon

The first Normans in southern Italy came as pilgrims to the great Mediterranean shrine of St Michael at Monte Sant'Angelo in Puglia. Obviously, they could have saved themselves a long trip by choosing instead to do whatever Michaelian pilgrims do at the saint's northern branch office, Mont Saint Michel. Monte Sant'Angelo must have had a reputation even then. Visit it today, and it won't take you long to realize you are in one of the most uncanny holy sites in Christendom. The light and air, the austere, treeless landscape and the dramatic mountaintop setting all conspire to strangeness.

Across Europe, the cult of St Michael was often associated with water, especially underground water. At Monte Sant'Angelo, the sanctuary is a cave that once had a flowing fountain in it. Souvenir stands outside peddle familiar images of the archangel spearing his dragon, or serpent, but it is likely that this tableau recalls something older and deeper than Christian legend – you won't find it anywhere in the Bible. Some mythologists speculate that, before they were demonized by Christian theologians, western dragons were really more like the benign Chinese sort, representing underground streams and currents of energy in the earth. On some of the other weird old churches of Monte Sant'Angelo, you will encounter the serpent again – a pair of them, usually, whispering into the ear of a fork-tailed mermaid or siren. Whoever this lady might be, she is portrayed in a quite alarming pose, with her tails spread wide to expose a part of mermaids seldom seen in churches.

Nearly every site dedicated to St Michael has something mysterious about it but this one would be hard to beat. There is a suggestion of something ancient and a bit heretical, something that could be openly portrayed in the anarchically tolerant 12th century, but was later suppressed or just disappeared, leaving no trace. One Italian scholar suggests the mermaids were a symbol of a Dionysiac dancing cult – but your guess is probably as good as his. The Church has any number of explanations for the depiction of the mermaid: she is the Church itself, personified wisdom or personified vice, or else just meaningless decoration. Unfortunately, all of these explanations are utterly contrived and false. If you meet the local priests and monks, you find they don't want to talk about her at all. Mermaids do not only occur in Puglia; you can see them in medieval churches all over Italy and southern France, especially those dedicated to St Michael. In many small churches they are hidden – look hard and you'll find her peeking out from the back of a pier, or on a capital in a dimly lit corner.

Nevertheless, Puglia is the lady's special province. In Monte Sant'Angelo, she seems to be the reigning deity, and she turns up in a conspicuous place in churches all over the region. If you follow her tracks as far as they lead, you'll see her in the mosaic floor of Otranto cathedral, near Puglia's Land's End on the Salentine peninsula. The smiling, spread-tailed mermaid here presides over the whole crazy Creation portrayed in this unique mosaic, seated next to King Solomon himself. There is an inscription around the figure that probably explains everything – only it is in Arabic Kufic script and nobody knows what it says.

The *Civitas Hippocratica*

As the industrial world struggles with its problems of healthcare – costs, ethical issues and disconcerting technology – it is refreshing to go back a thousand years to Salerno, where the first medical school of modern Europe was founded in the 11th century. Established, according to tradition, by the 'Four Doctors' – an Italian, a Greek, a Jew and an Arab – it was for centuries the finest in Europe, the *Fons Medicinae* as Petrarch called it. Its doctors and teachers played an important role in the transmission of Greek and Arab science into Europe. Before the teachings of Salerno became widespread in Europe, what succour existed lay in the hands of monks and priests, who often blamed any illness on divine wrath. Salerno's school marked a definite improvement, by going back to Hippocrates and seeking natural causes.

The school also marked the beginnings of medicine as a commercial enterprise, giving its students sound advice on collecting bills: 'When the patient is nearly well, address the head of the family, or the sick man's nearest relative, thus: "God Almighty having deigned by our aid to restore him whom you asked us to visit, we pray that He will maintain his health, and that you will now give us an honourable dismissal. Should any other member of your family desire our aid, we should, in grateful remembrance of our former dealings with you, leave all else and hurry to serve him."' At the same time, a natural sliding fee was the order of the day; a king was expected to pay a hundred times more for his cure than a small merchant.

Much of Salerno's medical theory was based on numerology and astrology, following the science of the time, but there was a more practical side, too. Medieval doctors sought to maintain a balance between the four humours of the body: phlegm (cold and moist), blood (hot and moist), bile (hot and dry) and black bile (cold and dry) – a poetic, metaphorical way of looking at things but one that experience found instructive for centuries. To judge the soundness of this approach, consider the Health Rule of Salerno. Famous throughout the Middle Ages, the Rule was compiled by a certain Robert of Normandy, who was wounded during the First Crusade and convalesced in the city. Originally in Latin verse, its recommendations were translated into English by an Elizabethan, Sir John Harington:

A king that cannot rule him his diet
Will hardly rule his realm in peace and quiet.

For healthy men may cheese be wholesome food,
But for the weak and sickly 'tis not good.

Use three doctors still, first Dr Quiet,
Next Dr Merry-man and Dr Diet...

Wine, Women, Baths, by art of nature warme,
Us'd or abus'd do men much good or harme.
Some live to drinke new wine not fully fin'd.
But for your health we wish that you drink none,
For such to dangerous fluxes are inclin'd,
Besides the lees of wine doe breed the stone.
But such by our consent shall drink alone.
For water and small biere we make no question
Are enemies to health and good digestion;
And Horace in a verse of his rehearses,
That water-drinkers never make good verses.

The Camorra: Oil for the Madonna

Sotto questo cielo non nascono sciocchi
(Under these skies no fools are born)
Neapolitan proverb

Camorra means a short jacket, of the kind the street toughs of Naples used to wear in the days of the Bourbon kings. But, as with Sicily's Mafia, the origin of the Neapolitan Camorra is lost in legend. Some accounts put it in the slums of the *Quartieri Spagnuoli*, under the rule of the Spanish viceroys of the 16th century. Spanish soldiers of that time lived the life of picaresque novels – or at least tried to – and the fathers and brothers of the district did their best to defend their girls from such picaresqueness, which usually meant a knife in the back in some dark alley.

There may be some truth to that, or it could all be romantic bosh. Criminals in southern Italy seem always to have been well organized with a hierarchy, a set of rules and a code of *omertà* (silence). Foreign visitors to the city in the 1700s wrote that, when something was stolen, they were able to get in touch with the 'King of Thieves' who would magically get it restored – stealing from guests, after all, was a discourtesy.

It's doubtful they were ever so polite to their fellow citizens, for as long as there has been a Camorra, it has lived mainly by extortion, with a fat finger in whatever rackets of the age looked most profitable. For a long time, the gang's biggest takings came from the prisons, which they controlled. In the old days, prisoners in Naples, as anywhere else, had to pay for their upkeep and each new arrival would be met by the *Camorristi* with a subtle request for 'money for oil for the Madonna' – that is, to keep the light burning at the shrine in the Camorra's favoured church, the Madonna del Carmine in the Piazza del Mercato. You can imagine that the Madonna required rather a lot of fuel.

Relations between the Camorra and the authorities have always been rather complex. In the last days of Bourbon rule, Ferdinand II made use of Camorra gangs as a kind of anti-liberal secret police. In 1860, it is said, Garibaldi was forced to make a deal with them, handing them control of the city government in return for nobody shooting at him and his army when he entered the city.

The new Italian state (run by northerners) tried to wipe out the Camorra by vigorous police action. The gangsters trumped that by going into politics, setting the pattern of close alliance between organized crime and centre-rightist parties that continues in Italy to this day. In an irony of parliamentary democracy, the titled gentry of the ruling class and the thugs found that their interests coincided, and by 1900, the theory and practice of southern machine politics had been honed to perfection.

Like the Mafia in Sicily, the Camorra took some hard knocks under Mussolini. If there was any cream to be skimmed, the Fascists wanted it all for themselves and the ambience of a dictatorship proved wonderfully convenient for getting around the legal niceties of arrest and conviction. But, also like the Mafia, the Camorra was able to manipulate the post-1944 Allied Military Government and get back on its feet.

It's possible the Americans felt the mobsters would be a useful ally in an impossible situation, or maybe they got a message that a little co-operation would save their army a lot of trouble (accidents can happen...). In any case, it seems to have been the Allies' policy on the Italian front to throw open the prisons in every town they captured.

In 1944, top American mobster Lucky Luciano went to Sicily to arrange things. He was swindled royally by his supposed brothers, demonstrating that there has always been less of a connection between the native and foreign Mafias than one might suppose. One of his New York lieutenants, Vito Genovese, grew up around Naples. He went back there and had more luck than Lucky, insinuating his way into the confidences of the Allied High Command. From the 'Triangle of Death' – the old Camorra stronghold in the villages north of the city – and from the *bancarelle* of the Forcella market, Genovese oversaw an orgy of black-market wheeling and dealing, largely in stolen army supplies, while old Camorra hands revived the ancient and hallowed traditions of extortion.

Today, while the recent crackdown on the Sicilian Mafia has enjoyed some success, the Camorra is proving a tough nut to crack. It is estimated that there are 6,000 Camorra members, divided into 100 or so 'families', and that 60 per cent of all businesses in the Naples area pay protection money to the Camorra. The gang takes its cut from most sorts of common crime and, like the Mafia, it has become heavily involved in drugs – not so much exporting them as pushing them on their neighbours. Unlike the Mafia, however, the Camorra has no recognized central authority. Factions settle their differences with reciprocal assassinations – conducted in the streets of the old quarters where all may enjoy them.

In recent years, with many top Camorra men in prison, a feature of the Neapolitan crime scene has been the increasing prominence of women within this traditionally men-only organization. The original model was Rosetta 'Ice Eyes' Cutolo, immortalized in the film *Il Camorrista*, who ran operations for her imprisoned brother Rafaele for 30 years until she gave herself up in 1993. More recently, two other women – Erminia Giuliano, who ran the Forcella neighbourhood, and Maria Licciardi, who controlled the Secondigliano district – were key players in the Neapolitan underworld, until both were arrested in 2001. The women proved as bloody as their fathers and brothers. Licciardi unleashed a drug war that left 13 people dead, while in May 2002, three women were killed in a shoot-out at Lauro (a small town east of Naples) – the first time women had opened fire on each other in the streets. Other southern regions also have their Mafia-type organizations. Apart from the Sicilian Mafia itself, there is the Sacra Corona Unita in Puglia and the 'Ndrangheta ('heroism' or 'virtue') in Calabria.

There are estimated to be 5,000 'Ndrangheta members, divided into 200 or 300 groups in the remote rural villages of the region. Like the Camorra, the 'Ndrangheta is made up of independent groups with no hierarchical structure, making it hard for anti-Mafia investigators to crack. Indeed, the 'Ndrangheta may have benefited from the crackdown on the Sicilian Mafia, which has allowed it to take over some of that organization's 'markets'. In recent years, it has even been investigated for smuggling Russian weapons and nuclear materials.

The Sacra Corona Unita is a more recent arrival, dating from 1983. It has been particularly involved in drugs and the smuggling of illegal Albanian immigrants into Italy. It is believed to have around 1,000 members.

The New Science

It is the driest, obscurest, metaphysicalest book I ever got hold of. Confucius is a more lucid writer. Mortgages and remainders are pleasanter to peruse.

John Fiske, a Harvard scholar (1858)

Probably only a Neapolitan, living in the shadow of Vesuvius, could have written *La Nuova Scienza*, and Giambattista Vico was a true son of the city. Born in a little room over his father's bookshop on Via San Biagio dei Librai, he spent most of his life among the mouldering alleys of the Spacca and the University. Vico tells his very Neapolitan story in his *Autobiography*, a classic of unintentional hilarity. The fun starts on the first page; after getting his birth date wrong by two years, Vico continues (writing in the third person):

He was a boy of high spirits and impatient of rest, but at the age of seven he fell head first from the top of a ladder to the floor below, and remained a good five hours without consciousness... The surgeon, indeed, observing the broken cranium and considering the period of unconsciousness, predicted that he would either die of it or grow up an idiot. However, by God's grace, neither part of his prediction came true, but as a result of this mischance, he grew up with a melancholy and irritable temperament, such as belongs to men of ingenuity and depth, who thanks to the one, are quick as lightning in perception, and thanks to the other, take no pleasure in verbal cleverness or falsehood.

The rest of the autobiography is pretty much in the same tone, with lofty, pompous phrasings befitting a man who held the chair of rhetoric at Naples University, and with a prickly defensiveness that came from a lifetime of being ignored or laughed at by his colleagues and nearly everyone else. Teaching rhetoric earned Vico a measly 100 ducats a year, and to get by, he had to squander his talent writing fulsome eulogies and panegyrics for the king and the grandees of Naples. All the while the poor philosopher was spending much of his time feeding and caring for his flock of children, a job his horrible, illiterate wife didn't much care for.

A turning point in Vico's life came at the age of 55, when he tried to secure appointment to the much better-paying chair of law. For the occasion, he composed a brilliant treatise on the philosophical basis of law and delivered it to the assembly blissfully unaware that almost all his fellows had been bribed to support one of the other candidates. The winner, best known as 'a notorious seducer of servant girls', eventually tried to publish a book and was found out as a plagiarist. The disgusted Vico gave up trying to get ahead, and devoted the rest of his life to his great work, the *New Science*. To get it printed, in 1726, he had to sell his diamond ring, and even then, he could only afford to do it in type so small it could barely be read.

Nevertheless, the work brought him some fame and respect in his last years, and the position of Official Historiographer to the King. Vico died in 1744; at the funeral, a quarrel broke out between his fellow professors and his religious confraternity over who would carry the coffin to the church; somehow this degenerated into a general neighbourhood brawl and Vico's corpse was abandoned in the middle of Via dei Tribunali. Finally, someone carted him off to the Girolamini Church, and 50 years later, his last surviving son got around to putting up a marker on the tomb, where it can be seen today. As James Joyce put it (writing of Finnegan, and maybe Vico):

A good clap, a fore marriage, a bad wake, tell hell's well.

But Vico has had the last laugh. In our troubled times, when the airy certainties of Voltaire and Locke begin to look a bit superficial, Vico may well be the only thinker of the 18th century still worth a serious reading; his strange and utterly subversive book has increased its renown and influence with every generation since his death. Vico called the *New Science* an essay on the 'principles of Humanity'.

His system is expressed in the language of myth, partly from Vico's own imaginative turn of mind, and possibly also from a desire not to arouse the Inquisition, still in business in 18th-century Naples. Vico has been called an 'Orphic voice', an oracle. He explains the development of language, for example, as beginning in a 'mute speech' of gestures and signs, a 'divine poetry'. The next stage is symbols – like heraldic arms; only then comes conventional speech. After a spin through the Wonderland of the *New Science*, this begins to make sense. The major theme of the book is an exploration of the origins of culture and society, and the circular 'course the nations run' through four stages: first a theocratic age, founded by giants out of barbarism; next comes the age of heroes, an aristocratic society, and then 'human' government, where equality is recognized, though this inevitably declines into monarchy (like Augustus' Rome). At last, through what Vico calls 'the barbarism of reflection', man's egotism causes disintegration and fall, and the stage is cleared for the whole cycle to start afresh. Scholars today emphasize Vico's contributions to social thinking – somewhat primitive ones, in their view – and he has been called the 'first political scientist'. They do not get the point. James Joyce did, and he turned the *New Science* inside out and tickled and teased it to make an even stranger book: *Finnegan's Wake*. As Norman O. Brown put it, 'Joyce wore his eyes out staring at Europe and seeing nothing'. Western civilization, for him, was over, simply biding time until the barbarians come (who could argue?), and he arranged his murky masterpiece in four parts, following Vico's four stages of history.

Goethe Takes a Holiday

In 1786, at the age of 38, Goethe suffered a severe midlife crisis at the court in Weimar and bolted for Italy when no one was looking. Famous all over Europe as the author of Werther, he travelled under a false name and did much to blaze the Grand Tour with his *Italian Journey*, published from his letters and notes in 1816. Many have used it as their guide, at least to Naples, but only a minority of Grand Tourists even now take up his challenge to sail on down to Sicily. 'To me, Sicily implies Asia and Africa,' he wrote, a sentiment that would make any northern Italian smile in agreement. But Goethe's interests were historical and classical; he longed 'to stand at that miraculous centre upon which so many radii of world history converge'.

Goethe was one of the greatest poets who ever lived, but his *Italian Journey* could have been written by an awestruck insurance salesman; his insights are ponderous and trite, his opinions on art marvels of philistine conformity. Everything is beautiful, or important, or simply fills him with emotion. Much of it hides what he was probably really thinking about – sex. Its easy availability in Italy did much to make the country so irresistible to the Romantic poets and artists of northern Europe.

Two hundred years ago, it took three or four days to sail from Naples to Palermo. Goethe was so seasick he couldn't stand up, but he still managed to compose an act or two of a play. On the return sail from Messina, his ship came within inches of crashing into the sheer cliffs of Capri; its neutral flag served to keep pirates at bay.

We take cameras to record our travels; Goethe took his own artist. In Naples, he hobnobbed with Sir William and Lady Hamilton. In Palermo, he impersonated an Englishman to meet the mother and relatives of Cagliostro. He was entertained by the viceroy, counts and princes, and had an amusing encounter with the gruff governor of Messina. Inns, however, were few and far between. In one especially desperate establishment, Goethe described how the beggars fought the dogs for his sausage skins and apple parings. In other towns, Goethe and his artist had to buy a chicken from a peasant, and hire his pots, stove, dishes and table; and they were grateful for a pestilent mattress to sleep on in the barn. Italy may be more comfortable nowadays, but fewer modern visitors have such luxury to dawdle. But then a journey was a more serious business then – a once-in-a-lifetime experience. Not only did Goethe see the sights, but he theorized on the 'primal plant', measured temples and ancient sculpture, read the *Odyssey* in Greek and began a new play.

But most of all, Goethe travelled to learn about Italy, and about himself, and his journey took on the weight of an archetype as old as the Odyssey itself: 'If I cannot come back reborn, it would be much better not to come back at all.'

Music and Opera

Italy has contributed as much to Western music as any country – and perhaps more. It was an Italian monk, Guido d'Arezzo, who devised the musical scale. It was a Venetian printer, Ottavino Petrucci, who invented a method of printing music with movable type in 1501 – an industry Italian printers monopolized for years (which is why, for instance, we play *allegro* but not *schnell*). Italy also gave us the piano – originally the pianoforte, because unlike the harpsichord you could play both soft and loud – and the accordion, which was invented in the Marches, while the violins of the Guarneri and Stradivarius of Cremona set a standard for that instrument that has never been equalled.

But Italy is most famous as the mother of opera, in many ways the most Italian of arts. Italian composers first came into their own in the 14th century, led by the blind Florentine Landini, whose *Ecco la Primavera* is one of the first Italian compositions to come down to us. Even in such early Italian works, musicologists note a special love of melody, as well as a preference for vocal music over the purely instrumental.

Landini was followed by the age of the *frottolas* (secular verses accompanied by lutes), which were especially prominent in the court of Mantua. The *frottolas* were forerunners of the madrigal, the greatest Italian musical invention during the Renaissance. Although sung in three or six parts, the text of the madrigals was given serious consideration and was sung to be understood. At the same time, church music had become so polyphonically rich and sumptuous (most notably at St Mark's in Venice) that it drowned out the words of the Mass. Melodies were co-opted from secular (and often bawdy) songs, and the bishops at the Council of Trent (1545–63) seriously considered banning music from the liturgy. The day was saved by the Roman composers, led by Palestrina. His solemn, simple but beautiful melodies set a standard for all subsequent composers.

Two contrasting developments near the end of the 16th century led to the birth of opera. On the one hand, there was the Baroque love of spectacle and the urge to make everything more beautiful, elaborate and showy. Musically, there were the lavish Florentine *intermedii*, performed on special occasions between the acts of plays. The *intermedii* used elaborate sets and costumes, with songs, choruses and dances to set a mythological scene. At the same time, also in Florence, a group of humanist intellectuals who called themselves the 'Camerata' came to the conclusion from their classical studies that ancient Greek drama was not spoken, but sung. They took it upon themselves to try to recreate this pure and classical form. One of their chief theorists was Galileo's father Vincenzo, who studied Greek, Turkish and Moorish music and advocated the clear enunciation of the words (as opposed to the Venetian tendency to merge words and music as a single rich unit of sound).

The first result of the Camerata's debates was court musician Jacopo Peri's *L'Euridice*, performed in Florence in 1600. Peri used a kind of singing speech (*recitative*) to tell the story, interspersed with a few melodic songs. But the first full-blown opera had to wait a few years, until the Duchess of Mantua asked her court composer, Claudio Monteverdi (1567–1643), to compose something like the work she had heard in Florence. Monteverdi went far beyond Peri. He brought in a large orchestra, designed elegant sets, and added dances and many more melodic songs, called arias. His classic *L'Orfeo* (1607), which is still performed today, and *L'Arriana* (unfortunately lost except for fragments) were the first operatic successes. Monteverdi moved on to bigger audiences in Venice, which soon had 11 opera houses. After he died, though, Naples took over top opera honours, gaining special renown for clear-toned *castrati*.

Other advances were taking place in the more pious atmosphere of Rome, where Corelli was perfecting the *concerto* and composing his famous Christmas Concerto. In Venice, Vivaldi greatly expanded the genre by composing some 400 *concerti* for whichever instruments happened to be played in the orchestra of orphaned girls where he was concert master.

The 18th century saw the sonata form perfected by harpsichord master Domenico Scarlatti. Opera was by now rid of some of its Baroque excesses and a division was set between serious works and the comic *opera buffa*. Pergolesi (1710–36 – his *Il Flaminio* was the basis for Stravinsky's *Pulcinella*) and *Cimarosa* (1749–1801) were the most sought-after composers, while Salieri (the antagonist of Mozart depicted in the film

Amadeus) charmed the court of Vienna. Another Italian, Sammartini, helped develop the modern symphony, and Italian composers held sway throughout Europe, contributing much to the creation of modern classical music.

Italy innovated less in the 19th century. By this time, most of its musical energies were devoted to opera, which had become the reviving nation's clearest and most widely appreciated medium of self-expression. All of the most popular Italian operas were written in the 19th and early 20th century, most of them by the 'Big Five' – Bellini, Donizetti, Rossini, Verdi and Puccini. For Italians, Verdi (1813–1901) is supreme. He was a national idol even in his lifetime, and his rousing operas were practically the battle hymns of the Risorgimento. Verdi, more than anyone else, put Italy back on the musical map; his works were Italy's melodic answer to the ponderous turbulence of Richard Wagner. After Verdi, Puccini held the operatic stage, though not entirely singlehandedly: the later 19th century gave us a number of composers best remembered for only one opera – Leoncavallo's *Pagliacci*, Mascagni's *Cavalleria Rusticana*, Cilea's *Adriana Lecouvreur*, and many others, down to obscure composers like Giordano, whose *Fedora* (famous for being the only opera with bicycles on stage) is revived frequently in his home town of Foggia. More recent Italian and Italian-American composers have included Respighi (whose works were the only 20th-century productions that the great Toscanini deigned to direct) and Gian Carlo Menotti – who is perhaps best loved not for his operas but for founding the Spoleto Festival. The innovative post-war composers Luigi Nono and Luciano Berio are two of the most respected names in contemporary Italian academic music.

Alongside this great classical tradition, remnants of Italy's traditional folk music still remain. The pungent sound of the Italian bagpipes (*zampogna*), the ancient instrument of the Apennine shepherds, can still be heard in many of the cities of southern Italy, especially at Christmastime. There are also the lively tarantellas of Puglia; the country accordion music heard at many a rural festa. And last, but by no means least, there is the great song tradition of the country's music capital, Naples, which has given the world such cornball classics as 'O Sole Mio', as well as many haunting, passionate melodies of tragedy and romance that are rarely heard abroad.

The best place to hear opera in southern Italy – if you can find and afford a ticket – is undoubtedly Naples' Teatro San Carlo. Opened in 1737, it is the world's oldest surviving opera house and, in Italy, second in prestige only to La Scala in Milan (which opened 41 years after the San Carlo). The theatre, which was completely rebuilt after the original burnt down in 1816, is both beautiful and known for its perfect acoustics. Almost every leading opera singer has sung at the San Carlo. Curiously, one of the least successful performances was by one of Naples' own sons. Enrico Caruso was born in 1873 in a poor neighbourhood near the Albergo dei Poveri, the 18th of 20 children. Although he has come to be regarded as the greatest operatic tenor in history, and had already triumphed at La Scala in Milan, Caruso was booed and hissed on his San Carlo debut in 1901. Stung by this humiliation, he vowed never to perform in his home town again – a promise he kept.

Food and Drink

04

There are those who eat to live and those who live to eat, and then there are the Italians, for whom food has an almost religious significance, unfathomably linked with love, *La Mamma*, and tradition. In a country where millions of otherwise sane people spend much of their waking hours worrying about their digestion, standards both at home and in the restaurants are understandably high. Few Italians are gluttons, but all are experts on what is what in the kitchen; to serve a meal that is not properly prepared and more than a little complex is tantamount to an insult. For the visitor this national culinary obsession comes as an extra bonus to the senses – along with remarkable sights, music and the warm sun on your back, you can enjoy some of the best tastes and smells in the world, prepared daily in Italy's kitchens and fermented in its countless wine cellars.

The Cuisine of Southern Italy

Regional Specialities

Naples gave the world (or at least, the Western world) both pizza and spaghetti, as well as the world's favourite dessert: ice cream. (The first sorbets appeared in Naples in 1660, followed by milk-sweetened ice creams in 1664.)

A genuine Neapolitan pizza cooked in a wood-fired brick oven is the archetypal local eating experience and watching it being made, whirled and slapped high in the air with lightning speed is just as much of an entertainment as consuming it. The popular *marinara* is anointed with tomato, garlic and oregano. *Calzoni* are half-moon envelopes of pizza dough, often filled with ham and cheese and sold as street snacks. Pasta often appears with engaging simplicity, smothered in oil and garlic, or tomato and basil. In the south, factory spaghetti gives way to the real monarch of pasta – nothing more than thick homemade spaghetti, but unmistakably different from the mass-produced commodity. *Mozzarella*, rather than parmesan, appears most often in pasta sauces. *Mozzarella in carrozza* is a fried sandwich of cheese, often sold as a street snack.

Campania tends to be overly modest about its cuisine. Its biggest favourites are simple enough: *pasta e fagioli* (pasta and beans) and *spaghetti alle vongole* (spaghetti with baby clams). The seafood, as everywhere else along the southern coasts, is superb. Besides the ubiquitous clams, squid, octopus and mussels, *zuppe di cozze* (mussels in a hot pepper sauce) appear frequently, along with oily fish like mackerel and sardines. Vegetables often served as *contorni* (an appetizing assortment) are excellent, too. Aubergines and courgettes make their way into many local dishes, especially *melanzane parmigiana* (aubergine baked with tomato and mozzarella), *misto di frittura* (deep-fried potato, aubergine and courgette flowers) or *zucchini a scapace* (courgettes in tomato sauce). In Campania, specialities tend to be hotter and spicier than in the north, and are often seasoned with condiments like capers, garlic, anchovies, lemon juice, oregano, olives and fennel. Dishes described as *alla napoletana* usually contain tomato, capers, black olives and garlic.

As far as the level of cooking is concerned, **Calabria** and **the Basilicata** are probably the most improved regions of Italy compared to 10 years ago – a little prosperity makes any corner of Italy blossom. Back in ancient Sybaris, the gourmet centre of the Greek Mediterranean, and in the other towns of Magna Grecia, public gastronomical revues rivalled athletic contests in popularity. Good recipes for fish sauces were treated as state secrets and slaves who happened to be good cooks were worth enormous sums. Calabrian cooking today is not that distinctive, except perhaps in a fondness for really hot peppers, but with the simple, fresh ingredients they use, it won't often be disappointing either. The biggest treat is the seafood, including the best swordfish anywhere, caught fresh from the Straits of Messina.

Puglia is more prosperous and the Puglians take their cuisine a little more seriously. *La cucina pugliese* (Puglian cooking) makes especially good use of seafood and you won't meet anyone in the region who isn't convinced theirs is the best in Italy. Bari is famous for fish, while Taranto has excellent mussels, mostly from the Mare Grande – called *mitili* instead of *cozze*. You'll taste varieties of shellfish in Puglia seen nowhere else: *fasulare*, small and roundish with tan-coloured shells, and *piedi di porco*, small, rugged black shells. Puglians scoff at the *vongole* served in *spaghetti alle vongole* everywhere else in Italy. Those tiny clams are really *guttuli*, they say. Real Puglian *vongole* are much bigger, and equally tasty, and you will even encounter *vongole imperiale*, giants among the clams.

The local olive oil is dark and strong, closer to that of Greece than the lighter oils of Tuscany and Umbria. The olives are smaller and fuller-flavoured, coming from trees whose roots have to dig deep into the soil to reach water.

As in most of southern Italy, sheep make up a great part of the livestock and the region's sheep's cheeses include the local styles of pecorino and ricotta. Look out for the unusually strongly flavoured *ricotta forte*. It goes particularly well in sauces with the favourite Puglian pasta, *orecchiette* ('little ears'), which is formed by shaping the uncooked pasta with the thumb. One popular dish is *orecchiette con cima di rape* (with turnip greens).

Puddings and cakes are rich and sweet all over the south. *Pasteria* is one of the most celebrated local sweets: a ricotta pie full of wheat berries, candied fruit and spices, traditionally eaten at Easter. Another irresistible speciality of Naples is *sfogliatella* (flaky pastry which may be stuffed with ricotta and candied peel), sometimes eaten for breakfast. Best of all (in season) is a fresh peach, naked and unadorned.

Pizza Paradise

Its origins are almost certainly Arab. Some people maintain the word may derive from pitta, the unleavened bread eaten in Greece, Turkey and the Middle East. But wherever it hails from, pizza as we know it is certainly an invention of Naples. Neapolitans are rightly and fiercely proud of this versatile dish and disdainful of imitations and the variations made by others. The thin-crusted affair served in Roman *pizzerie* is enough to make a Neapolitan cry and as for the deep-pan version invented in Chicago and served in many British and American pizza parlours... the less said the better.

For Neapolitans, a real pizza must have an uneven base and be cooked in a real wood-fired oven. Some say the secret is in the flour, others in the water. But all agree that the technique for flattening the dough is crucial. Not for the Neapolitans the pedantic practice of stretching out the dough with a rolling pin. In Naples, the *pizzaiolo* is a flamboyant character, flinging the dough up into the air, smashing it down on the marble table and swinging it round his head until it reaches the required shape and thickness. The best *pizzaioli* are much in demand and take home very respectable salaries.

As for the topping, the most authentic is *pomodoro fresco* – fresh tomatoes chopped over a bed of *mozzarella*, sprinkled with fresh basil and liberally doused with olive oil. Another Neapolitan favourite is the *ripieno*, a gut-buster of a pizza folded in two and stuffed with fresh *ricotta*, *mozzarella*, pieces of salami and cooked ham.

However you order it, pizza should really be eaten with beer rather than wine. Many pizzerias only serve fizzy, bottled wine, which is much more expensive and best left alone. Pizza is usually eaten as a meal in itself, sometimes for lunch but more often in the evening, preceded by an *antipasto* of *bruschetta* – slices of thick toasted bread soused in olive oil and garlic and topped with tomatoes and basil, or fried bite-sized chunks of *mozzarella* and vegetables.

For anyone on a tight budget – Neapolitans and tourists alike – the *pizzeria* is a lifeline. The bill for a pizza and a beer comes to about half that of a meal in a normal restaurant. In Naples, particularly good *pizzerias* are rewarded by a *vera pizza* (real pizza) emblem to hang outside. Two of the best are Lombardi a Santa Chiara and the exceptional Da Pasqualino, now in its fourth generation (*see* p.76).

Pasta Perfect

Pasta (or at least, noodles) was most likely invented by the Chinese and/or ancient Egyptians at least 3,000 years ago and probably brought to Italy by Saracen traders from North Africa. Italians would disagree, claiming an independent Etruscan or Roman origin. In any case, medieval recipe books show that pasta was known in Italy since at least the 11th century, long before Marco Polo was said to have brought it back from China (in 1292). Whatever its origins, the durum wheat was tough and hard to mill, and pasta remained a luxury dish until the invention of a mechanical mill in the 17th century allowed it to be produced cheaply enough for the masses.

Campania's climate, soil and proximity to the sea (the sea breezes helped to dry the wheat) proved ideal for producing dried pasta and Naples, along with Genoa, became one of the two centres of the new pasta industry. Between 1700 and 1785, the number of pasta shops in Naples increased from 60 to 280. Pasta hung from every balcony and street vendors cooked spaghetti and macaroni on charcoal-fired stoves. It was served plain, accompanied by grated Romano cheese; customers would hold up the long strands and lower them into their mouths, or suck them straight off the plate.

Macaroni, in particular, was particularly Neapolitan, and as it became the staple of the masses, it came to be associated with another symbol of the Neapolitan poor – the downtrodden, ever-hungry and miserable Pulcinella (who became the English 'Punch'); in Naples, you'll often see images of Pulcinella eating macaroni.

In the 1840s, pasta-makers from Amalfi set up the world's first fully mechanized pasta factory in Torre Annunziata, just south of Naples. Around this time, too, pasta first met tomato, the basis of so many modern pasta sauces. The tomato had been imported from Mexico by the Spanish in the 15th century but it took Europeans some time to accept that it was edible (it belongs to the often-poisonous nightshade family of plants). Tomato, boiled in a pot with a pinch of salt and a few basil leaves, was used in the early 1800s by Neapolitan street vendors for seasoning macaroni; pizza began to be topped with tomato sauce and mozzarella a few decades later.

Ice Cream Insights

As if giving the world – or at least the Western world – pizza and spaghetti wasn't enough, Naples also gave us our favourite dessert: ice cream. As with pasta, the Chinese got there first, developing a method that kept ice frozen for extended periods by mixing it with salt 1,000 years before Christ. The method was introduced to Europe in the 1660s, with first sorbets and then ices made with sweetened milk appearing in Naples in 1664. For the next two decades, Naples was the centre of the ice cream universe, leading the world in rich and innovative creations.

It's not surprising, then, that Naples still has some of the finest *gelaterie* in Italy. Look out for ones that offer *produzione propria* (made on the premises) or at least *produzione artigianale* ('homemade' but somewhere else). A local speciality is *granita di limone* (shavings of ice with lemon juice) often served from roadside stalls. There is also *semifreddo* (a smoother, mousse-like type of ice cream).

In a typical piece of marketing irony, the bland tri-coloured slab of artificially flavoured strawberry, vanilla and chocolate that you find in supermarkets under the name Neapolitan does not come from Naples at all but was concocted in America.

Drinks

Wine and Spirits

Italy is a country where everyday wine is cheaper than Coca-Cola or milk, and where nearly every rural family owns vineyards or has relatives who supply most of their daily needs – which are not great. But even though they live in one of the world's largest wine-growing countries, Italians imbibe relatively little and only at meals.

If Italy has an infinite variety of regional dishes, there is an equally bewildering array of regional wines, many of which are rarely exported because they are best drunk young. Unless you're dining at a restaurant with an exceptional cellar, do as the Italians do and order a carafe of the local wine (*vino locale* or *vino della casa*).

Most Italian wines are named after the grape and district they come from. If the label says DOC (*Denominazione di Origine Controllata*), it means that the wine comes from a specially defined area and was produced according to a certain traditional method. DOCG (*Denominazione di Origine Controllata e Garantita*) is allegedly a more rigorous classification, indicating that the wines not only conform to DOC standards, but have been tested by government-appointed inspectors. At present, only a few wines, mainly from Tuscany, have been granted this status but the number should increase steadily.

Limoncello

This lemon-flavoured liqueur is a speciality of the Sorrento peninsula.

1 litre alcohol for cooking (gin or vodka would do)
1 litre water
10 unwaxed large lemons
750g sugar

Peel the lemons, discarding the pith. Marinate the peel in the alcohol for at least 48 hours. Dissolve the sugar in a litre of boiling water and mix with the alcohol. Filter the mixture through a thick cloth. Serve chilled.

Italians are fond of postprandial brandies (to aid digestion) – the famous Stock or Vecchia Romagna labels are always good. Grappa (*acqua vitae*) is usually tougher and often drunk in black coffee after a meal (a *caffè corretto*). Other members of any Italian bar include Campari, the famous red bitter drunk on its own or in cocktails; popular aperitifs/digestives such as Vermouth, Fernet Branca, Cynar and Averno; and liqueurs including almond-flavoured Amaretto, cherry Maraschino and aniseed Sambuca. Or try one of the many locally brewed elixirs, often made by monks, found throughout southern Italy. Two of the best-known are Strega, the 'witch's potion' from Benevento, and *limoncello*, a lemon liqueur made on the Sorrento peninsula.

Campania was known for wine in Roman times. The legendary full-bodied Falerno was highly regarded by the ancients, and praised by Horace and Pliny. Today the region produces surprisingly little, and not much of any note. The most famous is Lacrima Christi, grown on the slopes of Vesuvius and only recently granted DOC status. Others to look out for include the white Greco di Tufo or Fiano di Avellino, or the deep, heavy red Taurasi.

Some good wines come from Calabria, though nothing especially distinguished. Ciró from the Ionian coast is a strong red (also white and rosé) wine best drunk in large quantities. Calabrians claim it is the oldest wine in Italy, made since the time of the Greeks in the area north of Crotone. A new DOC wine similar to Ciró, and made in a neighbouring region, is Melissa. Other good, strong DOC wines include Savuto and Pellaro. There is also a famous dessert wine, Greco di Gerace, and similar Grecos from the southern *terrazze* of Aspromonte. The Basilicata doesn't produce much wine, but it's certainly worth trying the excellent Aglianico red from Monte Vulture.

Puglian wine, like its cuisine, tends to be strong and full-bodied, and has had a high reputation since Roman times. Today there are about 24 different wines produced in Puglia including whites, reds, rosés, sparkling and the particularly sweet Muscat. One that is worth looking out is Cerignola, a powerful red from Foggia province. Other rich reds include Copertino and Salice Salentino (both these DOC denominations come in rosé, too). Look out for the famous and formidable Primitivo of Manduria, Puglia's oldest and strongest wine – it can be as much as 18 per cent alcohol. The best white is the comparatively light, delicate dry wine from Locorotondo.

Coffee Culture

Some people like it straight, a short sharp shot of rich dark liquid, usually downed in one gulp while standing at the bar. Others temper their favourite brew with a dash of hot milk – a *caffè macchiato*, literally, a stained coffee. In Italy, there are almost as many ways of taking a *caffè* as there are of eating pasta, and Naples is generally regarded as the capital of the country's coffee culture.

There is also the *latte macchiato* – a long glass of hot milk with a dash of coffee to give it colour and flavour, a wimp's drink by macho Neapolitan standards. The *cappuccino* (an *espresso* coffee topped with steam-whipped milk) is known to all but it can be ordered in myriad ways – *con schiuma* (with froth), *senza schiuma* (without froth), *freddo*, *tepido* or *bollente* (cold, warm or piping hot). It may be *scuro* or *chiaro* (dark or light), depending on the amount of milk desired. And it will always be restricted to the first coffee of the day. The foreign tourists' habit of ordering a milky *cappuccino* after lunch or dinner is enough to make any Neapolitan stomach heave. Coffee is usually served already sugared. (If you want it without, ask the barman for a *caffè amaro*.)

In Naples the all-important act of going out to the bar for a fix of caffeine is a ritual that is repeated every few hours. For Neapolitans, coffee is a sacred thing, its preparation an art form. At the best bars, barmen in starched white jackets with gleaming brass buttons serve the dark syrupy brew with a glass of water to prepare the palate for the treat in store.

Every Neapolitan has his favourite bar, but the 150-year-old Caffè Gambrinus on Piazza Trieste e Trento is widely recognized as the most venerable temple of them all. Also favoured are the Verdi in Via Verdi, the Caflish in Via Toledo and La Caffettiera in Piazza dei Martiri, a popular spot with well-dressed Neapolitan ladies after a busy morning's shopping.

And on summer evenings, outside the bars along the seafront at Mergellina, you'll see Neapolitans indulging in the ultimate bliss – a cup of coffee served to them in the comfort of their own car, on trays which slot conveniently over the window.

As any Neapolitan barman worth his salt will tell you, the perfect *espresso* is made with a blend of arabica coffees, with water passed through at a temperature of 90°C, for precisely 30 seconds. Connoisseurs can tell if the coffee will be good or not before they even taste it. The foam is the giveaway: it should be a uniform light brown colour, dappled with darker brown. Very dark brown or greyish foam is a clear warning sign that the barman is an amateur or the coffee second rate. Most self-respecting Neapolitans would rather leave such a brew untouched on the counter and head for another bar. A bad cup of coffee can cast a blight over the entire day.

Restaurant Basics

In Italy the various **types of restaurants** – *ristorante*, *trattoria* or *osteria* – have become much less distinct. Nowadays, a *trattoria* or *osteria* can be just as elaborate as a restaurant, though rarely is a *ristorante* as informal as a traditional *trattoria*. Unfortunately, the old habit of posting menus and prices in the windows has fallen from fashion, so it's often difficult to judge variety or prices. The least expensive type of restaurant is the *vino e cucina* – simple places serving simple cuisine. In general, the fancier the fittings, the fancier the bill, though neither has anything at all to do with the quality of the food. If you're uncertain, look for lots of locals.

When you eat out, mentally add to the **bill** (*conto*) the bread and cover charge (*pane e coperto*, between €1.50 and 2.50), and a 15 per cent service charge. This is often

Italian Menu Reader

Antipasti

These before-meal treats can include almost anything; the most common include:

antipasto misto mixed *antipasto*
bruschetta garlic toast (often with tomatoes)
carciofi (sott'olio) artichokes (in oil)
frutti di mare seafood
funghi (trifolati) mushrooms (with anchovies, garlic and lemon)
gamberi ai fagioli prawns (shrimps) with white beans
mozzarella (in carrozza) cow or buffalo cheese (fried with bread in batter)
prosciutto (con melone) cured ham (with melon)
salsicce sausages

Minestre (Soups) and Pasta

These dishes are the principal first courses (*primi*) served throughout Italy.

agnolotti ravioli with meat
cacciucco spiced fish soup
cappelletti small ravioli, often in broth
crespelle crêpes
fettuccine long strips of pasta
frittata omelette
gnocchi potato dumplings
minestra di verdura thick vegetable soup
minestrone soup with meat, vegetables and pasta
orecchiette ear-shaped pasta, often served with turnip greens
panzerotti ravioli filled with mozzarella, anchovies and egg
pappardelle alla lepre pasta with hare sauce
pasta e fagioli soup with beans, bacon and tomatoes
pastina in brodo tiny pasta in broth
penne all'arrabbiata quill-shaped pasta with tomatoes and hot peppers
polenta cake or pudding of corn semolina
risotto (alla Milanese) Italian rice (with stock, saffron and wine)
spaghetti all'Amatriciana with spicy sauce of salt pork, tomatoes, onions and chilli
spaghetti alla Bolognese with ground meat, ham, mushrooms etc.
spaghetti alla carbonara with bacon, eggs and black pepper
spaghetti al pomodoro with tomato sauce
spaghetti al sugo/ragù with meat sauce
spaghetti alle vongole with clam sauce
stracciatella broth with eggs and cheese
tagliatelle flat egg noodles
tortellini al pomodoro/panna/in brodo pasta caps filled with meat and cheese with tomato sauce/with cream/in broth

Carne (Meat)

abbacchio milk-fed lamb
agnello lamb
animelle sweetbreads
anatra duck
arista pork loin
arrosto misto mixed roast meats
bocconcini veal fried with ham and cheese
bollito misto stew of boiled meats
braciola chop
brasato di manzo braised beef with vegetables
bresaola dried raw meat similar to ham
capretto kid
capriolo roe-buck
carne di castrato/suino mutton/pork
carpaccio thin slices of raw beef served with a piquant sauce
cassoeula winter stew with pork and cabbage
cervello (al burro nero) brains (in black butter sauce)
cervo venison
cinghiale boar
coniglio rabbit
cotoletta (alla Milanese/alla Bolognese) veal cutlet (fried in breadcrumbs/with ham and cheese)

included in the bill (*servizio compreso*). If not, it will say *servizio non compreso* and you'll have to do your own arithmetic. Additional tipping is at your own discretion, but never do it in family-run places.

Breakfast (*colazione*) is no lingering affair, but an early morning wake-up shot to the brain: a *cappuccino* (*espresso* with hot foamy milk, often sprinkled with chocolate – first thing in the morning is the only time of day at which any self-respecting Italian will touch the stuff), a *caffè latte* (white coffee) or a *caffè lungo* (a generous portion of

fagiano pheasant
fegato alla veneziana liver (usually of veal) with filling
lombo di maiale pork loin
lumache snails
maiale (al latte) pork (cooked in milk)
manzo beef
osso buco braised veal knuckle with herbs
pancetta rolled pork
pernice partridge
petto di pollo (sorpresa) boned chicken breast (stuffed and deep fried)
piccione pigeon
pizzaiola beef steak with tomato and oregano sauce
pollo (alla cacciatora/alla diavola/alla Marengo) chicken (with tomatoes and mushrooms/ grilled/fried with tomatoes, garlic and wine)
polpette meatballs
quaglie quails
rane frogs
rognoni kidneys
saltimbocca veal scallop with *prosciutto*, sage, wine, butter
scaloppine thin slices of veal sautéed in butter
spezzatino beef or veal pieces, usually stewed
spiedino meat on a skewer or stick
stufato beef in white wine with vegetables
tacchino turkey
vitello veal

Pesce (Fish)

acciughe or ***alici*** anchovies
anguilla eel
aragosta lobster
aringa herring
baccalà dried salt cod
bonito small tuna
branzino sea bass
calamari squid
cappe sante scallops
cefalo grey mullet
coda di rospo angler fish
cozze mussels
dentice dentex (perch-like fish)
dorato gilt head
fritto misto mixed fried delicacies, mainly fish
gamberetto shrimp
gamberi prawns
gamberi di fiume crayfish
granchio crab
insalata di mare seafood salad
lampreda lamprey
merluzzo cod
nasello hake
orata bream
ostriche oysters
pesce azzurro various small fish
pesce di San Pietro John Dory
pesce spada swordfish
polipi/polpi octopus
rombo turbot
sarde sardines
seppie cuttlefish
sgombro mackerel
sogliola sole
squadro monkfish
stoccafisso wind-dried cod
tonno tuna
triglia red mullet (rouget)
trota trout
trota salmonata salmon trout
vongole small clams
zuppa di pesce mixed fish in sauce or stew

Contorni (Side Dishes, Vegetables)

asparagi asparagus
alla fiorentina with fried eggs
broccoli broccoli
carciofi (alla giudia) (deep fried) artichokes
cardi cardoons/thistles
carote carrots
cavolfiore cauliflower
cavolo cabbage
ceci chickpeas

espresso), accompanied by a croissant-type roll called a *cornetto* or *brioche*, or one of the other fancy pastries that are a special talent of Naples. This can be consumed in any bar and repeated during the morning as often as necessary. Breakfast in most Italian hotels seldom represents great value.

Lunch (*pranzo*), generally served around 1pm, is the most important meal of the day, traditionally with a minimum of a first course (*primo piatto* – any kind of pasta dish, broth or soup, rice dish or pizza), a second course (*secondo piatto* – a meat dish,

cetriolo cucumber
cipolla onion
fagioli white beans
fagiolini French (green) beans
fave broad beans
finocchio fennel
funghi (porcini) mushrooms (boletus)
insalata (mista/verde) salad (mixed/green)
lattuga lettuce
lenticchie lentils
melanzane aubergine/eggplant
patate potatoes
patate fritte chips, French fries
peperoncini hot chilli peppers
peperoni sweet peppers
peperonata stewed peppers, onions, etc.
piselli (al prosciutto) peas (with ham)
pomodoro(i) tomato(es)
porri leeks
radicchio red chicory
radice radish
rapa turnip
rucola rocket
sedano celery
spinaci spinach
verdure greens
zucca pumpkin
zucchini courgettes

Formaggio (Cheese)

Bel Paese a soft white cow's cheese
cacio/caciocavallo pale yellow, sharp cheese
fontina rich cow's milk cheese
groviera mild cheese (gruyère)
gorgonzola soft blue cheese
mozzarella soft cheese
parmigiano Parmesan cheese
pecorino sharp sheep's cheese
provolone sharp, tangy; ***dolce*** is less strong
ricotta creamy white cheese
stracchino soft white cheese

Frutta (Fruit, Nuts)

albicocche apricots
ananas pineapple
arance oranges
banane bananas
cachi persimmon
ciliege cherries
cocomero watermelon
datteri dates
fichi figs
fragole (con panna) strawberries (with cream)
lamponi raspberries
limone lemon
macedonia di frutta fruit salad
mandarino tangerine
mandorle almonds
melagrana pomegranate
mele apples
mirtilli bilberries
more blackberries
nespola medlar fruit
nocciole hazelnuts
noci walnuts
pera pear
pesca peach
pesca noce nectarine
pinoli pine nuts
pompelmo grapefruit
prugna/susina prune/plum
uva grapes

Dolci (Desserts)

amaretti macaroons
cannoli crisp pastry tubes filled with ricotta, cream, chocolate or fruit
coppa gelato assorted ice cream
crema caramella caramel-topped custard
crostata fruit flan
gelato (produzione propria) ice cream (homemade)
granita water ice, usually lemon or coffee
monte bianco chestnut pudding with cream

accompanied by a *contorno* or side dish – usually a vegetable, salad or potatoes), followed by fruit or dessert and coffee. Nowadays; few restaurants blink if you only order a bowl of pasta. You can, however, begin with a plate of *antipasti*. Italians do these appetizers brilliantly and they can range from warm seafood delicacies to raw ham (*prosciutto crudo*), salami in a hundred varieties, lovely vegetables, savoury toasts, olives, pâté and many, many more. There are restaurants that specialize in *antipasti* and they usually don't take it amiss if you decide to forget the pasta and meat and

panettone sponge cake with candied fruit
panforte dense cake of chocolate, almonds and preserved fruit
saint honoré meringue cake
semifreddo refrigerated cake
sorbetto sorbet/sherbet
spumone a soft ice cream
tiramisù layers of sponge, mascarpone, coffee and chocolate
torrone nougat
torta cake, tart
torta millefoglie layered pastry and custard cream
zabaglione hot dessert made with eggs and Marsala wine
zuppa inglese trifle

Bevande (Beverages)

acqua minerale mineral water
con/senza gas with/without fizz
aranciata orange soda
birra (alla spina) (draught) beer
caffè (freddo) (iced) coffee
cioccolata (con panna) chocolate (with cream)
gassosa lemon-flavoured soda
latte (intero/scremato) (whole/skimmed) milk
limonata lemon soda
succo di frutta fruit juice
tè tea
vino (rosso, bianco, rosato) (red, white, rosé) wine

Cooking Terms (Miscellaneous)

aceto (balsamico) vinegar (balsamic)
affumicato smoked
aglio garlic
alla brace on embers
bicchiere glass
burro butter
cacciagione game
conto bill
costoletta/cotoletta chop
coltello knife
cucchiaio spoon
filetto fillet
forchetta fork
forno oven
fritto fried
ghiaccio ice
griglia grill
in bianco without tomato
magro lean meat/pasta without meat
marmellata jam
menta mint
miele honey
mostarda candied mustard sauce
olio oil
pane bread
pane tostato toasted bread
panini sandwiches (in roll)
panna cream
pepe pepper
piatto plate
prezzemolo parsley
ripieno stuffed
rosmarino rosemary
sale salt
salmi wine marinade
salsa sauce
salvia sage
senape mustard
tartufi truffles
tavola table
tazza cup
tovagliolo napkin
tramezzini triangular sandwiches
umido cooked in sauce
uovo egg
zucchero sugar

just nibble on these scrumptious *hors d'œuvres* (though in the end it will probably cost more than a full meal). Most Italians accompany their meal with wine and mineral water (*acqua minerale*) with or without bubbles (*con* or *senza gas*), which supposedly aids digestion – concluding their meals with a *digestivo* liqueur.

Dinner (*cena*) is eaten around 8pm and often later in the south. It is similar to *pranzo* except lighter and without the pasta; typically, a pizza and beer, eggs or a fish dish. Restaurants, however, will offer all the courses both at lunch and in the evening.

People who haven't visited Italy for years and have fond memories of eating full meals for under a pound will be amazed at how much **prices** have risen, though eating out in Italy is still a bargain, especially when you figure out how much all that wine would cost you at home. Many restaurants offer a *menu turistico* – a set meal of usually meagre inspiration for €12–15. More imaginative chefs often offer a *menu degustazione* – a set-price gourmet meal that allows you to taste their specialities and seasonal dishes. Both of these are cheaper than ordering the same food à la carte. When you leave a restaurant, you will be given a receipt (*scontrino* or *ricevuta fiscale*) which, according to Italian law, you must take with you out of the door and carry for at least 60m. If you aren't given one, it means the restaurant is probably fudging on its taxes and thus offering you lower prices. There is a slim chance the tax police (*guardia di finanza*) may have their eye on you and the restaurant, and if you don't have a receipt, they could slap you with a heavy fine.

There are several **alternatives to sit-down meals**. The 'hot table' (*tavola calda*) is a stand-up buffet where you can choose a simple prepared dish or a whole meal. The food in these can be truly impressive (especially in the centre of Naples, where the sign out front may read *Degustazione*; some of these offer the best gourmet delights to be had in the south and are always crowded). Many offer only a few hot dishes, pizza and sandwiches, though in every fair-sized town there will be at least one *tavola calda* with seats where you can contrive a complete dinner outside the usual hours. Little shops that sell pizza by the slice are common in city centres.

At any grocer's (*alimentari*) or market (*mercato*) you can buy materials for a **picnic**; some places in the smaller towns will make the sandwiches for you. For really elegant picnics, have a *tavola calda* pack up something nice. And there's always the railway station – bars will at least have sandwiches and drinks, and occasionally some surprisingly good snacks you've never heard of before. Some station bars also prepare *cestini di viaggio*, full-course meals in a basket for long train trips – less common now that most long-distance trains have their own restaurants. Common snacks include pizza, *panini* of cheese and tomatoes, *prosciutto* or other meats, and *tramezzini* (little sandwiches on plain, square white bread) that are always much better than they look.

Travel

05

Getting There

With the growth of the budget airlines in Europe, flying is now not only the quickest way to get to Naples, but often the cheapest.

As well as more low-cost flights, there are interesting new developments on airports around Italy that will allow tourists to reach destinations previously considered remote and difficult to get to: from 2005, 15 military airports will become civil airports. Among them: Vicenza, Udine, Capua and Grazzanise in Campania; Marenostrum Airport in Comiso (Sicily); Oristano on the west coast of Sardinia; Aosta in the alpine northeast; and Pantelleria and L'Aquila (Preturo) in Abruzzo. A new budget airline, AirSal, will link Salerno-Pontecagnano Airport in Campania, gateway to the Amalfi coast, to London and Dublin.

By Air

From the UK and Ireland

Flying is obviously the quickest and easiest way of getting to **Naples**. British Airways lists both Naples and Bari on its new low-fare network. There are two daily services from London Gatwick to Naples, with return tickets going for as low as £80 including taxes. There are three flights a week (Tuesday, Thursday and Sunday) from London Gatwick to Bari in Puglia, with tax-inclusive return fares starting from £129.

Alitalia flies from London to **Reggio di Calabria** via Milan or Rome. Tickets cost around £200, with good last-minute or off-peak deals.

Among the budget airlines, easyJet have flights from Gatwick and Stansted to Naples from £70 return and Ryanair fly to Rome Ciampino, three hours from Naples by train.

From Ireland, Aer Lingus and Alitalia have direct flights to Rome.

From the USA and Canada

The main gateway for flights to southern Italy from North America is Rome, from where you can travel on south by air or train. Alitalia has the most options, or you could take a cheap flight to London and fly on from there.

From North America standard scheduled flights on well-known airlines are expensive but reassuringly reliable and convenient. Older travellers or families may prefer to pay extra for such a long flight (9–15 hours). Resilient, flexible and/or youthful travellers may be willing to shop around for budget deals on consolidated charters, stand-bys or perhaps even courier flights (but remember that you can usually only take hand luggage with you on the last).

Check in the Yellow Pages for courier companies. For discounted flights, try the small ads in newspaper travel pages (e.g. *New York Times*, *Chicago Tribune*, *Toronto Globe & Mail*). Numerous travel clubs and agencies also specialize in discount fares, but may require an annual membership fee.

By Rail

From London the journey time to Naples is about 21 hours. Two rail routes lead to Rome, either through France or through Belgium, Luxembourg, France and Switzerland; services run daily. You have to change stations in Paris, from Gare du Nord to Gare de Lyon.

Interail (UK) or **Eurail** (USA/Canada) passes for under-26s allow you to see a lot of other places on the way, giving unlimited travel throughout Europe. Various other cheap youth fares (BIJ tickets, etc.) are also available; buy them before leaving home.

Rail travel is not necessarily any cheaper than flying, even if you can take advantage of student or youth fares. A month's full Interail pass costs around £295, although if you just want to see Italy, you can buy a cheaper zonal pass covering three or four countries only.

Naples is a major rail hub and many services from the northern cities terminate here, rather than in Rome. There are hourly trains from Rome to Naples (journey time is about 2½ hours) and you can get a train straight from the airport without going into the city.

Rail Europe, **UK** 178 Piccadilly, London W1V 0BF, **t** 08705 84 88 48, *www.raileurope.co.uk*; **USA** 44 South Broadway, White Plains, NY 10601, **t** 877 257 2887, *www.raileurope.com*; **Canada t** 800 361 RAIL, *www.raileurope.com*.

Airline Carriers

UK and Ireland

Aer Lingus, UK **t** 0845 084 4444; Ireland **t** 0818 365 000, *www.aerlingus.com*.
Alitalia, UK **t** 0870 544 8259, *www.alitalia.co.uk*; Ireland **t** (01) 677 5171, *www.alitalia.ie*.
British Airways, UK **t** 0870 850 9850 (24 hours), *www.ba.com*.
easyJet, UK **t** 0870 607 6543, *www.easyjet.com*.
Ryanair, UK **t** 0871 246 0000; Ireland **t** 0818 30 30 30, *www.ryanair.com*.

USA and Canada

Air Canada, **t** 888 247 2262, *www.aircanada.ca*; operates from Toronto and Montreal.
Alitalia, USA, **t** 800 223 5730, *www.alitaliausa.com*; Canada, **t** 800 268 9277, *www.alitalia.ca*.
British Airways, **t** 800 AIRWAYS, *www.ba.com*.
Delta, **t** 800 241 4141, *www.delta.com*.
Northwest Airlines, **t** 800 447 4747, *www.nwa.com*.

Charters and Discounts

UK and Ireland

Italflights, 125 High Holborn, London WC1V 6QA, **t** (020) 7405 6771.
Italia Nel Mondo, 6 Palace St, London SW1E 5HY, **t** (020) 7834 7651.
Magic Travel Group, Kings Place, 12–42 Wood Street, Kingston-upon-Thames KP1 1JF, **t** 0800 980 3378, *www.magictravelgroup.co.uk*.
Trailfinders, 215 Kensington High St, London W8 6BD, **t** (020) 7937 1234, *www.trailfinders.co.uk*.
Budget Travel, 134 Lower Baggot St, Dublin 2, **t** (01) 631 1111, *www.budgettravel.ie*.
United Travel, Stillorgan Bowl, Stillorgan, Dublin, **t** (01) 215 9300, *www.unitedtravel.ie*.

USA and Canada

Airhitch, **t** (212) 864 2000, *www.airhitch.org*; last-minute seats on a 'space available' basis.
Last Minute Travel Club, 41, 1154 Chemong Rd, Peterborough, Ontario K9H 7J6, **t** 877 970 3500.
Now Voyager Travel, 45 West 21st Street, Ste.5A, New York, NY 10010, **t** (212) 459 1616, *www.nowvoyagertravel.com*; courier flights.

Student Fares

UK and Ireland

Europe Student Travel, 6 Campden St, London W8, **t** (020) 7727 7647.
STA, 6 Wrights Lane, London W8 6TA. STA has over 50 branches in the UK. For details, **t** 08701 600 599, *www.statravel.com*.

USA and Canada

Council Travel, 205 East 42nd St, New York, NY 10017, **t** 800 2 COUNCIL; major specialists in student and charter flights; many branches.
STA Travel, 10 Downing St, New York, NY 10014, **t** 800 781 4040, *www.statravel.com*.
Travel Cuts, 187 College St, Toronto, Ontario M5T 1P7, **t** (416) 979 2406, or toll free **t** 866 246 9762, *www.travelcuts.com*; Canada's largest student travel specialist, with many branches.

Websites

These websites specialize in cheap air fares:
www.bargainholidays.com
www.cheapflights.com
www.expedia.com
www.lastminute.com
www.opodo.com
www.skydeals.co.uk

By Road

By Coach

Eurolines (London–Naples return from £182, **t** 08705 80 80 80, *www.eurolines.com* or *www.gobycoach.com*) is Europe's largest international bus operator, serving over 500 cities in 25 European countries. It has offices in Italy and a wide range of other countries, booked through National Express. Services to Italy terminate at Rome, where you have to change for destinations further south.

It's a long journey and not much cheaper than flying or the train. However, if it isn't dark at the time, you'll get a glimpse of Mont Blanc, Milan, Venice, Bologna, Florence and Rome on the way.

By Car

To bring a GB-registered car into Italy, you need a vehicle registration document, full driving licence and insurance papers. Non-EU citizens should have an international driving licence with an Italian translation incorporated. Your vehicle should display a nationality plate indicating its country of registration.

The distance from London to Naples is about 1,750km (1,050 miles) – the best part of 24 hours' driving time even if you stick to fast toll roads. The most scenic and hassle-free route is via the Alps, avoiding crowded Riviera roads in summer, but if you drive through Switzerland, expect to pay for the privilege. In winter, the passes may be closed and you will have to stick to the tunnels.

For more information on driving in Italy, contact the **AA**: **t** 0870 600 0371, *www.theaa.com*; or **RAC**, **t** 0870 572 2722, *www.rac.co.uk* in the UK; **AAA**, **t** (212) 757 2000, or **t** 800 222 4357, *www.aaa.com*, in the USA.

By Ferry

Besides the ferries and hydrofoils connecting Naples with resorts further down the coast and the islands in the Bay of Naples, regular boat services also link Naples with more far-flung destinations including Reggio di Calabria, Milazzo and the Aeolian Islands. Siremar and Tirrenia are the main long-distance ferry companies operating from Naples (*see* p.68).

Entry Formalities

Passports and Visas

EU nationals with a valid passport can stay in Italy for as long as they like.

Citizens of the USA, Canada, Australia and New Zealand need only a valid passport to stay up to three months. If you want to stay longer, you need to get a visa in advance from an Italian embassy or consulate:

UK, 14 Three Kings Yard, London W1K 4 EH, **t** (020) 7312 2200; 32 Melville St, Edinburgh EH3 7HA, **t** (0131) 226 3631; Roadwell Tower, 111 Piccadilly, Manchester M1 2HY, **t** (0161) 236 9024; *www.embitaly.org.uk*.

Ireland, 63–65 Northumberland Rd, Dublin, **t** (01) 660 1744; 7 Richmond Park, Belfast BT9 5EF, **t** (02890) 668 854, *www.italianembassy.ie*.

USA, 690 Park Avenue, New York, NY, **t** (212) 439 8600; 12400 Wilshire Blvd, Suite 300, Los Angeles, CA 90025, **t** (213) 820 0622, *www.italconsulnyc.org*.

Canada, 136 Beverley St, Toronto M5T IY5, **t** (416) 977 1566, *www.toronto.italconsulate.org*.

Australia, Level 45, The Gateway Building, 1 Macquarie Place, Circular Quay, Sydney 2000, NSW, **t** (02) 9392 7939.

New Zealand, PO Box 463, 34 Grant Rd, Thorndon, Wellington, **t** (04) 473 5339.

Customs

EU nationals over the age of 17 can now import a limitless amount of goods for personal use. Non-EU nationals have to pass through the Italian Customs, which are usually benign. How the frontier police manage to recruit such ugly, mean-looking characters to hold the sub-machine-guns and dogs from such a good-looking population is a mystery, but they'll let you be if you don't look suspicious. You are allowed to bring in up to 200 cigarettes or 100 cigars, a litre of spirits or three bottles of wine, two cameras, a movie camera and 10 rolls of film for each, a radio, tape recorder, record player, one canoe, sports equipment for personal use and one TV (though you'll have to pay for a licence for it).

Pets must be accompanied by a bilingual Certificate of Health from your local Veterinary Inspector. You can take the same items listed above home with you without hassle – except of course your British pet. USA citizens may return with $400 worth of merchandise but keep your receipts.

Currency

There are no limits to how much money you can bring into Italy: legally you may not export more than €10,300 (a sum unlikely to trouble most of us), though officials rarely check.

Getting Around

By Sea

A complex network of ferries and hydrofoils run by half a dozen different companies links Naples with the islands in the bay as well as several further afield (Sardinia, Malta, Corsica, Sicily), and other resorts down the coast.

During the summer, up to six ferries and 20 hydrofoils cross daily to Capri, and as many to Ischia, with regular departures to Procida.

In addition, there are ferries and hydrofoils daily from Sorrento to Capri, from Pozzuoli to Procida, and between the islands of Ischia and Procida. All are very short rides and, in most cases, day trips are quite viable ways of exploring the local islands.

Services for Capri, Sorrento, Ischia, Procida, Forio and Casamicciola depart from the Molo Beverello in front of the Castel Nuovo in Naples. Boats for Palermo, Reggio di Calabria, Milazzo and the Aeolian Islands leave from the Stazione Marittima.

Hydrofoils also serve the bay islands from Mergellina, another important terminal in the western suburb of Naples.

You can usually buy your tickets when you turn up at the port. Return tickets don't generally offer any savings over two separate single tickets.

Ferries are, as you'd expect, cheaper than the faster hydrofoil services and less affected by rough weather.

The daily newspaper, *Il Mattino*, gives a full list of current timetables.

By Rail

Trenitalia train information: **t** 89 20 21 (*open 7am–9pm*); *www.trenitalia.com*.

Naples, the main rail hub for southern Italy, is served by a full range of Regionale, Diretto, Espresso, Intercity, EuroCity and ETR 450 fast trains. From the centre (the main station is Stazione Centrale at Piazza Garibaldi), a cat's cradle of funiculars and national and local lines straggles out through the disparate suburbs and down the coast via Pompeii and Herculaneum to Sorrento and beyond.

The state-run **FS** line offers a fast service between Naples and Salerno; for other coastal destinations, you will probably rely on local rail systems. Inland, erratically scheduled and complicated train services head for Caserta, Capua and Benevento from Naples' Stazione Centrale. South of Salerno, Paestum and most destinations on the Cilento coast are served by the main rail route from Naples to Reggio di Calabria.

For coastal journeys, the **Circumvesuviana** is the most useful service, trundling right round the Bay of Naples every half-hour or so from dawn till quite late at night, stopping just about everywhere. This is the best way to reach Pompeii, Herculaneum and Sorrento. The Neapolitan terminus is a modern station on Corso Garibaldi, but trains stop at Stazione Centrale, too. Main lines run east via Ercolano (the Herculaneum station), then diverge, passing Pompeii on opposite sides.

One line takes you to Sorrento, the other to Sarno, east of Vesuvius. The journey to Sorrento takes about an hour. You can also get to Nola and Baiano on a separate line. You'll need to catch a bus from Sorrento or Salerno to the towns of the Amalfi coast.

If you're heading westwards from Naples, you can take the Naples underground (or **Metropolitana**) which crosses the city centre and ends up at Pozzuoli-Solfatara, a half-hour run. Both the **Ferrovia Cumana** (running along the coast) and the **Circumflegrea** (via Cumae) take you as far as Torregaveta.

Elsewhere in the south, train services are regular along the coasts, and if you plan ahead carefully, you can see all the larger towns in the interior, too.

It will be complicated, though, inevitably involving strange connections and sometimes a ride on one of the several old narrow-gauge private railways that are still in business in the south. See the 'Getting Around' sections in the Calabria and the Basilicata and Puglia chapters for more details.

The Pendolino (high-speed tilting trains) is the fastest and most expensive service, then Eurostar, Intercity and Diretto. Most large stations now have ticket machines , but they often only give the expensive options and don't always give change.

By Road

By Bus

The main bus station in Naples is just in front of the central railway station. From here, a mass of routes heads for all the main towns and places of interest in Campania, and threads through the maze of suburbs and dormitory towns to outlying villages. Many are run by the **Naples Public Transport Board**, **t** 081 700 1111, which has information offices in Piazza

Garibaldi. Other services are operated by **SITA**, **t** 081 552 2176, Via Pisanelli 3–7, and **Curreri**, **t** 081 801 5420.

In Naples, there are various all-inclusive passes for bus and rail (*see* **Naples**: 'Getting Around', p.69).

The Italian bus system is not the easiest to crack. Indications of destination and departure point are often mystifying and it's best to ask before you get on.

Buy tickets in advance from tobacconists, newsstands or ticket booths at the bus stations, and validate them on the bus by punching them in the machine. Many people don't bother buying tickets, but you can be heavily fined if you are caught travelling without one, or with an unvalidated ticket.

There are regular services from Naples to Salerno (SITA), Benevento, Caserta and Avellino (Naples Public Transport Board). Curreri runs a useful service from Capodichino Airport to Sorrento. The Circumvesuviana railway is generally easier to use for destinations in the bay to the east of Naples, such as Pompeii, but you can take buses, too.

Buses really come into their own on the islands of the bay, which are too small to have their own railways.

The same is true for the Amalfi coast, which is not served by train; buses are the cheapest way to hop from place to place. SITA services are frequent between Sorrento and Salerno. Buy tickets in advance in local bars or shops with the SITA sign, or from terminus depots.

Paestum is an easy bus ride from Salerno (about every half-hour). ATAC buses serve the Cilento coast, from Salerno to Sapri.

In the rest of the south, buses are quicker than train travel, although they are also a bit more expensive. Compared with most of Europe, the Italian intercity bus system is excellent and it will take you to places the train won't. The provincial capitals are always the main centres, with a station (usually near the rail station) that has a fat timetable of buses to every outlying village in the province, and a few beyond.

By Car

A car is the best and most convenient way to get to the more remote parts of the Mezzogiorno, but sheer hell in Naples, whether moving or stationary. Driving isn't much fun in any southern town really. The streets weren't made for cars, and most modern Italians wouldn't be caught dead walking (except maybe for the evening *passeggiata*). In any place of more than 10,000 people, expect solid traffic jams from about 11am to 2pm, and again in the evening from about 5 until 10 or 11. If you must drive in or out of a town, try to do it at night, or when the Italians are having their *pranzo*.

If you must bring a car into Naples or Bari, make sure you leave it securely in a guarded parking lot with nothing valuable inside. On the streets, if the thieves don't get it then a tow-truck may offer a similar service – take care not to leave it in a *zona rimozione*.

In Italy, third-party insurance is a minimum requirement, but you should be a lot more than minimally insured, as many of the locals have none whatsoever. Obtain a Green Card from your insurer, which gives automatic proof that you are fully covered. Also get hold of a European Accident Statement form, which may simplify things if you are unlucky enough to have an accident. Always insist on a full translation of any statement you are asked to sign. Breakdown assistance insurance is a sensible investment (e.g. AA's Five Star or RAC's Eurocover Motoring Assistance).

Don't give the local police any excuse to fine you on the spot for minor infringements such as worn tyres or burned-out sidelights.

A red triangular hazard sign is obligatory. Also recommended are a spare set of bulbs, a first-aid kit and a fire-extinguisher. Spare parts may be tricky to find for non-Italian cars. Petrol (*benzina*; unleaded is *benzina senza piombo*, and diesel *gasolio*) is still expensive in Italy (around €1.10–1.30 per litre) and the motorway (*autostrada*) tolls are quite high. Services can be hard to find in remote areas and are usually closed all afternoon.

Italians are famously anarchic behind a wheel, and nowhere more so than within the city of Naples, where all warnings, signals and generally recognized rules of the road are ignored. The only way to beat the locals is to join them by adopting an assertive and constantly alert driving style.

Bear in mind the old maxim that he/she who hesitates is lost (especially at traffic lights, where the danger of crashing into someone at the front is less great than that of being rammed from behind). All drivers from boy racers to elderly nuns seem to tempt providence by overtaking at the most dangerous bend, and no matter how fast you are hammering along the *autostrada* (toll motorway), plenty of cars will whizz past at what seem like supersonic rates.

North Americans used to leisurely speed limits and gentler road manners will find the Italian interpretation of the highway code especially stressful. Speed limits (generally ignored) are officially 130kph on motorways (110kph for cars under 1100cc or motorcycles), 110kph on main highways, 90kph on secondary roads, and 50kph in built-up areas. Speeding fines may be as much as €250, and you can also be fined €50 for jumping a red light (a popular Italian sport).

If you are undeterred by these caveats, you may actually enjoy driving in Italy, at least away from the congested tourist centres. Signposting is generally good and roads are usually excellently maintained. Some of the roads (e.g. the Amalfi corniche and some of the mountain roads in Calabria) are feats of engineering that the Romans themselves would have admired; bravura projects suspended on cliffs, crossing valleys on vast stilts and winding up hairpins.

Buy a good road map, such as one from the excellent Italian Touring Club series.

The **Automobile Club of Italy** (ACI), *www.aci.it*, is a good friend to the foreign motorist. Besides having bushels of useful information and tips, they offer a free breakdown service, and can be reached from anywhere by dialling **t** 803 116 – also use this number if you have to find the nearest service station. If you need major repairs, the ACI can check the prices charged are according to their guidelines:

Naples: Piazzale Tecchio 49/d, **t** 081 593 7940.
Salerno: Via Picenza, **t** 089 386 7914.
Caserta: Via N. Sauro 10, **t** 0823 216 721.
Benevento: Via S. Rosa 24–26, **t** 0824 355 430.

Hiring a Car

Hiring a car or camper van is usually simple but not particularly cheap. In Italian it's called *autonoleggio*.

There are the familiar international firms (through which you can reserve a car in advance) and local agencies, which often have lower prices. Air or train travellers should check out possible discount packages.

Most companies will require a credit card imprint, or a deposit amounting to the estimated cost of the hire. They also usually require that you are at least 21 (23 in some cases) and have held a driving licence for three years. You must show your licence and a passport when you hire.

Several major companies have offices in Naples, mainly on Via Partenope (near the port), and at the airport or main station:

Avis, UK **t** 0870 010 0287, *www.avis.co.uk*;
USA **t** 800 230 4898, *www.avis.com*;
Canada **t** 800 272 5871.
Hertz, UK **t** (020) 7026 0077, *www.hertz.co.uk*;
USA **t** 800 654 3131, *www.hertz.com*;
Canada **t** 800 263 0600;
Ireland **t** 01 676 7476.
National Car, UK **t** 0870 400 4581,
www.nationalcar.co.uk.

A hefty surcharge is levied in Naples because of the local theft problem. If you hire a car outside Naples, check that you are allowed to drive within the city without penalty. You can take a car to Capri or Ischia, but rental is only available on Ischia.

Hitch-hiking

It is illegal to hitch on the *autostrada*, though you may pick up a lift near one of the toll booths. Don't hitch from the city centres; head for suburban exit routes instead. For the best chances of getting a lift, travel light, look respectable and take your shades off. Two or more men may encounter some reluctance.

Women should not hitch on their own in southern Italy.

By Motorcycle or Bicycle

You may have trouble hiring a *motorino* (moped) or *vespa* (scooter) in Naples because of theft, but they are available in most resorts and on the islands. You must be at least 14 to hire a *motorino* and 16 for anything more powerful. Helmets are compulsory. Costs for a *motorino* range from about €30–50 per day.

Special Interest Holidays

UK and Ireland

Andante Travels, The Old Barn, Old Road, Alderbury, Salisbury, Wiltshire SP5 3AR, **t** (01722) 713 800, *www.andantetravels.co.uk*; offers art, architecture and archaeological sites.

Brompton Travel, 3 Hinchley Way, Hinchley Wood, Esher, Surrey KT10 0BD, **t** (020) 8398 3672, *www.bromptontravel.co.uk*; southern Italy, city tours and opera in Naples.

Camper & Nicholsons, 25 Bruton St, London W1J 6QH, **t** (020) 7491 2950, *www.cnconnect.com*; does specialist yacht charters.

Italiatour, 71 Lower Road, Kenley, Surrey CR8 5NH, **t** 0870 733 3000, *www.italiatour.co.uk*; tours to Puglia and Campania.

LAI Travel, 185 Kings Cross Road, London WC1X 9DB, **t** (020) 7837 1477, *www.laitravel.co.uk*; charter flights on British Midland; holidays to Naples, Pompeii and Sicily.

Magic Travel Group, Kings Place, 12–42 Wood Street, Kingston-upon-Thames KP1 1JF, **t** 0800 980 3378, *www.magictravelgroup.co.uk*; offers package tours and tailor-made holidays.

Martin Randall Travel, 10 Barley Mow Passage, London W4 4GF, **t** (020) 8742 3355, *www.martinrandall.com*; archaeological and art history tours, plus visits to villas and gardens.

Prospect Music & Art, 36 Manchester Street, London W1U 7LH, **t** (020) 7486 5704 *www.prospecttours.com*; organizes art, architecture, music and archaeology tours.

Travel for the Arts, 12–15 Hanger Grn, London W5 3EL, **t** (020) 8799 8350, *www.travelforthearts.com*; music and opera tours.

USA and Canada

Dailey-Thorp Travel, PO Box 670, Big Horn, Wyoming 82633, **t** 800 998 4677, *www.daileythorp.com*; music and opera.

Italiatour, 666 5th Ave, New York, NY 10103, USA **t** 800 845 3365, Canada **t** 888 515 5245, *www.italiatourusa.com*; fly-drive trips.

Stay and Visit Italy, 4971 Ringwood Meadow, Sarasota, Florida 34235, **t** 877 782 9878, *www.stayandvisit.com*.

Bicycle hire costs €20–30 per day, which may make buying one (€100–250) an option if you plan to spend much time in the saddle. You can usually take your bike quite cheaply on slower trains.

By Taxi

Try not to take taxis if you're on a budget. They are invariably expensive at the best of times and foreign tourists are unfortunately sitting ducks for overcharging. Naples used to be notorious for rip-offs, although now that most taxis have meters, the situation is a bit better. But even a short trip may clock up an alarming bill because of the traffic jams. Don't try to flag a taxi down on the street; head for a taxi rank on a main square, or dial one through **Radiotaxi Napoli**, **t** 081 556 4444. In other places, taxis aren't such bad news, but they are still expensive.

Practical A–Z

06

Climate and When to Go

Average Temperatures in °C	Jan	April	July	Oct
Naples	9	14	25	18
Capri	11	13	24	17
Bari	6	13	27	18
Reggio	11	16	26	19

Southern Italy can be diabolically hot in summer, with daytime temperatures soaring to an enervating 35°C, but the drought that scorches every scrap of inland vegetation by July is relieved by occasional bouts of torrential rain. Temperatures are more moderate on the coast, refreshed by breezes, while annual rainfall is considerably higher in Amalfi than Rome or London. You don't really need an umbrella in summer, but take a light jacket for cool evenings. August is the most unforgiving month to stump through southern Italy. Transport facilities are stretched to capacity, prices are at their highest and Naples and the main sights, such as Pompeii, are abandoned to hordes of tourists, while the locals sensibly remain indoors, or take to the beach.

Spring and early autumn are far more appealing: spring for the infinity of wild flowers in the countryside, autumn for the colour of trees in the hills. Temperatures are milder, there are fewer people and you shouldn't need raingear until October. From December to March, you can find solitude at reasonable temperatures anywhere close to the coasts. In the mountains (and even around the Bay of Naples), it can rain and rain, with valleys shrouded for days on end beneath banks of mist.

Consulates

In Italy

Australia: Via Antonio Bosio 5, Rome, **t** 06 852 721.
Canada: Via G Carducci 29, Naples, **t** 081 401 338.
Ireland: Largo del Nazarenos, Rome, **t** 06 678 2541.
New Zealand: Via Zara 28, Rome, **t** 06 440 2928.
UK: Via dei Mille 40, Naples, **t** 081 423 8911.
Via Terribile 9, Brindisi, **t** 0831 568 340.
USA: Piazza della Repubblica 2, Naples, **t** 081 583 8111.

Abroad

Australia: Level 45, Macquarie Place, Sydney 2000, NSW, **t** (02) 9392 7900.
Canada: 136 Beverley St, Toronto MST 1YS, **t** (416) 977 1566, *www.italconsulate.org*.
Ireland: 63–5 Northumberland Rd, Dublin, **t** (01) 660 1744, **f** (01) 668 2759; 7 Richmond Park, Belfast BT9 5EF, **t** (02890) 668 854.
New Zealand: PO Box 463, 34 Grant Rd, Wellington, **t** (04) 473 5339.
UK: 38 Eaton Place, London SW1 8AN, **t** (020) 7235 9371; 32 Melville St, Edinburgh EH3 7HA, **t** (0131) 226 3631, *www.embitaly.org.uk*.
USA: 690 Park Ave, New York, NY, **t** (212) 737 9100, *www.italconsulnyc.org*; 12400 Wilshire Bd, Suite 300, Los Angeles, CA, **t** (310) 820 0622, *www.conlang.com*.

Crime and the Police

Emergencies: t 112

Southern Italy has more than its fair share of opportunist criminals. Naples and Bari, in particular, are notorious for street crime; here kindly waiters will tuck your necklace out of sight, and remind you as regularly as bus conductors to hang onto your camera. Local crime syndicates (the Camorra in Naples, the 'Ndrangheta in Calabria and the Sacra Corona Unita in Puglia) keep a toehold on most walks of life, financed by drug dealing, protection rackets and the proceeds of the *toto nero* (illegal football pools). Pickpocketing, purse snatchings, minor thievery of the white-collar kind (always check your change and the taxi meter), car break-ins and theft are rife.

Violent crime is fairly rare, though injuries are sometimes caused by scooter-borne bag-snatchers; stay on the inside of the pavement and keep a firm grip on your property. Pickpockets generally strike in crowded buses and gatherings: don't carry more cash than you need, and split it up so you won't lose the lot at once. Don't leave valuables in hotel rooms.

In Naples, avoid carrying a bag with you at all and don't wear valuable jewellery. Particular areas to be aware of in Naples are around Piazza Garibaldi in the old centre, and anywhere near the Quartieri Spagnuoli (although you will now notice that there is a large police presence around the main tourist sights). Look out for anyone who's behaving suspiciously around you (you'll be spoilt for choice, so don't get too paranoid), particularly groups of young men clustering around you with one or two on foot and one on a moped. If you feel you've reason to be suspicious, don't be shy – dive into a shop or café until they've gone. Also be aware of groups of noisy children, or 'gypsy' women asking for money – they may be entirely honest but they may alternatively be surprisingly quick at relieving you of your wallet. As if this weren't enough, there are numerous street scams in Naples – a good rule of thumb is: don't buy anything from a less-than-permanent-looking stall or just from a lone pedestrian and always be vigilant in train stations.

If possible, avoid taking a car anywhere near Naples. Theft is so common that some car-hire firms refuse to rent certain models for use in the city. If your car is stolen, ring the police, **t** 081 599 1475, but don't expect much sympathy. Always park cars in garages, well-lit streets or guarded lots with anything remotely portable or valuable removed if possible, or at least well out of sight.

For police emergencies, **t** 113 or **t** 112 connects you to an English-speaking service.

Outside Naples, organized crime is much less evident. The *vigili urbani* take care of minor everyday problems in towns. They are generally more easy-going and courteous than the quasi-military *carabinieri* who, along with the *polizia statale*, watch over the rural areas. Traffic offences are dealt with by the *polizia stradale*, who patrol the highways.

The *Guardia di Finanza* is the tax police (only in Italy...). You'll see quite a lot of them, patrolling the coastal waters for smugglers and haunting the towns for businesses cheating on their income statements. It's true that they stop people outside bars and ask to see their receipts – they once fined an eight-year-old boy on a beach for buying an ice-cream cone and not taking away the *scontrino*. The case was dismissed because the boy hadn't had any pockets in his swimming trunks.

You may see soldiers protecting courthouses and other public buildings, and occasionally in the countryside. Often their only purpose is cosmetic, an effort by the government to make people in the Mafia areas feel a little more secure. The tall fellows with the feathers in their alpine hats are *bersaglieri* (sharpshooters), Italy's élite troops.

Avoid travelling after dark in Aspromonte, which is renowned for bandits, and be aware that possession of any type of questionable substances could subject you to a hard time in drug-ridden southern Italy – despite your theoretical legal right to carry a few grams of soft stuff for personal use.

Disabled Travellers

Italy has been slow off the mark in providing for disabled visitors. Uneven pavements, the appalling traffic conditions, crowded public transport and endless flights of steps in many public places are all disincentives, although things are slowly getting better. A national support organization in your own country may have information on facilities in Italy, or will at least be able to provide general advice. The Italian tourist office, ENIT, or the state travel agency, CIT (*see* p.62), can also advise on hotels, museums with ramps, etc. If you book rail travel through CIT, you can request assistance if you use a wheelchair.

Royal Association for Disability & Rehabilitation (RADAR), 12 City Forum, 250 City Road, London EC1V 8AF, **t** (020) 7250 3222, **f** (020) 7250 0212, *www.radar.org.uk*; sell a guide, *Holidays & Travel Abroad: A Guide for Disabled People* (£3.50).

Mobility International, PO Box 10767, Eugene, Oregon 97440, **t** (541) 343 1284, *www.minsa.org*.

Society for Accessible Travel and Hospitality (SATH), 347 Fifth Avenue, Suite 610, New York, NY 10016, **t** (212) 447 7284, *www.sath.org*.

Australian Council for the Rehabilitation of the Disabled (ACROD), PO Box 60, Curtin, ACT 2605, **t** (02) 6682 4333, **f** (02) 6281 3488, *www.acrod.org.au*.

If you need help while you are in Naples or the resorts of Campania, contact the local tourist office. Provincial tourist boards provide lists of hotels with specialized facilities, museums with wheelchair access, and so on.

Eating Out

Southern Italians typically eat lunch around 1pm and dinner at 8pm or after; the

Calendar of Events

January

6 Re-enactment of the Magi's visit to Bethlehem in Lizzano, Taranto.
17 Festa d'o' Cippo di Sant'Antonio in Naples: a procession for the protector of animals. Bonfires and games in Novoli, Lecce.
Jan–April Chamber music at the Teatro delle Palme in Naples.
Jan–mid-July Opera at the San Carlo in Naples.

February

16 Dec–Feb Italy's longest carnival at Putignano, Bari. The Carnevale Dauno at Manfredonia lasts four weeks, but not much happens until the final week.

April

Holy Week Celebrations have a Spanish flavour, with processions of floats carried by robed and hooded *confraternities*; the best are in Taranto. There is a passion play nearby at Ginosa and a torchlight procession for Good Friday in Nemoli, Potenza. Orthodox Albanian Easter celebrations take place at Lungro in Calabria.

May

Weekends Cultural events in Naples.
Last half International music festival in Naples.
3rd week Comic strip and illustration show in Naples.
28–29 Festival of San Gerardo in Potenza.

June

2 La Scamaciata in Fasano, Brindisi – a costume parade and festivities.
7 June–mid-July Music festival in Ravello.
27 Sant'Andrea in Amalfi: fireworks, costumes and processions. The Festa dei Gigli in Nola, near Naples: a procession of giant 'lilies' (wooden-tower floats) that recalls the homecoming of Bishop Paolino from Africa in 394. The Challenge of the Trombonieri at Cava de' Tirreni, Salerno: an arquebus shooting contest in period costume, celebrating a victory over the Angevins.

farther south you go, the later it happens. Breakfast generally consists of a coffee and a pastry, and is usually taken at any time of the morning.

Many restaurants offer a *menu turistico* for €12–15. Some have a *menu degustazione* of local and house specialities; this is usually better and more expensive than the *menu turistico*, but still cheaper than à la carte.

The cost of your meal will include a cover charge (*pane e coperto*, between €1.50–2.50), and a 15 per cent service charge. This is often included in the bill (*servizio compreso*); if not, it will say *servizio non compreso*. Additional tipping is not usually expected. For further information about eating in southern Italy, including local specialities, wine and a menu decoder, *see* the **Food and Drink** chapter, p.33.

Restaurant Price Categories

Prices are based on a three-course meal with wine, per person.

very expensive over €45
expensive €30–45
moderate €20–30
cheap up to €20

Festivals

In Campania, any excuse will do for throwing a party, especially if it can be combined with having a day off work, and the region hosts some of Italy's most spectacular and colourful *feste*. Most of them are linked to religious events and feast days. The Madonna features prominently, often decked out with fairy lights and gaudy flowers and hauled through the streets atop tiny Fiats hastily covered with red velvet (with peep holes for the driver), or on platforms stoically borne by the village's strongest young men. Many of the celebrations have a strong pagan flavour, especially those linked to the land and the harvest, and some feast-day paraphernalia is unmistakably phallic (towers and obelisks are an obvious giveaway).

Whatever the occasion, a village *festa* is a chance to see local traditions and ancient rites in full swing. They are jolly affairs, and outsiders are nearly always welcome. A visit to a *festa* will invariably involve consuming vast quantities of food, often superbly cooked in makeshift kitchens organized by the local women and served at knockdown prices.

July

2 Madonna della Bruna in Matera: a religious procession with a huge allegorical float that is torn to pieces at the end of the day.

26 Feast of St Anne in Ischia: a torchlight procession of boats, transformed into floats, to honour the island's patron saint.

27 Feast of St Pantaleone in Ravello: an extravagant firework display accompanies the liquefaction ceremony of the 4th-century saint. (A vial of his blood in the town's *duomo* is said to liquefy on this day each year.)

August

6–8 Feast of San Nicola Pellegrino in Trani: a waterfront festival.

14–16 Madonna della Madia in Monopoli, Bari: a water festival celebrating an icon of the Madonna that floated ashore.

15 Wheat festival in Foglianise, Benevento: a procession of decorated tractors, with a light pageant in the evening. Feast of the Assumption in Positano: an ancient celebration in honour of the Virgin.

22 Procession on the sea and fireworks in Porto Cesareo, Lecce.

September

First 10 days Neapolitan song contest and fireworks in Piedigrotta, Naples.

19 Feast of San Gennaro, Naples, where the faithful gather to watch the liquefaction of the saint's blood.

End Puglian handcrafts show in Foggia.

November

10 Feast of San Trifone in Adelfia, Bari: a procession of children dressed as angels.

December

Throughout Christmas Fair, across the region: selling decorations for *presepi* (Christmas cribs).

8 Immaculate Conception sausage and polenta festival in San Bartolomeo in Galdo, Benevento.

24 *Presepi* at the Zinzalusa grotto in Castro, Lecce. Midnight mass and tableaux at Grottaglie (Taranto) and Nardo (Lecce).

The table above lists some of the best, but also check notices in town and village piazzas.

Health and Emergencies

Ambulances: t 118

Citizens of EU countries can get reciprocal healthcare in Italy's national health service and a 90 per cent discount on prescriptions. You need to bring a **Form E111** with you: it's available in the UK from post offices. The E111 does not cover all medical expenses – there are no repatriation costs, for example, and no private treatment – so it is advisable to take out separate travel insurance for full cover.

Australia also has a reciprocal healthcare scheme with Italy but other non-EU countries, such as New Zealand, Canada and the USA, do not. Citizens of these countries should check that they have adequate insurance for any medical expenses and the cost of returning home. However, if you have health insurance, a student card or a credit card, these may give you some medical cover abroad.

In an emergency, **t** 118 for an ambulance (*ambulanza*); in Naples, **t** 081 752 8282 (24 hours). The hospital (*ospedale*) in Naples is Policlinico, Via Sergio Pansini, **t** 081 746 1111, though this is a regular subject of horror stories in the local newspapers. Less serious problems can be treated at a *pronto soccorso* (casualty/first aid department) at any hospital, or at a local health unit (*azienda sanitaria locale* – ASL). Airports and the main railway stations also have first-aid posts. If you have to pay for any health treatment, make sure you get a receipt.

Pharmacies are generally open 8.30am–1pm and 4–8pm. Pharmacists are trained to give advice for minor ills and administer simple first aid. All large towns have a pharmacy that stays open 24 hours. Others take turns to stay open (the address rota is posted in the windows of pharmacies and in the newspaper *Il Mattino*). The 24-hour pharmacy in Naples is Carducci, Via Carducci 21–23, **t** 081 417 283.

No specific vaccinations are required or advised for citizens of most countries before visiting Italy. The main health risks are the usual travellers' woes of upset stomachs or the effects of too much sun. Occasional, much-publicized outbreaks of more serious diseases have occurred in Naples in recent years (cholera, for example), but these are unlikely to affect travellers. Take a supply of useful medicines with you (including insect repellent, anti-diarrhoeal medicine, sun lotion and antiseptic cream), and any drugs you need regularly. Stick to bottled water (dehydration is a serious risk) and avoid uncooked shellfish around the polluted Bay of Naples.

Maps and Publications

It's worth investing in a good, up-to-date regional map before you leave home. They are available from the following bookshops:

Stanford's, 12–14 Long Acre, London WC2 9LP, **t** (020) 7836 1321, *www.stanfords.co.uk*.

The Travel Bookshop, 13 Blenheim Crescent, London W11 2EE, **t** (020) 7229 5260.

The Complete Traveler, 199 Madison Ave, New York, NY 10016, **t** (212) 685 9007.

Excellent maps are produced by Touring Club Italiano, Michelin and Istituto Geografico de Agostini. They are available at all major bookshops in Italy (e.g. Feltrinelli) and some newsstands. Italian tourist offices are helpful and can often supply good maps and plans.

Naples has an excellent English language bookshop, **Universal Books**, at Corso Umberto I 22, **t** 081 252 0069.

Money and Banks

On 1 Jan 2002, Italy adopted the **euro** as its official currency. It comes in €1 and €2 coins, and €5, €10, €20, €50, €100, €200 and €500 notes, and 1, 2, 5, 10, 20 and 50 cent coins.

Remember that Italians indicate decimals with commas and thousands with full points.

Exchange rates at the time of going to press were €1 = £0.69, $1.23, CDN$1.55, A$1.70.

Banking hours vary, but core times are usually Monday to Friday, 8.30–1.20 and 3–4, closed weekends and on local and national holidays (*see* opposite).

Getting cash in Italy can be a frustrating business involving much queueing and form filling. Major banks and exchange bureaux licensed by the Bank of Italy give the best exchange rates. Hotels, private exchanges in resorts and FS-run exchanges at railway stations usually have less attractive rates, but are open outside banking hours.

In Naples, you can also change money at the post office, in hotels and some travel agents.

You'll find cash machines in the big cities such as Naples. They take the usual credit cards and have instructions in English. You can expect to pay around 4 per cent commission when withdrawing cash.

Most banks will also give you cash on a recognized credit card or Eurocheque with a Eurocheque card (for little or no commission), although MasterCard (Access) is less widely accepted in Italy than other major cards.

Large hotels, resort area restaurants, shops and car-hire firms will accept credit cards as well, but many smaller places will not – from sad experience, Italians are wary of plastic.

You can also have money transferred to you through an Italian bank, which will take one or two days. You need to show your passport as identification when you collect it. Sending cheques by post is inadvisable.

Banks in Italy have security guards with guns outside. Before you enter, you have to put your handbag into a locker, then pass through a metal-detecting revolving door.

National Holidays

Most museums, as well as banks and shops, are closed on the following national holidays:

1 January (New Year's Day)
6 January (Epiphany)
Easter Sunday and Monday
25 April (Liberation Day)
1 May (Labour Day)
15 August (Assumption, or Ferragosto, peak of the Italian holiday season)
19 September (San Gennaro – **Naples** only)
1 November (All Saints' Day)
8 December (Immaculate Conception)
25 December (Christmas Day)
26 December (Santo Stefano, St Stephen's Day)

Opening Hours, Museums and Churches

Although it varies from region to region, most of Italy closes down at 1pm until 3 or 4pm to let everyone eat and properly digest the main meal of the day. Afternoon hours are 4–7, sometimes 5–8 in the hot summer months. Bars are often the only places open during the early afternoon. Shops are usually closed on Sundays and often on Monday mornings, too.

Italy's churches have always been a target for art thieves, and are usually locked when there isn't a caretaker to keep an eye on things. All churches, except for the really important cathedrals and basilicas, close in the afternoon, and the little ones tend to stay closed. Always have some coins for the light machines in churches, or the work of art you came to inspect will remain shrouded in ecclesiastical gloom. Don't do your visiting during services, and don't come to see paintings and statues in churches the week preceding Easter – you will probably find them covered with mourning shrouds. Many churches are becoming less strict about dress, but don't wear shorts or sleeveless tops when visiting cathedrals.

Many of Italy's museums are magnificent, many are run with shameful neglect, and many have been closed for 'restoration' for years, with slim prospects of reopening in the foreseeable future. With an estimated two works of art per inhabitant, Italy has a hard time financing the preservation of its national heritage; it's as well to enquire at the tourist office to find out what is open and what is 'temporarily' closed before setting off on a wild goose chase.

Generally, Sunday afternoons and Mondays are dead periods for the sightseer – you may want to make them your travelling days. Places without specified opening hours can usually be visited on request – but it's best to go before 1pm.

We have listed the hours of important sights and museums, and specified which ones charge admission: expect to pay between €3–10, although important sites, such as Pompeii, may cost more. EU citizens under 18 and over 65 get free admission to state museums by presenting their passports.

Post Offices

Dealing with *la posta italiana* has always been frustrating and time-consuming. One of the scandals that has mesmerized Italy in the past few years was the one involving the minister of the post office, who disposed of literally tons of backlog mail by tossing it in the Tiber. When the news broke, he was replaced – the new minister, having learned his lesson, burned all the mail the post office was incapable of delivering. Not surprisingly, fed-up Italians view the invention of email as a gift from the Madonna.

If you want to take your chances, post offices are usually open Monday to Saturday from 9am until 1pm, or until 6 or 7pm in a large city. To have your mail sent poste restante (*fermo posta*), have it addressed to the central post office and allow three to four weeks for it to arrive. Make sure your surname is clearly written in block capitals. To pick up your mail, you must present your passport and pay a nominal charge.

Stamps (*francobolli*) may be bought in post offices or tobacconists (*tabacchi*, identified by their black or blue signs with a white 'T').

Prices fluctuate. The rates for letters and postcards (depending how many words you write!) vary according to the whim of the tobacconist or postal clerk.

There's now a more efficient *posta prioritaria* service, costing €0.62 for a letter, which arrives next day in Italy and within three days in Europe. If your letter is bigger than a small envelope, you have to put on two stamps. *Tabacchi* regularly run out of stamps, so you might have to go to the post office.

Note that the enormous queues in most post offices are rarely for stamps, but consist of people paying bills – check you're in the right line for posting letters or you'll be there forever.

You can also have money telegraphed to you through the post office. If all goes well, this can happen in a mere three days, but expect a fair proportion of it to go into commission.

In Naples, the **main post office** is in Piazza Matteotti, **t** 081 551 1456, near Via Toledo, and is open Monday to Friday 8.30am–7pm, Saturday 8am–12 noon. You can also send faxes and telegrams from there.

Shopping

You'll find some of the lowest shopping prices in **Naples**, especially its street markets.

Amalfi's specialities are fine stationery (paper-making was already a major industry here in the Middle Ages) and ceramics – mostly tourist bric-a-brac, but some very well done.

Every conceivable luxury item Italy makes is sold in the shops of **Sorrento**. If you come in the off season (December and January are best) you'll find bargains in fashions, glass and other trinkets. Sorrento's own speciality is *intarsia*, inlaid wood scenes on tables or trays, or simply framed for hanging. They are exquisite things, and prices are often reasonable.

Prices for **clothes** in Italy are generally high, and sizes are tailored for slim Italian builds.

Sports and Activities

Fishing

Many lakes and streams are stocked, while sea fishing from the shore or boats (though not much with an aqualung) is possible almost everywhere without a permit.

To fish in fresh water you need to purchase a year's membership card from the **Federazione Italiana della Pesca Sportiva**, which has an office in every province (Naples: **t/f** 081 622 129). They will inform you about any local conditions and restrictions.

Football

Soccer (*il calcio*) is a national obsession. For many Italians, its importance outweighs tedious issues like the state of the nation, government of the day, or any international event – not least because of the weekly chance (slim but real) of becoming an instant euro millionaire in the *Lotteria Sportiva*. The sport was actually introduced by the English, but a Renaissance game that was a cross between football and rugby has existed in Italy for centuries. Modern Italian teams are known for their grace, precision and teamwork. Rivalries are intense and scandals, especially bribery and cheating, are rife. The tempting rewards offered by big-time entertainment attract all manner of corrupt practices, although crowd violence is rare.

The only Southern Italian team currently in Serie A (the equivalent of the Premiership) is Lecce, much to the annoyance of Neapolitan football fans; Napoli SSC was once a great club, winning titles in the late 1980s with Diego Maradona at the helm. A brief flurry in Serie A in the 2001–2 season has since been overshadowed by financial disaster, with the club passing hands between a string of shady chairmen, one of whom was detained in a Rome jail while magistrates scrutinized his business activities. The club was declared bankrupt in August 2004, only to be saved from ignominy by film mogul Aurelio De Laurentiis (he produced *Hannibal*), who bought the club and renamed it Napoli Soccer.

Almost any weekend (matches are generally played on Sunday afternoons) you should find a good game somewhere in the region. Tickets for the top matches cost €15–60.
In Naples, the main ground is the Stadio di San Paolo in Fuorigrotta (a western suburb – take Ferrovia Cumana to Mostra; the stadium is directly outside), **t** 081 735 4310 or 800 00 16 16.

Hiking

Southern Italy cannot match the mountains of the north, but there's no shortage of rugged, off-the-beaten track countryside. The principal national parks of the south all offer good hiking and scenery: the Cilento in southern Campania, Pollino National Park in northern Calabria/southern Basilicata, the Gargano peninsula in Puglia, and the Sila and Aspromonte in Calabria.

For information about national parks, contact the **Federazione Italiana Parchi e Riserve Naturali**, Via Cristoforo Colombo 149, 00147 Roma, **t** 06 5160 4940, **f** 06 5143 0472, *www.parks.it*. The website has details of local hiking guides and facilities in each park.

In the Bay of Naples, head for the hills of the Sorrento peninsula (accessible via the funicular from Castellammare di Stabia to Monte Faito) and the interiors of Capri and Ischia.

Useful walking maps include the green Touring Club Italia (TCI) series, as well as the Club Alpino Italiano (CAI) map of the Monti Lattari for the Sorrento peninsula.

Don't expect trails to be clearly marked and easy to follow; if you want to explore, ask at local tourist offices for local guiding services.

Sailing

Almost all the islands have some facilities for yachts, though they may not be equipped for a long stay. You can bring your own boat to Italy for six months without any paperwork if you bring it by car; if you arrive by sea you must report to the port authority. The harbour master (*capitaneria di porto*) at your first Italian port of call will give you a document called a *costituto*, which you will have to produce for subsequent harbour masters. This permits the purchase of tax-free fuel. For further information, contact the Italian State Tourist Office or write to:

Mare Club d'Italia (MACI), Via A. Bargoni 8, 00135 Rome, **t** 06 589 4046, **f** 06 589 7084.

Other useful addresses are:

Federazione Italiana Vela (Italian Sailing Federation), Piazza Borgo Pila 40, Genoa, **t** 010 54 45 60, **f** 010 59 28 64, *www.federvela.it*.

Federazione Italiana Motonautica (Italian Motorboat Federation), Via Piranesi 44/b, Milan, **t** 02 7016 3001, **f** 02 7016 3525.

The main Bay of Naples yacht harbours are Posillipo (Naples), Capri, Procida and Porto, Casamicciola, Lacco Ameno and Forio d'Ischia on the island of Ischia.

Tennis

Many of the expensive hotels have courts, and non-residents may be able to use them by arrangement with the hotel or local tourist office. There are public courts in Naples: contact **Federazione Tennis**, Via Giochi del Mediterraneo, Naples, **t** 081 570 3912, and Ischia Porto, Lungomare Colombo, **t** 081 985 245, *www.federtennis.it*.

Watersports and Beaches

At most resorts, you can hire boats and equipment, and go windsurfing, waterskiing, or diving; in Naples, contact the **Subacquei Napoletani**, Via Caracciolo 2, **t** 081 761 1985.

Capri is good for watersports, with some of the cleanest waters in the Bay of Naples. For scuba diving, waterskiing, sailing, canoeing and boat hire, contact the **Sea Service Centre**, Marina Piccola, Via Mulo 63, **t** 081 837 0221.

Sorrento, Positano, Amalfi and Salerno also offer a range of watersports and cruises.

Many southern Italian beaches are flat, with lines of parasols and sunbeds. Those in the Bay of Naples tend to be of grey volcanic sand; the free public ones are crowded and neglected, with few facilities. To enjoy Italian beaches, you'll have to pay: most of the best stretches (and some of them are artificial) are private concessions.

For the most attractive resort beaches, head for Positano, Minori or Maiori. Despite the pollution immediately around Naples, the water off the islands of Ischia, Procida and Capri is generally clean and inviting, while the Amalfi coast is scenically the most dazzling stretch of shoreline in the whole of Italy.

Below the Gulf of Salerno, the Cilento coast is generally rocky rather than sandy. Good beaches do exist, however, and are much less crowded than the beaches of the Amalfi coast. The area is popular for scuba diving.

Elsewhere, there are hundreds of kilometres of empty beaches. Don't expect them to be clean, although the water is usually fine if you steer clear of the big industrial centres.

Telephones

Naples area code: t 081

Public telephones for international calls may be found in the offices of **Telecom Italia** (Italy's telephone company). In the last few years, other companies have appeared, so rates for long-distance calls vary, but they remain high. Calls within Italy are cheapest after 10pm; international calls after 11pm.

Most phone booths now take phone cards (*schede telefoniche*), sold in tobacconists and at newsstands in units of €1, €2.50 and €5. To use, rip off the serrated corner of the card where marked. There is also a range of international phonecards (*schede internazionali*), some of which you can use from your own mobile.

In smaller villages and islands, you can usually find *telefoni a scatti*, with a meter on them, in at least one bar (a small commission is generally charged). Avoid telephoning from hotels, which often add 25 per cent to the bill. Naples has phone centres in the Stazione Centrale, at Via Depretis 40, and in the Galleria Umberto I.

Note that you have to dial the area prefix when making a call. Even if you are calling a Naples number from within Naples, you have to dial **t** 081 followed by the number and, if calling from abroad or from your foreign mobile, you have to dial **t** 00 39 081 followed by the number. If you own an American mobile and want to call home from Italy, you need a tri-band mobile phone .

You can make direct international calls from Italian public phones. Codes from Italy are:

UK t 0044
Ireland t 00353
USA and Canada t 001
Australia t 0061
New Zealand t 0064

Time

Italy is one hour ahead of Greenwich Mean Time and six hours ahead of Eastern Standard Time. From the last weekend of March to the end of October, Italian Summer Time (daylight saving time) is in effect.

Tourist Information

Italy's state tourist board, ENIT (*www.enit.it*), has offices or booths in most major towns and resorts. They are generally open 8–12.30 or 1 and 3–7, and possibly longer in summer. Few open on Saturday afternoons or Sundays.

These offices, known as EPT, AAST or APT, provide hotel lists, town plans and (often terse) information on transport and local sights. English is spoken in the main centres. However, queues can be long and you may get more sense out of a travel agency.

ENIT also has overseas offices:

Australia: Level 26, 46 Market St, NSW 2000, **t** (02) 9262 1666, *www.italiantourism.com.au*.
Canada: 175 Bloor St E, Suite 907, Toronto, Ontario, M4W 2AY, **t** (416) 925 4882, *www.italiantourism.com*.
UK: 1 Princes St, London W1B 2AY, **t** (020) 7399 3562, *www.italiantouristboard.co.uk*.
USA: 630 Fifth Ave, Suite 1565, New York, NY 10111, **t** (212) 245 4822; 12400 Wilshire Blvd, Suite 550, LA, CA 90025, **t** (310) 820 1898; 500 N. Michigan Ave, Suite 2240, Chicago, IL 60611, **t** (312) 644 0996; *www.italian tourism.com*.

You can also consult the Italian state-run travel agency **CIT** before travelling:
UK: Marco Polo House, 3–5 Lansdowne Rd, Croydon, Surrey CR9 1LL, **t** 0870 901 4013, *www.citalia.co.uk*.
USA: 15 West 44th St, 10th floor, New York, NY 10036, **t** 800 CIT-TOUR, *www.cit-tours.com*.
Canada: 7007 Islington Avenue, Suite 205, Woodbridge, Ontario, **t** (905) 264 0158 or **t** 1 800 387 0711.

Where to Stay

All accommodation in Italy is classified by the provincial tourist boards. Price control, however, has been deregulated since 1992. Hotels now set their own tariffs, and in some places, prices have rocketed. High-season prices are given, which often just applies to a couple of weeks in August. At other times, these might be halved.

The quality of furnishings and facilities has improved in all categories in recent years. But you can still find plenty of older-style hotels and *pensioni* whose eccentricities of character and architecture (in some cases, undeniably charming) may frequently be at odds with modern standards of comfort or even safety.

In Naples, good, affordable accommodation is scarce and should be booked ahead, while Capri's ritziest establishments vie with any in Italy on price. Beyond the Bay of Naples, however, prices are generally lower.

Hotels and Guesthouses

Italian *alberghi* come in all shapes and sizes. They are rated one to five stars, depending on their facilities (not their quality, style or charm). The star ratings are some indication of price levels, but for tax reasons not all hotels choose to advertise themselves at the rating to which they are entitled, so you may find a modestly rated hotel just as comfortable (or more so) than a higher rated one. Conversely, you may find that a hotel offers few stars to attract budget-conscious traveller but charges as much as a more highly rated neighbour.

Pensioni are traditionally more modest establishments, though the distinction between these and ordinary hotels is becoming blurred. *Locande* used to indicate even more basic lodgings, but these days the term may denote somewhere fairly chic.

Other cheap accommodation is sometimes known as *alloggi* or *affittacamere*. There are usually plenty of cheap dives around railway stations; for somewhere more salubrious, head for the historic quarters. Whatever the

Hotel Price Categories

For a double room with bath/shower.
luxury over €230
very expensive €150–230
expensive €100–150
moderate €60–100
cheap up to €60

shortcomings of the furnishings and fittings, you can usually rely at least on clean sheets.

Price lists, by law, must be posted on the door of every room, along with meal prices and any extras (such as air conditioning, or even a shower in cheap places). Low-season rates can be a third lower than peak-season tariffs, and some resort hotels close down altogether for several months a year.

During high season you should always book ahead to be sure of a room. If you have paid a deposit, your booking is valid under Italian law, but don't expect a refund if you cancel. Tourist offices publish regional lists of hotels and pensions with current rates, but will not make reservations for visitors. Large railway stations generally have accommodation booking desks; inevitably, a fee is charged.

If you arrive without a reservation, begin looking for accommodation early in the day. If possible, inspect the room before you book, and check the tariff carefully. Italian hoteliers may legally alter their rates twice during the year, so prices on tourist board lists (and guidebooks) can quickly become outdated. Hoteliers who overcharge can be reported to the local tourist office. You will be asked for your passport for registration purposes.

You can expect to pay about two-thirds the rate for single occupancy, though in high season, you may be charged the full double rate. Extra beds are usually charged at about a third of the room rate and rooms without private bathrooms 20–30 per cent less. Most places offer discounts for children sharing parents' rooms, and/or children's meals. A *camera singola* (single room) may cost from €30 upwards. Double rooms are normally twin-bedded (*camera doppia*). For a double bed, specify a *camera matrimoniale*.

Breakfast is usually optional in hotels and *pensioni*. You will normally get better value in a bar or café if you have a choice. In high season, you may be expected to take half board in resorts if the hotel has a restaurant, and one-night stays may be refused.

Bed and breakfast and apartment rental can be organized by the **Rent A Bed** booking agency, based in Naples but covering the whole of the Bay of Naples, including the bay's islands and the Amalfi Coast down to the Cilento. They also arrange *agriturismo* stays.

Rent A Bed, Vico Sergente Maggiore 16, Naples, **t/f** 081 417 721, *www.rentabed.com*.

Youth Hostels

There aren't many of these in Italy (known as *alberghi* or *ostelli per la gioventù*), but the ones that do exist are generally pleasant and sometimes located in historic buildings. An international membership card lets you stay in any of them: cards can be purchased on the spot in many hostels. Hostels around Naples include **Agerola-S. Lazzaro** or **Mergellina** (Naples) and **Irno** (Salerno). Rates are usually €10–16 for a place in a dorm and breakfast. There are discounts for senior citizens, and some family rooms. You generally have to check in after 5pm and pay for your room before 9am. They often close in the daytime and many operate a curfew. In summer, it's best to book ahead: contact them direct. For a full list, contact **Associazione Italiana Alberghi per la Gioventù** (Italian Youth Hostel Association, or AIG), Via Cavour 44, 00184 Roma, **t** 06 487 1152, **f** 06 488 0492. The **International Youth Hostel Federation** (**t** (01707) 324 170, *www.iyhf.org)* publishes *Hostelling International, Vol 1: Europe* (£5.50), listing all hostels in Europe.

Camping

Most sites are near beaches, though there are a few inland in scenic areas or near major tourist centres such as Pompeii or Paestum. Camping is not the fanatical holiday activity it is in, say, France, nor is it a great bargain, but it is popular with many holiday-making families in August, when you will find many sites full to bursting. Unofficial camping is generally frowned on. Camper vans (and facilities for them) are increasingly popular.

Charges range from about €6–7 per adult, plus an extra €6 for a vehicle. Extra charges may also be levied for hot showers and electricity. To obtain a camping carnet and book ahead, write to the **Centro Internazionale Prenotazioni Campeggio**, Casella Postale 23, 50041 Calenzano, Firenze, and request their list of campsites and a booking form. The **Touring Club Italiano** (TCI) also publishes an annual guide to campsites and tourist villages throughout Italy. Write to: TCI, Corso Italia 10, 20122 Milan, **t** 02 85261, or try regional tourist offices for lists of local sites.

Self-catering Operators

A number of agencies organize self-catering holidays on the coast or in rural settings, sometimes also offering discounted air fares and fly-drive schemes.

HotelPronto.com, 98 Great North Road, London N2 0NL, **t** 0870 405 9455, **f** 0870 405 9456, *www.hotelpronto.com*.

Apartment Service, 5–6 Francis Grove, London SW19 4DT, **t** 020 8944 1444, **f** 020 8944 6744, *www.apartmentservice.com*. Selected apartments for city stays.

CV Travel, 43 Cadogan St, London SW3 2PR, **t** (020) 7591 2800, **f** (020) 7591 2802, *www.cvtravel.net*. Distinctly unpackaged villa and hotel holidays.

First Choice Holidays, First Choice House, London Rd, Betts Way, Crawley, West Sussex RH10 9GX, **t** (01293) 560 777 or **t** 0870 850 3999, *www.firstchoice.co.uk*. Villas and apartments in Ravello and Sorrento.

Interhome, 383 Richmond Rd, Twickenham, TW1 2EF, **t** (020) 8891 1294, *www.interhome.co.uk*.

Long Travel, The Stables, Dudgeley House, All Stretton, Shropshire, SY6 6LB; **t** (01694) 722 193, **f** (01694) 724 291, *www.long-travel.co.uk*. Villas in authentic unspoilt Italy.

Vacanze in Italia, Manor Courtyard, Bignor, nr Pulborough, W. Sussex, RH20 1QD, **t** 0870 078 0193, *www.indiv-travellers.com*. Villas .

Hometours International, PO Box 11503, Knoxville, TN 37939, USA; **t** 865 690 8484, *http://thor.he.net/~hometour*.

The closest campsite to Naples is the **Circolo Campeggiatori Napoletani**, Via Monteruscello 351a, Pozzuoli, **t** 081 524 5540, close to the bubbling, rotten-egg-smelling volcanic crater of Solfatara, west of the city. It's usually crowded. Camping is forbidden on Capri, although there are sites on Ischia and Procida.

Agriturismo

For a breath of rural fresh air, the normally gregarious Italians head for a spell on a working farm, in accommodation (usually self-catering) that often approximates to the French *gîte*. Often, however, the real pull of the place is a restaurant in which you can sample some homegrown produce (olives, wine, etc.). Outdoor activities may also be on tap (riding, fishing, and so forth). This branch of the Italian tourist industry has burgeoned in recent years and every region now has several Agriturist offices. And prices for farmhouse accommodation, compared to the over-hyped 'Tuscan villa', are still reasonable.

Agriturismo isn't as well established in southern Italy as in Tuscany or Umbria, but it does exist. However, it's as well to have a little Italian under your belt before burying yourself in an olive grove. Local tourist offices will have information on this type of accommodation in their areas. The national organization **Agriturist**, Corso Vittorio Emmanuele 101, 00186 Rome, **t** 06 685 2337, **f** 06 685 2424, *www.agriturist.it*, publishes a complete listing, available both online and in Italian bookshops. The office of **Agriturist Campania** in Naples is at Corso Lucci 137, **t** 081 284 077, **f** 081 281 397.

Women Travellers

With the heritage of Casanova, Don Giovanni and Rudolf Valentino, Italian men are confident of their role as Great Latin Lovers, but the old horror stories of gangs following the innocent tourist maiden are way behind the times. Italian men these days are often exquisitely polite and flirt on a far more sophisticated level. Still, women travelling alone may frequently receive hisses, wolf whistles and unsolicited comments or 'assistance' from local swains – usually of the balding, midlife-crisis variety. Attitudes in Calabria have changed least. A confident, indifferent poise is usually the best policy. Failing that, a polite 'I am waiting for my *marito*' (avoiding a damaged ego), followed by a firm '*no*!' or '*Vai via!*' (Scram!) will generally solve the problem. Flashers and wandering hands on buses may be an unpleasant surprise, but rarely present a serious threat (unless they're after your purse).

Travelling with a companion of either sex buffers you from such nuisances. Also, use your common sense: avoid lonely streets, parks and stations after dark, and choose restaurants close to public transport. As in most countries, women should avoid hitch-hiking alone in Italy.

Naples

Naples
VIA PIETRO CASTELLINO
VIA GIACINTO GIGANTE
VIA MATTEO RENATO IMBRIANI
VIA SALVATORE ROSA
V. M. D. VITO PISCICELLI
V. G. B. RUOPPOTO
PZA MEDAGLIE D'ORO
VIA SIMONE MARTINI
SANTA CROCE
VIA G.
VIALE MICHELANGELO
Montesanto
CORSO VITTORIO EMMANUELE
VIA ACITILLO
VOMERO
Montesanto Funicular
VIA TITO ANGELINI
Quattro Giornate
VIA LUCA GIORDANO
PZA VANVITELLI
VIA A. SCARLATTI
Vanvitelli
Castel Sant'Elmo
Certosa di San Martino
VIA FRANCESCO CILEA
VIA ANIELLO FALCONE
VIA DOMENICO CIMAROSA
Funicolare Centrale
QUARTIERI SPAGNUOLI
Funicolare di Chiaia
Villa Floridiana
VIA ANIELLO FALCONE
VIA TORQUATO TASSO
Amadeo
VIA DI PARCO MARGERITA
PZA AMEDEO
Stazione V. Emmanuele (F. Cumana)
VIA FRANCESCO CRISPI
VIA DEI MILLE
VIA MICHELANGELO SCHIPA
Museo principe de Aragona Pignatelli
PZA DEI MARTIRI
RIVIERA DI CHIAIA
Villa Comunale
PZA VITTORIA
PZA DELLA REPUBBLICA
VIA FRANCESCO CARACCIOLO
Mergellina
VIA PIEDIGROTTA
VIA GIORDANO BRUNO
VIALE ANTONIO GRAMSCI
Tomba deVirgilo
PZA SANNAZZARO
MERGELLINA

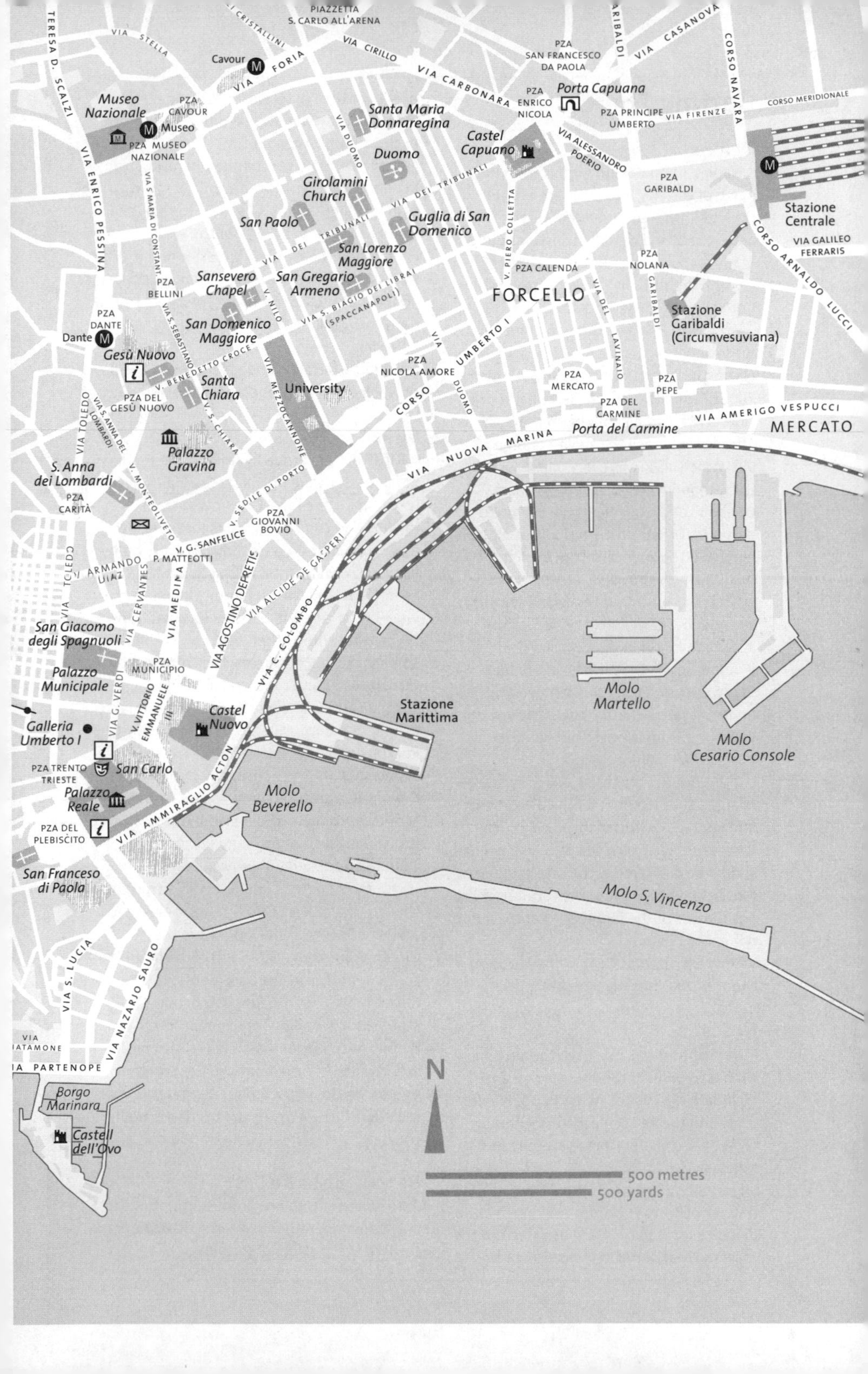

PIAZZETTA S. CARLO ALL'ARENA
VIA CRISTALLINI
VIA STELLA
TERESA D. SCALZI
VIA FORIA
VIA CIRILLO
VIA CARBONARA
PZA SAN FRANCESCO DA PAOLA
VIA CASANOVA
CORSO NAVARA
Cavour
Museo Nazionale
PZA CAVOUR
Museo
PZA MUSEO NAZIONALE
Santa Maria Donnaregina
PZA ENRICO NICOLA
Porta Capuana
PZA PRINCIPE UMBERTO
VIA FIRENZE
CORSO MERIDIONALE
Castel Capuano
VIA ALESSANDRO POERIO
VIA DUOMO
Duomo
VIA ENRICO PESSINA
VIA S MARIA DI CONSTANT.
Girolamini Church
VIA DEI TRIBUNALI
PZA GARIBALDI
Stazione Centrale
San Paolo
Guglia di San Domenico
V. PIERO COLLETTA
CORSO ARNALDO LUCCI
VIA GALILEO FERRARIS
San Lorenzo Maggiore
PZA NOLANA
PZA BELLINI
Sansevero Chapel
San Gregario Armeno
PZA CALENDA
FORCELLO
VIA DEL LAVINAIO
GARIBALDI
Stazione Garibaldi (Circumvesuviana)
VIA S. BIAGIO DEI LIBRAI (SPACCANAPOLI)
V. NILO
PZA DANTE
Dante
San Domenico Maggiore
VIA S. SEBASTIANO
Gesù Nuovo
V. BENEDETTO CROCE
CORSO UMBERTO I
PZA NICOLA AMORE
PZA MERCATO
PZA PEPE
Santa Chiara
University
VIA MEZZOCANNONE
PZA DEL GESÙ NUOVO
VIA TOLEDO
VIA S. ANNA DEI LOMBARDI
V. S. CHIARA
DUOMO
PZA DEL CARMINE
Porta del Carmine
VIA AMERIGO VESPUCCI
MERCATO
Palazzo Gravina
VIA NUOVA MARINA
S. Anna dei Lombardi
PZA CARITÀ
V. MONTEOLIVETO
V. SEDILE DI PORTO
PZA GIOVANNI BOVIO
V. G. SANFELICE
P. MATTEOTTI
V. ARMANDO DIAZ
VIA ALCIDE DE GASPERI
V. CERVANTES
VIA MEDINA
VIA AGOSTINO DEPRETIS
VIA C. COLOMBO
San Giacomo degli Spagnuoli
Palazzo Municipale
PZA MUNICIPIO
Molo Martello
Stazione Marittima
V. VITTORIO EMMANUELE III
VIA G. VERDI
Castel Nuovo
Galleria Umberto I
Molo Cesario Console
PZA TRENTO TRIESTE
San Carlo
Palazzo Reale
Molo Beverello
VIA AMMIRAGLIO ACTON
PZA DEL PLEBISCITO
San Franceso di Paola
Molo S. Vincenzo
VIA S. LUCIA
VIA NAZARIO SAURO
VIA PARTENOPE
Borgo Marinara
Castell dell'Ovo
N
500 metres
500 yards

Getting There

By Air

Naples' **Capodichino Airport** is on the north of the city, relatively close to the centre. It has frequent direct services to and from all major Italian destinations and many foreign cities, including London (several flights daily). Airport information: **t** 081 789 6259, *www.gesac.it*.

From 6.30am to 11.30pm, the blue Alibus runs every 30mins between the airport, Piazza Garibaldi (for the train station) and Piazza Municipio (for the ferry harbour). Tickets (€2) can be bought on the bus. Alternatively, take the slower orange 3S bus, which also runs every half-hour but with frequent stops, including Piazza Garibaldi and Molo Beverello (for the ferry harbour). Tickets cost €0.77 and must be purchased before travelling, from the *tabacchi* in the airport.

A bus run by Circumvesuviana (**t** 081 772 2444, *www.vesuviana.it*, €4) leaves the airport three times a day for Pompei (Pompei Scavi). Buy tickets on the bus. Lastly, **Curreri** (**t** 081 801 5420, every 1½ hours till 7pm, €6) runs buses to Sorrento, departing from the stop outside the Arrivals hall (on the right).

If you opt for a **taxi**, you will officially be charged supplements for the airport trip and luggage on top of the meter fare. If in doubt, ask to see the price list, which should be displayed in the cab, or agree a fare before getting into the cab. If traffic is not too heavy, the fare to the centre should not exceed €25.

There's a Thomas Cook (*8am–11.30pm*) at the airport – the only one in Naples.

By Sea

Naples' port has more sea connections than anywhere in the Mediterranean, including the islands in the Bay of Naples, Sicily and the Aeolian Islands. Generally, ferries are cheaper than hydrofoils, but take twice as long.

Ferries and hydrofoils leave from three different points in Naples. Most long-distance ferries arrive and depart from the **Stazione Marittima** in the centre of the port near the Castel Nuovo. Consult individual companies for timetables or look in the daily newspaper *Il Mattino* or in *Qui Napoli*. The main companies operating from Stazione Marittima are **Tirrenia** (**t** 199 123 199) for Palermo and Cagliari; **Siremar** (**t** 081 580 0340 or 199 123 199) for the Aeolian Islands and Milazzo in Sicily; **Medmar** (**t** 081 551 3352) to Tunisia; and **TTT Lines** (**t** 800 915 365) to Catania. **SNAV** (**t** 081 761 23 48) runs a daily hydrofoil from Mergellina quay to Palermo.

For more details of boat services to the Bay of Naples and its islands, *see* p.102 and p.125.

By Rail

Most visitors arrive by train at the modern Stazione Centrale on Piazza Garibaldi, also a junction for the local Circumvesuviana railway and city buses. Trains for Rome or Reggio di Calabria pass through every half-hour or so. Many trains also stop at Napoli Mergellina and Napoli Campi Flegrei, in the west of the city, and at other local stations.

There are three other local railway lines serving the Bay of Naples. The **Ferrovia Circumvesuviana** runs to Herculaneum, Pompeii and Sorrento. The **Ferrovia Cumana** goes to the Campi Flegrei area, including Pozzuoli and Baia, from the station at Piazza Montesanto. A third company, the **Ferrovia Circumflegrea**, runs trains to and from Piazza Montesanto west to Licola and Cuma. The last trains are: Circumflegrea 8.30pm, Cumana 9pm and Circumvesuviana 10.30pm. For details of rail services around the Bay of Naples, **t** 800 892 021, or *see* p.102.

Piazza Garibaldi station, where the Circumvesuviana, Metro and some mainline trains depart, is in the basement of Stazione Centrale. (It's poorly signposted; take the stairs from the main forecourt.) Tickets can be purchased from machines (which rarely work) or ticket desks, or from the travel agency on the ground floor behind the stairwell. Circumvesuviana trains also call at the nearby station in Corso Garibaldi.

By Long-distance Bus

Most services to and from destinations in Campania operate from Piazza Garibaldi in front of the Stazione Centrale.

SITA (**t** 081 552 2176) runs a bus service to Salerno with stops on the Amalfi coast. Buses depart from the Molo Immacolatella, walking from the ferry harbour with the sea on your right and signposted for SITA.

By Car

The A2 *autostrada* from Rome approaches Naples from the north, via Caserta. On the city's outskirts, just east of the airport, it meets a series of massive road junctions: the A16 turns east for Avellino and Bari, then two roads head west: the P1 for the coast and Naples' inner ring road, the *tangenziale*, The *tangenziale* lets you reach much of Naples avoiding the centre. If you're heading further south, stay on the A2 until it meets the A3, avoiding the city entirely.

Getting Around

Naples' main **landmarks** are Castel Sant'Elmo and the huge, fortress-like monastery of San Martino, neighbours on the steep Vomero hill that slopes down to the sea near the port, dividing the city into old and new quarters.

To the west is **modern Naples** – the busy, pleasant districts of Mergellina, Vomero and Fuorigrotta, where middle-class Neapolitans retreat after work on creaking old funicular railways. East, towards Vesuvius, lies the **old centre**. The oldest districts are along and east of Via Toledo, where tall tenements jam into a grid of narrow streets, climaxing in the crowded markets around Piazza Garibaldi.

Walking is often the best and fastest way of getting around. Otherwise take public transport – don't even think about driving.

For just €13 (€8 for under-25s), the new **Artecard** (*www.campaniaartecard.it*) gives three days' travel on metro, buses, trains and funiculars, plus a return trip to Sorrento on the Circumvesuviana and travel on the Metro del Mare. The Artecard also gives discounted car parking and free or half-price entry to major museums and sites in Campania – including Pompeii, Herculaneum and Paestum. You can buy it at the airport, museums or hotels. (There's also a seven-day version for €28, which includes free entry to all sites in Naples and around the Bay, but not transport. If you are staying longer, a monthly pass (€23) covers buses, funiculars and metro.

By Bus

Given the problems involved in using cars and even taxis in Naples, visitors often find themselves left with the buses. These will be slow and indecently crowded and there are no schedules or maps. The confusion is compounded by the recent division of services run by the old bus company Atam under its successor ANM and other smaller companies. Most bus lines start at either Piazza Garibaldi or Piazza del Plebiscito. Some that might be useful are: R2, from Piazza Garibaldi to Corso Umberto and Piazza Municipio; R3, from Piazza Municipio to Riviera di Chiaia and Mergellina; 137 or 160, from Piazza Garibaldi to Piazza Cavour and Capodimonte.

Many bus stops now have electronically updated information telling you when buses are due to arrive – a vast improvement on the previous chaos. If you buy the Artecard, the accompanying booklet provides excellent maps and itineraries for key routes.

The Artecard also includes the Linea dei Musei hop-on-hop-off bus service, which runs every 45 minutes between principal museums and sites from Fridays to Sundays. The useful new **Giranapoli** ('Around Naples') bus tickets come in two types, one lasting 90 minutes for €0.77 and a day ticket for €2.34.

By Metro and *Funicolare*

Naples used to have a shabby, single-line underground, running from Gianturco to Pozzuoli – really a part of the state railway, using the same underground tracks as the long-distance trains. Currently, you'll find much of the city torn up for gigantic excavations, as a major expansion is underway. For now, the Metro will be helpful for reaching the station (Piazza Garibaldi), the Archaeological Museum, points in Vomero and Fuorigrotta, Solafatara and Pozzuoli. Note that the old line is number 2, while the new one being built will be number 1.

A much more agreeable way to travel, though you can't go very far, is on the three *funicolari*, or inclined railways, up to Vomero. The longest – one of the longest in the world, in fact – is the **Funicolare Centrale**, which leaves from Via Toledo, just behind the Galleria, and heads up to Via Cimarosa. The **Funicolare di Chiaia** also ends nearby in the same street, having started from Piazza Amedeo in Chiaia. Finally, the **Funicolare di Montesanto** travels up to Via Morghen from Montesanto Station, the start of the suburban Circumflegrea and Cumana rail lines. All three *funicolari* bring you out near the San Martino Museum and the Castel Sant'Elmo. All run daily until about 10pm. Ticket inspections are frequent and fines issued if you fail to present a ticket. You must validate your ticket when you climb aboard. If the machine doesn't work, write the time and date on the reverse.

By Taxi

Neapolitan taxi drivers have a reputation for scamming tourists, but they are striving to improve their reputation and most now display charges inside the cabs. There are plenty of taxi ranks, or call **Radiotaxi Napoli**, **t** 081 556 4444. Don't get into one that's trying to poach you from the queue (they will rip you off) and watch your change. Tipping is optional – 50 cents is plenty. In the city centre, traffic is often so thick that short journeys can take as long as walking.

By Car

Thinking of driving in Naples? Don't. Cars are stolen with alarming regularity, traffic moves at a crawl, and drivers ignore all road rules and signals. Fatalities are common.

Instead, check with hotels to see if they have secure parking (*parcheggio custodito*). If not, you might want to use the private car parks. Typical costs are: €0.30 per hour, €7.20 per day. Included with the Artecard are 20 per cent discounts for two car parks, one near the station at the Porto exit from the *tangenziale* (ANM Brin), the other in Vomero (ANM Colli Aminei). Both have good bus connections into central Naples. **ANM**: **t** 081 763 2827.

For breakdowns, the AA or RAC both have a reciprocal arrangement with Italy's equivalent, the ACI (**t** 803 116 for emergencies or 081 239 4511 for information, or see *www.aci.it*).

Car hire starts from around €40 a day.

Avis (Station, **t** 081 554 3020);
Hertz (Piazza Garibaldi 91, **t** 081 206 228);
Europcar (Airport **t** 081 780 5643 or **t** 800 014 410);
Inter-rentacar (Via Partenope 37, **t** 081 764 5060).

For traffic news, see *www.posteggInapoli.it* or *www.anm.it*. For scant sympathy about stolen cars, call the city police on **t** 081 794 1435.

Tourist Information

The best place for information about Naples itself is the friendly information booth run by the city's **Azienda Autonoma di Soggiorno** on Piazza del Gesù Nuovo, **t** 081 552 3328 or 081 551 2701, in the Old Town (*open Mon–Sat 9–8, Sun and hols 9–3*). There are other tourist offices in the Royal Palace, **t** 081 252 5711, **f** 081 418 619, and opposite the Teatro San Carlo in the Galleria Umberto I, **t** 081 402 394. Details of excursions outside the city are available from the less helpful provincial tourist office **EPT**, Piazza dei Martiri 58, **t** 081 410 7211.

The EPT has another office at the Stazione Centrale, **t** 081 268 779, which may help in finding a hotel. Two others are to be found at the airport, **t** 081 789 6259, and the Stazione Mergellina, **t** 081 761 2102.

Look out for the excellent free monthly handbook *Qui Napoli*, available at tourist offices; some hotels are available for download at *www.inaples.it*, which carries a great deal of useful information, timetables, listings and calendars of events. The EPT produce good free maps The tourist office map contains four *itinerari artistici* – tourist circuits in the old centre. They are clearly marked and well worth a stroll.

Two associations organize tours of underground Naples. **Napoli Sotterranea** meets outside the church of San Paolo Maggiore at Piazza San Gaetano (**t** 081 296 944, *www.napolisotterranea.com*; *weekdays 12–4, weekends 10–6*). **Laes** (Libera Associazione Escursionisti Sottosuolo; **t** 081 400 256, *www.lanapolisotterranea.it*) meets outside Caffé Gambrinus and runs three visits a day on Saturdays and Sundays and one on Thursday evening.

For **Internet access**, try Multimedia, Via Sapienza 43, **t** 081 298 412. Alcott's principal clothing store on Via Toledo also has an Internet café – if you buy a drink, you can check your mail. Try also Caffé Liberty (**t** 081 544 5797), in Galleria Principe di Napoli, opposite the Archaeological Museum.

Crime

Police: t 112, for an English-speaking operator. Naples has a reputation for crime. Although exaggerated, it's not entirely undeserved. Tips for a safe stay include leaving valuables in your hotel room or safe and avoiding looking too much like a tourist in poor areas. This means not waving your camera around or pulling out maps if you can avoid it. Keep your bag in front of you on buses and in crowds. And leave your car in a secure car park.

Areas where particular care is advised – especially after dark – are on buses and at train stations, around Piazza Garibaldi, the Forcella markets, the Quartieri Spagnuoli and near the botanical gardens.

Shopping

No one thinks of Naples as one of Italy's prime shopping destinations but there are as many things to be bought here as anywhere else, and usually at lower prices. The back streets around Spaccanapoli and other old sections are still full of artisan workshops. The Royal Factory at Capodimonte makes the **porcelain and ceramic figures** that are sold at the fancier shops in the city centre. Another old Naples tradition is the making of **cameos** from special seashells; the shops outside the Certosa di San Martino have the best selection at relatively low prices.

Via San Biagio dei Librai – the middle stretch of the Spaccanapoli – contains some of the best antiquarian book-dealers in Italy, but this street is also full of odd surprises. Many of the religious goods shops, for instance, have surprisingly good works in terracotta. The **Doll Hospital** at No. 81, **t** 081 203 067, is one of the most charming shops in Naples. **Scriptura**, at Vico San Domenico Maggiore 3, is a tiny shop that specializes in beautiful handmade leather diaries, notebooks, photo albums, etc.

In the back streets near the Archaeological Museum there are many antique and junk shops. The swankiest antique shops tend to be along Via Merelli off Piazza dei Martiri in Chiaia. There's also a huge twice-monthly antiques market, the **Fiera dell'Antiquariato**, on alternate Saturday and Sunday mornings in the Villa Comunale gardens. You can buy lovely old prints at **Bowinkel**, Piazza dei Martiri 24, **t** 081 764 4344, while the 150-year-old **Fonderia Chiurazzi**, Via della Resistenza 26, **t** 081 712 3418, makes artistic bronzes, including reproductions of works in the Archaeological Museum. **Intramoenia**, a publishing house and literary café in Piazza Bellini, has a good selection of cards, books and posters of old Naples. For **clothes**, Via dei Mille, which runs from Piazza Amedeo down to Via Chiaia, has several local designer boutiques (such as Barbaro), while Via Calabritto off Piazza del Martiri is the home of Prada and Versace.

For **department stores**, go to Coin on Vomero's pedestrianized Via Scarlatti or try La Rinascente on Via Toledo. The **street markets** near Piazza Garibaldi are fascinating places – especially the daily catch of fish, live squid and octopus in the lively market on Via Ferrara, to the east of Corso Navara – although it's not very safe.

Sports and Activities

For coming events, see the local newspaper *Il Mattino*, the free multilingual monthly guide *Qui Napoli* and the daily freesheets *Metro* and *Leggo*. Many of Naples' attractions are in Fuorigrotta, to the west of Mergellina. **Edenlandia**, **t** 081 239 1182, *www.edenlandia.it*, is a big amusement park there, on Viale Kennedy in the Mostra d'Oltremare, Naples' big trade fair site. Take the Ferrovia Cumana to the station of the same name. There is also a small **zoo** (**t** 081 239 5943, *open daily 9–5; adm*) in the area. Bus 152 passes the gates.

Anything a Neapolitan can bet on flourishes here. The **racetrack** (Ippodromo di Agnano, **t** 081 570 1660), with horse and trotting races, is out west in Agnano, 10km from the city centre along the *tangenziale*. And, of course, there's **football**. With the help of Maradona, Napoli won the league title in 1987. Since then, the club has fallen on harder times, but every big victory still calls forth wild celebration and a live match is unforgettable. Matches are played at the Stadio San Paolo, Piazzale Vincenzo Tecchio, **t** 081 735 4310 or 800 00

1616; take the Ferrovia Cumana to Mostra or the Metropolitana to Campi Flegrei.

The sea within the city is not especially clean. If you want a swim, there is a **pool**, the Piscina Scandone, Via Giochi del Mediterraneo, also in Fuorigrotta, **t** 081 570 2636. **Tennis** can be played at Tennis Club Napoli, Viale Dohrn, **t** 081 761 4656, in the Villa Comunale, Tennis Club Vomero, Via Rossini 6, **t** 081 579 8917, and at the Virgilio Sporting Club, Via Tito Lucrezio Caro 6, **t** 081 575 5261. **Bowling Oltremare** (**t** 081 624 444) are popular 20-lane bowling alleys in Fuorigrotta, near the zoo, Edenlandia and the NATO base at Bagnoli. They are open daily until late.

Where to Stay

Naples ✉ 80100

There's a shortage of good, affordable accommodation in Naples – book ahead if you can. The best area to stay is undoubtedly down on the waterfront around Santa Lucia and Castel dell'Ovo, where you have easy access to shopping, museums and good restaurants. It's less claustrophobic, too. There are thousands of cheap rooms near Piazza Garibaldi, but most are in horrible dives. The hotel-booking service at the station or airport can find you a room for a small fee.

Luxury

Naples has fewer than its share of quality hotels. The Germans, inexplicably, blew up a few of them before their retreat in 1944. Three of the best are located in a row along Via Partenope, overlooking the Castel dell'Ovo, where the views over the bay more than compensate for the traffic noise below.

*****Excelsior, Via Partenope 48, **t** 081 764 0111, **f** 081 764 9743, *www.excelsior.it*. Visiting sheiks, kings and rock stars favour this, Naples' finest hotel, with its beautiful suites and a tradition of perfect service since 1909. You pay for space – elegant lounges, a beautiful rooftop solarium and restaurant, rooms with large beds and antique-style furniture. This is a place for those who think the hotel is the most important part of the holiday. It sits on the right of three other plush hotels and faces Vesuvius.

*****Parker's, Corso Vittorio Emmanuele 135, **t** 081 761 2474, **f** 081 663 527, *www.grandhotelparkers.com*. Further inland (near the Corso Vittorio Emmanuele stop on the Cumana line) this delightful hotel is Naples' oldest. The airy rooms have ample charm, with plenty of polished wood, chandeliers and comfortable furniture. Choose a sea-facing room with a balcony for the palm-fronted vista of Vesuvius and distant Capri. The view is even more spectacular from the award-winning restaurant on the terraced roof.

*****Santa Lucia, Via Partenope 46, **t** 081 764 0666, **f** 081 764 8580, *www.santalucia.it*. This beautifully restored 18th-century *palazzo* is sandwiched between the others. In face of the competition and its lack of roof garden, the management has clearly opted for the corporate crowd, with extensive conference facilities.

*****Vesuvio, Via Partenope 45, **t** 081 764 0044, **f** 081 764 4483, *www.vesuvio.it*. In spite of its name, this grandiose hotel lacks the head-on view of Vesuvius, but it's where Bill Clinton and the Italian football team stay, so it must be doing something right. It has a lovely roof garden for dining (important since none of the rooms have good balconies) and a health spa. *Wheelchair accessible*.

Very Expensive

*****Miramare, Via Sauro 24, **t** 081 764 7589, **f** 081 764 0775, *www.hotelmiramare.com*. A gem. Manager Enzo Rosalino exudes plenty of old-world charm. There are personal touches in each of the 30 rooms and the atmosphere is cosy and intimate. Some rooms are small but the old lift and the lavish breakfast laid out on the rooftop solarium more than make up. Rooms not facing the sea are quieter.

*****Paradiso, Via Catullo 11, **t** 081 247 5111, **f** 081 761 3449, *www.bestwestern.it* A good bet, if a little corporate, with stunning views over the bay – book a sea-facing room.

*****Angioino, Via de Pretis 123, **t** 081 552 9500, **f** 081 552 9509, *www.mercure.com*. Owned by the French Mercure hotel chain, it offers 86 good-sized rooms and a central location (a minute from Piazza Municipio), with efficient service that makes it popular with the business crowd. The views are unspectacular, the furnishings functional, but all rooms are comfortable and it provides a good base. *Wheelchair accessible*.

***Cavour**, Piazza Garibaldi 32, **t** 081 283 122, **f** 081 287 488, *www.hotelcavournapoli.it*. A decent, well-run hotel in an otherwise desperate area. Book the top-floor suites for little more than a standard room. These enjoy ample terraces, good views over Vesuvius and are a respite from the bustle below. Rooms are nicely decorated in the omnipresent Liberty style. Bathrooms are good in an area where the plumbing hasn't been overhauled since the Greeks, and the restaurant gets two Michelin *fourchettes*. *Wheelchair accessible*.

Expensive

***Chiaia Hotel de Charme**, Via Chiaia 216, **t** 081 415 555, **f** 081 422 344, *www.hotelchiaia.it*. A quiet, clean, extremely comfortable hotel in an aristocratic *palazzo* two minutes' walk from San Carlo and Piazza del Plebiscito. 27 rooms furnished with antiques (some have a jacuzzi bathtub). Friendly and well priced.

***Palazzo Doria D'Angri**, Piazza 7 Settembre 28, **t** 081 790 1000, *www.albergosansevero.it*. This new hotel, just off Piazza Dante, is in a lovingly restored 18th-century palace designed by the Bourbons' architect, Luigi Vanvitelli. The eight large bedrooms lead to a beautifully proportioned circular breakfast room, a bar and an oval ballroom with its original mirroring and exquisite friezes and frescoes by Fischietto. Boasting its own private chapel, the Palazzo Doria once played host to Garibaldi himself, who proclaimed the unification of the south of Italy with the north from its balcony in September 1860.

***Rex**, Via Palepoli 12, **t** 081 764 9389, **f** 081 764 9227, *www.hotel-rex.it*. In the Santa Lucia district near Piazza del Plebiscito, this hotel offers simple rooms with bare brown wood and breakfast in bed – there are no public areas – this is a good base.

Albergo San Severo, Via S. M. Di Costantinapoli 101, **t** 081 790 1000, *www.albergosansevero.it*. A real find. Tucked within an elegant *palazzo* near the Archaeological Museum, it is quiet and well furnished, the staff are warm and friendly. If the Albergo San Severo is full, the family also own two other reasonable hotels in historic *palazzi* close by and in the same price range: the **Soggiorno San Severo** at Piazza San Domenico Maggiore 9 (**t** 081 551 5742) or the **Albergo San Severo Degas** at Calata Trinità Maggiore 53 (**t** 081 551 1276).

Ausonia, Via Caracciolo 11, **t/f** 081 682 278 or 081 664 536. A clean, comfortable *pensione* with 20 rooms and a nautical theme – portholes around the room numbers and nautical design bedspreads. Well-appointed rooms, each with TV and video player (tapes also available in English). Located within a *palazzo*, looking onto an interior courtyard, this is a quiet option in the Mergellina area.

Moderate

*Duomo**, Via Duomo 228, **t** 081 265 988. In the same street as the cathedral, this *pensione* has a family feel and 12 clean and spacious rooms with bathrooms.

Fontane al Mare, Via N. Tommaseo 14, **t** 081 764 3470. It is definitely worth booking in advance for a room at this hotel. There are only 21 rooms located on the last two floors of an old *palazzo* next to the Chiaia Gardens. Ask for rooms without a bathroom for the best sea view (and value). It's a well-known hotel and popular with the local *carabinieri* college. To use the lift, you need 10 cent coins.

*Margherita**, Via Cimerosa 29, **t** 081 556 7044 or 081 578 2852. With 20 rooms, on the 5th floor of a *palazzo* high on Vomero hill, this is basic but clean. There are six bathrooms (shared) and you need 5 cents for the lift. It is in a safe area and next door to the Funiculare Centrale which runs until 1am and takes you down to the Via Toledo in 10 minutes.

Hotel Ginevra, Via Genova 116, **t** 081 554 1757 or **t** 081 283 210 for information in English, *www.hotelginevra.it*. A clean and friendly hotel in the least seedy corner of Piazza Garibaldi. Bright, cheery and recently modernized, it's a far cry from the fleapit room-by-the-hour hotels typical of the area and offers cheap double en suite rooms.

Cheap

Naples has a distinct dearth of pleasant budget hotels. Many of the cheap places are around Stazione Centrale and the Piazza Garibaldi; the hotels here are invariably substandard – at best, a place to sleep and certainly not a good holiday base. Another area for cheap lodging is Via Mezzocannone, south of Spaccanapoli. This street borders the university and, with so many students, it can be hard to find a vacancy. Like Piazza Garibaldi, it is also a little grotty.

Soggiorno Imperia, Piazza Miraglia 386, **t** 081 459 347. With just nine rooms, the Imperia has a prime location, just around the corner from Piazza Bellini. Only one room (No. 8) is en suite with a TV; the other eight share two bathrooms. The staff are friendly and rooms 5 and 6 have wonderful views. Its drawback is there's no lift and it's on the fifth floor.

Ostello Mergellina, Salita della Grotta 23, **t** 081 761 2346, **f** 081 761 2391. This is Naples' youth hostel, near the Mergellina metro station. IYHF cards are required but you can buy them at the hostel.

Eating Out

Neapolitan cuisine is simple – one of the most celebrated dishes is *spaghetti alle vongole* – and, even in some of the more pretentious places, you will see favourites of the Neapolitan *cucina povera* sneaking onto the menu, like *pasta e fagioli*. There are few bad restaurants or tourist traps in the city and many excellent family-run *trattorie* or *pizzerie*.

For authentic Neapolitan pizza, look for the genuine Neapolitan pizza oven, a built-in, bell-shaped affair made of stone with a broad, clean tile floor. The fire (for which only certain kinds of wood will do) is at the back, nice and close to the pizza, not hidden underneath.

Watch out in restaurants for the house wines. In cheaper places this is likely to be Gragnano from nearby Monte Faito – detestable, rough stuff. On the other hand, you can find some real surprises from Campania: a dry white called Greco di Tufo; or Taurasi, a distinguished red; or Falerno, descendant of the ancient Falernian that Latin poets never tired of praising.

Naples has some of the cheapest restaurants in Italy – they cheat on their taxes. Others can be alarmingly expensive, especially for fish. Restaurants in all price ranges are spread pretty evenly around town. For a romantic meal, try **Borgo Marinara** beside the Castel dell'Ovo, where the whole marina is set aside for dining, or try **Mergellina**. Nearer the old centre, you'll find character; pokey streets with pokey restaurants whose chefs pop over to local street stalls for their fresh veg.

Some of the cheapest and homeliest places can be found on or around **Via Speranzella**, a block west of Via Toledo in the Tavoliere, where few tourists penetrate. Most restaurants around Piazza Garibaldi and the station are best avoided but this area, and also Piazza Mercato, is an open bazaar, and you can enjoy snacking from bars and stalls on slices of pizza, heavy *arancini* and the flaky pastries called *sfogliatelle* – another Naples speciality.

Very Expensive

Da Cicciotto, Calata Ponticello a Marechiaro 32, Posillipo, **t** 081 575 1165. On the front of Marechiaro, along from Mergellina, Da Cicciotto's setting is very romantic. A stone's throw from the sea with the temple of Fortuna as backdrop, fish is the order of the day here. There is no fixed menu – the waiter explains what's on offer each day – but a typical meal is fresh *mozzarella di bufala* accompanying huge quantities of mixed grilled or fried seafood *antipasti*, followed by lobster. The kitchen is fast-moving and queues form in the evenings. It's best to book ahead.

Dora, Via Ferdinando Palasciano 30 (off Riviera di Chiaia), **t** 081 680 519. Booking ahead is advised. Dora is a Neapolitan institution. Extremely cosy and unpretentious, with friendly staff and a convivial atmosphere, it serves only fish and attracts visiting celebrities and guests from the 5-star hotels at Santa Lucia. With a colourful tile mural and old-fashioned nautical paraphernalia, the specialities are *antipasti misto mare*, *linguine alla dora* and fish cooked *alla brace*, while their grilled prawns are to die for. *Closed Sun and mid-Aug*.

La Cantinella, Via Nazario Sauro 23, **t** 081 764 8684. Near the Castel dell'Ovo on the esplanade, this is believed by many to be Naples' finest – also the place to be seen for the Parthenopeans, with a telephone on each table which they retain despite the invention of mobile telephones. Their *linguine Santa Lucia*, made with homemade pasta, octopi, squid, prawns, clams and fresh baby tomatoes, takes some beating. The risotto is also excellent. Though it isn't cheap, you can easily spend more in other places nearby. The atmosphere is smart but relaxed and the service welcoming and friendly. *Closed Sun and Aug 12–17.*

Expensive

La Bersagliera, Borgo Marinara 10, **t** 081 764 6016. In an excellent location beneath the Castel dell'Ovo, this large 1900s restaurant cuts an elegant image despite the tacked-on 80s extension. The fish is delicious and the wine is good, too, especially the white Fiano de Avellino. *Closed Tues.*

Ciro, Borgo Marinaro, **t** 081 764 6006. A smart place on the Borgo Marinaro beneath the Castel dell'Ovo. Go ahead and order *pasta e fagioli* or any other humble pasta dish. It's what the place is famous for – typical Naples cuisine at its best. They also do Pizza trail, although refurbishment has stripped out much of its character. *Closed Wed.*

Jap-One, Via Santa Maria Cappella Vecchia 30, **t** 081 764 6667, *www.jap-one.it*. This sushi restaurant, with chefs from Tokyo and Koji and stylish minimalist interior, is a trendy addition to Naples' culinary scene. Not easy to find, at the end of a safe but narrow road beside Feltrinelli at Piazza dei Martiri. Booking is essential. *Eves only, closed Mon and Aug, booking essential.*

La Sacrestia, Via Orazio 116, **t** 081 664 186. Run for generations by the Ponsiglione family, this is another temple of Neapolitan gastronomy. It has a superb location, too, overlooking the Bay of Naples from the heights at Mergellina near San Goachino funicular station. Try the *risotto con neonati di seppietta* (risotto with baby squid). *Closed Sun eves, Mon lunch; Aug.*

Moderate

Mimì alla Ferrovia, Via Alfonso d'Aragona 19, **t** 081 553 8525. A nice surprise in the area at the end of Piazza Garibaldi and popular with the local media posse. Again, you'll find no new-fangled concoctions, just honest dishes based on fresh ingredients and recipes handed down for generations. Try the seafood and *pasta e ceci*, a khaki green soup of flat pasta and chick peas. Ignore the brusque service. *Closed Sun and mid-Aug.*

Don Salvatore, Via Mergellina 5, **t** 081 681 817. Over 40 years on the Mergellina esplanade, this place has built a reputation for turning out fine Neapolitan dishes, accompanied by some of the area's best wines. There are set menus for those who want an introduction to Naples' best, and pizza for those who want to keep the bill down. *Closed Wed.*

La Cantina di Triunfo, Riviera di Chiaia 64, **t** 081 668 101. This small restaurant on the north of Piazza della Repubblica has Neapolitan *cucina povera* raised to an art form – wintry soups of chestnuts and lentils, or lighter versions using broad beans and fresh peas in spring, *polpette di baccalà* (small balls of minced salt-cod, fried or served in a fresh tomato sauce) and mouthwatering pasta dishes. Desserts are good, too – try the *crostata d'urance e mandorle* (an orange and almond tart). The wine list is exceptional, and there are 80 types of grappa to choose from, many of them homemade. Be sure to book as space is limited. *Closed lunch, Sun and Aug.*

Taverna e Zi Carmela, Via Niccolò Tommaseo 11/12, **t** 081 764 3581. On the Via Partenope esplanade (beyond the Castel dell'Ovo but before the Villa Communale), seafood is the speciality here. *Closed Wed.*

Brandi, Salita Sant'Anna di Palazzo 1/2, **t** 081 416 928, *www.brandi.it*. This lively *pizzeria* off Via Chiaia claims to have invented the *margherita*, Naples' most famous pizza (mozzarella, tomatoes and basil) in honour of the 19th-century queen whose favourite dish it apparently was. She would pick up pizza on the way back from balls to eat cold in the morning. They have two floors and a small terrace. The seafood pizza includes octopi cooked with their ink sacs intact.

Cheap

Castel Nuovo, Piazza Francese 42, **t** 081 551 5524. Located where Piazza Municipio meets Molo Beverello, this restaurant is handy for the ferry to Capri. Excellent service accompanies fresh, well-prepared pasta dishes, such as *spaghetti alle cozze*, *rigatoni* with squash and prawns or penne with walnuts. The pizzas are equally good.

Da Michele, Via Sersale 1, **t** 081 553 9204. Good for a quick snack. Neapolitans cluster outside. The superb, giant pizzas come in two models: *margherita* and *marinara*.

Da Pasqualino, Piazza Sannazzaro 78/9, **t** 081 681 524. At this old *pizzeria* near Mergellina quay, you can get two superb pizzas and lots of easy-drinking local wine for the price of a plate of pasta in smarter places. *Closed Tues.*

Pizzeria Port'Alba, Via Port'Alba 18, **t** 081 459 713. Founded in 1830, this little place in the historic centre does excellent pizzas. You can also get full dinners, including the house speciality, *linguine al cartoccio* – oven-baked seafood pasta: it's vast, so go easy on the *antipasti*. You can sit outside, under the Port'Alba or inside (upstairs is cosier).

Bellini, Via Santa Maria di Costantinopoli 80, **t** 081 459 774. More good pizza and pasta dishes at this *trattoria* just beyond the Port'Alba, with a few outdoor tables in summer. Try the *linguine al cartoccio* if it is on offer or *pesce alla griglia*. *Closed Sun.*

Lombardi a Santa Chiara, Via Benedetto Croce 59, **t** 081 552 0780. Slightly more up-market, this busy restaurant off Piazza del Gesù Nuovo offers great pizza, and *antipasti* of fried courgettes, baby mozzarella and artichokes. If you can't face another pizza, the *bucatini al pomodoro* is a treat. Noisy but friendly, it fills up quickly, so book ahead.

Da Pietro, Via Luculliana 27. There are a handful of tables here and no menu, but it occupies a million-dollar position on the Borgo Marina. Enjoy tasty seafood dishes (but little else) at reasonable prices while you relax next door to far more prestigious establishments.

Trattoria Nennella, Vico Lungo Teatro Nuovo 103–105, **t** 081 414 338. This amazing bargain in the Quartieri Spagnuoli offers true Neapolitan food and spirit in a simple setting (paper cups and tablecloths and photocopied menus). You are likely to be the only foreigner. *Closed Sun.*

Cafés and *Gelaterie*

Neapolitans are Italy's most dedicated coffee consumers. However, the best (and cheapest) coffee is to be found in the many stand-up places, where you pay at the till, bang the receipt and a tip down on the bar and bark your order. If you like it without sugar, ask for a *caffè amaro*. Good bars should give you a glass of water with your coffee.

Good stand-up coffee bars include **Caffè del Professore** (Corso Novara opposite the station), **Bar Mexico** (Piazza Garibaldi 72, Piazza Dante and Via Scarlatti 69 in Vomero), **Bar Nilo** on Spaccanapoli (Via San Biagi dei Librai 129) and **Caffè Roma** (Via Toledo 325).

The locals tend to leave sitting to tourists, but the city does have a crop of elegant, ornate (and often faded) 19th-century *gran caffè*, mostly close to the Galleria and the Piazza del Plebiscito. The best is **Gambrinus**, Piazza Trieste e Trento, but it's not cheap.

For people-watching, try **La Caffetteria** (Piazza Vanvitelli 10 in Vomero and Piazza di Martiri 30 in Chiaia), **Caffè San Domenico** (Piazza San Domenico di Maggiore 11) and **Caffè Amadeus** (Piazza Amedeo 2). Other good areas for a sit-down coffee include Borgo Marinara and Mergellina harbour (especially **Chalet Ciro**) and the cafés in Piazza Bellini (although watch out for purse-snatchers).

Naples is hailed for its locally roasted coffee. Look out for Moreno, Passalacqua and Tico. Naples also produces some great ice cream and pastries. *Gelaterie* can be found all over town but **Scimmia**, Piazza della Carità 4, just off the Via Toledo near Spaccanapoli, has for long been regarded as one of the city's best. For an ice cream with a view, try **Bilancione**, Via Posillipo 238. Other good *gelaterie* include **Chiquitos** (Piazza Barbaia Mergellina) and **La Tortiera** (Via Filangieri 75 in Chiaia).

For *sfogliatelle*, **Scaturchio** (Piazza San Domenico Maggiore) is acclaimed as the best *pasticceria* in Naples, although the following are good, too: **Pintauro** (Via Toledo 275), **Bar Cimmino** (Via Filangieri 12, in Chiaia), **Moccia** (Via San Pascuale a Chiaia 21 in Chiaia) and **Dolcezze Siciliane** (inside the port).

Entertainment and Nightlife

For concerts, shows, and other cultural events – Naples always has plenty – the best information on programmes and times will be found in the newspaper *Il Mattino* or in the free monthly guide *Qui Napoli*.

Opera, Classical Music and Theatre

For opera lovers, the ultimate experience is a night at the **San Carlo** (Via San Carlo, **t** 081 797 2111), but tickets are very hard to come by and very pricey. Hotels may be able to get them most easily, or go to the box office in person. If you do get a ticket, be sure to dress up. You may have more luck catching a concert at the **Auditorium RAI-TV**, Via Guglielmo Marconi (Fuorigrotta), **t** 081 725 1111; at the **Conservatorio San Pietro a Maiella**, Via San Pietro a Maiella, **t** 081 564 4411; or at the **Associazione Alessandro Scarlatti**, Piazza dei Martiri 58, **t** 081 405 637, which holds concerts for jazz, chamber and other music.

Check with the tourist office or in *Qui Napoli* for programmes, and don't forget that many, often free, concerts are staged in the city's churches. You can get tickets for many events at the ticket offices in the **Box Office**, Galleria Umberto I 15–16, **t** 081 551 9188, and at **Concerteria**, Via Schipa 23, **t** 081 761 1221.

The best theatres to try are the **Politeama**, Via Monte di Dio, **t** 081 764 5016; the **Cilea**, Via S. Domenico, **t** 081 247 2684; the **Bracco**, Via Tarsia 40, **t** 081 564 5323; and the **Sannazaro**, Via Chiaia 157, **t** 081 411 723.

Clubs, Bars and Discos

Neapolitans are night owls, probably thanks to their Spanish heritage, and many, especially in summer, don't even think about going out to dinner until 10pm. That doesn't leave too much time for partying, once the 2–3 hour ritual of eating is over, but there are some reasonable clubs and late-night bars.

One thing to remember is that some areas are best left well alone after midnight, most notably the Forcella–Piazza Garibaldi area near the station and the Quartieri Spagnuoli, the narrow side streets that run off the Via Toledo. And if the vampish hookers seen at every street corner after dark take your fancy, take a second look – those girls could well be boys. Naples is famous even in drag-obsessed Italy for its transvestites and some of them are positively remarkable.

For late-night **bars**, Piazza Bellini, one block north of Santa Chiara in the Old Town, is the spot where the young and trendy come to see and be seen, especially in summer. It is also one of the few piazzas in Naples whose cafés have outside tables. Try to get a table at **Intra Moenia**, the literary café-cum-publishing house, **t** 081 200 720, *www.intramoenia.it*. The Via Paladino, next to the university, and the piazzas del Gesù and San Domenico Maggiore on Spaccanapoli, are also popular on a Saturday night. The bars at Mergellina and on the Borgo Marinara stay open until 2am and are lively in summer, while Via Martucci, in Chiaia, is another good bet for a bar crawl.

It's worth checking with the locals where their most popular **nightclubs** are since the popularity of haunts can change with the current fads. Borgo Marinara is a good spot to try. Neapolitans tend to bop the weekends away, so very few open during the week. You will rarely pay over €15 to get in – the fairer sex often get in for less or even for free – which normally includes a drink. Remember that things never kick off until after midnight, so if you turn up before that, you need to bring your own crowd.

A list of clubs can be found in *Qui Napoli*.

La Mela, Via dei Mille 40, **t** 081 410 270. Good reports from the young and beautiful.

Madison Street, Via Sgambati 47, **t** 081 546 566. Naples' biggest disco is an institution, with different theme nights (Saturday is gay night) and an affluent young crowd.

My Way, Via Cappella Vecchia 30/c, **t** 081 245 1887. Popular nightspot.

Velvet Garage, Via Cisterna dell'Olio. An alternative disco with a rougher edge.

Otto Jazz Club, Piazzetta Cariati 23, **t** 081 551 7453. Jazz which looks for inspiration as much to Neapolitan folk songs as to New Orleans. It also serves light meals, with a well-stocked bar serving 200 cocktails (their specials are beer-based!). Don't take too much cash with you, as this otherwise very pleasant club is in a pretty hard area – when you leave, it's best to get a taxi rather than walk around much outside. *Open Thurs–Sun.*

Virgilio Sporting Club, Via Tito Lucrezio Caro 6, **t** 081 575 5261. A much more tranquil nightclub, set in its own parkland up on Posillipo hill, with tables outside in fine weather. *Open Fri–Sun, midnight–4am.*

The most loathsome nest of human caterpillars I was ever forced to stay in – a hell with all the devils imbecile in it.

John Ruskin

***...it reveals itself only to the* simpatici.**

Peter Gunn

For many, Naples is the homeland of a particular Italian fantasy, the last bastion of singing waiters and red-checked tablecloths, operatic passion and colourful poverty, balanced precariously between Love's own coastline and the menace of Vesuvius. But mention Naples or the Neapolitans to any modern, respectable north Italian and as they gesticulate and roll their eyes you will get a lesson in the dynamics of Italy's eternal 'Problem of the South'. Many Italians cannot accept that such an outlandish place can be in the same country as them, a sentiment that probably contains as much envy as contempt. Naples, the city that has given the world Enrico Caruso, Sophia Loren, pizza and syphilis (the disease appeared here in 1495, and was immediately blamed on the French garrison), has also long been Italy's urban problem child.

Whatever it might have been that so spooked the delicate Ruskin, among Italians Naples used to conjure up a very different image – a city of grace and joy, laughter and song and plenty of good food. 'You are the empire of harmony, O Naples', as the famous traditional song *Santa Lucia* put it. Harmony got a rude jolt adjusting to the modern industrial world, and an even worse one with World War II and the nightmarish poverty and depravity of the Allied occupation that followed. In the ensuing decades, visitors saw Naples at its worst. The Allies had allowed organized crime to re-establish itself, and it came to dominate the city and its institutions. In a world where corruption ruled all, urban problems got out of hand. Drugs and crime flourished – the contraband pack of Marlboros came to rival Vesuvius as the city's best-known symbol, while at one point, the smugglers formed a union to protect themselves against the police. The pollution and traffic problems became Italy's worst. Illegal building spoiled much of the bay, while at the same time, a horrific housing problem left Neapolitans living in abandoned buses and stolen cargo containers.

In the 18th century, when the city and its incomparable setting were a highlight of the Grand Tour, the saying was 'See Naples and die...'. By the 70s and 80s, when things were arguably at their worst, this had become a macabre joke. The good news is, signs are everywhere that Naples is slowly, fitfully, recovering its old graces. Long-neglected monuments are being restored, public services run a little better; a new metro is under construction and much of the centre has been closed to traffic. A huge modern business centre, the Centro Direzionale, has appeared out of the old wastelands behind Piazza Garibaldi. There's still no shortage of problems, though. Rubbish pick-up is a crying scandal these days, as you'll surely notice, and the Camorra still makes the headlines daily with its grisly clan wars.

As the man in the hotel put it: 'It's not quite Zurich yet' and we both agreed one could be thankful for that. Zurich is hardly *simpatico*, and the thought of a tidy, orderly Switzerland on the Bay sends a chill through the soul. Naples' real attraction is a priceless insight into humanity, at the hands of a population of 2.2 million spirited anarchists. The Napoletani may be numbered among the few peoples of urban Europe who truly realize they are alive and try to enjoy it as best they can. Their history being what it is, this manifests itself in diverse ways.

The Napoletani do not stand in lines, fill out forms or stop for traffic signals if they can get away with avoiding them; they will talk your ears off, run you over in their ancient Fiats, criticize the way you dress, whisper alarming propositions, give you sweets, try to pick your pockets with engaging artlessness, offer surprising kindnesses and, with a reassuring smile, they will always, always give you the wrong directions. In an official capacity, they will either break the rules for you or invent new ones; in shops and restaurants, they will either charge you too much or too little. A bus ticket officially costs 77 cents, but even the employees of the bus line round it off to 75; life is too short to worry about pennies.

If the accounts of long-ago travellers are to be believed, Naples has always been like this. Too much sunshine, and living under such a large and ill-mannered volcano, must contribute much to the effect. It would be somewhat harder to explain some of Naples' ancient distinctions. First and foremost, Naples is Italy's city of philosophers. Her greatest, Giambattista Vico, was a Neapolitan, and others, such as St Thomas Aquinas and Benedetto Croce, spent much of their time here.

Naples can also claim to be first in music. Among native composers are Gesualdo, Scarlatti and Leoncavallo, and Neapolitans claim their conservatory is the oldest in Europe. Even today, members of the opera company at San Carlo look down on their colleagues at Milan's La Scala as a band of promising upstarts who could stand to take their jobs a little more seriously. Neapolitan popular song, expressive and intense, is an unchained Italian stereotype; the Napoletani maintain its traditions as jealously as they do their impenetrable dialect – flavoured with Arabic and Spanish galore – one of the most widely spoken and robust in modern Italy.

Along with these, the aural ambience takes in plenty of fireworks, slamming doors, impromptu arias, screams, ambulance sirens and howling cats. The only thing subtle about Naples is its charm and the city may win your heart at the same time it is deranging your senses.

History

Naples' rise to become the metropolis of Campania was largely the result of the lucky elimination of her rivals over the centuries. Capua, Cumae and Benevento rose and fell, and Pompeii and Herculaneum disappeared under volcanic ash, but fortune has always seemed to protect Naples from the really big disasters. As a Greek colony founded by Cumae in 750 BC, the city began with the name *Neapolis* (New City) and prospered moderately throughout the periods of Greek, Samnite and Roman rule. Belisarius, Justinian's famous general, seized the region for Byzantium in AD 536, after invasions of the Goths and Vandals, but a duke of Naples declared the city independent in 763, acknowledging only the authority of the pope.

The chronicles are understandably slim for this period; early medieval Naples offers us more fairytales than facts. Many of its early legends deal with none other than the poet Virgil; somehow, folklore in the Dark Ages transformed the greatest Latin poet into Master Virgil, a mighty magician who was given credit for many of the unexplainable engineering feats of the ancient Romans. Naples claimed him for its founder and its legends told of how he built the Castel dell'Ovo, balancing it on an egg at the bottom of the harbour. Master Virgil also built a talking statue that warned the city of enemies, earthquakes or plagues, and medieval chroniclers mention the bronze horses and bronze fly he built over two of the city's gates, still to be seen then, and said to be magical charms on which the city's fortunes depended.

Naples lost its independence to the Normans in 1139, later passing under the rule of the Hohenstaufen emperors along with the rest of southern Italy. Charles of Anjou took over in 1266, and lopped off the head of the last Hohenstaufen, Conradin, in what is now Piazza del Mercato. Under the Angevins, Naples for the first time assumed the status of a capital. The Angevin kings of Naples, however, did little to develop their new realm, expending most of their energy in futile attempts to recapture Sicily, lost to them after the Sicilian Vespers revolution of 1282. After their line expired in 1435 with the death of Giovanni II, the kingdom fell to Alfonso V of Aragon – a fateful event, marking Spain's first foothold on the Italian mainland.

Habsburgs and Bourbons

Aragonese rule seemed promising at first, under the enlightened Alfonso. Later, though, it became clear that the Spaniards were mainly interested in milking Italy for taxes with which to finance further conquests. The city itself, as the seat of the viceregal court, prospered greatly; by 1600, its population of 280,000 made it the largest city on the Mediterranean. The long period of Spanish control did much to give Naples its distinct character, especially during the 17th and 18th centuries, when the city participated almost joyfully in the decadence and decay of the Spanish empire. This period saw the construction of the scores of frilly, gloomy Baroque churches – now half-abandoned, with bushes growing out of the cornices – that add so much to the Neapolitan scene. In manners especially, the imperial Spanish influence was felt. 'Nothing', in the words of one observer, 'is cheaper here than human life.'

In 1707, during the War of the Spanish Succession, Naples passed under the rule of Archduke Charles of Austria. Prince Charles of Bourbon, however, snatched it away from him in 1734, and mouldering, picturesque Naples for the next century and a half made the perfect backdrop for the Rococo shenanigans of the new Bourbon kingdom. The new rulers were little improvement over the Spaniards, but immigrants from all over the south poured into the city, chasing the thousands of ducats dropped by a free-spending court. Naples became the most densely populated city in Europe (a distinction it still holds today); crime and epidemics became widespread.

Nevertheless, this was the Naples that attracted 18th- and 19th-century aesthetes doing the Grand Tour. Goethe flirted with contessas here, while English poets flirted with dread diseases and Lord Nelson made eyes at Lady Hamilton. The Neapolitans are frank about it: Naples owed its prominence on the tour less to Vesuvius and the ruins of Pompeii than to good old-fashioned sex – Naples at the time was the easiest place in Europe to find some, and everyone knew it, saving Goethe and the rest the trouble of ever mentioning the subject in their travel accounts and letters home.

The Bourbon restoration after Napoleon's occupation meant the return of political decadence and reaction. The Neapolitans rebelled in 1821 and forced Ferdinand I to grant a charter, though he soon took it back. Still, the city was generally happy under the light Bourbon rule. And neither it nor its rulers were as backward as their reputation would have it. Under the last Bourbons, Naples built Italy's first railroad and its steamship.

Garibaldi's army entered Naples in February 1861. As the new Italy's biggest basket case, the city has since received considerable assistance with its planning and social problems – though, unfortunately, not nearly enough to make up for the centuries of neglect. The Second World War didn't help: for four days in late September 1944, the city staged a heroic and successful revolt against the Germans, the 'Quattro Giornate'; more damage was done by Allied bombing; and the retreating Nazis rounded off the destruction by destroying the city's port and utilities as they left.

While the post-war period saw considerable rebuilding, it also brought new calamities. Illegal and speculative building projects grabbed most of the already-crowded city's open space (you'll notice the almost total absence of parks) and turned the fringe areas and much of the once beautiful Bay of Naples shore into a nightmare of human detritus, one of the eeriest industrial wastelands of Europe.

In the postwar era, organized crime ran the city directly, as under the shadowy mayor Achille Lauro (1950-58), or else in partnership with the major parties. In the political turmoil of the 1990s, with the collapse of the old parties, Naples saw a big rise in support for both the Communists and the neo-Fascist MSI. Crime interests countered attempts at reform with political obstruction, and occasionally, violence. Nevertheless, much has been accomplished. In 1993, the state stepped in and dissolved Naples' crooked government; in mayoral elections the next year, Communist reformer Antonio Bassolino narrowly beat Alessandra Mussolini, Benito's granddaughter (and Sophia Loren's niece). Bassolino was overwhelmingly re-elected for a second term in 1998, and his two terms saw the worst of the ghettos around the port demolished, while tourist trails across Spaccanapoli were encouraged, and churches and sites long closed were reopened. The grand Piazza del Plebiscito, for a long time choked by traffic and fated to remain the city's car park, was emptied and cleaned up.

Most spectacularly of all, Naples planned and built the Centro Direzionale, a huge modernistic skyscraper development on the lines of Paris's La Défense. In spite of a few hiccups, most notably when the new palace of justice was mysteriously burnt to the ground (no prizes for guessing by whom), the project provides a striking new centre for the regional economy. But the excitement has fizzled out – Camorra families are still collecting extortion money and bombing each other right in the middle of town and Bassolino has lost his halo. He is accused of addressing only the outer layer of Naples' problems rather than tackling major issues. Still, the Left is holding on. His successor, Rosa Iervolina Russo, still occupies the Municipio and she has become a politician of national stature, while Bassolino sits as President of the Campania regional council. Even though things are looking up, you may still find discussions of the city's problems in the press are conducted in apocalyptic tones. Leave some room for exaggeration – the Napoletani probably couldn't enjoy life without a permanent state of crisis.

Around Piazza del Plebiscito and Via Toledo

Piazza del Plebiscito and the Palazzo Reale

After years as a parking lot, the immense and elegant **Piazza del Plebiscito**, the centre of modern Naples, has been rescued and restored to the city. Children now come here to kick a football under the eyes of adoring parents. Shows staged here by the city for the benefit of national television have even forced some northern Italians to revise their opinions of Naples and admit that it may not be all bad after all.

The huge domed church, embracing the piazza in its curving colonnades as does St Peter's in Rome, is **San Francesco di Paola**. King Ferdinand IV, after the British restored him to power in 1815, made a vow to construct it. The classical portico and great dome were modelled after Rome's Pantheon. There's little to see in the austere interior, and anyone with an understanding of Naples will not be surprised to find the colonnades given over to light manufacturing and warehouse space.

Across the square rises the equally imposing bulk of the **Palazzo Reale** (*Royal Palace;* ***t*** *081 580 8111, open Thurs–Tues 9–9; adm*). Begun by the Spanish viceroys in 1600, it was expanded by the Bourbons and finished by the kings of Italy. Umberto I added the eight giant figures on the façade, representing the eight houses that have ruled at Naples. It seems the 19th-century sculptors had trouble taking some of them seriously; note the preposterous figures of Charles of Anjou, whom the Neapolitans never liked, and Vittorio Emmanuele II, the latter probably an accurate portrayal. There are Ruritanian stone sentry boxes and stone peacocks in the courtyard to recall the Bourbons.

A number of rooms inside have been restored and can be visited, including a grand staircase, a theatre and the royal apartments in 18th-century style. The theatre saw the premieres of many of the works of Alessandro Scarlatti. In the Palatine chapel there is an exquisite 1674 altar of semiprecious stone, and an outstanding 18th-century crib or *presepio* – a handful of its 210 figures are by master sculptor Sammartino.

The newly restored roof garden offers wonderful views over the bay while the rear of the palace, now home to Naples' important **Biblioteca Nazionale**, faces a pretty, little-visited garden, across from the Castel Nuovo, where you can eat a pizza in peace.

Teatro San Carlo and Galleria Umberto I

The Bourbons were great opera buffs and built Italy's largest opera house, the **Teatro San Carlo**, right next to their palace. Begun in 1737 (making it older than La Scala in Milan), the theatre was sumptuously restored after a fire in 1816, during a period when Naples was the unquestioned capital of opera. So important was the theatre to the people of Naples that King Ferdinand made sure the workmen got the job done in record time – 300 days. Today, the San Carlo is still among the world's most prestigious opera houses (the Neapolitans, of course, would place it first). Each season at least one lesser-known Neapolitan opera is performed. Tickets are as expensive as opera anywhere – they can cost over €100 on an opening night. On weekends, brief tours of the theatre (***t*** *081 797 2111*) cost much less.

Opposite the San Carlo is the grandest interior in southern Italy, the **Galleria Umberto I**. This great glass-roofed arcade, perhaps the largest in the world, was begun in 1887, nine years after the Galleria Vittorio Emmanuele in Milan. The arcade is cross-shaped, with a pretty mosaic of the zodiac on the floor at the centre, and its arching dome is 184ft tall. The Galleria complex covers an entire block; tucked in the corner facing Piazza Trieste e Trento is the old Bourbon court church, **San Ferdinando**, with a wild Baroque interior in the manner of Cosimo Falzago.

Castel Nuovo

The port of Naples has been protected by this odd, beautiful castle, looming over the harbour behind the Palazzo Reale and San Carlo, for some 700 years now. Charles of Anjou built it in 1279; many Neapolitans still call it by the curious name of Maschio Angioino, the 'Angevin Boy'. Most of what you see today, however, including the eccentric, ponderous round towers, is the work of Guillermo Sagrera, the great Catalan architect who built the famous Exchange in Palma de Mallorca.

Between two of these towers at the entrance, the conquering Aragonese hired the finest sculptors from all over Italy to build Alfonso's Triumphal Arch, a masterpiece of Renaissance sculpture and design inspired by the triumphal arches of the ancient Romans. The symbolism, as in the Roman arches, may be a little confusing. The figure at the top is Saint Michael; below him are a matched pair of sea gods, and further down, allegorical virtues and relief panels portraying Alfonso's victories and wise governance.

The castle currently houses parts of the Naples city administration and a number of cultural societies. If you come during office hours, someone will probably be around to show you the **Sala dei Baroni**, where the city council meets. It has a cupola with an unusual Moorish vaulting – an eight-pointed star made of interlocking arches. King Ferrante used this as his dining hall: it takes its name from the evening he invited a score of the kingdom's leading barons to a ball and then arrested the lot.

The castle also houses the **Civic Museum** (***t** 081 795 5877; open Mon–Sat 9–7; adm; disabled access*), with some lovely 14th – and 15th-century frescoes set in the Gothic Cappella Palatina, next to the council hall. In the south wing, meanwhile, there are paintings and a collection of silver and bronzes from the 15th century to the present.

Castel dell'Ovo

The hill called **Pizzofalcone** rises directly behind the Piazza del Plebiscito. Around it was the site of Parthenope, the Greek town that antedated Neapolis and that was eventually swallowed up by it (though Neapolitans still like to refer to themselves as Parthenopeans). Parthenope had a little harbour, formed by an island that is mainly covered by the strangely shaped fortress of the Castel dell'Ovo (***t** 081 764 0590*) – the one Master Virgil is said to have built balanced on an egg (hence the name). Most of it was really built by Frederick II and expanded by the Angevins.

The island has been the scene of many unusual events. It contained the villa of the Roman general and philosopher Lucullus, victor over Mithridates in the Pontic Wars; Lucullus curried favour with the people by throwing his sumptuous gardens and his famous library open to the public. In the 5th century AD, the villa became a home in exile for Romulus Augustulus, last of the Western Roman emperors. The Goths spared him only because of his youth and simple-mindedness, and pensioned him off here.

King Ferrante's Dungeons

Guillermo Sagrera was the Frank Lloyd Wright of the Renaissance – a brilliant and iconoclastic architect who dreamed up shapes and forms never seen before. In his rebuilding of the Castel Nuovo, with its arch and massive and eccentric towers, he and his intelligent patron, King Alfonso, must have been aware of the revolutionary design statement (as we might call it today) they were making – a castle meant to be not only a royal residence and stronghold, but a landmark and symbol for Naples.

Even before the arrival of the Spanish, the Castel Nuovo had witnessed a good deal of history. Here, when the castle was brand-new, Charles of Anjou had received the news of the Sicilian Vespers, and reportedly cried out: 'Lord God, since it has pleased you to ruin me, let me only go down by small steps!' King Robert the Wise kept his great library here, and received Petrarch and Boccaccio in his apartments.

Poor Sagrera would be sad to hear that the Castel Nuovo seems somewhat dark and sinister to many Italian visitors today, thanks to the monstrous King Ferrante. The illegitimate son of Alfonso the Magnanimous (or just as likely, people whispered, of a certain Moor of Valencia), Ferrante took the throne of Naples in 1458. He was a devious and capable ruler, just the sort of man the state needed for the dangerous intrigues and ever-shifting political alliances of Renaissance Italy. But he is better remembered for his calculated cruelty. On one occasion, he invited an enemy back to Naples, professing great affection, and treated him to a month of parties before arresting him and sending him to the torture room. An invitation to the king's table for dinner was often as good as a death warrant. Ferrante was known to keep a 'museum of mummies' of executed foes and rebellious barons at the castle, each dressed in his own clothes. It was said he kept a crocodile in the castle's dungeons, which was fed on live prisoners.

In 1294, Pope Celestine V – a simple and slow-witted hermit in the Abruzzo before his surprise election – paid a visit. The church bosses, who wanted a stronger hand on the papal throne, meant to get rid of him as soon as possible, and in this castle, they tricked him into abdicating by whispering into his room through a hidden tube, claiming to be the voice of God and commanding him to quit.

The castle holds regular art exhibitions and conferences. If you ask, you should be able to go in and have a look round: the views across the bay are wonderful.

Squeezed onto the rest of the island below the castle, **Borgo Marinara** is a small harbour flanked by cafés and restaurants. In the evenings, it's a safe and pleasant area, full of romancing couples, fortune-tellers and buskers.

Via Toledo

From the landward side of Piazza del Plebiscito and the Palace, Naples' most imposing street, recently pedestrianized Via Toledo, runs northwards past the Galleria Umberto I through Piazza Carità (*marked on some maps as Piazza S. D'Acquisto*). Its name commemorates its builder, Don Pedro de Toledo, Spanish viceroy at the beginning of the 16th century and a great benefactor of Naples. Stendhal, in 1817, called this 'the most populous and gayest street in the world', and it is still the city's main business and shopping street, eventually leading up to Capodimonte and the northern suburbs. Don Pedro's elegant Renaissance tomb, among others, can be seen in the little church of **San Giacomo degli Spagnuoli**, now swallowed up by the 19th-century **Palazzo Municipale** (*marked on some maps as the Palazzo S. Giacomo*) complex, originally home to the Bourbon royal bureaucracy.

To the right of Via Toledo, Naples' half-crumbling, half-modern business centre contains a few buildings worth a look. The **Palazzo Gravina** on Via Monteoliveto is a fine palace in the northern Renaissance style, built between 1513 and 1549. It now houses Naples University's Faculty of Architecture. Almost directly across the street, the church of **Sant'Anna dei Lombardi** (*marked on some maps as the Chiesa di Monteoliveto; open Mon–Fri 8.30–12, Sat 8.30–12 and 5.30–6.30*) is a little treasure house of late Renaissance sculpture and painting, with tombs and altars in the chapels by southern artists like Giovanni da Nola and Antonio Rosellino, as well as some frescoes by Vasari.

After passing Spaccanapoli, Via Toledo continues northwards to **Piazza Dante**, one of the most animated corners of the city.

Quartieri Spagnuoli

When you are walking north along Via Toledo, any street on your left can be the entrance to the dense, crumbling, sinister inner sanctum of the Neapolitan soul, the vast slum called the Quartieri Spagnuoli. It can be a fascinating place to walk around, in daytime at least, but it can be dangerous even then. Lately, thanks to battling factions of the Camorra, the *Quartieri* has achieved even more than its accustomed share of notoriety; for a while, the hoods were bumping each other off at a rate of one per week. Though the *Quartieri* covers almost all the area sloping up to San Martino and Vomero, the most populous and colourful part is that immediately adjoining Via Toledo, a grid of narrow streets laid out by Don Pedro de Toledo and now called the **Tavoliere** or chessboard. Be careful if you venture into this neighbourhood, as the side streets around here are used as getaway funnels for muggers.

Spaccanapoli and the Old Town

The district east of Via Toledo is called after the familiar name of its main street: *Spaccanapoli* means 'Split-Naples', and that is exactly what this long, narrow thoroughfare has done for the last 2,600 years. On the map it changes its name with alarming frequency – Via Benedetto Croce and Via San Biagio dei Librai are two of the most prominent – but, in Roman times, you would have found it by asking for the *decumanus inferior*, the name for the second east–west street in any planned Roman city. No large city in all the lands conquered by Rome has maintained its ancient street plan as completely as Naples (the Greeks laid out these streets, of course, but the Romans learned their planning from them). It is easier to imagine the atmosphere of a big ancient city here than in Rome itself or even in Pompeii The narrow, straight streets and tall *insulae* cannot have changed much; only the forum and temples are missing.

This is the heart of old Naples – and what a street it is, lined with grocery barrows and scholarly bookshops, shops that sell old violins, plaster saints, pizza or used clothes

Four Days in Naples

The contempt that many northern Italians often display towards this city and its accomplishments can look a bit silly when compared with the facts. Just for the record, we note that in September 1944, Naples did more than its part in redeeming Italian honour by becoming the first city to liberate itself, and the only one to do so until the German collapse at the end of the war.

At the time of the Allied landings in Salerno, the city was in a bad way. Rations of everything were extremely short, sometimes nonexistent, and the Germans were preparing to dynamite all the important facilities in case the Allied advance should reach Naples. Worst of all, SS units were combing every quarter for able-bodied males to ship off to forced labour camps in the north of Italy or in Germany.

No one knows exactly what particular incident touched off the great revolt. In the excellent 1960s film account, *Quattro Giornate a Napoli*, a group of men who had escaped from the Germans in the Quartieri Spagnuoli is recaptured and lined up against a building to be shot.

A basket on a string suddenly appears among them, of the type old women would send down from their windows in the tall tenements to buy fresh tomatoes or chestnuts from the street vendors. This time, though, the basket contained a gun – unexpected aid from heaven has always been a common theme in Neapolitan mythology.

pegs. Not so long ago, the Spacca was a Felliniesque stage for arch-Neapolitan characters , manic motorists; and long alleys of impossibly tall tenements, down any of which you might have seen a hundred full clotheslines swelling bravely in the breeze. Visitors will probably find that claustrophobia is right around the corner – this is the Naples that was the most densely packed city in Europe, courtesy of a 1555 Spanish decree that forbade building outside the walls. Increasing prosperity is thinning it out now; you won't see nearly as many clotheslines. What's more, the city has banished the cars and taken a fair start on fixing up the scores of historic churches and palaces. The Spacca that had decayed to a picturesque slum is now, slowly, regaining its place as Naples' proud *centro storico*.

Piazza del Gesù Nuovo

Coming from Via Toledo, your introduction to the Spacca is Piazza del Gesù Nuovo. It's decorated by the gaudiest and most random of Naples' monuments, the **Guglia della Immacolata**. A *guglia* (pinnacle) is a kind of Rococo obelisk, dripping with frills, saints and *putti*. The unsightly and unfinished façade behind the Guglia, covered with pyramidal extrusions in dark basalt, belongs to the **church of Gesù Nuovo** (*open daily 6.45–1 and 4–7.30*). As strange as it is, the façade, which was originally part of a late-15th-century palace, has become one of the landmarks of Naples. The interior is typically lavish Neapolitan Baroque, gloriously overdone in acres of coloured marbles and frescoes, some by Solimena.

One of his best works is here, above the main door inside. Dating from 1725, it depicts three angels driving the Syrian magician Eliodorus out of the Temple of Jerusalem. In the second chapel on the right, you will see a bronze statue of Naples' newest saint

But however it started, the uprising spread like a prairie fire through the city. Pistols and old rifles came out from their hiding places, and the police arsenals were broken into for more. *Scugnizzi* (street children) waited in doorways with stolen grenades, ready to try and tip one into a passing Nazi truck or tank. The prisons were thrown open and, while many inmates scuttled off into the shadows, plenty of others took what arms they could find and joined in the fight. Then the rebels surrounded the heavily defended football stadium in Vomero, full of captured Neapolitans waiting to be sent to Germany. They took it, despite heavy casualties, and freed the lot.

At the beginning, the rebels carried on without any leadership whatsoever – except, of course, among the Communists. The completely anarchic, overwhelming, totally spontaneous movement of the city's people was something that few cities but Naples could ever produce. The Germans found it the ultimate Neapolitan experience; it was as if they had kicked over a beehive. They responded with brutality – massacres of prisoners and tanks firing point-blank into apartment blocks – but stung and pestered on every side, they simply could not endure long. A hastily formed committee went to negotiate terms with the exasperated German commander and a deal was cut. The troops would depart immediately and attacks on them would cease.

An eerie silence fell over the city and indifferent faces watched from their windows as the German columns filed out. And then Naples went back to being Naples.

– Saint Giuseppe Moscati. He was a doctor who lectured at Naples University and otherwise devoted himself to caring for the poor, and died on 12 April 1927.

Chiesa di Santa Chiara

This church, just across the piazza, dates from the early 14th century. It once had a Baroque interior as good as the Gesù's, until Allied bombers remodelled it to suit modern tastes in 1943. Only a few of the original Angevin tombs have survived. To get some idea of what the interior must have been like, stop in and see the restored **Majolica Cloister**, nothing less than the loveliest and most peaceful spot in Naples – especially in contrast to the neighbourhood outside. The cloister can be visited as part of the new **Complesso di Santa Chiara** (***t** 081 797 1256; open Mon–Sat 9.30–1 and 2.30–5.30, Sun and hols 9–1; adm*), which includes a museum housing the church treasures, marbles and an area of archaeological excavations from the Roman period. So much in Naples shows the Spanish influence (such as the use of the title 'Don', now largely limited to Camorra bosses) and here someone in the 1740s transplanted the Andalucían love of pictures done in painted *azulejo* tiles, turning a simple monkish cloister into a little fairyland of gaily coloured arbours, benches and columns, shaded by orange and lemon trees – the only trees in the whole district.

Recently, during the restoration of a vestibule off the cloister (reached via the back of the church), it was discovered that beneath the indifferent 17th-century frescoes were some earlier, highly original paintings of the Last Judgement. They have since been uncovered and restored, revealing an inspired 16th-century vision of the event. Their style is utterly unlike the slick virtuosity of the time, with plenty of novel tortures for the damned and angels welcoming cute naked nuns among the elect.

Piazza San Domenico and Around

A few streets down Via Benedetto Croce is Piazza San Domenico with monuments from Naples' three most creative periods. **San Domenico Maggiore**, built between 1283 and 1324, was the Dominican church in Naples; St Thomas Aquinas lived in the adjacent monastery. Later this became the favourite church of the Spanish and it contains some interesting Renaissance funerary monuments. A better one lies across the square in the **church of Sant'Angelo a Nilo** – the tomb of Cardinal Brancaccio, designed by Michelozzo, with a relief of the Assumption of the Virgin by Donatello (the two artists had collaborated before on the Baptistry in Siena). The second of the area's three Baroque pinnacles decorates the piazza, the **Guglia di San Domenico**, built after a plague in 1650.

Near San Domenico, a block south of the Spacca, is **Naples' University**, one of Europe's oldest and most distinguished. Emperor Frederick II founded it in 1224, as a 'Ghibelline' university to counter the pope's 'Guelph' (*see* **Glossary**, p.273) university at Bologna, as well as to provide scholars and train officials for the new state he was trying to build. It still occupies its ancient, woefully overcrowded quarters around Via Mezzocannone.

Behind the university walls is the **Museo delle Scienze Naturali** (*Via Mezzacannone 8; **t** 081 253 5163; open Mon and Thurs 9–1.30 and 3–5, Tues, Wed and Fri 9–1.30, Sat–Sun 9–1; adm*), with sections on mineralogy, zoology, anthropology and palaeontology.

Sansevero Chapel

***t** 081 551 8470; open Mon–Wed 10–8, hols 10–1.30; adm.*

Just around the corner from the Piazza San Domenico, on Via F. de Sanctis, you can inspect Neapolitan Rococo at its queerest in the Sansevero Chapel. Prince Raimondo di Sangro (b. 1701) was responsible for the final form of this, his family's private chapel. He was a strange bird, a sort of aristocratic dilettante mystic. Supposedly there is a grand allegorical scheme behind the arrangement of the sculptures and frescoes he commissioned, but a work like this, only 200 years old, seems as foreign to our modern sensibilities and understanding as a Mayan temple.

The sculptures, by little-known Neapolitan artists like Giuseppe Sammartino and Antonio Corradini, are inscrutable allegories in themselves, often executed with a breathtakingly showy virtuosity. Francesco Queirolo's *Il Disinganno* ('Disillusion') is an extreme case; nobody else, perhaps, has ever tried to carve a fishing net, or the turning pages of a book, out of marble. Others, such as Sammartino's *Cristo Velato*, display a remarkable illusion of figures under transparent veils. There are a dozen or so of these large sculptural groups, all under the crazy heavenly vortex of the ceiling fresco by Francesco Mario Russo.

Down in the crypt there are two complete human cardiovascular systems, removed and preserved by Prince Raimondo in the course of his alchemical experiments.

Sansevero to the Duomo

Continuing east on the Spaccanapoli (now Via San Biagio dei Librai), just around the corner on Via San Gregorio is the **church of San Gregorio Armeno**, with another gaudy Baroque interior. If the gilding and the painting by Luca Giordano of the Arrival of

Presepi

It would not be easy to explain why the genius of Naples should have chosen Christmas cribs as a subject to elevate to an art form. But, after philosophy, pizza and music, it's what this city does best. Churches and private homes have always had a little competitive edge on when they begin their displays (sometime in November, if not earlier). The most extreme cases are assembled inside the Museo Nazionale di San Martino (*see* p.96). One is as big as a bus and must have taken someone a lifetime; another is fitted inside an eggshell – still with over 100 figures in it. The best parts are the large, finely carved individual wooden or ceramic figures. Most represent Neapolitans of two or three centuries ago from every walk of life; with their painstakingly detailed and expressive faces, each is a genuine portrait. To have them all here in one place is like old Bourbon Naples appearing before your eyes.

For do-it-yourself modern cribs, Via San Gregorio (*see* below) is the place to go. At Christmastime, the street is taken over by stalls of artisans who make and sell figurines for cribs, as well as little trees, sheep, donkeys, amphorae, pots, Turks, salamis, dogs, chickens, angels, cheese wheels and all the other items without which no Neapolitan *presepio* would be complete.

Convention requires that, apart from the Holy Family and the standard angels, shepherds and animals, certain things be present in every crib. A Roman ruin is a must, as are Turks in Ottoman empire dress (useful if one of the Three Kings gets lost). A band of musicians is also expected – all the better if they, too, are Turks. Beggars and dwarfs earn envy for the crib-maker – there is a whole display of figures called the 'deformities' – but, above, all there must be tons of food. The best cribs have the busiest cooks and the most bulging pantries, with tiny wooden roast pigs, eggs, sausages, plates of macaroni and even a pizza or two. Go to the Galleria Umberto at Christmas time to see Neapolitans throw money at the giant *presepio* there to pay for its upkeep for another year.

Saint Basilio are not your cup of tea, try the cloister (*open daily 9.30–noon*). This is another oasis of tranquillity and a step back to the 16th century. Since the 1500s, the cloister has served the convent of Benedictine nuns. At the centre of the cloister there is a fountain sculpted in 1733 depicting Christ meeting the Samaritan woman. On the way out, note the revolving drums used for communicating with the outside world before 1922, when the monastic order was totally closed off from the profane. A caustic note by the nuns on one of them dismisses the popular misconception that they were for abandoned newborn babies.

In December, this street and others around it become Naples' famous **Christmas Market**, where everyone comes to buy figurines of the Holy Family, the Three Kings and all the other accessories required for their Christmas *presepsi* (manger scenes), one of the most devotedly followed of local traditions (*see* above). For several weeks, hundreds of stands fill up the neighbourhood's narrow streets; any time of the year, it's the place to find your Neapolitan souvenirs.

A little further north up Via San Gregorio is the late 13th-century **San Lorenzo Maggiore** (*open Tues–Sun 8–12 and 5–7*), one of Naples' finest medieval churches; Petrarch lived for a while in the adjacent monastery. Recent excavations have uncovered extensive Greek and Roman remains on the site; entering through the cloister, where the base of a Roman *macellum* (marketplace) is being excavated, head down the stairs at the back to see this fascinating piece of subterranean Naples. **San Paolo**, across the street, isn't much to see now but, before an earthquake wrecked it in the 17th century, its façade was the portico of an ancient Roman temple to Castor and Pollux. Andrea Palladio studied it closely and it provided some of the inspiration for his classical villas and churches in the Veneto. Napoli Sotterranea tours (*see* 'Tourist Information', p.70) start outside the church.

After Spaccanapoli, **Via dei Tribunali** is the busiest street in old Naples, as it has been since it was the Roman *Decumanus Maximus*. The arcades that line the street in places, a sort of continuous covered market, are 1,000 years old or more. Here, at the otherwise unremarkable **Girolamini church** (*open Mon–Sat 9.30–1*), you may see frescoes by Luca Giordano, paintings by Ribera and Guido Reni, among many others, as well as the modest tomb of Naples' greatest philosopher, Giambattista Vico.

Northwest of the Girolamini, around **Via Anticaglia**, you'll find a few crooked streets, the only ones in old Naples that do not stick to the rectilinear Roman plan. These follow the outline of the **Roman theatre**, much of which still survives, hidden among the tenements. A few arches are all that is visible from the street.

Duomo

The wide Via Duomo is a breath of fresh air in this crowded district – exactly what the city intended when they ploughed it through Old Naples after the cholera epidemic of 1884. The Duomo itself is another fine medieval building, though it is hidden behind an awful pseudo-Gothic façade pasted on in 1905. The best things are inside: the Renaissance **Cappella Minutolo**, the tomb of Charles of Anjou and the **Cappella San Gennaro** (also known as Il Tesoro), glittering with the gold and silver of the cathedral treasure, and with frescoes by Domenichino and Lanfranco, the latter a swirling *Paradiso* in the dome (1643).

The **Basilica Santa Restituta**, a sizeable church in its own right, is tacked onto the side of the cathedral. Its columns are thought to be from the temple of Apollo that once occupied the site. Begun in 324, though often rebuilt, this is the oldest building in Naples. The ceiling frescoes are by Luca Giordano.

Just off the basilica, the 5th-century **baptistry** contains a good Byzantine-style mosaic by the 14th-century artist Lello di Roma; the baptismal font itself probably comes from an ancient temple of Dionysus. From Santa Restituta's chapel, you can access a collection of archaeological remains dating from the Greeks to the Middle Ages (*open daily 8–12.30 and 4.30–7; adm*).

The last and most elaborate of the area's *guglie*, the **Guglia San Gennaro**, designed by Cosimo Fanzago, can be seen just outside the south transept. You can also visit the **crypt of San Gennaro**, patron of Naples, with elaborate marble decoration from the Renaissance, and the tomb of Pope Innocent IV.

On a small piazza just north of the Duomo, **Santa Maria Donnaregina** offers more overdone Baroque. To the side of this 17th-century work is the smaller, original church,

The Legend of San Gennaro

San Gennaro (St Januarius) was a bishop from Benevento who was executed with other martyrs at the Solfatara in Pozzuoli in 305 during the persecution of Christians under Diocletian. Initially, he was sentenced to death by being torn apart by wild animals in the amphitheatre at Pozzuoli but, because the Roman governor was not present, this was commuted to being beheaded at the Solfatara. After the execution, his body was taken to the Catacombs of S. Gennaro (*see* p.93). It was moved at the beginning of the 5th century and, from this date on, he became identified as the patron of Naples, protecting it from destruction by Vesuvius and other disasters.

The saint's head is now kept upstairs in the chapel named after him, along with two phials of his blood that miraculously 'liquefy' three times each year – the first Sunday in May, 19 September and 16 December – so as to prove that San Gennaro is still looking out for the city. The only time the miracle has ever failed, during the Napoleonic occupation, the people of the city became enormously excited and seemed ready to revolt. At this the French commander, a true son of the Enlightenment, announced that San Gennaro had 10 minutes to come through – or else he'd shoot the Archbishop. Somehow, just in time, the miracle occurred.

built in 1307 by Queen Mary of Hungary (the wife of Charles of Anjou; her Hungarian title only reflected a claim to that throne). Her elaborate tomb, and some good frescoes from the first half of the 12th century, are the sights of the church.

South of the cathedral in the Via Duomo is the **Filangieri Museum** (***t*** *081 203 175; open Tues–Sun 9.30–2 and 3.30–7, hols 9.30–1.30*), housed in the 15th-century Palazzo Cuomo, with a small collection of china, armour and curiosities.

Piazza Garibaldi and Around

The Market Districts

In Italian, the word for a market stall is *bancarella*. In Naples, they are as much a part of life today as they were in the Middle Ages; the city has as many of them as all the rest of Italy put together. The greatest concentration can be found in the **Forcella market district**, in the narrow streets east off the Via del Duomo, selling everything from stereos to light bulbs. According to government economists, at least one-third of Naples' economy is black, or at least grey: either outright illegal, not paying taxes or subject to any regulation. In the post-war decades, specialities included bootleg cassette tapes, untaxed American cigarettes, and plenty of designer labels (if they're real, don't ask where they came from). There's been a strong crackdown lately, and the Forcella is smaller, calmer and much more respectable; eventually this will pass, and things will get back to normal.

Bootleg CDs are a current favourite. Naples is one of the world leaders in this thriving industry, and you'll have your choice of thousands of titles along these streets, though you should get them to play your CD before you part with any money. Hundreds of tired-looking folk sit at little tables selling contraband American cigarettes, and you'll see plenty of designer labels on the *bancarelle*. If they're real, don't ask where they came from. Take note, though: Forcella may be a fascinating peek into the true heart of Naples, but it is controlled by the Camorra and not a safe area after dark. Don't carry valuables and avoid waving maps and cameras and such tourist paraphernalia.

Piazza Mercato, one of the nodes of the Neapolitan bazaar, has probably been a market square since Roman times. Today it's well out of the mainstream, home to sellers of ladders, cement mixers and garden furniture. In the old days, this was also the site of major executions, most notably that of 16-year-old Conradin, the rightful heir to the throne, by Charles of Anjou in 1268, an act that shocked all Europe. Charles ordered him buried underneath the piazza – he couldn't be laid in consecrated ground since he had just been excommunicated for political reasons by Charles' ally, the pope.

In 1647 Masaniello's revolt started here during the festival of Our Lady of Mount Carmel. Masaniello (Tommaso Aniello), a young fisherman of Amalfi, had been chosen by his fellow conspirators to step up in the middle of the ceremonies and proclaim to the people and the viceroy that the new tax the viceroy had introduced 'no longer existed'. As the plotters had hoped, a spontaneous rising followed, and for a week, Masaniello ruled Naples while the frightened viceroy hid in Castel Sant'Elmo.

In Naples, unfortunately, such risings can burn out as quickly as a match. The viceroy's spies first secretly drugged Masaniello, so that he appeared drunk or mad to the people, and then, in an unguarded moment, they murdered him and sent his head to the viceroy. That was the end for Naples, but the incident sparked off a wave of revolts across the south that took the Spaniards three years to stamp out.

Masaniello met his end in the **convent of S. Maria del Carmine**, on the adjacent Piazza del Carmine, where the church has the most spectacular Baroque campanile in Naples (1631). The narrow streets between the port and Corso Umberto I are on the main route for smuggled contraband – be it drugs, guns or fake Prada. Again, keep a low profile when walking around the Piazza Mercato area and don't go near it after dark.

Porta Capuana

Northwest of the Piazza Garibaldi, some of Naples' shabbiest streets lead towards the **Piazza Enrico de Nicola**, once the city's main gate. The **Porta Capuana**, built in 1484, seems a smaller version of the Castel Nuovo's triumphal arch, crowded in by the same squat round towers. Here it is traditional to eat *zuppa alle cozze* (mussel soup) – in summer, about a dozen pavement restaurants appear in the square, heaving with assertive locals. Get a ticket and stand in line for a truly Neapolitan experience.

The **Castel Capuano** began life as a residence for the Hohenstaufen kings. Since its construction in the 13th century, it has been reshaped so many times it doesn't look like a castle any more; for four centuries, it has served as Naples' law courts.

Facing the Porta Capuana is **Santa Caterina a Formiella**, a church by the obscure architect Romolo Balsimelli that is one of the masterpieces of 16th-century Italian architecture. Completed in 1593, the church's bulky, squarish form was an important stepping-stone towards the Baroque. Despite long neglect (during which its dome seemed to tilt at an ever-more precarious angle), the church has reopened to the public and further projects are under way for the conservation of its interior.

North of the Old Town

To the north of Spaccanapoli, the traffic-clogged Via Foria follows the line of the old city walls and marks the northern boundary of the historic centre. To the north are three working-class districts – El Virgini, Miracoli and Sanita – rising to Capodimonte. The main sights in this area are the great Museo Archeologico Nazionale and the superb collection of paintings in the palace of Capodimonte (both described below). The area does have other attractions, however, although these are poor parts of town where once again you'd be well advised to keep valuables to a minimum. If you're just heading up to Capodimonte, it's safer to take the bus.

Directly north of the Porta Capuana on Via Foria is the huge, derelict **Albergo dei Poveri** (*restoration is apparently complete but it is not yet open to the public*). Begun in 1751 by King Charles III, this workhouse for the poor was meant to be five times its present size but the project was never completed. Even so, it is still claimed to be the largest public building in Europe. Next to the Albergo is the **Orto Botanico**. Founded by Joseph Bonaparte in 1807, it is one of Italy's best botanical gardens and a quiet oasis in this busy part of town. To the northwest is another Bourbon project, the **Osservatorio Astronomico** (*t 081 557 5111; Mon–Fri by appointment; adm*), built in 1819 by Ferdinand IV and housing a museum of old telescopes and scientific instruments.

Over on the western side of this zone, Via Santa Teresa degli Scalzi – a continuation of Via Toledo – climbs northwards through the Sanita district from the Archeological Museum to Capodimonte. On the way, after changing its name to Corso Amedeo di Savoia, the street passes three Christian underground burial vaults, with an extraordinary total area of over 100,000 square metres, only a small part of which has been completely explored. Two may be visited. The **catacombe di San Gaudioso** (*t 081 544 1305; tours daily at 9.45 and 11.45; adm*) lie under the attractive Baroque church of **Santa Maria della Sanità** on Piazza della Sanità. They include the 5th-century tomb of San Gaudioso himself, a martyred African bishop. Further up the hill, the **Catacombe di San Gennaro** (*t 081 741 1071; entrance through the courtyard of the Basilica dell'Incoronata a Capodimonte; look for the yellow signs; tours daily at 9.30, 10.15, 11.00 and 11.45; adm*) is the more interesting, with an extensive collection of early Christian frescoes and mosaics, some from as early as the 2nd century.

Museo Archeologico Nazionale

*Piazza Museo 19, **t** 081 440 166; open Wed–Mon 9–8; adm.*

Naples has the most important collection of Roman art and antiquities in the world, thanks to Vesuvius (for burying Pompeii and Herculaneum) and the sharp eyes and deep pockets of the Farnese family. Many of the best works here come from the collection they built up over 300 years. On the ground floor, room after room is filled with **ancient sculpture**, generally in need of a good dusting. Many of the pieces on view are the best existing Roman-era copies of lost Greek statues, including some by Phidias and Praxiteles. Some are masterpieces in their own right, such as the huge, dramatic ensemble called the Farnese Bull, the Tyrannicides (with other statues' heads stuck on them) and the truly heroic Farnese Hercules that once decorated the Baths of Caracalla. A number of provocative Aphrodites compete for your attention, along with several formidable Athenas, the famous Doryphorus (spear-bearer) and enough Greek and Roman busts to populate a Colosseum.

The museum's famous collection of Roman pornography, the **Gabinetto Segreto** (Secret Room), contains a veritable cornucopia of embarrassing expressions and inflated manhoods – a fascinating insight into the love life of ancient Rome. The room has been regularly closed by outraged royals and curators since 1819 (it was shut from 1971 until 2000, supposedly for 'restoration') but now welcomes sniggering visitors over the age of 11. Book your visit at the ticket desk when you arrive.

Upstairs, most of the museum's rooms are given over to finds from **Pompeii**. The collection of Roman mosaics, mostly from Pompeii and Herculaneum, is one of the best of its type anywhere; the insight it provides into the life and thought of the ancients is priceless. One feature it betrays clearly is a certain silliness – plenty of chickens, ducks and grinning cats, the famous *Cave canem* (beware of the dog) mosaic from the front of a house, comic theatre scenes, and especially, one wonderful panel of crocodiles and hippopotami along the Nile.

Some of the mosaics are very consciously 'art' – including one showing a detailed scene of the Battle of Issus, where Alexander the Great defeated the Persian king, and another with a view of the Academy of Athens that includes a portrait of Plato.

A recent addition is a section devoted to the Temple of Isis at Pompeii. Five rooms display sculptures, frescoes and paintings from the temple, discovered in 1765.

The museum also houses a superb collection of **Roman murals** (*see* pp.112–3). Much of it is fascinatingly modern in theme and execution; many of the walls of Pompeiian villas were decorated with architectural fantasias that seem strangely like those of the Renaissance. Other works show an almost Baroque lack of respect for the gods – *The Wedding of Zeus and Hera*. Scholars do indeed denote a period of 'Roman Baroque' beginning around the 2nd century. From it come paintings graced by genuine winged *putti*, called *amoretti* in Roman days. Among the most famous pictures are *The Astragal Players* – young girls shooting craps – and the beautiful *Portrait of an Unknown Woman*, a thoughtful lady holding her pen to her lips who has become one of the best-known images from Roman art. Other attractions of the museum include large collections of jewellery, coins, fancy gladiators' armour, Greek vases, decorative bronzes and a highly detailed, room-sized scale model of all excavations up to the 1840s at Pompeii (lovingly restored since the memorable assault on it by the authors' baby boy back in 1980). The Egyptian collection is not a large one, but it is fun, with a dog-headed Anubis in a Roman toga, some ancient feet under glass and a mummified crocodile.

Museo Nazionale di Capodimonte

Via Miano 1, t 081 749 9111; open Tues–Sun 8.30–7.30; adm.

At the top of the hill north of the museum is the **Parco di Capodimonte**, a well-kept and exotic park created as a hunting preserve by the Bourbons in the 18th century.

Charles III built a royal palace here in 1738, which is now Naples' art gallery, the Museo Nazionale di Capodimonte. On the first floor, the **Royal Apartments** are still much the way the Bourbons left them. Persevere through the score of overdecorated chambers to the **Salotto di Porcellana** of Queen Maria Amalia. Originally built for the royal palace at Portici in 1757, the room was dismantled and moved to Capodimonte in 1866. It contains over 3,000 pieces of Capodimonte porcelain.

The collection of **paintings** on the second floor is the best in the south of Italy and especially rich in works of the late Renaissance. Some of the works you shouldn't miss: an *Annunciation* by Filippino Lippi; a Botticelli *Madonna*; the mystical portrait of the mathematician Fra Luca Pacioli by an unknown *quattrocento* artist; Giovanni Bellini's *Transfiguration*; two wry homilies by the elder Brueghel, *The Misanthrope* and *The Blind*; Masaccio's *Crucifixion*; Caravaggio's *Flagellation of Christ;* Titian's *Danae*; and a hilarious picture by Lotto of St Peter Martyr conversing nonchalantly with the Virgin Mary – with a hatchet sticking out of his head. Look out, too, for paintings by Neapolitan artists Luca Giordano and Artemesia Gentileschi. The fiery Gentileschi, one of the few female artists of her day, was the victim of a well-publicized rape; she exorcized her demons with violent paintings featuring avenging women, such as her *Judith and Holofernes*. The top floor showcases contemporary art and is well worth a look just to see Andy Warhol's *Vesuvius*, erupting Pop Art-style.

The museum also contains a fine **armoury** collection, while an entire wing is filled with delightfully frivolous 18th-century **porcelain** figurines. The Bourbons maintained a royal factory for making such things at Capodimonte, which now houses an institute for the porcelain and ceramics industry.

West of Piazza del Plebiscito

Some of Naples' nicest suburbs, home to the city's middle classes, lie to the west of Piazza del Plebiscito, including Vomero, on the hilltop above Via Toledo, and the waterfront districts of Chiaia, Mergellina and Posillipo.

Vomero

Until the Second World War, the hill above Quartieri Spagnuoli was a quiet, semi-rural area, but the countryside is now buried beneath a rash of post-war buildings. It does, however, contain two major sights – the Castel Sant'Elmo and the Certosa di San Martino – and commands tremendous views over Naples and the Bay. Vomero can be reached by three cable cars – the Funicolari di Montesanto, Centrale and Chiaia. You can also walk up (or down) the long flights of stairs connecting it to the streets below.

Via Scarlatti, Vomero's main drag, is an elegant, pedestrianized street lined with plane trees: this is a much more affluent area than the Quartieri Spagnuoli down below. To the south, on Via Cimarosa near the top of the Funicolare di Chiaia, the **Villa La Floridiana** is set in a large, wooded park. It's one of the loveliest gardens in Naples, although currently rather overgrown and undergoing restoration. There's a great view from the southern terrace.

The Villa itself, which was originally a present from Ferdinand I to his second wife, the Duchess of Floridia, is now the **Museo Duca di Martina** (*also known as the Museo Nazionale della Ceramica;* **t** *081 578 8418; open for tours Tues–Sun at 9.30, 11 and 12.30; adm*). It houses one of Italy's greatest collections of porcelain, majolica, glass, ivory, coral, tortoiseshell and mother-of-pearl.

On Vomero's highest point, looking down over the city, the 17th-century **Castel Sant'Elmo** (*t 081 578 4120; open Mon–Sat 9–2; adm*) is an impressive Baroque fortification, partly built of the tufa rock on which it stands. Today, the castle holds temporary art exhibitions, and in summer, there are late-night films on the terrace.

Certosa and Museo Nazionale di San Martino

Largo San Martino 5, **t** *081 578 1769; open Tues–Sun 8.30–7.30; adm.*

Next to the castle, and hogging the best view in Naples, is the Certosa di San Martino (charterhouse), supported by a gargantuan platform visible for kilometres out to sea and containing enough stone to construct a small pyramid. The Carthusians built their original, modest, monastery here some time in the early 14th century. Two centuries later, like most Carthusian branch offices, they were rolling embarrassingly in lucre, and building the poshest monastery in all Italy was the only thing to do. Most of the present building was built between the 16th and 18th centuries, particularly by the 17th-century architect Cosimo Fanzago.

Upon entering the complex, the first attraction is the **church**, one of the glories of Neapolitan Baroque, with an excess of lovely coloured inlaid marble to complement the overabundance of painting. The work over the altar, the *Descent from the Cross*, is one of the finest of José Ribera. This tormented artist, often called *Lo Spagnuolo* in Italy, has paintings all over Naples. This is not entirely due to his artistic talent, for he is said to have formed a cartel with two local artists and hired a gang of thugs to harry other painters out of town.

The newly restored cloister, the **Chiostro Grande** (Large Cloister), is another masterpiece of Baroque, elegantly proportioned and gloriously original in its decoration. The creepy sculptures by Fanzago resemble vampires in priestly robes and mitres, while the walls are topped with gleaming marble skulls. Since 1866, the **Museo Nazionale di San Martino** has occupied the rooms around the cloister. Dedicated to Neapolitan life and culture, it contains a collection of Naples' unique *presepi* (Christmas cribs – *see* p.89), plus costumes, maps, paintings, ship models and every sort of curiosity.

On the south side of the building, the lavish 17th-century **Quarto del Priore** (Prior's Quarters) has been recreated as it looked during that period, with exquisite furniture, a fine art collection and superb views over the city. At the corners of the complex, belvederes command more fine views of Naples, as do the series of lovely **terraced gardens** in front of the building.

Chiaia

West of Castel dell'Ovo, Chiaia district occupies a handsome sweep of waterfront. This is one of the most pleasant parts of the new city. Here the long, pretty **Villa Comunale**, central Naples' only park, follows the shore. Inside the park, the **Aquarium** (*t 081 583 111; open Tues–Sat 9–6 in summer, 9–5 in winter, Sun 9–2; adm*), built by the German naturalist Dr Anton Dohrn in the 1870s, is perhaps the oldest in the world. All the fish, octopi and other marine delicacies here are from the Bay of Naples; depending on the hour, you may either find them fascinating or appetizing. When the Allies marched into town in 1943, the Neapolitans put on a party for the officers; there being practically nothing left to eat anywhere in Naples, they cleaned out the aquarium and managed to put on an all-seafood feast. General Mark Clark, the commander, is reputed to have got the aquarium's prize specimen, a baby manatee – although how they prepared it is not recorded.

Ask to see the murals and you'll be led upstairs to see Dohrn (who was, incidentally, a friend and colleague of Charles Darwin) and other buddies depicted by the German artist Hans von Marees. The wall opposite has local boys frolicking naked under the orange groves. Recently restored after the 1980 earthquake, the murals are an insight into the secret life of aquariums.

Behind the park, on the Riviera di Chiaia, the **Museo Principe di Aragona Pignatelli Cortes** (*t 081 761 2356; open Tues–Sun 9–2, closed Mon; adm*) will show you more of the same kind of decorative porcelain as at Capodimonte, as well as 18th- and 19th-century carriages, furniture and art.

Mergellina and Posillipo

Beginning a few streets beyond the western end of the Villa Comunale, **Mergellina** is one of the brightest and most popular quarters of Naples, a good place for dinner or a *passeggiata* around the busy **Piazza Sannazzaro**. Its centre is the **Marina**, where besides small craft there are hydrofoils to Sorrento and the islands in summer, and excursion boats for tours of the shore between Castel dell'Ovo and Posillipo.

From the harbour, Mergellina rises steeply into the surrounding hills; there is a funicular to the top (every 15 minutes), although it is somewhat run-down and not entirely safe. On the hillside, between the railway bridge and the tunnel that leads under the hill to Fuorigrotta, is a small park containing a Roman funerary monument that tradition has always held to be the **Tomb of Virgil** (*open Tues–Sun 9–1*). The poet died in Brindisi in 19 BC on his way back from a trip to Greece. Neapolis was a city dear to him – he wrote most of the Aeneid here – and Virgil was brought here for burial, though ancient authors attest that the tomb was closer to the Aquarium. Just below the monument, you can see the entrance to one of the little-known wonders of the ancient world. The **Crypta Neapolitana** (*open daily 9–1*) is a 1,988ft road tunnel built during the reign of Augustus to connect Neapolis with Pozzuoli and Baia – the longest such work the Romans ever attempted.

West of Mergellina lies the up-market suburb of **Posillipo**, on a hill overlooking the bay. The area was popular in Roman times and is dotted with 17th-century aristocratic villas but, as with Vomero, unregulated post-war development has lessened the natural beauty of the area. On the clifftop at the western end of Posillipo, reached by the 140 bus from Santa Lucia or the C27 from Piazza Amedeo, the beautifully restored

Parco Virgiliano has amazing views over the Bay of Naples. You can also peer down on the devastated beauty around Italsida, the huge, defunct steel plant at Bagnoli then meander down the narrow lanes to **Marechiaro**, where you can eat like a king and bathe safely – one of the few places in Naples where the water is clean enough.

The Bay of Naples

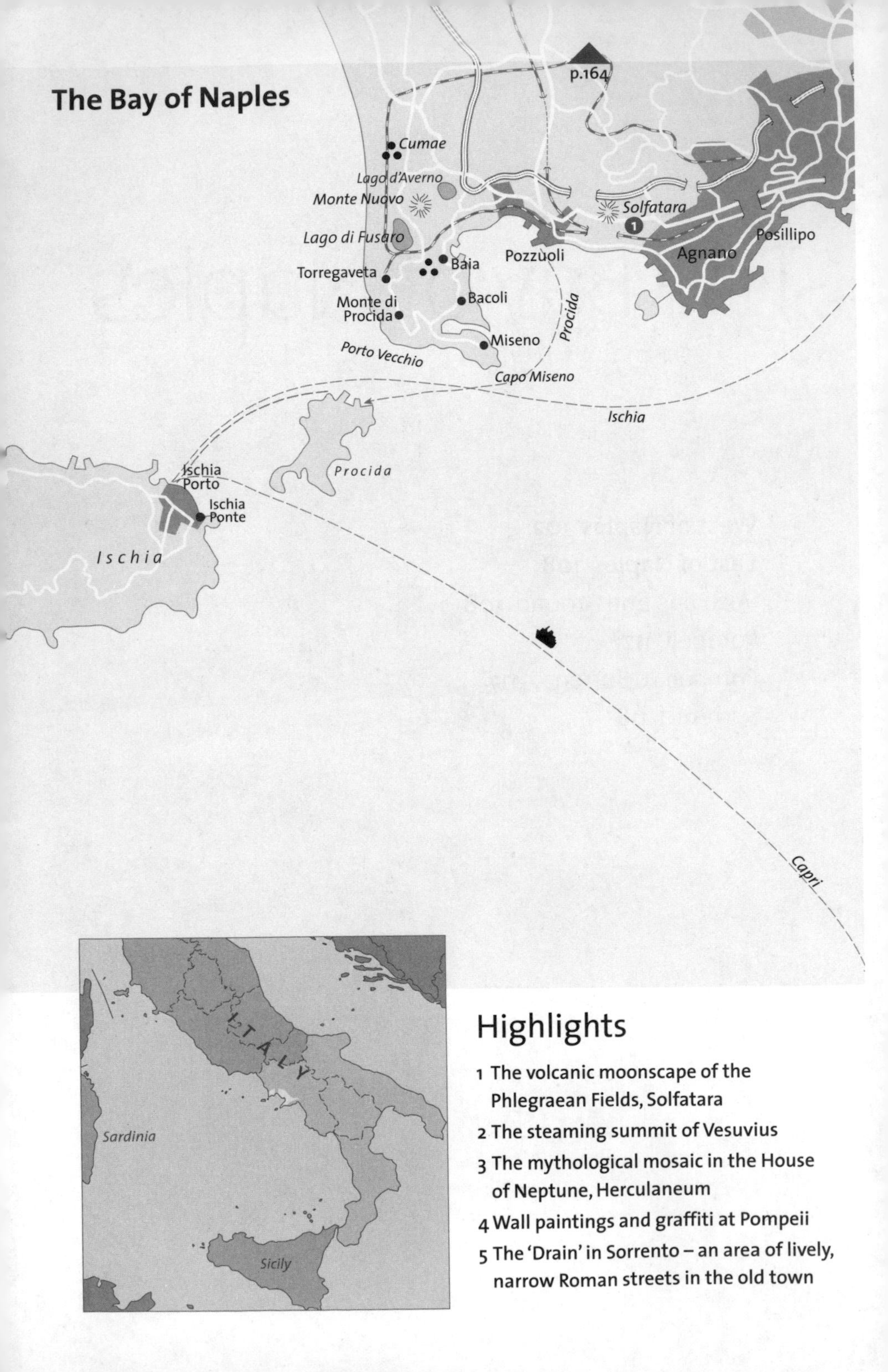

Highlights

1 The volcanic moonscape of the Phlegraean Fields, Solfatara
2 The steaming summit of Vesuvius
3 The mythological mosaic in the House of Neptune, Herculaneum
4 Wall paintings and graffiti at Pompeii
5 The 'Drain' in Sorrento – an area of lively, narrow Roman streets in the old town

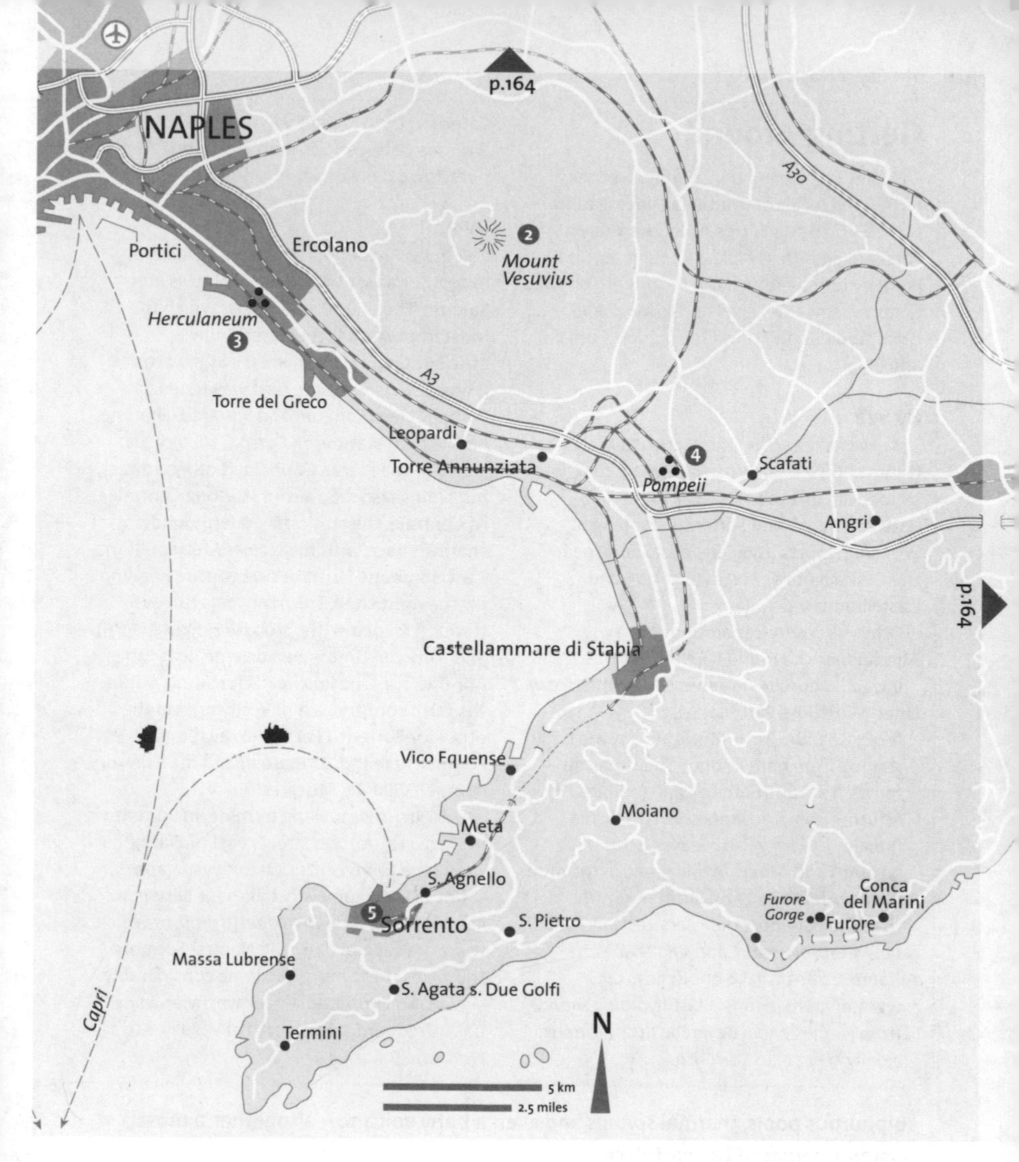

In the Bay of Naples, creation left nothing half-done or poorly done; against any other part of the monotonous Italian coastline, the Campanian shore seems almost indecently blessed, possessing the kind of irresistibly distracting beauty that seduces history off the path of duty and virtue. Today, for all the troubles that come seeping out of Naples, this coast is still one of the capitals of Mediterranean languor.

In Roman days, it was nothing less than the California of the ancient world: fantastically prosperous, lined with glittering resort towns and as favoured by artists and poets as it was by rich patricians. Like California, though, the perfume was mixed with a little whiff of insecurity. Vesuvius would be enough, but even outside of the regularly scheduled eruptions and earthquakes, the region is Vulcan's own curiosity shop. West of Naples especially, there are eternally rising and sinking landscapes,

Getting Around

Naples is the bay's transport hub; buses, ferries and local commuter rail lines lead from the city to all points (*see* p.68). The 3-day **Artecard** pass (*see* **Naples**: 'Getting Around', p.69) includes a return trip to Sorrento on the Circumvesuviana, travel on the Metro del Mare, and bus/rail travel to Pozzuoli, Cuma and Baia.

By Sea

A new ferry service, the **Metro del Mare** (**t** 199 44 66 44; *www.metrodelmare.com*) was introduced in 2002. The MM1 route runs between Bacoli and Sorrento, stopping at Pozzuoli, Naples (Molo Beverello dock, near the Castel Nuovo), Portici/Ercolano and Castellammare.

Other ferry services around the bay:

Alimar does the round trip from Naples' Molo Beverello dock to Sorrento three times a day.

Linee Marittime Partenopee, t 081 551 3236 (**t** 081 807 1812 in Sorrento), runs seven daily returns from 9am to 9pm. They also run ferries from Sorrento to Capri (40mins return, 5 daily), Positano (6 daily), Ischia (1 daily, 9.30am, return leaves Ischia at 5.20pm) and Amalfi (3 daily), and a hydrofoil from Sorrento to Capri (20mins return; 16 daily). In winter, their services only run between Sorrento, Capri and Naples.

Alilauro, t 081 551 3236 or 081 507 1345, *www.alilauro.it*, runs a fast hydrofoil service from Naples' Molo Beverello dock (30mins, 7 daily, 9–7.30) to Sorrento.

Caremar, t 199 123 199, *www.caremar.it*. Runs ferries between Sorrento and Capri (20mins return; 4 daily).

By Rail

Regular FS trains aren't much help here, except for a fast trip between Naples and Salerno. There are local lines, of which the most important is the refreshingly efficient **Circumvesuviana** (**t** 081 772 2111, *www.vesuviana.it*), the best way to reach Pompei, Herculaneum and Sorrento. This line has its own station, on Corso Garibaldi just south of the Piazza Garibaldi (**t** 081 772 2444), but trains also stop at the Stazione Centrale. At Centrale, the station is underground, sharing space with the Naples Metropolitana – ask someone to make sure you are heading for the right train. The main lines run east through Ercolano (the stop for Herculaneum) and Torre del Greco, then diverge near Torre Annunziata. One line heads for Sarno, out in the farm country east of Vesuvius, and the other for Sorrento. For the excavations at Pompei, take the Sorrento line to the Scavi di Pompei/Villa dei Misteri stop.

The Circumvesuviana terminal in Sorrento is in Piazza Lauro, two streets east of Piazza Tasso, the town centre. Circumvesuviana trains usually run every half-hour between 5am and 10.45pm. On a *direttissima*, of which there are several daily, the Naples–Sorrento trip takes 1hr 10mins; locals are considerably slower. An additional Circumvesuviana line has infrequent trains north of Vesuvius to Nola and Baia.

sulphurous pools, thermal springs and even a baby volcano – altogether, a most unstable corner of the earth's crust.

West of Naples

The pretty coastal road leaving the city has views of Vesuvius all through the district of Posillipo. Naples' suburbs continue through **Agnano**, a town of spas and hot springs set around a mile-wide extinct crater, and stretch as far as Pozzuoli.

Pozzuoli

Sophia Loren's birthplace is a modest little city with only its ruins to remind it of the time when Roman Puteoli, and not Naples, was the metropolis of the bay. In the time

For the west bay, Naples' own **Metropolitana FS** (**t** 800 568 866; trains every 15mins) goes as far as Pozzuoli-Solfatara. The two other regional lines both have trains about every half-hour from Piazza Montesanto station, near the Piazza Dante. The **Ferrovia Cumana** (**t** 800 001 616, *www.sepsa.it*) runs along the shore through Fuorigrotta, Bagnoli, Pozzuoli and Baia to Torregaveta (trains every 10mins). The **Circumflegrea** (also **t** 800 001 616; trains every 20mins) also finishes at Torregaveta, but usually goes only as far as Licola. Six trains a day stop at the archaeological site of Cumae.

By Bus

Naples city bus 152 from Piazza Garibaldi and Via Mergellina travels to Solfatara and Pozzuoli. A blue bus run by **Sepsa** (**t** 800 001 616, *www.sepsa.it*) departs from Piazza Garibaldi and stops at Solfatara, Pozzuoli and Baia. From the bus stop in the centre of Baia, there are connecting buses to Cumae, Bacoli and Cape Miseno.

Although the Circumvesuviana makes buses unnecessary for most of the east bay, there is a bus from the airport to Sorrento three times a day. The express bus from Naples to Salerno, which usually runs every half-hour, leaves from the **SITA** office on Via Pisanelli, just off the Piazza Municipio, **t** 081 552 2176, and arrives in Salerno at the terminal at Corso Garibaldi 117, **t** 089 226 604. SITA buses go to Pompeii from Naples and Salerno.

SITA also runs buses from Salerno for the Amalfi coast, with regular departures for Sorrento (in front of the Circumvesuviana station), stopping at Amalfi, Ravello and other towns en route. They are usually so frequent that it is easy to see all the main coast towns on a day trip, hopping from one to the next. Buses are the best way to do it; driving can be a hair-raising experience.

By Car

Drivers heading for the west bay area and wishing to arrive quite quickly should get on to the *tangenziale* out of Naples and stay on it until past Pozzuoli, before turning off on to the (by then) more tranquil SS7, which runs around the Miseno peninsula. Alternatively, you can take the SS7 all the way from the harbour in Naples via the Mergellina tunnel, or the pretty but slow coastal road – initially the Via Posillipo – around Cape Posillipo.

If you are heading towards Pompeii and the east bay – where the distances are greater, and so a car is much more useful – then it's advisable to use the A3 *autostrada* to get out of Naples if you don't want to spend a long time on the SS18 coast road through the suburbs. You can leave the A3 at Ercolano or Pompeii, or Castellammare for SS145 to the Sorrento peninsula.

As the region is so well served by public transport, **car hire** is hardly essential, but **Avis** have an office in Sorrento on Viale Nizza 53, **t** 081 878 2459, **f** 081 807 1143, *www.avisautonoleggio.it*.

Don't be tempted into hiring a **moped**. The small roads are always busy with tour coaches and natives impatient to overtake, making it extremely dangerous.

of Caesar and Augustus, it was the main port of Italy; at one point, the Senate actually considered the bizarre idea of digging a canal all the way to Rome to make shipping safer. The city's decline began in the 2nd century with Emperor Trajan's expansion of the port of Ostia, closer to Rome. During the 5th-century barbarian invasions, most of Puteoli's citizens took refuge in better-defended Naples.

The **Amphitheatre** (***t*** *081 526 6007; open Wed–Mon 9am–one hour before sunset; adm*), on Via Domiziana near the railway station, was the third largest in the Roman world (after Rome and Capua), with 60 gates for letting in the beasts. It is remarkable for the preservation of its subterranean structure where the scenery, changing rooms and cells for storing wild animals prior to shows (*venationes*) were located. The long cavity in the centre was for hoisting up scenery. Unlike the chambers underneath, which were buried in mud and landslides, the exposed stands were stripped of their masonry through the ages (visitors are not allowed onto them).

The Amphitheatre was started by Nero and finished by Vespasianus, who renamed the city Colonia Flavia Augusta Puteoli, in thanks to Puteoli for its aid in the civil war that made him emperor. It was the second amphitheatre in Pozzuoli – a few broken arches of the older one, probably used for gladiatorial combats, survive 100m to the north.

Pozzuoli's other important ruin is a little embarrassment to the town. For centuries, people here were showing off the ancient **Serapeum** – temple to the popular Egyptian god Serapis – until some killjoy archaeologist proved the thing to be an unusually lavish *macellum* (market). Only the foundations remain, now forming the centrepiece of the Piazza Serapide, near Pozzuoli's small harbour.

For all ancient Puteoli's size and wealth, little else remains. The reason is *bradyseism* – a rare seismic phenomenon that afflicts this town and other spots around the bay. It manifests itself in the form of 'slow' earthquakes. The level of the land fell nearly 20ft in the 1,000 years after the fall of Rome, only to begin rising again in the 15th century. Currently falling again, the bits of ancient Puteoli that have not been gently shaken to pieces over the centuries are now underwater. Roman *moles* and docks can still sometimes be made out beneath the surface.

Works for the development and restoration of the historical area of **Rione Terra** (*t 848 800 288; open Sat–Sun 9–6*) started in 2002. The site has disclosed the remains of a Roman settlement dating from 194 BC, and it should become a larger archaeological site within a few years.

Solfatara

t 081 526 2341; open daily 9–7.30 in summer, 9–4.30 in winter; adm.

What's troubling Pozzuoli can be seen clearly just outside the town at Solfatara, the storm centre of what the Greeks called the **Phlegraean (fiery) Fields** – in Italian, the *Campi Flegrei*. To the Romans, it was the Forum Vulcani and a major attraction of the Campanian coast. It hasn't changed much since. Solfatara is the crater of a collapsed volcano, but one that just can't be still; sulphur gas vents, bubbling mud pits and whistling superheated steam fumaroles decorate the eerie landscape. Dangerous spots are fenced off and guides are sometimes available to lead you around. Their favourite trick is to hold a smoking torch to one of the *fumaroles* – making a dozen others nearby go off at the same time. (The effect is produced by the steam condensing around smoke particles.) Solfatara is perfectly safe, even though the ground underneath feels hot and sounds strangely hollow. It is; scientists keep a close watch on the huge plug of cooled lava that underlies the area around Pozzuoli, and they say the pressure from below is only about one-third as much as it was under Vesuvius in AD 79.

The easiest way to reach Solfatara is on the 152 bus from Naples. Otherwise, it is a 25-minute trudge uphill from Pozzuoli train station.

Baia

Baia, the next town along the coast, was nothing less than the greatest pleasure dome of classical antiquity. Anybody who was anybody in the Roman world had a villa here, with a view of the sea, beach access and a few hundred slaves to dust the statues and

Getting Around

In addition to the services at the start of the chapter, the **Archeobus Flegreo** (**t** 800 001 616) tours the archaeological sites of Pozzuoli, Cumae, Baia and Capo Miseno in 16 stops, every hour between 9am and 7pm.

Tourist Information

Pozzuoli: Pza Matteotti 1/A, **t** 081 526 6639, **f** 081 526 5068. *Open 9–2 and (June–Sept) 4–8.*

Eating Out

As it is close enough to Naples for an easy day trip, nobody has made the west of the Bay of Naples a base for a holiday since sometime around the 4th century AD. However, there are a few decent restaurants for lunch. In addition, the mini-market in **Sulfatara** is a good place to pick up a *panino* for a picnic on the acropolis at Cumae, while at **Baia** there is a mini-market opposite the station.

Pozzuoli

The harbour is not particularly scenic, but there are two recommendations.

La Granzeola, Via Cupa delle Fescine 33, **t** 081 524 3430 (*expensive*). On the way out of Pozzuoli along the coastal road. Carmine Russo, the owner-chef of this restaurant, turns fish bought directly off the boats into an array of tasty dishes. Try the *rigatoni con ragù di cozze* (short pasta with a delicious mussel sauce). *Closed Sun eves and Mon.*

Il Capitano, Via Cristoforo Colombo 10, **t** 081 526 2283 (*moderate*). A good rendezvous for fish-lovers. It also has five rooms for rent. *Closed Thurs.*

Baia to Cuma

L'Altro Cucchiaro, Via Lucullo 13, **t** 081 868 7196 (*expensive*). Divine concoctions of seafood and pasta, as well as superb fish. Between Baia's railway station and harbour, it's perfectly placed if you're visiting the archaeological park. *Closed Mon and Aug.*

La Ninfea, Via Italia 1, Lake Lucrino, **t** 081 866 1326 (*expensive*). On the road from Baia to Pozzuoli, you can bask on the lakeside terrace as you dine on fresh fish and simple grilled meats. Try the *linguine* with prawns.

Giardino degli Aranci, Via Cuma 75, **t** 081 854 3120 (*expensive*). This fish restaurant is a safe bet after visiting the archaeological site at Cuma. *Closed Tues in low season.*

Villa Chiara, Via Torre di Cappella 10, **t** 081 868 7139 (*moderate*). One of several decent seafood places between Cuma and Fusaro. *Closed Mon.*

Anfiteatro Cumano, Via Cuma 576, **t** 081 854 3119, *www.anfiteatrocumano.com* (*cheap*). Another good fish restaurant near the archaeological site.

Torregaveta

Restaurants in shabbyish Torregaveta are generally cheaper than in the bay.

Villa Aragonese, Via Spiaggia Torregaveta, **t** 081 868 9180 (*expensive*). Full dinners for reasonable prices. *Closed Tues, 2 weeks in Aug and Oct–April.*

clean up after the orgies. You'll find little hint of that today: Goths, malaria and earthquakes have done a thorough job of wrecking the place. Most of ancient Baia is now underwater, a victim of the same *bradyseism* that afflicts Pozzuoli. In summer, a **glass-bottomed boat** departs from Baia harbour to see this Roman Atlantis (**Associazione Aliseo**, ***t*** *081 523 3797; tours depart Sat 12 and 4, Sun 10.30, 12 and 4, and last 70 mins; also scuba-diving trips to the ruins*). Modern Baia is a pleasant small town but its lovely bay has been consigned to use as a graveyard for dead freighters. Nevertheless, the extensive but humble remains of the imperial villa can be visited at the **Parco Archeologico** (***t*** *081 868 8868; open Tues–Sun 9–one hour before sunset; adm*). Not much is labelled or explained, but the ruins include a part of the famous baths – a thermal spa for wealthy Romans that was probably the largest and poshest such establishment in the ancient world, and an inspiration for the great baths of Rome and other cities.

The wonderful **Baia Castle** (*t 081 523 3310; open daily 9–one hour before sunset in summer, 9–3 in winter*) dominates the Golfo di Pozzuoli, with views as far as Capri. It's worth a visit. Begun by the Aragonese in 1495 to protect the bay from a feared French invasion, it was rebuilt by Pedro di Toledo after the earthquake of 1538. The castle contains the **Archaeological Museum of the Phlegraean Fields**, with some impressive Roman frescoes and statues. Take a bus towards Miseno from Baia's Cumana station.

Bacoli to Cumae via Capo Miseno

The coast curves south towards **Bacoli**. This pleasant village has two sights: a covered Roman reservoir called the **Piscina Mirabile**, a vaulted chamber like the one in Istanbul; and the **Cento Camarelle**, the '100 little rooms' (*t 081 523 3690; closed for renovation*), a vast ruin of a villa that might have belonged to Julius Caesar.

South of Bacoli lies **Capo Miseno** (Cape Misenum), a beautiful spot that for centuries was the greatest naval base of the Roman empire, home to 10,000 sailors. As at Baia, foundations and bits of columns and cornices are everywhere, though nothing of any real interest has survived intact. Nearby **Lake Miseno**, also called the 'Dead Sea', was once a part of the base, joined to the sea by a canal dug by Augustus' right-hand man, Cornelius Agrippa, in 37 BC.

Caligula once ordered a double row of boats to be made across the bay all the way from Bacoli to Pozzuoli. Suetonius wrote that the purpose was to fulfil a prophecy that Caligula would never become emperor until he rode across the bay on his horse (which he proceeded to do). It's more likely, though, that he did it to impress the Persian ambassador with the strength of the Roman navy.

That same distance was covered by the famous 'boy on a dolphin' – a story that inspired many classical works of art. Many reliable witnesses attested to Pliny that a little boy from the peninsula befriended a dolphin, which gave him a ride every day to lessons with his tutor in Puteoli. Pliny records that the boy died after an illness and that the dolphin, after waiting faithfully for his friend for several days, beached himself and died, too. The two were burned together.

More lakes, created as a result of volcanic action, lie north of Cape Miseno. **Lago di Fusaro** is a large, shallow oyster farm, cut off from the sea by a sand bar near the woebegone fishing village of **Torregaveta**, the terminus of the Circumflegrea and Cumana railways. The decaying rococo palace on an island in the centre is the **Casina** (*t 081 687 080; open daily 9–one hour before sunset*), built in 1782 by the Bourbon kings' favourite architect, Luigi Vanvitelli.

Nearby is the baby volcano we promised you at the start of the chapter. **Monte Nuovo** is only about 460ft tall and an easy climb up to the crater (you can have a picnic inside it). It has been quiet for some time, passing up the opportunity to celebrate its 450th birthday on 29 September 1988 – the same 1538 earthquake that wrecked much of Pozzuoli gave birth to this little cone. The eruption also filled in half of **Lago di Lucrino**, which is separated from the sea by a narrow strip of land. The lake has always been renowned for its oysters. Sometime around 90 BC, a sharp Roman named C. Sergius Orata had the idea of farming oysters here and selling them to the rich owners of the villas around the bay. The business was one of the most profitable in antiquity. There is a nature reserve here (*open daily 9–one hour before sunset*).

Lago d'Averno (Lake Avernus) may ring a bell from your school days. It's the mouth of Hell, according to the ancient Greeks, who believed any passing bird would be suffocated by the infernal fumes rising from it. Cornelius Agrippa didn't have much respect for mythology and he turned the lake into a part of the naval base by cutting another canal. Among the ruins that surround the lake are the remains of a domed building, perhaps a temple or a sort of spa, originally as big as the Pantheon in Rome. Emperor Nero was fond of this area and built a covered canal lined with colonnades from the lake all the way to Pozzuoli. No trace remains of this now.

Cumae

t 081 854 3060; open daily 9–one hour before sunset; adm.

North of Monte Nuovo and the lakes, near the modern town of Cuma, is the main archaeological site west of Naples – the Greek city of Cumae. As one of the first Greek settlements in Italy, the city was the mother colony for Naples and many other cities of Magna Grecia. In 421 BC, it lost its independence to the Samnites and declined steadily from then on. Arab raiders, who did so much damage elsewhere in Campania, finally wiped the city off the map in the 9th century AD. They did a good job and there is little to see at the site – only the foundations of a few temples on the high acropolis, worth the climb for the views around Capo Miseno and the famous Cave of the Sibyl.

One of the ruins is a famous **Temple of Apollo**, rebuilt by Augustus in thanks to the god after his victory at Actium. Another is the **Temple of Jupiter**, also dating from the Augustan age and converted into a Christian basilica in the 5th or 6th century.

Just below the summit is the **Cave of the Cumaean Sibyl**, discovered by accident in 1932. This was the setting of Aeneas' famous encounter with the Sibyl who led him into the underworld, as described in Book 6 of Virgil's *Aeneid*. It is a place of mystery, a long series of strange, trapezoidal galleries cut out of solid rock – impressive enough, even stripped of the sumptuous decoration they must once have had (all ancient oracles were marvellously profitable). Nobody has a clear idea how old it is, but by classical times, it took the form of an oracle quite like the one at Delphi. At the far end of the cave, a plain alcove with two benches marks the spot where the Sibyls would inhale fumes over the sacred tripod, chew laurel leaves and go into their trance. Legend has it that King Tarquin of Rome came here, to the most venerable and respected oracle in all the western Mediterranean, with the intention of purchasing nine prophetic books from the Cumaean Sibyl. Unwisely, he said they were too dear, whereupon the Sibyl threw three of the books into the fire and offered him the remaining six at the same price. Again he complained, and the Sibyl put three more in the flames. Finally, Tarquin gave up and took the last three at the original price. It was a good bargain. The Sibylline Books guided Rome's destiny until they, too, were burned up in the great fire of 82 BC.

The cult was in decline by the 2nd century when Trimalchio, a character in Petronius' *Satyricon*, claims he saw the ancient Sibyl's remains in a jar hanging in the cave.

East of Naples

From Naples to Sorrento by way of Pompeii and Vesuvius, this short but celebrated stretch of the Campanian coastline, in the shadow of southern Italy's most famous mountain, contains the region's most-visited tourist attraction and most popular resort – as well as some unattractive industrial suburbs of Naples.

Vesuvius and Around

Naples' eastern suburbs and satellite towns spread along the shore of the bay in the shadow of Mount Vesuvius as far as Torre Annunziata. The coastal road passes through unattractive industrial zones and modern housing blocks – many thrown up to rehouse the homeless after the 1980 earthquake.

Tempting though it is to bypass all this and head straight for Pompeii on the A3 *autostrada*, the area does have two great attractions: the splendid Roman ruins at Herculaneum and Vesuvius itself, which is accessed from Ercolano, the modern town built on top of those ruins. There are also traces of the splendid villas of the Bourbon aristocracy along the once-glorious Golden Mile, and another fine Roman villa at Oplontis (all covered below).

The modern towns along this stretch of coastline – Portici, Ercolano, Torre del Greco and Torre Annunziata – are less appealing, although Torre del Greco is known for the production of coral artwork. (These days, most of the coral comes from Asia.)

Vesuvius

***t** 081 777 5720; open daily 9–5; adm.*

Despite its fearsome reputation and formidable appearance looming over Naples, Mount Vesuvius is a midget as volcanoes go – only 4,202ft. No one even suspected it was a volcano, in fact, until it surprised the people of Pompeii, Herculaneum and Stabiae on 24 August 79. That titanic eruption did not include much lava. Instead, it buried Herculaneum under mud and the other two cities under cinders and ash, while coating most of Italy with a thin layer of dust. After the explosion, Roman writers noted that the plume of smoke and ash over the volcano looked exactly like a young pine tree; observers have noted the same sinister tree shape in many eruptions in more recent years. Over 100 eruptions have since destroyed various towns and villages, some more than once. But, as at Mount Etna in Sicily, people just can't stay away from Vesuvius' slopes. Volcanic soil grows grapes and olives in abundance, though the novelty of it often makes the Italians exaggerate their quality. The AD 79 explosion hasn't been matched since. It blew the top of the mountain clean off, leaving two peaks, with the main fissure in between. The lower one is called Monte Somma or *nasone* ('big nose') by the Neapolitans; the higher, parallel peak is Vesuvius proper.

Vesuvius was last heard from in 1944. That eruption left the lava flows you'll see on the upper slopes. It also sealed the main fissure, putting an end to the permanent

Tourist Information

Pompei: Via Sacra 1, 80045, **t** 081 850 7255, f 081 863 2401, *www.pompeiisites.org*. *Open Mon–Sat 8.30–7*. There's also a branch near the Porta Marina entrance to the Pompeii site. Detailed guidebooks are sold in the stands outside the ruins.

Where to Stay

With the picturesque Sorrentine peninsula and its excellent collection of hotels only 40 minutes away in one direction, and with Naples about the same in the other, there's little point staying overnight in this built-up, semi-industrial area.

Eating Out

As well as the following, the harbour at **Castellammare di Stabia** is much favoured by locals, who come to dine *al fresco* in the hot summer evenings.

Ercolano

Note that there are no restaurants or cafés inside the **Herculaneum** ruins.

Cagnano, Via Roma 17 (*cheap*). This simple *trattoria* is a short walk up the hill from the ruins of Herculaneum and serves huge bowlfuls of pasta, including a memorable *spaghetti alle vongole*.

Bar degli Amorini, opposite the entrance to the ruins. Has a deceptively small front, but upstairs there is a reasonable dining area, good for a snack or pizza.

Pompei

There is a restaurant in the ruins, just beyond the forum area through the Arch of Tiberius. The food from the self-service is nothing special; to escape the crowds opt for waiter service and sit out under the colonnade adjoining the ancient baths.

Restaurants in modern Pompei tend to cater for the captive tourist market, with ubiquitous multilingual menus. Among the best are:

Al Gamberone, Via Piave 36, **t** 081 850 6814 (*cheap*). Close to Pompei's main church, you can feast here on prawns doused in cognac and other good fish dishes. In summer, you may dine outside under the lemons and oranges. If you do not want fish there is an array of other dishes including a good *cannelloni*. *Closed Tues*.

Anfiteatro, Via Plinio 9, **t** 081 850 6042 (*cheap*). One of the few places in Pompei where you'll see *baccalà* (salt cod) on the menu, along with truly good *spaghetti alle vongole*. It is just outside the excavations' exit next to the amphitheatre.

Zi Caterina, Via Roma 20, **t** 081 850 7447 (*cheap*). With live lobsters in the tank and other good seafood dishes, this is also a good place to try Lacrima Christi wine from the slopes of Vesuvius. *Closed Tues eves*.

plume of smoke that was once such a familiar landmark. You can bet the scientists are watching Vesuvius but there is no reason to expect another eruption soon – although if it were to explode now, it would cause a catastrophe, as the area around the volcano has become one of the most densely populated in all of Italy. In an attempt to shift this trend, the government has offered €25,000 to families if they move from the slopes of the volcano.

To visit the main crater (between the two peaks), take the Vesuvius bus from the Circumvesuviana stop in Ercolano. You then have a stiff half-hour climb up the ash path. Dismiss all hopes of an easy ascent to the top singing 'Funiculi, funicula' from the legendary Thomas Cook cable railway, long since defunct. The white scar on the side of the crater is the result of work on a second funicular, which was meant to have replaced the old chairlift. Work halted after an argument over its control between the communes of Torre del Greco and Ercolano – while they were arguing, the money mysteriously 'disappeared'.

Portici to Ercolano: The Golden Mile

It's hard to believe, as you pass through the sprawling industrial outskirts of southern Naples, but this was once a beautiful coastline of forests and elegant villas. In 1738, Charles II, always keen on any place with good hunting, had a royal palace built at Portici. The aristocracy of the Bourbon court followed suit, constructing over 120 villas between Naples and Torre del Greco, and the area became known as Il Miglio d'Oro – the Golden Mile. The villas commanded fine views over the bay and were decked out with frescos and other imitations of the Roman villas of antiquity.

After the fall of the Bourbons in 1860, the courtiers sold their great mansions. Today many are abandoned or converted into apartments, but an organization called **Ente Ville Vesuviane** (***t*** *081 732 2134*) has taken on the task of restoring some of them to their former glory, and a few are open to visitors.

The **Palazzo Reale** (*Via Universita 100, Portici*), built between 1738 and 1742, has been home to the Agriculture School of the University of Naples since 1873. You can walk in and have a look, although most of the palace's original contents are now in the Museo Nazionale Archeologico.

Another mansion that is open to visitors is the **Villa Campolieto** (*Corso Resina 283, Ercolano; open Tues–Sun 10–1*), dating from 1760 and with a magnificent circular portico, the setting for an annual summer concert season. The Ente Ville Vesuviane offices are located here. Next door is the **Villa Ruggiero** (*Via Alessandro Rossi; open Tues–Sun 10–1).* Also in Ercolano, you can visit the beautiful gardens of the **Villa Favorita** (*Via Gabriele D'Annunzio*) with its lovely pavilions and sea views (although you can't visit the house itself).

Herculaneum

Open daily April–Oct 8.30–7.30, Nov–Mar 8.30-5; last tickets 90mins before closing; adm.

The drab suburb of Ercolano is built on the mass of rock that imprisons ancient Herculaneum, a smaller and less famous victim of the great AD 79 Vesuvius eruption than Pompeii, but equally worth visiting. Vesuvius destroyed them in different ways. Pompeii was buried under layers of ash, while Herculaneum, much closer to the volcano, drowned in a sea of mud. Over time, the mud hardened to a soft stone, preserving the city and nearly everything in it as a sort of fossil – furniture, clothing and even some goods in the shops have survived.

Like Pompeii, Herculaneum was discovered by accident. In the early 1700s, an Austrian officer named Prince Elbeuf had a well dug here. Not far down, the workmen struck a stone pavement – the stage of the city's theatre. The Bourbon government began some old-fashioned destructive excavation, but serious archaeological work began only under Mussolini. Only about eight blocks of shops and villas, some quite fashionable, have been excavated. The rest is covered not only by tens of yards of rock, but also by a dense modern neighbourhood; bringing more of Herculaneum to light is a fantastically slow and expensive operation, but new digs are still going on. At any given time, most of the buildings will be locked, but the guards wandering about have all the keys and will show you almost any of them upon request (they are not supposed to accept tips, though you will find they often seem to expect them).

But unlike Pompeii (which was an important commercial centre), Herculaneum seems to have been a wealthy resort, and is only about a third of Pompeii's size. Many of the most interesting houses can be found along **Cardo IV**, the street in the centre of the excavated area. On the corner of the *Decumanus Inferior*, the **House of the Wooden Partition** may be the best example we have of the façade of a Roman house: inside there is an amazingly preserved wooden screen (from which the house gets its name) used for separating the *tablinum* – the master's study – from the atrium. Next door, the **Trellis House** was a much more modest dwelling, with a built-in workshop; the **House of the Mosaic Atrium**, down the street, is another luxurious villa built with a mind to the sea view from the bedrooms upstairs. On the other side of the Decumanus, Cardo IV passes the **Samnite House** (so named because of its early-style atrium), and further up, a column with police notices painted on it stands near the **House of Neptune**, with a lovely mythological mosaic in the atrium.

The **Suburban Baths**, near the entrance to the site, were built not long before Vesuvius erupted, and are probably the best-preserved baths of antiquity. Inside, there are stucco reliefs depicting warriors, some remarkably well-preserved wooden doors and window frames, a central furnace that is perfectly intact, and marble floors and seats throughout. Other buildings worth a visit include the **House of the Deer**, with its infamous statue of a drunken Hercules relieving himself, the well-preserved **Forum Baths**, and the **Palaestra** (gym), with its unusual serpent fountain and rather elegant, cross-shaped swimming pool.

Villa Poppaea at Oplontis

***t** 081 862 1755; open daily April–Oct 8.30–7.30, Nov–Mar 8.30–5; last tickets 90mins before closing.*

Torre Annunziata is another sorry place with a serious drug problem and a penchant for pasta production. However, the Roman villa excavated on Via Sepolcri, known as the Villa Poppaea at Oplontis, is well worth a detour. If you are arriving on the Circumvesuviana, exit the station, walk downhill over the crossroads and head for the open area on the left opposite the military zone.

Two-thirds of the villa has been fully excavated, revealing an extremely opulent pad with its own bath complex, servants' quarters, monumental reception rooms and ornamental pool. There are beautiful wall paintings (*see* box, pp.112–3) depicting scenes of monumental halls hung with military arms, a magnificent tripod set between a receding colonnade, bowls of figs and fresh fruit and vignettes of pastoral idylls – including one showing Hercules under a tree with the apples of the Hesperides, which he persuaded Atlas to retrieve during his penultimate labour. The part of the villa near the road is dominated by the atrium hall and the family quarters. The wing farther from the road seems to have been the servants' quarters. Here you can still see amphorae stacked up in a storeroom. Outside the latrines, partitioned for each sex, it may have been a slave who left his name, scrawled in Greek, 'Remember Beryllos'.

Roman Frescoes

Not surprisingly, Pompeii and Herculaneum have been of prime importance in the study of Roman painting. It is impossible to know how much of this art was borrowed from the Greeks or the Etruscans, although by the time of Augustus, it appears that Rome and Campania were in the vanguard. New fashions set in the palaces of the Palatine Hill were quickly copied in the villas of Roman Campania – or perhaps it was the other way round.

Wealthy Romans tended to regard their homes as domestic shrines rather than a place to kick off their *caligae* and relax after a hard day at the forum (the public baths served that role – the ancient Italians behaved much like the modern ones, who do everything in groups of 10 and can't bear being alone). At home, they used as many mosaics and wall paintings as they could afford to lend the place the necessary dignity. In Pompeii and Herculaneum, four styles of painting have been defined by art historians, although as you roam the ruins, you'll find that they often overlap.

Style I (2nd century BC) was heavily influenced by Hellenistic models, especially from Alexandria. Walls are divided into three sections, often by bands of stucco, with a cornice and frieze along the top and square panels (*dados*) on the bottom. The middle sections are skilfully painted to resemble rich marble slabs. A predilection for deep colours, combined with a lack of windows, often makes these small rooms seem somewhat claustrophobic (*see* the Samnite House, Herculaneum, p.111).

Later Romans must have felt the same lack of air and space for, in about 90 BC, they moved on to the 'architectonic' **Style II**. Columns and architraves were painted around the edges of the wall, and an architectural screen added to provide an illusion of depth and space on the large central panels. At first, the centres consisted of more pseudo-marble, but landscapes and mythological scenes soon became more popular.

An amphora marked with the name Poppaea has given rise to the suggestion that the villa may have belonged to the wealthy Roman family, the *gens* Poppaea, who also owned the House of Menander at Pompeii. The most infamous member of this family was Sabina Poppaea, a woman with everything but virtue. She used her charms to captivate the emperor Nero, leaving her second husband Otho – another future emperor – who was rapidly dispatched to Lusitania. Spurred on by her, Nero killed off his mother Agrippina and his first wife. Nero eventually killed Sabina by mistake in a fit of rage in AD 65, viciously kicking her in the abdomen while she was pregnant.

Pompeii

Open daily April–Oct 8.30–7.30, Nov–Mar 8.30–5; last tickets 90mins before closing.

Herculaneum may have been better preserved, but to see an entire ancient city come to life, the only place on earth you can go is this magic time capsule left to us by the good graces of Mount Vesuvius. Pompeii is no mere ruin. Walking down the old Roman high street, you can peek into the shops, read the graffiti on the walls, then wander

The Villa of the Mysteries (*see* p.117) near Pompeii is a prime example. It is also one of the oldest to have portraits of real people or at least local character types.

Vitruvius, the celebrated writer on architecture, sternly disapproved of **Style III**, which abandoned pretence and architectural dissimulation in favour of more playful compositions in perspective, still always done with a strict regard for symmetry. A favourite motif was patterns of foliage, fountains and candelabras, decorated with delicate, imaginative figures. These would be called 'grotesques' in the Renaissance, when Raphael and his friends rediscovered some in a Roman 'grotto' that was really a part of Nero's Golden House. The middle panels are often done in solid colours, with small scenes at the centre to resemble framed paintings. In Pompeii, examples include the Houses of Lucretius Fronto and the Priest Amandus, the latter done by a remarkable artist who comes close to scientific perspective, albeit with several vanishing points.

The last fashion to hit Pompeii before Vesuvius did, **Style IV**, combines the architectural elements of Style II and the framed picture effects of Style III, but with a much greater degree of elaboration and decoration. Additional small scenes are placed on the sides – among the subjects covered are landscapes, still lifes, genre scenes from everyday life and architectural *trompe l'oeil* windows done with a much more refined use of perspective (*see* the House of the Vettii, p.116). Sometimes an entire stage would be painted, with the curtain pulled aside to show a scene from a play. Borders are decorated with garlands of flowers, leering satyrs, grotesques and frolicking Cupids (Italians call these *amoretti*). Humorous vignettes of the gods and incidents from Virgil's *Aeneid* were popular, along with images of Pompeii's divine patroness, Venus. She also inspired the subject matter of the frescoes you have to bribe the guards to see.

off down the back streets to explore the homes of the inhabitants and appraise their taste in painting – they won't mind a bit if you do. Almost everything we know for sure concerning the daily life of the ancients was learned here, and the huge mass of artefacts and art dug up over 200 years is still helping scholars to re-evaluate the Roman world.

Though a fair-sized city by Roman standards, with a population of some 20,000, Pompeii was probably only the third or fourth city of Campania, and a trading and manufacturing centre of no special distinction. Founded perhaps in the 7th century BC, the city came under the Roman sphere of influence around 200 BC. In the fateful year of AD 79 it was still a cosmopolitan place, culturally more Greek than Roman. Vesuvius' rumblings and the tall, sinister-looking cloud that began to form above it, gave those Pompeiians with any presence of mind a chance to leave, and only about 10 per cent of the population perished.

After the city was buried under the stones and ash of the eruption, the upper floors still stuck out. These were looted and gradually cleared by farmers, and eventually, the city was forgotten altogether. Engineers found it while digging an aqueduct in 1600 and the first excavations began in 1748 – a four-star attraction for northern Europeans on the Grand Tour. The early digs were far from scientific; archaeologists

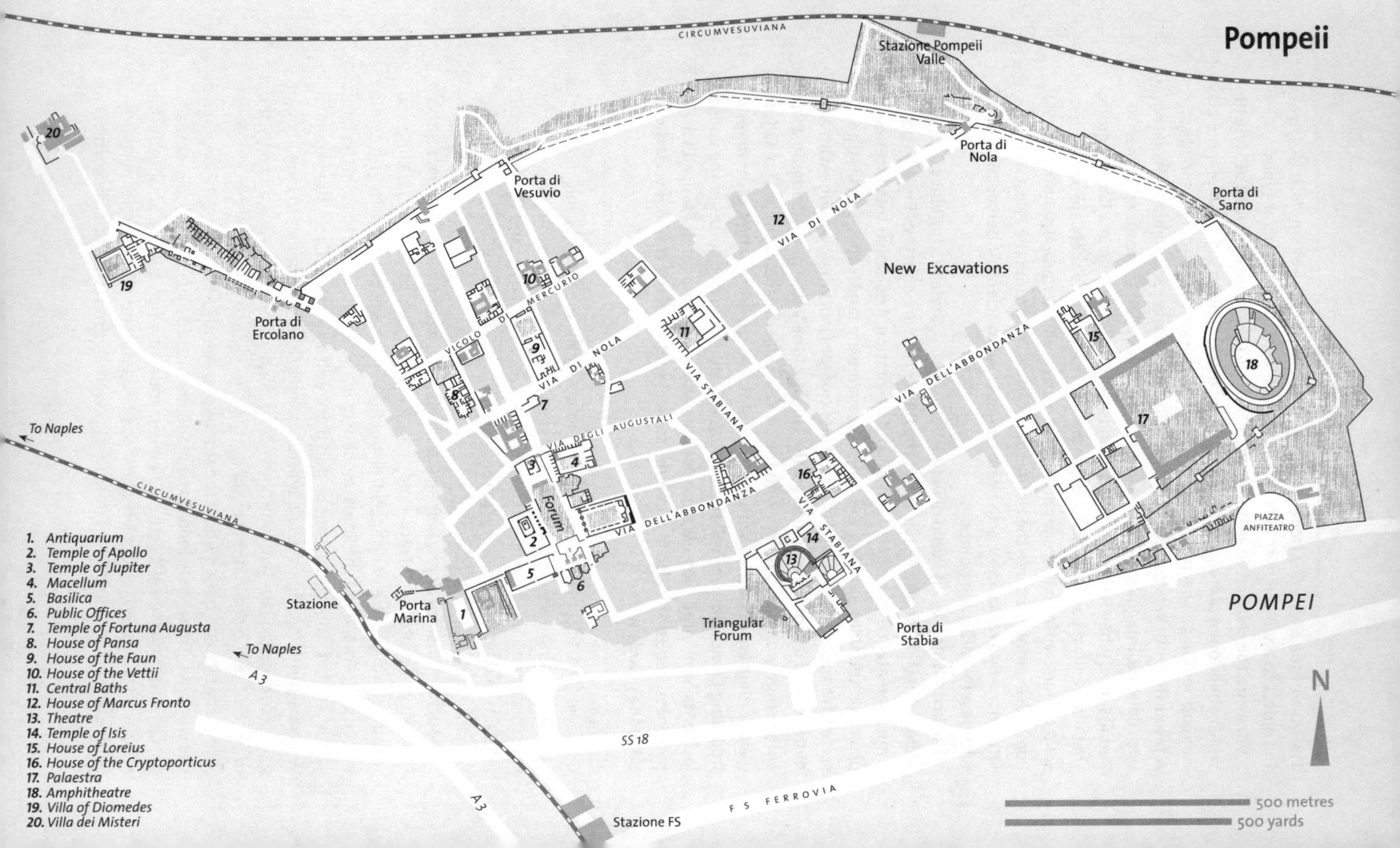

Pompeii

CIRCUMVESUVIANA
Stazione Pompeii Valle
Porta di Vesuvio
Porta di Nola
Porta di Sarno
Porta di Ercolano
New Excavations
VIA DI NOLA
VICOLO DI MERCURIO
VIA STABIANA
VIA DELL'ABBONDANZA
VIA DEGLI AUGUSTALI
Forum
To Naples
CIRCUMVESUVIANA
Stazione
Porta Marina
Triangular Forum
Porta di Stabia
PIAZZA ANFITEATRO
POMPEI
To Naples
A3
SS 18
F S FERROVIA
Stazione FS
N
500 metres
500 yards

1. *Antiquarium*
2. *Temple of Apollo*
3. *Temple of Jupiter*
4. *Macellum*
5. *Basilica*
6. *Public Offices*
7. *Temple of Fortuna Augusta*
8. *House of Pansa*
9. *House of the Faun*
10. *House of the Vettii*
11. *Central Baths*
12. *House of Marcus Fronto*
13. *Theatre*
14. *Temple of Isis*
15. *House of Loreius*
16. *House of the Cryptoporticus*
17. *Palaestra*
18. *Amphitheatre*
19. *Villa of Diomedes*
20. *Villa dei Misteri*

today complain that they did more damage than Vesuvius. Resurrected Pompeii has had other problems: theft of artworks, a good dose of bombs in the Second World War, and most recently, the earthquake of 1980. The damage from that is still being repaired today, though almost all the buildings are once more open to visitors.

There are two ways to see Pompeii. You can spend two or three hours on the main sights or devote a day to scrutinizing details for a total immersion in this ancient world that you won't find anywhere else. Your ticket also entitles you to entrance to the Villa dei Misteri (Villa of the Mysteries), five minutes' walk up the Viale Villa dei Misteri (to the left on exiting the Circumvesuviana).

Pompeii isn't quite a perfect time capsule. The site today is all too serene, with a small-town air. Remember that almost every building was two or three storeys high, and that most streets of a Roman town were permanent market places. When the volcano struck, much of the town was still in the process of being rebuilt after the damage caused by an earthquake in AD 62.

As long as daylight lasted, Pompeii would have been crowded with improvized *bancarelle*; any wagon driver who wished to pass would need all manner of creative cursing. At least the streets were well-paved – better than Rome itself in fact. Campania's cities, the richest in western Europe, could well afford such luxuries. All the pavements were much smoother and more even than you see them now. The purpose of the flat stones laid across the streets should not be hard to guess. They were places to cross when it rained – streets here were also drains – and the slots in them allowed wagon wheels to pass through.

The shops, open to the street in the day, would be sealed up behind shutters at night, just as they are in old parts of Mediterranean cities today. Houses, on the other hand, turned a blank wall to the street. They got their light and air from skylights in the *atrium*, the roofed court around which rooms were arranged. Later, fancier villas have a second, open court directly behind the first, designed after the Greek *peristyle*.

As in Rome, there was no 'fashionable district'. Elegant villas are everywhere, often between two simple workmen's flats. And don't take the street names too seriously. They were bestowed by the archaeologists, often, as with the Via di Mercurio (Mercury Street), after mythological subjects depicted on the street fountains.

Around the Forum

Past the throng of hawkers and refreshment stands, the main site entrance takes you through the walls at the **Porta Marina**. Just inside the gate, the **Antiquarium** displays some of the artworks that haven't been spirited off to the museum in Naples, as well as some truly gruesome casts of fossilized victims of the eruption, caught in their death poses.

Two blocks beyond the Antiquarium and you're in the **Forum**, orientated towards a view of Vesuvius. Unfortunately, this is the worst-preserved part of town. Here, you can see the tribune from which orators addressed public meetings and the pedestals that held statues of heroes and civic benefactors, as well as the once-imposing **Basilica** (law courts), **temples to Apollo and Jupiter**, a public latrine and a **Macellum** (market) decorated with frescoes.

Around Mercury Street

There are some interesting houses around the Via di Mercurio. The real attractions in this part of town, though, are a few lavish villas in the side streets, including the enormous **House of Pansa** and the **House of the Faun**, with the oldest-known welcome mat (set in the pavement, really).

The best of these villas is the wonderful **House of the Vettii**, owned by a pair of wealthy brothers who were oil and wine merchants. It contains several rooms of excellent, well-preserved paintings of mythological scenes, as well as the famous picture of Priapus.

This over-endowed character, in legend the son of Venus and Adonis, together with a couple of wall paintings along the lines of the *Kama Sutra*, has managed to make Pompeii something more than a respectable tourist trap. There are a few paintings of Priapus showing it off in the houses of Pompeii, besides the phallic images that adorn bakers' ovens, wine shops and almost every other establishment in town.

The Pompeiians would be terribly embarrassed, however, if they knew what you are thinking. They were a libidinous lot, like anyone else fortunate enough to live on the Campanian coast during recorded history but the omnipresent phalluses were never meant as decoration. Almost always they are found close to the entrances, where their job was to ward off the evil eye. This use of phallic symbols against evil probably dates from the earliest times in southern Italy; the horn-shaped amulets that millions of people wear around their necks today are their direct descendants. Even so, not so very long ago, women visiting Pompeii were not allowed to set eyes on the various erotic images around the site, and were obliged by the guides to wait chastely outside while their spouses or male companions went in for a peek.

Nearby Via di Nola, one of Pompeii's main streets, leads northwest past the **Temple of Fortuna Augusta**, the **Central Baths** – which were not yet completed when Vesuvius went off – and the **House of Marcus Fronto**, which has more good paintings and a reconstructed roof.

The Triangular Forum

Beginning in 1911, the archaeologists cleared a vast area of Pompeii around what was probably the most important thoroughfare of the city, now called the Via dell'Abbondanza. Three blocks west of the Forum, this street leads to the **Via dei Teatri** and the Triangular Forum, bordering the southern walls.

Two **theatres** here are worth a visit: a large, open one seating 5,000, and a smaller, covered one for concerts. The big quadrangle, originally a lobby for the theatres, seems to have been converted at one point into a gladiators' barracks. This is only one of the disconcerting things about Pompeii. The ruined temple in the Triangular Forum was already long ruined in AD 79, and scholars who study the art of the city find that the last (fourth) period betrays a growing lack of skill and coarseness of spirit. It seems 1st-century Pompeii had its share of urban problems and cultural malaise.

Next to the theatres, a small **Temple of Isis** testifies to the religious diversity of Pompeii; elsewhere around town, there is graffiti satirizing that new and troublesome cult, the Christians.

The Via dell'Abbondanza and Via delle Tombe

The Via dell'Abbondanza is one of Pompeii's most fascinating streets. Among its shops are a smith, a grocer, a weaver, a laundry and a typical Roman tavern with its modest walk-up brothel. The most common are those with built-in tubs facing the street – shops that sold wine, or oil for cooking and lamps. Notices painted on walls announce coming games at the amphitheatre or recommend candidates for public office.

Some of the best-decorated villas in this neighbourhood are to be found along the side streets: the **House of Loreius**, the **House of Amandus** and an odd underground chamber called the **Cryptoporticus**. Pompeii's two most impressive structures occupy a corner just within the walls: the **Palaestra**, a big colonnaded exercise yard, and the **Amphitheatre** – the best-preserved in Italy, with seating for about 20,000. Tacitus records that a fight broke out here between the Pompeiians and rival supporters from Nocera during games staged in AD 59. Nero exiled those responsible for the games and forbade further spectacles for 10 years.

The Romans buried their dead outside their cities. The manner of burial depended on wealth and status, but around the **Via delle Tombe** (or 'Necropoli'), which lies outside the town walls through the **Porta di Noceria** (near the Palaestra), you can see some impressive funerary monuments to local dignitaries and their families.

The Villa dei Misteri

The famous **Villa dei Misteri** is a country villa northwest of the city through the Porta di Ercolano. It is thought to have been a place of initiation in the forbidden Bacchic (or Dionysiac) Mysteries, one of the cults most feared by Rome's Senate, and later, by the emperors. On the walls are scenes from the myth of Dionysus and of the ritual itself.

Pompei to Sorrento

Modern Pompei

The town of Pompei (the modern town has one 'i') is an important pilgrimage centre and worth a visit, if for nothing else than the wonderfully overdone church, dedicated to the **Madonna di Pompei** (*open daily 6.15am–7.30pm*). For a good view over the town and the excavations, take the lift up the tower (*open daily 9–1 and 3–5; adm*). The Madonna of the church holds a special place in the affections of Neapolitan women. You'll probably see them busily saying their rosaries, asking for the Madonna's intercession to help sort out their problems. If they have bare feet, this is not poverty but devotion – usually the fulfilment of a personal pledge to the Madonna in thanks for a favour received: Neapolitans who ask for the Madonna's help often promise to walk here barefoot from Naples (26km) if their prayers are met. It is only justice that

Pompei should play host to the **Vesuvian Museum** (*Via Colle San Bartolomeo;* ***t*** *081 850 7255; open Mon–Sat 9–2*), a couple of minutes' walk from Piazza B. Longo in front of the church. This has more than enough to satisfy most basic volcano questions: prints of the volcano erupting, exhibits on the materials produced in eruptions and much more that is explosive.

Along the Coast to Sorrento

Beyond Pompeii, the coastline begins to curve out towards Sorrento. At the foot of the peninsula lies **Castellammare di Stabia**, which little suggests the beauty farther on. Roman Stabiae was the port of Pompeii and the third big town to be destroyed by Vesuvius. Most famously it was where Pliny the Elder, who was in command of the fleet at Misenum during the AD 79 eruption, met his death as he tried to bring help to those fleeing the catastrophe. The description of the eruption and these events are recorded for posterity in his nephew's letter to Tacitus. Today, beneath a 12th-century **Hohenstaufen Castle**, you'll find the modern shipyards of the Italian navy.

From Castellammare, you can take a short ride in the cable car (*open April–Oct*) up to **Monte Faito**, a broad, heavily forested mountain that may be the last really tranquil spot on the bay – though a few hotels have already appeared. It is a good starting point for some pleasant walks in the hills of the Sorrento peninsula.

Back down on the coast, the first clue that you are entering one of the most beautiful corners of all Italy comes when the busy road from Castellammare begins to climb into a corniche at **Vico Equense**, a pretty village that is fast becoming a small resort to absorb some of the overflow from Sorrento. There is a nice beach under the cliffs at the back of the town.

Sorrento

Sorrento began its career as a resort in the early 19th century, when Naples began to grow too piquant for English tastes. The English, especially, have never forsaken it. Sorrento's secret is a certain perfect cosiness, comfortable like old shoes or a favourite cardigan. Visitors get the reassuring sense that nothing distressing is going to happen to them and, sure enough, nothing ever does. It helps that Sorrento is a lovely, civilized old town. Not many resorts can trace their ancestry back to the Etruscans or claim a native son like the poet Torquato Tasso. Today, Sorrento is more proud of a songwriter named De Curtio, whose *Come Back to Sorrento,* according to a local brochure, ranks with *O Sole Mio* as one of the 'two most familiar songs in the world'. There's a bust of De Curtio in front of the Circumvesuviana station.

Sorrento doesn't flagrantly chase after your money, unlike many other places in Italy, and it lacks the high-density garishness of, say, Rimini. The town's one big drawback is its lack of a decent beach – though at some of the fancier hotels you can take a lift down to the sea. There are also several piers (called *stabilimenti*), which are kitted out with loungers and beach umbrellas for hire.

Tourist Information

Vico Equense: Via San Ciro 16, **t** 081 801 5752, *www.vicoturismo.it*.
Sorrento: Via L. de Maio 35, **t** 081 807 4033, **f** 081 877 3397, *www.sorrentotourism.it*. *Open 8.45–7, closed Sun and hols.*
Massa Lubrense: Viale Filangieri 11, **t** 081 808 9856.

Where to Stay

Vico Equense ✉ 80069

★★★★**Capo La Gala**, Località Scrajo, **t/f** 081 801 5758, *www.capolagala.com* (*very expensive*). A beautiful modern resort hotel at nearby Scrajo, where there are sulphur springs. Rooms have terraces overlooking the beach and there's a pool. *Closed Nov–Mar.*

Sorrento ✉ 80067

There are some 90 hotels in Sorrento, making it a good base for exploring Campania. The town isn't the status resort it once was, but rates are still high. Many up-market places, however, are good value: converted villas by the sea are almost indecently elegant.

Luxury

★★★★★**Excelsior Vittoria**, Piazza Tasso 34, **t** 081 807 1044, **f** 081 877 1206, *www.exvitt.it*. Set in its own park, complete with orange and olive groves, overlooking the sea, this is the place if you want a taste of the Grand Tour. Byron, Wagner, Dumas, Nietzsche, Oscar Wilde, Marilyn Monroe, Sophia Loren and Pavarotti have all stopped by.

★★★★**Imperial Tramontano**, Via V. Veneto 1, **t** 081 878 2588, **f** 081 807 2344, *www.tramontano.com*. With incredible tropical gardens, this place has long been favoured by British travellers, from Byron and Shelley on. Private beach and a pool. *Closed Jan–Mar.*

Very Expensive

★★★★**Bellevue-Syrene**, Piazza della Vittoria 5, **t** 081 878 1024, **f** 081 878 3963, *www.bellevue.it*. A villa-hotel with lush gardens, beautifully restored rooms and a lift to the beach. The clifftop colonnade is a lovely spot for a drink even if you're not staying – ignore the pompous staff. The building was originally a Roman villa, rebuilt in the 18th century. *Wheelchair accessible.*

★★★★**Ambasciatori**, Via Califano 18, **t** 081 878 2025, **f** 081 807 1021, *www.manniellohotels.it*. One of the Manniello family's good-value quality hotels. It may be a bit removed from the centre, but the palatial interior, pool, lush gardens and sea-bathing platform more than compensate. *Closed Jan–Mar.*

★★★★**Royal**, Via Correale 42, **t** 081 807 3434, **f** 081 877 2905, *www.manniellohotels.it*. Also owned by the Manniellos, this beautifully remodelled hotel has a pool and beach access and is perched atop the cliffs above the Riviera Massa. Most rooms have good balconies, so opt for the sea view. *Closed Nov–April. Wheelchair accessible.*

★★★★**President**, Via Colle Parise, **t** 081 878 2262, **f** 081 878 5411, *www.acampora.it*. A good option if you have a car, set in its own park with lovely views and good-sized pool. Take the coast road past the Marina Grande, turning left up the SS145.

Expensive

★★**La Tonnarella**, Via Capo 31, **t** 081 878 1153, **f** 081 878 2169, *www.latonnarella.com*. An attractive villa with great views, a private beach and a good restaurant to boot. It's best to reserve early. *Closed Jan–Feb.*

★★★**Minerva**, Via Capo 30, **t** 081 878 1011, **f** 081 878 1949, *www.acampora.it*. East out of town, this hotel has 50 nice rooms, some with stunning sea views. *Closed Nov–Mar.*

Moderate

★★**Loreley et Londres**, Via Califano 2, **t** 081 807 3187, **f** 081 532 9001. The friendly staff make up for dreary décor, while the terrace has the most romantic sunsets in town. In summer, take half board if you want a room with a view and away from the noisy road. There is a sea-bathing platform for guests. *Closed mid-Nov–mid-Mar. Wheelchair accessible.*

★**City**, Corso d'Italia 221, **t/f** 081 877 2210. Simple hotel in the centre. *Closed mid-Nov–mid-Dec.*

★**Nice**, Corso Italia 257, **t** 081 807 2530, **f** 081 878 3086, *hotelnice@hotmail.com*. A good find, on the main road just in front of the Circumvesuviana station. Rooms are clean and pleasant.

Cheap

Ostello delle Sirene, Via degli Aranci 160, **t** 081 807 2925, *www.hostel.it*. A budget hostel near the station; follow the signs.

Massa Lubrense ✉ 80061

Il Giardino di Vigliano, Via Vigliano 3, Località Villazzano, **t** 081 533 9823, *www.massa lubrense.it/vigliano.htm* (*cheap*). If you have a car, you can stay up on the hill at this *azienda agrituristica*, in a 17th-century building complete with Saracen tower – look out for the sign on the wall that marks the turn-off from the main road. The view of Capri from the roof terrace is breathtaking. Also half board and apartment rental.

Eating Out

Sorrento

Caruso, Piazza Tasso, **t** 081 807 3156 (*very expensive*). A vast, inventive menu comes with attentive service and an extensive wine list. Leave room for the sumptuous desserts. The restaurant has a small museum about opera singer Enrico Caruso. Booking essential.

O'Parrucchiano, Corso Italia 71, **t** 081 878 1321, *www.parrucchiano.it* (*very expensive*). This place claims to have invented *cannelloni*, back in 1870.

La Lanterna, Via S. Cesareo 23-25, **t** 081 878 1355 (*expensive*). Just off Piazza Tasso in the middle of town, with outside tables in the quieter alley area, pink stucco walls and a garden. Friendly and efficient service and impeccable *risotto alla pescatora*. *Closed Jan–Feb, Wed*.

Da Gigino, Via degli Archi 15, **t** 081 878 1927 (*moderate*). A bustling *trattoria* serving decent pizza and pasta alongside more sophisticated dishes such as *salmone e pesce spada affumicato con rucola* (smoked salmon and swordfish with rocket). *Closed Feb, Tues except Aug*.

Trattoria da Emilia, Via Marina Grande 62, **t** 081 807 2720 (*moderate*). This bustling *trattoria* has a terrace overlooking the sea and a fine menu based on local ingredients and recipes. Try the pasta and beans with mussels. *Closed Tues except high season*.

Panetteria-Pizzeria Franco, Corso Italia 265, **t** 081 877 2066 (*cheap*). Sit at one of the long wooden tables beneath the hanging hams to see your pizza prepared in front of you.

Taverna Artis Domus, Via San Nicola 56, **t** 081 877 2073 (*cheap*). In the basement of an old Roman villa, this is a lively place for a snack or drink. Live music every night in Summer.

Bars and Ice Cream

Holiday Inn Pub, Via P. R. Giuliani 65. Typical of the town's many English-style pubs, with a small selection of light dinners, a few English beers and music.

Fauno Bar, Piazza Tasso 13. A place to see and be seen. In the evening, sit back and watch people gather in the piazza.

Bar Rita, Corso Italia 219/A. This cosy little bar serves excellent pies, pastries and *panini*.

Davide, Via P. R. Giuliani 41. In a land where ice cream is culture, you can hardly go wrong, but this huge *gelateria* is truly exceptional. At least 50 flavours are on offer.

Nerano

Maria Grazia, Via Marina del Cantone 65, **t** 081 808 1011 (*expensive*). Maria is renowned for her melt-in-the-mouth *spaghetti con le zucchine*. *Closed Dec–Jan*.

Da Pappone, Via Marina del Cantone 23, **t** 081 808 1209 (*moderate*). This elegant restaurant specializes in fish fresh out of the sea. There are 16 guest rooms. *Closed Tues*.

Sant'Agata sui Due Golfi

Don Alfonso, Piazza Sant'Agata, **t** 081 878 0026, **f** 081 533 0226, *www.donalfonso.com* (*very expensive*). A fantastic Michelin three-starred restaurant, 9km outside Sorrento, reckoned by food critics to be the best in southern Italy. You can also stay in one of their three beautiful apartments. *Closed Mon, Thurs except high season, Jan–Feb*.

Massa Lubrense

Apreda Francesco, Via Tasso 6, **t** 081 878 2351. A delicatessen with a mouthwatering range of breads, hams, salami and cheeses, including the best Sorrentine *treccia*.

Sorrento sits on a long cliff overlooking the bay. A narrow ravine cuts the town in half. On one side is a suburban area of quiet, mostly expensive hotels, around Via Correale. On the other is the Old Town, still preserving its grid of narrow Roman streets. Sorrento was never a large town, though in the Middle Ages, it was for a while an important trading post. The Sorrentini still recall with pride that their fleet once defeated Amalfi's fleet (even though it was in 897). Today, the population is only 15,000, although this figure is inflated in the summer by the scores of coaches and cruise ships disgorging British and American passengers.

There isn't much of artistic or historical interest in Sorrento. Tiny **Via San Cesareo** is the heart of the Old Town – the sizeable community of British ex-pats call it 'The Drain'. It's the focus of the town's *passeggiata*, which goes on until late at night.

Half the shop windows here seem to be displaying *intarsia* – fine pictures in inlaid woods, a local craft for centuries. Look out for the laboratories, open to the street, producing perfume and *limoncello*, the distinctive lemon liqueur made from the lemons grown throughout the peninsula. The **Sedile Dominova**, built in 1349, was where the local nobility discussed the city's matters. Today, it is a working men's club where old men play cards under its 16th-century *trompe l'œil* cupola.

The church of **San Francesco** stands in the piazza of the same name, next to a small 14th-century arched cloister with arabesques. In summer, there are art exhibitions (*free*) and impromptu concerts here. The nearby public gardens offers the classic Sorrentine view along the clifftops, with the sea and Vesuvius in the distance. You can get down to the *stabilimenti* by taking the lift from here.

If you are stuck for something to do on a rainy day, visit the **Correale Museum**, a grab bag of assorted Neapolitan bric-a-brac (*Via Correale; **t** 081 878 1846; open Wed–Mon 9–2, closed Tues and hols; adm*). Another interesting museum is the **Museo-Bottega della Tarsialignea** (*Woodcarving Museum Workshop; Via San Nicola; **t** 081 877 1942; open Mon–Sat 10–1*).

Around Sorrento

As far as the mountains will allow, the area surrounding Sorrento is one of the great garden spots of Campania – a lush little plain full of vines and lemon groves tucked beneath a backdrop of soaring hills. From the town, you can follow the winding path to the west to the **Bagni Regina Giovanna**, a natural triangular seapool where you can see the scanty ruins of the Roman **Villa di Pollio**.

You can also take the short trip west to **Massa Lubrense**, an uncrowded fishing village with fine views stretching as far as the tip of the peninsula and the rugged outline of Capri beyond. These days, Massa Lubrense absorbs some of Sorrento's tourist overflow: although it will probably soon follow the fate of many of the Bay of Naples' erstwhile fishing villages and become a fully fledged resort in its own right, for now it retains a refreshingly simple charm.

There are some lovely walks from Massa and the nearby village of **Termini**, exploring the rugged tip of the peninsula with stupendous views of Capri, the Bay of Naples and the Amalfi coast: ask the Massa Lubrense tourist office for a walking map. In the old days, a permanent watch was kept on **Campanella Point** at the tip of the bay. It takes its name from the big bell that was hung here and rung to warn the towns around the bay when pirates were sighted. The bell used to hang in the ruined tower that stands on the point. Known as the Torre Minerva, it stands on the site of a Roman temple to the goddess of that name.

The waters around the point, including the uninhabited islands of Vetara and Vervece, have been made into a marine reserve to protect it from overfishing. Local diving clubs organize dive trips to the reserve – ask at the tourist office in Massa Lubrense or Sorrento for more information.

The Islands of the Bay of Naples

09

The Islands of the Bay of Naples

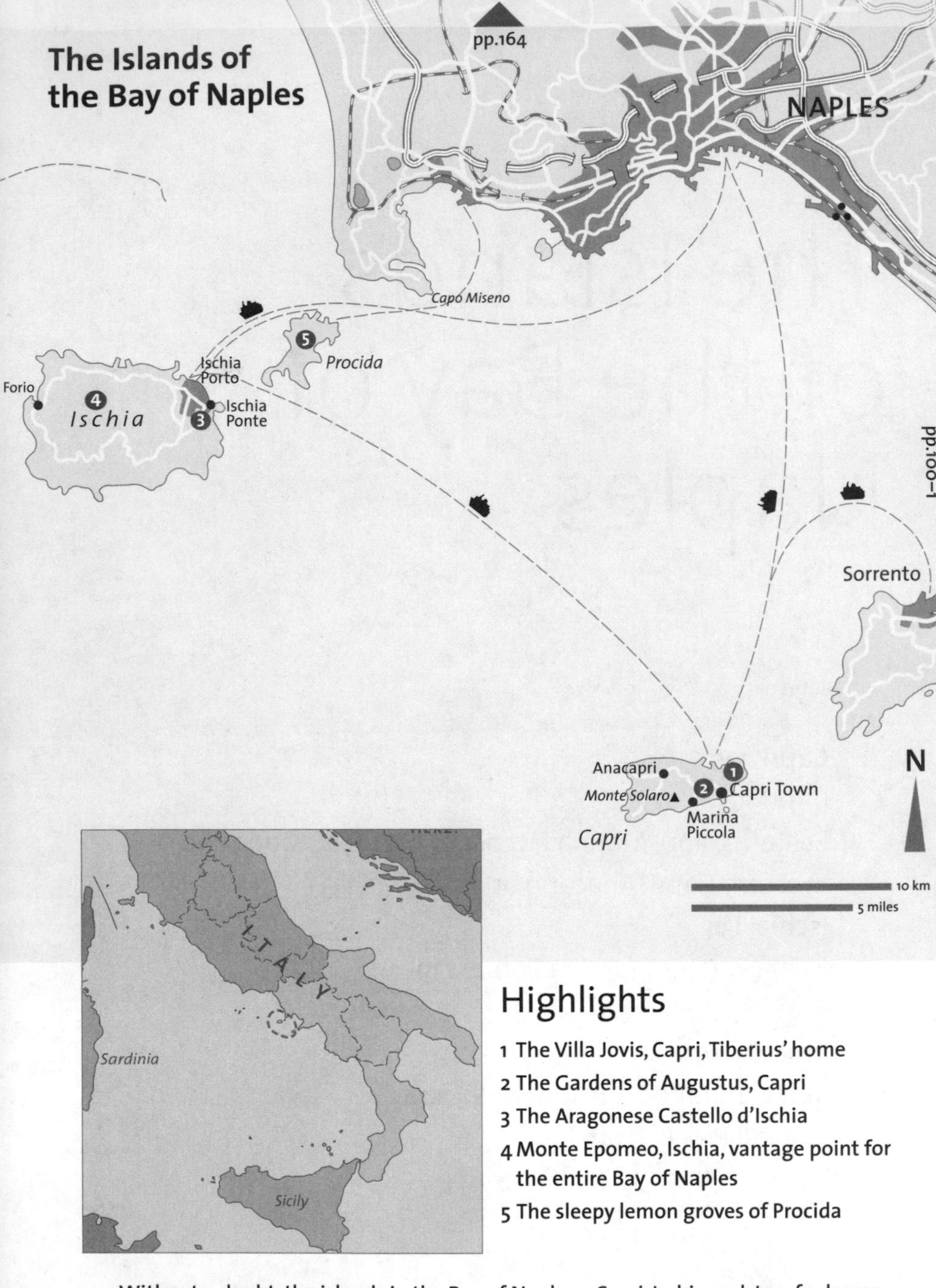

Highlights

1 The Villa Jovis, Capri, Tiberius' home
2 The Gardens of Augustus, Capri
3 The Aragonese Castello d'Ischia
4 Monte Epomeo, Ischia, vantage point for the entire Bay of Naples
5 The sleepy lemon groves of Procida

Without a doubt, the islands in the Bay of Naples – Capri, Ischia and, to a far lesser extent, Procida – are the holiday queens of the Italian islands. Every schoolchild has heard of Capri, the notorious playground of Emperor Tiberius and Norman Douglas' 'gentlemanly freaks'.

Getting to the Islands

In summer, there are frequent ferries and hydrofoils from Naples to the islands, from Sorrento to Capri and Pozzuoli to Procida and Ischia. In Naples they leave from Molo Beverello or Mergellina dock in Chiaia.

From Molo Beverello, Naples

Alilauro, t 081 761 1004, *www.alilauro.it*, hydrofoil to Ischia Forio and Ischia Porto (daily, every hour).

Caremar, t 199 123 199, *www.caremar.it*, runs 4 hydrofoils and 6 ferries daily to Capri, and 6 hydrofoils and 8 ferries to Ischia via Procida.

Linea Jet, t 081 550 763, *www.navlib.it*, ferries to Capri (daily about every hour).

Medmar, t 081 551 3352, *www.lineelauro.it*, ferries to Ischia (6 daily; every 90mins).

From Mergellina, Naples

Alilauro, *see Molo Beverello*.

SNAV, t 081 761 2348, hydrofoil to Capri (5 daily), Ischia (6 daily) and Procida (4 daily).

From Sorrento

Linee Marittime Partenopee, t 081 807 1812, ferries (20mins; 5 daily) and hydrofoils (10mins; 16 daily) to Capri.

Caremar, t 081 807 3077, f 081 807 2479, *www.caremar.it*, fast ferry service to Capri (10mins; 4 daily).

From Salerno, Amalfi, Positano

A ferry service called the *Faraglione* leaves Salerno's Molo Manfredi (situated towards the western end of town) at 7.30am each day, calling at Amalfi and Positano on the way to Capri.

Ischia, 50 years ago, was the favourite island of jet-setters jaded by Capri. Renowned in ancient times for its mud baths, it has become a home-from-home for the German bourgeoisie. If anyone tries to tell you it's still 'unspoiled', take this into consideration: Ischia is Italy's biggest buyer of spaghetti-flavoured ice cream.

Procida, on the other hand, has hardly been developed at all, though not through any lack of charm. For many Italians, the very name of the island, for years the home of a high security prison, conjures up the same associations that Alcatraz does for Americans – which has managed to keep the developers away until very recently.

Ischia and Procida are a part of the enormous submerged volcano of Campano, which stretches from Ventotene in the Pontine Islands down to Stromboli and the Aeolian Islands. In not too ancient times, the two islands were connected to each other and, if the Greek geographer Strabo is to be believed, also to the Phlegraean Fields on the mainland.

Strabo records how, during an eruption of the now dormant volcano Epomeo on Ischia, an earthquake split Ischia–Procida from the mainland, then, in another upheaval, jolted the once-united island in twain. In this same geological cataclysm, Capri broke off from the Sorrentine peninsula, a blow that shattered its coasts to form the island's famous cliffs.

Capri

Capri is pure enchantment, and can lay fair claim to being the most beautiful island in the Mediterranean, a delicious garden of Eden with over 800 species of flowers and plants cascading over a sheer chunk of limestone.

An Eden, but one where the angels have definitely let down their guard. Unlike Ischia and other, more recent, tourist haunts, Capri has the relaxed air of having seen it all.

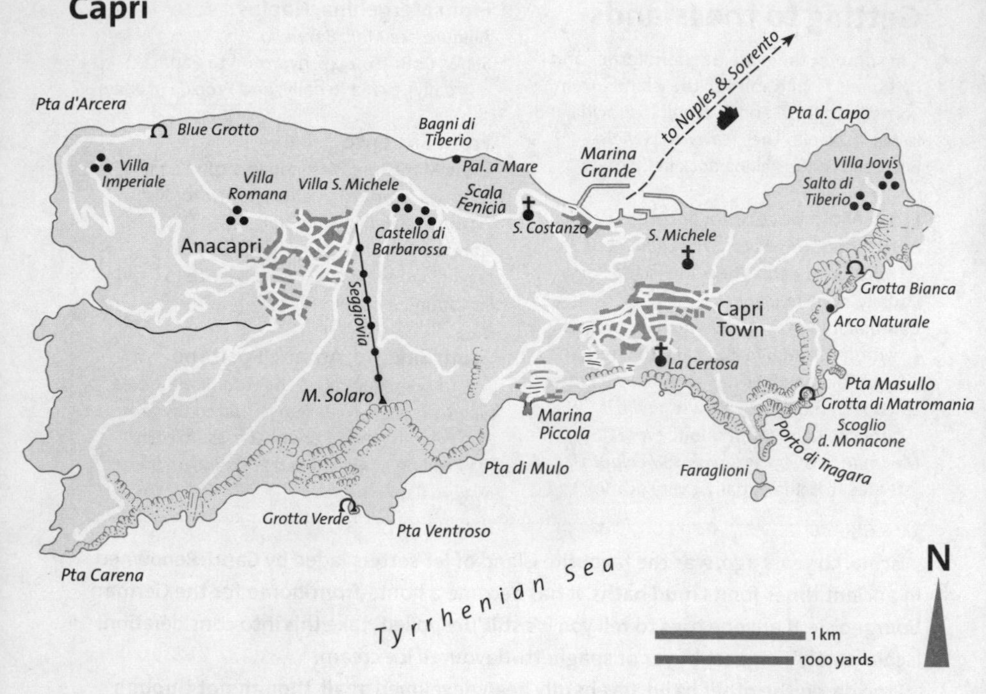

No room remains for property speculators; everything has been built and planted. The tourists come and go every day, almost invisible to the Capriots and other residents who have learned to turn a blind eye to them, knowing the space they occupy will be filled the next day by other anonymous camera-clutching tourists.

Between June and September, you begin to understand why the word 'trash' is inscribed on the bins in 30 different languages. However, if you don't mind all the trendy shops being closed, try coming in November or February when you may be lucky enough to enjoy a few brilliant days between the rains and feel like Adam or Eve (well, almost). It's worth the risk of a soaking or two.

There are various schools of thought on the etymology of the island's name. The belief that it came from the Latin word for goat (*capra*) is now out of favour; those who think it derived from the Greek *kapros* (boar) have fossils to back them up. Yet another group maintains that it comes from an ancient Etruscan word meaning 'rocky' (*capr–*), similar to Caprera (an island off Sardinia), Cabrera (off Majorca) and Caprara in the Tremiti Islands, to name just a few. Make sure you pronounce it CAPri, not CapRI like the Ford.

Capri is divided into two distinct halves by the rocky escarpment that runs north to south across the middle of the island. Until as recently as the 1870s, the two halves – the lower, eastern side around Capri town below the escarpment and the higher, western side around Anacapri – had little contact with one another, linked only by a single stairway, the Scala Fenicia.

History

In the Quaternary period, when Capri broke away from the Sorrentine peninsula, it took elephants and tigers with it. The first humans appeared in the Palaeolithic era. A strong tradition associates the island with the sirens of the Odyssey and with the mysterious Teleboeans from the Greek island of Kephalonia. Neolithic ceramicware decorated with red bands, first found here, has been designated the 'Capri style'.

Little is known of Capri at the time when Augustus arrived, except that it was still very Greek and that a dying ilex suddenly revived and sprouted new leaves. The emperor thought this was a good portent and traded Ischia to Naples for Capri to make the island one of his retreats. Life must have been good on Capri; at one point, Augustus called it Apragopolis (or 'Lubberland', as Robert Graves translates Suetonius' 'land of layabouts'). Augustus was succeeded by his stepson Tiberius, whose exploits, as reported by the same Suetonius, made Capri synonymous with decadence. The Roman writer turned the island into a dirty old man's dream come true, with Tiberius hurling his victims off the cliffs to add a touch of reality (*see* p.131). Tabloid journalism or not, his images of sexual acrobats dressing up as nymphs and frolicking in Tiberius' gardens, along with Sirens on the seashore, are an intrinsic part of the Capri myth. Under Tiberius, Capri was the capital of Rome between AD 27 and 37. The cliffs made it into a natural citadel from where the ageing emperor conducted (or neglected) the affairs of state as he pleased and nurtured the future Emperor Caligula.

After the death of Tiberius, Capri lost its lustre and is mentioned only occasionally as a place of exile. Then the Benedictine friars arrived and built chapels on the island, and it suffered the usual ravages of Saracens and pirates. In 1371 a Carthusian monastery (La Certosa) was founded on Capri on land granted by the Angevins. A plague in 1656 left the island all but abandoned; only the Carthusians stayed behind, safe inside the walls of the Certosa, picking up the titles to land that had no owners and becoming quite wealthy (and unpopular) in the process.

During the Napoleonic Wars, the English occupied Capri. Hudson Lowe, commander of the English garrison, fortified the island until it became 'a little Gibraltar' but still managed to lose it to the French in 1808 – a 'discreditable Lowe business' according to Norman Douglas, longtime resident and writer on things Capricious.

The last chapter of the island's history began with the 'discovery' of the Blue Grotto by a German artist called Kopisch in 1826; he swam into it 'by accident'. Perhaps it was just a coincidence that Kopisch's discovery followed a landslide that covered the entrance of another, even lovelier cave. Anyway, the magic of the name, Blue Grotto of Capri, proved irresistible and the Capriots converted their fishing boats into excursion boats to take tourists to the cave while farmers sold their land and built hotels.

Capri Town

The charming white town of Capri is daily worn down by the tread of thousands of her less ectoplasmic followers. The **megalithic walls** supporting some of the houses have seen at least 3,000 years of similar comings and goings, although certainly on a

Getting Around

From Marina Grande, you can ascend to Capri or Anacapri by one of the frequent **buses**, or take the **funicular** up to Capri Town (*daily, 6.30am–12.30am, every 15mins; Oct–April until 9pm*), although it gets crowded.

Regular **buses** run from Capri Town to Anacapri, Marina Piccola and Damecuta, and from Anacapri to Faro, the Blue Grotto, Marina Grande and Marina Piccola.

There's a **chairlift** from Anacapri to Monte Solaro (*12mins; summer 9.30–sunset; Nov–Feb 10.30–3; closed Tues*). Tours of the island by **motor launch** leave from Marina Grande (*June–Sept; first tour 9am*).

Finally, you can **walk** to most places. The trails across the island are major attractions, but pack a mac out of season, just in case.

Tourist Information

Capri Town: Piazza Umberto 1, 80073, **t** 081 837 0686, *infocapri@libero.it. Open April–Oct daily 8.30–8.30.*

Marina Grande: at Banchina del Porto, **t** 081 837 0634. *Open Nov–Mar 9–1 and 3.30–6.45.* They can help find accommodation.

Anacapri: Via G. Orlandi 59/a, 80071, **t** 089 837 1524, *touristoffice@capri.it. Open Mar–Nov 9–1 and 3.30–6.45, closed Dec–Feb.*

Where to Stay

Capri ✉ 80073

Hotel prices on Capri are well above average, and rooms for the summer months are often booked months in advance. Prices are often halved out of season.

Luxury

*****__Grand Hotel Quisisana__, Via Camerelle 2, **t** 081 837 0788, **f** 081 837 6080, *www.quisi.com*. If money is no object, this is the place to stay in Capri Town. It's set in its own grounds and equipped with pool, gym, tennis courts and just about everything else you could want. The building was originally a sanatorium built by a Scot, George Clark. With acres of white tiled floors, plush white sofas and lamps borne by carved ebony figures, it is not merely the luxury but the sheer size that impresses. *Closed Nov–Mar.*

*****__La Scalinatella__, Via Tragara 8, **t** 081 837 0633, **f** 081 837 8291, *www.scalinatella.com*. A jewel of a hotel with stunning views, 31 beautifully decorated rooms, a pool and a good restaurant, but no large public spaces. The hotel doesn't take tour groups.

****__Hotel Punta Tragara__, Via Tragara 57, **t** 081 837 0844, **f** 081 837 7790, *www.hoteltragara.com*. This deluxe resort hotel at Punta Tragara has pool, gym, restaurants and more in a building designed by Le Corbusier. The architect's distinctive modern style and the predominance of strong reds, oranges and dark wood fittings come at a price, but the views are spectacular. The hotel also boasts a lovely veranda restaurant and a nightclub in the rocks. *Closed Nov–Mar.*

****__Villa Brunella__, Via Tragara 24a, **t** 081 837 0122, **f** 081 837 0430, *www.villabrunella.com*. Further up on the way to the panoramic Punta Tragara, this is a pretty hotel with rooms on terraces that overlook Monte Solaro. There is a good restaurant and pool for lazing away hot afternoons. The emphasis is on villa-style accommodation and privacy, suiting those who are looking for a retreat. *Closed Nov–Mar.*

***__Floridiana__, Via Campo di Teste 16, **t** 081 837 0166, **f** 081 837 0434, *www.lafloridiana-capri.com*. Close to the Certosa of San Giacomo and the Gardens of Augustus, with fine sea panoramas. The management are upgrading many of its rooms in pursuit of

much smaller scale than you'll find here nowadays in August. Capri's architecture complements the island's natural beauty – much of what is typical and 'homemade' in Mediterranean building can be seen here in the older quarters: the moulded arches and domes; the narrow streets and stairways crossed by buttresses supporting the buildings; the ubiquitous whitewash; the play of light and shadow, another star from the tourist board. Single travellers merely pay half the cost of a double room. *Closed Nov–Mar.*

Very Expensive

★★★★**La Palma**, Via Vittorio Emmanuele 39, **t** 081 837 0133, **f** 081 837 6966, *www.lapalma-capri.com*. This is good value by Capri standards. Just above the Quisisana in Capri Town, it is set in its own gardens, with lovely majolica-tiled floors in the rooms and a pleasant airy feel. The staff are charming and the atmosphere more comfortable than at more expensive hotels. Established as a hotel in 1822, it's older than the Quisisana. *Closed Nov–Easter.*

Expensive

★★**Villa Krupp**, Viale Matteotti 12, **t** 081 837 0362, **f** 081 837 6489. This is one of the loveliest and most historic of the lower-priced hotels in Capri. Situated above the path up to the Gardens of Augustus, the hotel has enviable views, antique furniture and a relaxed and welcoming ambience where one can sit and compose letters all day. Trotsky stayed here and even left a samovar. Book well ahead to secure a room. *Closed Nov–Feb.*

★**Stella Maris**, Via Roma 27, **t** 081 837 0452, **f** 081 837 8662, *albergostellamaris@libero.it*. Clean, well run and centrally located close to the bus station, this is a cosy family-run affair. They have been here for generations and are proud of their hospitality, so you will not want for towels and other personal touches. Most rooms look down to the Marina Grande below and across to distant Ischia.

★**La Tosca**, Via D. Birago 5, **t/f** 081 837 0989, *www.latoscahotel.com*. Still in Capri Town, but overlooking the opposite coast, this hotel was refurbished in 2002, with clean tiled rooms and high ceilings. Ask for a room with a view. *Closed Nov–Mar.*

Eating Out

Capri Town

Very Expensive

I Faraglioni, Via Camerelle 75, **t** 081 837 0320. Delectable house specialities like *crêpes al formaggio* (thin pancakes filled with cheese) and *risotto ai frutti di mare*, with a fine wine list and a lobster hatchery.

La Capannina, Via delle Botteghe 12–14, **t** 081 837 0732, *www.capannina-capri.com*. Set in a secluded garden in Capri Town, this has long been Capri's best restaurant, with delicately prepared shellfish, pasta, fish and good desserts. *Closed Wed, Nov–Mar.*

Expensive

Da Paolino, Via Palazzo a Mare 11, **t** 081 837 6102. Eat in an arbour of lemon trees, tasting dishes mainly inspired by the fruit, between Capri Town and Marina Grande. *Eves only, closed Feb–Easter.*

Moderate

Da Gemma, Via Madre Serafina 6, **t** 081 837 0461, **f** 081 837 8947, *www.dagemma.com*. An island institution up the stairs past the cathedral and down the tunnel to the right, this welcoming *trattoria* has walls decked with brass pans and ceramic plates, and superb local dishes including a fine *risotto alla pescatora*. It also serves good pizza. *Closed Mon except Aug, mid-Jan to end of Feb.*

Anacapri

Da Gelsomina alla Migliara, Via La Migliara 72, **t** 081 837 1499 (*expensive*). About a half-hour's walk from the Piazzetta, this *trattoria* offers homemade wine to go with its homecooked island specialities, including mushrooms from Monte Solaro. The risotto here is a real treat. *Closed Tues except high season, Jan.*

and sudden little squares, just large enough for a few children to improvise a game of football. Most of the island's hotels are scattered throughout the town, generally very tasteful and surrounded by gardens. The supreme example is the famous Quisisana, a hotel whose register over the years reads like a *Who's Who* of the famous and pampered.

If you go up to Capri by *funicolare*, you'll surface next to the much-photographed **cathedral**, with its joyful campanile and clock. Built in the 17th century in the local Baroque style, the cathedral has a charming buttressed roof. The little square in the church's shadow is Piazza Umberto, commonly known as **La Piazzetta**. Its many outdoor cafés have been frequented by such a variety of past eccentrics, dilettantes and celebrities that each chair should have a historical plaque on it (but beware – the drinks are extraordinarily expensive!). On the other side of the piazza is a sheer drop down to Marina Grande.

In the Piazza Cerio next to the cathedral, the **Centro Caprense Ignazio Cerio** (***t*** *081 837 6681; open Fri–Sat and Tues–Wed 10–1, Thurs 3–7, closed Sun, Mon and hols; adm*) contains archaeological finds and fossils from Capri. Ignazio Cerio was not the first person on the island to take an interest in such things. Emperor Augustus founded a museum for the 'weapons of ancient heroes' and a collection of what he called his old 'Big Bones', then popularly believed to be the remains of monsters.

From the Piazza Umberto, take the Via Roma for the post office and buses to Anacapri. For exclusive boutiques, head towards the Via Vittorio Emmanuele to Via Camarelle and Via Tragara. Or you can take Via Vittorio Emmanuele (which becomes Via F. Serena, then Via Matteotti) to **La Certosa** (***t*** *081 837 6218; open Tues–Sun 9–2,*), the Carthusian charterhouse founded in 1371 by Giacomo Arcucci, member of a famous Capri family, and suppressed in 1808. Built over one of Tiberius' villas and topped by a 17th-century Baroque tower, the golden-hued church and cloisters are charming. It also contains some mediocre paintings from the 17th to 19th centuries.

A few minutes away from La Certosa are the **Gardens of Augustus**, founded by Caesar himself. A wide variety of trees and plants grow on the fertile terraces and belvederes overlooking one of the most striking views in the world.

On the other side of town the **church of Monte San Michele**, built in the 14th century, is a fine example of local architecture.

Eastern Capri: Marina Piccola to Marina Grande

From Capri Town, the narrow Via Krupp (built by the German arms manufacturer of that name, who spent his leisure hours studying lamprey larvae off the Salto di Tiberio) takes you down the cliffs in 100 hairpin turns to the **Marina Piccola**, the charming little port with most of Capri's bathing establishments: Da Maria, La Canzone del Mare, Le Sirene and Internazionale (all but the last connected to restaurants). On one side are the ruins of a **Saracen tower**. On the other is the **Scoglio delle Sirene** (Sirens' Rock); if you read the books of Norman Douglas and Edwin Cerio, son of Ignazio Cerio the archaeologist, they will convince you that this really was the home of the Sirens. There is a bus, fortunately, that makes the steep climb back up the cliffs to Capri Town.

East of Marina Piccola, back past the Certosa, the **Faraglioni** are three enormous limestone pinnacles that tower straight up in the ever blue-green sea. These rocks are home to the rare blue lizard (*Lacerta caerulea Faraglionensis*) and a rare species of

The Old Goat of Capri

London has its tabloids and ancient Rome had Gaius Suetonius Tranquillus, born *c.* AD 60. All of Suetonius' other books are lost, including such titles as the *Lives of Famous Whores* and the *Physical Defects of Mankind*, but enough copies of his scandalmongering classic, *The Twelve Caesars*, were written out to ensure that the whole juicy text has survived. Modern historians have always argued over Suetonius' reliability, but his stories have been confirmed by enough other sources to suggest that he couldn't have exaggerated that much. And, as chief secretary to Emperor Trajan, Suetonius had full access to the imperial archives.

One of the most entertaining chapters deals with the man who put Capri on the map – the Emperor Tiberius, adopted son of Augustus. A good general and, at first, a capable ruler, Tiberius had an unusual habit of declining honours and titles. Suetonius hints that the emperor knew – or suspected – that he would eventually go a bit mad and wanted no pointless flattery left behind for his enemies to mock later. Mad or not, Tiberius did have a mania for privacy. He left Rome in AD 26 for Capri, which he admired for its beauty and for the fact that it had only one landing port. The entire island became his pleasure garden, and while imperial decrees went out prohibiting 'promiscuous kissing' and ordering a clampdown on loose women, the emperor himself was whooping it up. According to Suetonius:

> *Bevies of young girls and men, whom he had collected from all over the empire as adepts in unnatural practices, and known as* spintriae, *would perform before him in groups of three, to excite his waning passions. A number of small rooms were furnished with the most indecent pictures and statuary imaginable, also certain erotic manuals from Elephantis in Egypt; the inmates of the establishment would know from these exactly what was expected of them.*

Once aroused, apparently, the imperial pervert would bore in on anything that caught his fancy, and the smaller the better. Suetonius pictures him rushing through a religious sacrifice to get at the little boy who was carrying the incense casket, and training other little boys, his 'minnows', to 'chase him while he went swimming and get between his legs to lick and nibble him... such a filthy old man he had become!' Even Suetonius is shocked. Distracted by such pleasures, Tiberius let the empire go to pot: the Persians invaded from the east, while Germanic bands roamed unchecked in Gaul. The generals and the civil service managed to see that no serious harm was done, but they could not stop the ageing Tiberius, in his island isolation, from turning into a murderous paranoid, torturing and killing anyone who opposed him (or seemed to). Suetonius names all the names and tells all the tales; nobody was ever better at capturing the essential vileness of imperial Rome.

One of the stories related by Suetonius about Tiberius' time on Capri is that of a fisherman who decided to surprise the emperor, bringing him a gift of an enormous mullet. Tiberius was so scared that he ordered his guards to rub the poor man's face raw with it. In agony, the fisherman shrieked, 'Thank Heavens I didn't bring that huge crab I caught!' Tiberius sent for the crab and had it used the same way.

seagull that supposedly guffaws. From Via Tragara, a stairway descends to the point and the **Porto di Tragara** where, for a price, you can take a swim from the platforms beneath the vertical rocks.

Nearby is the Tragara Terrace, with magnificent views, and the tall, skinny rock called Pizzolungo. Follow the main track along the coast and up the stairway to the **Grotta di Matromania.** This was the centre of the cult of the goddess Cybele (Mater Magna), whose worship was banned in Rome itself. Part of Capri's reputation as an island of orgies may derive from this ancient eastern cult's noisy hypnotic rituals, which would culminate with the self-castration of the priest. Only vestiges remain of the cave's elaborate décor.

From the Grotta di Matromania, a stepped path leads down to yet another famous eroded rock, the **Arco Naturale**, where dark pines – found everywhere on Capri – cling to every tiny ledge. On the way back to town, you'll pass some of the island's vineyards, which produce the rare and famous *Lacrimae Tiberii*.

The **Villa Jovis** (*www.villajovis.it; open 9–one hour before sunset; adm*) on Punta Lo Capo (1,017ft) was the most important of the 12 imperial villas on Capri: from here, Tiberius governed the Roman empire for his last 10 years. Although much has been sacked through the centuries, the extent of the remaining foundations and walls gives a fair idea of the scale on which the imperial pervert lived. The centre of the villa was occupied by vast cisterns for supplying the private baths, scene of so many naughty capers.

Close by, the **Faro** (lighthouse) was believed to have been part of a system for sending messages to the mainland. The great sheer cliff beside the villa, the **Salto di Tiberio**, is always pointed out as the precipice from which the emperor hurled his victims. It had already become a tourist attraction in Suetonius' day. Its view of both the Bay of Salerno and Naples is as spectacular as any, even if it's not altogether what the Neapolitans mean by 'see Naples and die'!

All the ferries and hydrofoils from the mainland call at **Marina Grande** (most pleasure boats anchor in the Marina Piccola on the other side of the island). Here, Capri's dependence on tourism is at its most evident. Marina Grande is little more than a commercialized station platform but it does its best to get you off to your destination as quickly as possible: the *funicolare* (cable railway) will lift you to the town of Capri; buses will wind you up to Anacapri; glorious old bathtub convertible taxis hope to trundle you off to your hotel; boats for the Grotta Azzurra and other excursions around the island bob up and down at their landings. There's even a genuine yellow submarine waiting to take you down for an underwater tour around the island.

In good weather, you can take a sea excursion around the island from Marina Grande. As well as visiting the island's lovely grottoes, the trip provides breathtaking views of the cliffs and Capri's uncanny rock formations.

On the north coast just west of Marina Grande are the so-called **Baths of Tiberius** and the meagre remains of Augustus' sea palace, the **Palazzo a Mare**. You can swim here at the establishment of Bagni di Tiberio. Above here, carved into the escarpment of Anacapri, is the **Scala Fenicia** ('the Phoenician Stair'), in truth Greco-Roman in origin and, until the 19th century, the only way to reach the upper part of the island. Originally 800 in number, the steps have now crumbled and are impassable today. Near here, on the road from Marina Grande to Anacapri, lies **San Costanzo**, the first Christian church on the island. According to legend, Costanzo was a bishop of Constantinople whose body, packed in a barrel, floated to Capri during the Iconoclasm in Greece. A church, which came with a reputation for defending the island from Saracens, was built for him in the 11th century over a Roman villa. It's in the form of a Greek cross with four ancient columns supporting the Byzantine dome.

Western Capri: Anacapri and Around

On top of the green plateau above the escarpment spreads the town of **Anacapri**, once a fierce rival to Capri, each town regarding the other as barbaric and uncouth. The construction of the roads in 1874 has slowly taught them to reconcile their differences. Although it has its share of hotels, Anacapri retains a rustic air, with its many olive trees and surrounding vineyards and its simple style of architecture – rather Moorish in style with cubic, flat-roofed houses. In Anacapri's Piazza San Nicola, the 18th-century **church of San Michele** (*www.sanmichele.org; open May–Sept 9–6; Oct and April 9.30–5, Mar 9.30–4.30, Nov–Dec 10.30–3.30*) contains a magnificent mosaic floor of majolica tiles by the Abruzzese artist Leonardo Chiaiese, based on a design by D. A. Vaccano, depicting Adam and Eve in the Garden of Eden and their expulsion. The **church of Santa Sofia**, nearby on the Piazza Diaz, was built in the Middle Ages and later Baroqued.

From Piazza Vittoria, a chairlift travels to the summit of **Monte Solaro**, the highest point on the island at 1,919ft. The views are stunning. Also from Piazza Vittoria, you can take Via Orlandi to Via Capodimonte and the **Villa San Michele** of Axel Munthe (1857–1949). Munthe, who spent most of his career in Paris, was one of the greatest physicians of his day and a leader in the field of psychiatry. Extremely generous, he donated his services to the victims of plagues, earthquakes and the First World War, and also found time to establish bird sanctuaries on Capri and elsewhere. In 1929 he wrote his best-selling autobiography, *The Story of San Michele*, to which his villa owes most of its fame. One of Munthe's hobbies was collecting stray animals and Roman artefacts; the latter are still on display (*open daily 9–sunset; adm*).

Near here is the ruined 8th–9th-century **Castello di Barbarossa**, named after the Turkish pirate captain who plagued the Mediterranean for so many years. Via Capodimonte continues through the valley to Santa Maria a Cetrella, another white church of local design. From the church, the road goes to the top of Monte Solaro. Another path from Piazza Vittoria (Via Caposcuro to Via Maigliara) skirts Monte Solaro, passing through the vineyards to the Belvedere della Migliara, from where you can see the Faraglioni and the entrance of the **Grotto Verde**. A bus leaves Anacapri every hour in the summer for **Punta Carena** and its lighthouse at the southernmost tip of the island. From the bus, the unusual arched doorways visible on the left belonged to the Torre di Materita. Further on, overlooking the Cala del Tombosiello, is a ruined watchtower. Punta Carena is the most out-of-the-way place for a quiet swim.

Another bus leaves from the piazza in Anacapri for the Blue Grotto (*see* below) and its bathing area, passing the old windmill and the **Villa Imperiale** – another of the summer residences built by Augustus and also known as 'the Damecuta'. Apart from the Villa Jovis, this is the best-preserved villa on Capri and has recently been further excavated (*open 9–one hour before sunset, closed Mon*).

The Blue Grotto (*Grotta Azzurra*)

Capri's most famous tourist sight is well named if nothing else – its shimmering, iridescent blueness is caused by the reflection of light on the water in the morning. Similar caverns are fairly common in the Mediterranean but Capri's is the yardstick by which they are measured.

In summer (*1 June–30 Sept*), boats for the Blue Grotto leave from Marina Grande at 9am, provided the sea is calm. The entrance to the cave is quite low and, if there's any swell on the sea at all, someone is sure to get a nasty knock on the head.

Ischia

Ischia is a remarkably lovely island and one quite able to hold its own with Capri in the glitterati sweepstakes. The sea of vineyards encircling the island's highest peak, volcanic Monte Epomeo (2,601ft), produces excellent wine named after the mountain, and the villages high on its slopes, like Fontana and Buonapane, remain untouched by the international onslaught at the resorts of Casamicciola, Forio, Lacco Ameno and Ischia Porto.

Unlike Capri, Ischia has many long, first-class beaches. On one – Maronti – the island's volcanic origins are more than evident. The hot mineral springs that gush all year round have attracted cure-seekers since Roman times and are still recommended today for people suffering from rheumatism, arthritis, neuralgia and obesity. Because many of the springs are radioactive, a doctor's permission is often required before you take a soak (there are physicians on the island who specialize in prescribing such treatments, and they charge a pretty penny). The hottest spring on the island is Terme Rita at Casamicciola, which belches from the earth at around 180°F. Try the renovated Terme Comunali at the port or the unique baths at Cavascura above Sant'Angelo.

History

Inhabited by 2000 BC, Ischia became an important stop along one of the earliest trade routes in the Mediterranean, from Mycenean Greece to the Etruscans of northern Italy and the mines of Elba. The prevailing currents and winds made it natural for the Greek ships sailing west to circumvent Sicily and land in the Bay of Naples – as did that most famous sailor, Odysseus.

As an island along the sea lane, Ischia was the perfect place to found an outpost to secure the route and trade, and here in 756 BC, Chalcidians and Eretrians from Euboea founded one of the first Greek colonies in western Europe. They called the island Pithekoussai, referring to its abundant pottery clay (pithos). However, when Montagnone

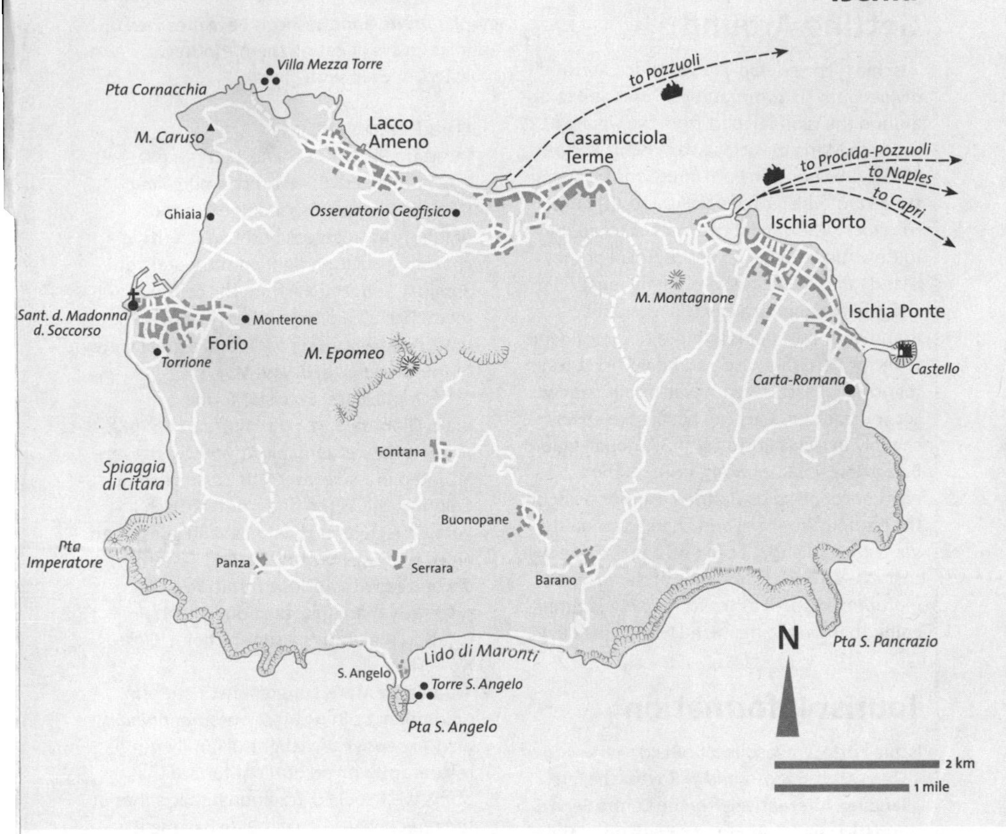

(a now-extinct volcano on Ischia) erupted, the colonists fled to the mainland, establishing themselves at Cumae, where they prospered. Roman writers later refer to the island as Eneria, where Aeneas stopped to repair his ships, or Inarime, a name of unknown origin. The name Ischia is believed to be a corruption of *insula*, or just plain old island. In the year AD 6, Augustus traded the larger, more fertile island of Ischia for Capri, which then belonged to Naples.

For most of its history, Ischia and its famous castle remained attached to that great city; but during one period in the early 16th century, the island outshone Naples as a cultural centre. This was due to one woman, Vittoria Colonna, who lived much of her childhood in the castle of Ischia, after her father's Roman estates were confiscated by Pope Alexander VI. She was betrothed at the age of six to another leading personage of the era, Francesco Ferrante, nephew of Constanza d'Avolas, the duchess who ruled Ischia for 50 years. On 27 December 1509, Vittoria and Francesco were married at the castle of Ischia in the celebrity wedding of the decade, but two years later, Francesco was drawn away by the wars in the north and only once returned to Vittoria and Ischia before he died. Vittoria was an accomplished poet but is best remembered for her spiritual friendship with Michelangelo, who wrote sonnets to her. Learned and gracious,

Getting Around

Ischia is considerably larger than Capri and divided into six communities. **Buses** and **taxis** around the island depart from the square next to Santa Maria di Portosalvo in Ischia Porto. **SEPSA** runs buses in both directions following the SS270, which circles the island. CD buses run clockwise while those marked CS do the route anticlockwise. An entire circuit of the island takes about two and a half hours.

If you're planning a day trip round the island, your best bet is to buy a ticket valid for 12hrs for €4. Otherwise a standard ticket (valid for 90mins) costs €1.20. A weekly bus pass will set you back €15. **Cars** can be hired relatively cheaply. In Ischia Porto, try the **Autonoleggio Balestrieri**, Via Jasolino 27, **t** 081 985 691, *www.autonoleggiobalestrieri.it*, inside a bar on the harbour front. In Forio, there's **Davidauto**, Via G. Mazzella 104, **t** 081 998 043. Car hire will cost €31–46 per day. You may prefer to rent a *motorino* (moped) as traffic here is less threatening than on the mainland (€21–31 per day).

Tourist Information

Ischia Porto, Via Jasolino, **t** 081 507 4211. *Open Mon–Sat 9–2 and 3–8.* Near the ferry landing. Alternatively, try the **Centro Servizi Turistici**, Via Jasolino 72, **t** 081 98 061, a travel agent which is better stocked with leaflets. A good website providing information on Ischia is *www.ischiaonline.it*.

Sports and Activities

There are **beaches** all around Ischia; these are listed in the text for each town.

There are public **tennis courts** (*open 8–11*) at Via C. Colombo, Ischia Porte, **t** 081 985 245.

Where to Stay and Eat

During peak season on Ischia, many of the hotels charge obligatory half board and have a minimum stay of up to a week.

On Ischia, fish features prominently on the menu and has inspired some imaginative local dishes. You will also find meat (especially rabbit: for some reason, Ischia is fairly hopping with rabbits, and the locals have dreamed up endless ways of eating them – in stews, roasted, or even with pasta).

Ischia Porto ✉ 80077

****__Mare Blu__, Via Pontano 44, **t** 081 982 555, **f** 081 982 938, *www.hotelmareblu.it* (*luxury*). You can also indulge in a spot of luxury at this sleek hotel, which sits in a charming position right on the waterfront and just a short walk from the centre of town. There's a private beach just over the road, two swimming pools and a great view of the castle. *Closed Nov–May.*

*****__Grand Hotel Excelsior Terme__, Via E. Gianturco 19, **t** 081 991 522, **f** 081 984 100, *www.excelsiorischia.it* (*very expensive*). Situated in a side street off Corso Vittoria Colonna, this is the finest hotel in Ischia Porto. It is quieter than most and guests can enjoy the fine pool and garden. Tastefully decorated with antique furniture and discreetly managed, the hotel's central location makes this a stylish choice. *Closed Nov–Mar.*

Zi Nannina a Mare, Lungomare Cristoforo Colombo 1, **t** 081 991 350, *www.zinannina.it* (*very expensive*). A delightful family-run restaurant with an outdoor terrace that offers well-cooked, traditional specialities of the region, based on either fish or meat. *Open daily April–Oct, open Fri–Sat Nov–Mar.*

Gennaro, Via Porto 66, **t/f** 081 992 917, *www.ristorantegennaro.it* (*expensive*). Gennaro Rumore is a charismatic and convivial host and probably the best-known restaurateur on the island. He has fed the likes of Tom Cruise, Nicole Kidman and Andrew Lloyd Webber, who gave him a superb write-up in the British press. He serves great giant prawns and delicious Ischian specialities. *Closed Oct–Mar.*

Il Damiano, Lungomare Cristoforo Colombo, **t** 081 983 093 (*expensive*). A well-established restaurant with beautifully cooked seafood and fish dishes – best of all is the *linguine all'aragosta* (with a lobster sauce). *Open eves only. Closed Oct–Easter.*

****__Villa Rosa__, Via G. Gigante 5, **t** 081 991 316, **f** 081 992 425, *www.lavillarosa.it* (*expensive*). An elegant hotel screened from the outside world by a leafy forecourt, where you can escape the heat and bustle of the streets for this cool inner sanctum. It's tastefully furnished with a minimum of fuss and surprisingly well priced for a hotel of such finesse. There's a small pool, garden and thermal treatments. *Closed Nov–Mar.*

★★★**Parco Verde**, Via Mazzella 43, **t** 081 992 282, **f** 081 992 773, *www.parcoverde.it* (*moderate*). Set in an attractive park amidst shady pines, this hotel has full thermal facilities and trained staff – making it a good bet for those who want to try out Ischia's famous thermal treatments for a bit less than at the smarter hotels. If you can do without mud baths, there's a pool in the grounds and it's a short walk to the beach. *Wheelchair accessible.*

★★**Macrì**, Via Jasolino 78a, **t/f** 081 992 603 (*moderate*). This well-run, relaxed hotel two steps from the harbour is named after the painter Antonio Macrì. A bargain that should prove popular with younger, independent travellers. Ask for a room on the first floor.

Da Cocò, Piazzale Aragonese, **t** 081 981 823 (*moderate*). On the seafront just before you reach the causeway, enjoy traditional food in unpretentious surroundings at this relaxed eatery run by Salvatore di Meglio, a retired fisherman who claims to be 'in love with the sea'. It's recommended by the locals, who cram into the noisy and friendly dining area. *Closed Wed except high season, Jan–Feb.*

Ischia Ponte ✉ 80077

★★★**Monastero**, Castello Aragonese 39, **t/f** 081 992 435, *www.castelloaragonese.it* (*expensive*). One of the best value hotels in Ischia Ponte, within the Castello Aragonese itself. There are 14 clean and simple en suite rooms, housed in the cells where monks once slept. It's a bit of a climb, but the view is unforgettable. *Closed Nov–Mar.*

Giardini Eden, Via Nuova Cartaromana 68, **t** 081 985 015 (*expensive*). A lovely restaurant with fantastic sea views and excellent seafood. Dine on the freshest fish, as it's as good as plucked out of the water. If you don't fancy the steep descent from the road, the restaurant offers a free taxi-boat (*eves only*) from the Via Pontana. The restaurant is surrounded by thermal pools, which you can try out at a price. *Closed Oct–April.*

Pirozzi, Via Seminario 51, **t** 081 991 121 (*cheap*). For a pizza or a lighter meal, try this popular and bustling *pizzeria*, where the smell of freshly cooked dough hangs in the air and the doors are flung open to the humming streets. Try the *parmigiana*. *Closed Mon except high season, Dec.*

Ciro e Caterina, Via Luigi Mazzella 80, **t/f** 081 993 122 (*cheap*). A well-priced restaurant not far from the castle. Tables spill out beneath a palm tree and local works of art are on show round a small fountain. Try the rich and tasty *gnocchi* dish and look out for the helpful, though mildly mad, owner. *Closed Thurs except high season.*

Casamicciola ✉ 80074

Monti, Calata S. Antonio 7, **t** 081 994 074, **f** 081 900 630 (*cheap*). Prices tend to be a bit lower in Casamicciola and this hotel has special reductions for families, too. High on the hill behind the main town, it's a lively spot with views, an excellent restaurant, swimming pool and parking. Given its position, a car is essential. Half board is obligatory. *Closed Nov–Dec.*

Lacco Ameno ✉ 80076

★★★★★**Regina Isabella**, Piazza Santa Restituta, **t** 081 994 322, **f** 081 900 190, *www.reginaisabella.it* (*luxury*). Right on the waterfront with a private beach, superb gym and some well-known spas, this is the swankiest hotel on Ischia. Typical of luxury resorts in Italy, it's a grandiose establishment straight out of the pages of *Hello!* magazine, with impeccable service and expansive style rather than warmth or intimacy. *Closed Nov–Mar. Wheelchair accessible.*

★★★★★**San Montano**, Via Monte Vico, **t** 081 994 033, **f** 081 980 242, *www.sanmontano.com* (*very expensive*). This resort hotel offers a pool, tennis courts and many other comforts, in addition to thermal baths. *Closed Nov–Mar. Wheelchair accessible.*

★★**Bristol**, Via Fundera 88, **t** 081 994 566, **f** 081 994 586 (*moderate*). With a small garden and swimming pool, this is your best bet if you can't afford the plusher hotels. The staff are very friendly. *Closed Nov–Mar. Wheelchair accessible.*

Al Delfino, Corso A. Rizzoli 116, **t** 081 900 252 (*expensive*). Try this restaurant for a great meal on the harbour front, especially the *spaghetti alle vongole*. Plates are carried from the kitchen across the street to the clientele in the glass-fronted restaurant. *Closed Wed except high season, Nov–Mar.*

Forio ✉ 80075

★★★★★**Grand Albergo Mezza Torre**, Via Mezza Torre 23, **t** 081 986 111, **f** 081 986 015, *www.mezzatorre.it* (*luxury*). An elegant place off the SS270 towards Lacco Ameno, through a terracotta archway. The building is a 16th-century tower, and its 60 rooms share the grounds of a small castle that belonged to film director Visconti (which, after much controversy, is now under restoration). With a spa, tennis courts and a pool just above the beach, it can't be beaten for old-fashioned luxury and country-house atmosphere. *Closed Nov–Mar.*

★★★★**Punta del Sole**, Piazza Maltese, **t** 081 989 156, **f** 081 998 209, *www.hotelpuntadelsole.it* (*very expensive*). Tucked away in a lovely flower-filled garden in the heart of town, this cool and restful hideaway is like an oasis, set among abundant bougainvillea. Leafy walks, helpful management and pretty balconies make this one of the most likeable hotels on the island. Half or full board only.

★★**Umberto a Mare**, Via Soccorso 2, **t/f** 081 997 171, *www.umbertoamare.it* (*expensive*). Old-fashioned and defiantly lacking in swanky accessories, this hotel sits right by the church of San Soccorso overlooking the sea. Inside is a good restaurant and you can swim from the rocks below. Minimum stay one week. *Closed Jan–Mar.*

Cava dell'Isola, Via Citara, **t/f** 081 997 452 (*expensive*). Right on the water's edge south of Forio and great for lunch, when hungry young people drop in for a bite to eat after a morning spent on the lovely stretch of beach outside. Good local specialities are the mainstay: there is a range of fresh fish and pasta dishes along with the local rabbit concoctions. *Closed Nov–Mar.*

Cavé Gran Diavolo, Via Bocca 56, **t** 081 989 282 (*cheap*). Outside town, heading to Santa Maria del Monte, this rustic restaurant serves more meat than fish, including Forio's speciality, *bucatini con sugo di coniglio* – fat, hollow spaghetti in a rich rabbit sauce. Good local wine. *Closed Wed except high season, only open weekends in winter.*

Sant'Angelo ✉ 80070

★★★★**Miramare**, Via Cte Maddalena 29, **t** 081 999 219, **f** 081 999 325, *www.hotelmiramare.it* (*luxury*). Built into the rockface in pretty Sant'Angelo, this is a lovely hotel with an attentive management and panoramic views over the small harbour. There is no swimming pool but guests are offered a discount at the affiliated Giardini Termali Aphrodite-Apollon, a series of 12 thermal pools set in pretty gardens beside the hotel. *Closed Nov–Mar.*

Serrara Fontana ✉ 80070

Conchiglia, Via Chiaia delle Rose 3, **t/f** 081 999 270 (*moderate*). *Al fresco* dining on a tiny but charming terrace overlooking the harbour. There's a handful of nice rooms (*cheap*) above the restaurant if you can't make it home. *Closed Nov–Mar.*

Da Pasquale, Via S.Angelo 79, **t** 081 904 208 (*cheap*). For delicious pizza follow a narrow stairway through the old centre of the village to this informal restaurant, popular with locals. Inside it's packed with long wooden tables and benches, from where you can watch your dinner cook in the belly of a wood-burning oven. Try the fresh rocket (*rucola*), either as a salad with parmesan or piled high on your pizza. *Closed Tues except high season, Nov–Mar.*

Barano ✉ 80070

★★★**St. Raphael**, Via Maronti 5, **t** 081 990 508, **f** 081 990 922, *www.saintraphael.it* (*moderate*). If you fancy staying up the hill from Maronti (Ischia's main beach), then this might be a good base. The rooms are a little sparse but there are good facilities, including a well-situated swimming pool and a spa where thermal treatments are available at an extra cost. The view of Sant'Angelo and the bay is lovely. Half or full board only. *Closed Dec–Feb.*

★**Camping Mirage**, Via Maronti 37, **t/f** 081 990 551 (*cheap*). At this large campsite on Lido di Maronti, you can step out of your tent right onto Ischia's longest stretch of sand.

she was on close terms with the most brilliant men of Rome. Her opinions were sought-after and her behaviour was always perfectly proper amidst the intrigues that surrounded her famously belligerent family. The contrast between the elegant court that surrounded her on Ischia and the ravages and slave-taking wrought on the island by the corsairs Barbarossa and Dragut only a few years after her departure for Rome, illustrate the extremities of the period.

Other writers of far-reaching influence also found inspiration on Ischia. One was the Neapolitan philosopher Giambattista Vico. In the mid-17th century, he was offered an easy tutoring job on the island, giving him the leisure to formulate his celebrated and murky New Science. Bishop George Berkeley, the Irish philosopher, visited the island at the beginning of the 18th century and wrote of it extensively in his journals; Henrik Ibsen spent the summer of 1867 at Casamicciola and wrote most of *Peer Gynt* there.

During the Napoleonic Wars, the island suffered in battles between the French and the English and, for a brief period, was Nelson's base. In the 19th century Ischia, like so many islands, was a political prison.

Ischia Porto and Ischia Ponte

The first hint of Ischia's volcanic origins comes when you enter the almost perfectly round harbour of Ischia Porto, formed by a sister crater of Monte Epomeo. It was only connected to the sea in 1855, when Ferdinand II's engineers carved a narrow outlet. Full of yachts, lined with restaurants and a step away from the tourist information office, it is everything a Mediterranean port should be. Note that ships dock to the left (as you look out to sea), while hydrofoils dock to the right, near the newly modernized **Terme Comunali**. Via Roma, the main shopping street of Porto, with cafés and boutiques, passes the **Chiesa dell'Assunta**, built in 1300 and later given a Baroque makeover. Further on, when Via Roma becomes the more fashionable Corso Vittoria Colonna, turn down Via V. F. d'Avalos for the numerous seaside *pensioni*, or down Via V. E. Cortese for the **Pineta** (pine wood) – the lovely shady divider between Ischia Porto and Ischia Ponte. From the summit of the extinct volcano behind the town, **Montagnone** (836ft), views stretch to the Phlegraean Fields on the mainland.

Ischia Ponte – once a separate fishing village – is slowly being gobbled up by the tourist sprawl of Ischia Porto. 'Ponte' refers to the causeway built by Alfonso (Il Magnifico) of Aragon in 1441 to the Castello d'Ischia on its offshore rock.

Popular **beaches** line many of the town's shores. In Ischia Porto, Ciro, Medusa, Lauro and Starace are private beaches for which you have to pay. Others, like the Spiaggia degli Inglesi (named after the English occupation at the beginning of the 18th century) and Dei Pini, are free.

Castello d'Ischia

***t** 081 992 834, www.castellodischia.it; open 9.30–sunset; adm.*

On the tiny islet across the causeway from Ischia Ponte, the fortress of the Castello d'Ischia (*also called the Castello Aragonese*) sits atop a rugged outcrop. With the large dome of its **abandoned church** in the centre, the fortress where Vittoria Colonna spent so many years looks like a fairytale illustration. There are atmospheric narrow streets and 500-year-old houses, and the views from the walls are superb. Do not miss the **crypt** with its lovely frescoes by Giotto's disciples and sad graffiti by Ischia's students. Come on 26 July for the festival of Sant'Anna to see the island's traditional *'ndrezzata*, a ritualistic dagger dance dating from the time of Vittoria Colonna, accompanied by clarinets and tambours.

Around Ischia

Besides the state highway (SS270) there are some scenic little roads zigzagging across the island if you have a car – or a sturdy constitution and a good pair of shoes.

Casamicciola Terme

A few kilometres west of Ischia Porto (buses every half-hour), the popular resort of Casamicciola Terme is the oldest spa on the island and the probable location of a Greek settlement. All remains of this, however, were obliterated by the earthquake of 1883 in which 2,300 people were killed, including 600 British tourists. Henrik Ibsen spent a summer in a nearby villa (see the medallion minted in his honour in the piazza). The mineral springs of Casamicciola are particularly potent – Rita and Gurgitello rate as the hottest – and contain large quantities of iodine.

Largely rebuilt, the resort of Casamicciola is more a conglomeration of hotels than a proper town, although there is a centre around shady **Piazza Marina** with shops, banks and car-hire firms. The rest of the town sprawls across the Gurgitello and Sentinella hills; be prepared for some steep walks if you're too impatient to wait for the bus which departs from Piazza Marina. As well as the Lido, there are also beaches at Suorangela and Castagna, and a heliport just west of the town. From Piazza Marina, an hour's walk will take you to the **Osservatorio Geofisico** (Geophysical Observatory) built in 1891. You can't go inside, but there are good views over the town.

Lacco Ameno

A half-hour's walk along the coast from Casamicciola leads you to the more fashionable Lacco Ameno, another large resort. The local landmark is the **Fungo**, a mushroom-shaped rock that dominates the harbour. In the centre of town, you can pay your respects to Ischia's patron saint at the pale pink **Sanctuary of Santa Restituta**. Martyred in the 3rd century, her body was thrown into the sea and floated ashore at Lacco Ameno, where they built her a basilica. This was replaced in 1036 by the current sanctuary. Excavations in the crypt have also revealed parts of the Roman baths. Greek and Roman tools and vases, found west of Lacco Ameno at Monte Vico and behind the town on Fundera plain, are displayed in the **museum** (*www.pithecusae.it; open Tues–Sun 9.30–12 and 3–7; adm*) next to the church, and the neo-Pompeian **Terme Regina Isabella**, connected to the Regina Isabella Hotel in Piazza Santa Restituta.

For the hardy, there is a charming country path, the **Calata Sant'Antonio**, leading from Lacco Ameno (off Via Roma) to the Chiesa dell'Immacolata in Casamicciola – the local milkmen, having delivered their wares fresh from door to door, would herd their goats home along this path in the evening.

Forio

Forio, the wine-producing centre of Ischia and a growing resort, is one of the island's prettiest towns and supports a small art colony. The town has four sights to include in a stroll through its centre. The first of these is the squat tower known as the **Torrione**, built by King Ferrante in 1480 on the site of an even older tower. It did little, however, to defend the island from pirate raids and was later converted to a prison. Today, it is a gallery of local art. Nearby **Santa Maria di Loreto** is a fine Baroque church built in the 14th century; the towers are decorated with majolica tiles.

Off Corso Umberto, a crumbling portal and dusty courtyard mark the entrance to **Santa Maria Visitapoveri** ('Visit the poor'), a tiny, atmospheric church built at the turn of the 17th century outside the customs house. Here poor children collected coins to buy lantern oil for a small street shrine to the Madonna. Faded majolica floor tiles and late 18th-century oval paintings by Alfonso di Spigna are among the treasures inside. On the westernmost point of town, right on the sea, is the pretty white **Santuario della Madonna del Soccorso**. Inside, little ships float on top of pillars, carved by local fishermen as votive offerings.

Behind Forio there are several paths leading up into the hills below Monte Epomeo towards Monterone, Sant'Antonio Abate and Santa Maria del Monte. There are also beaches on either side of Forio – the popular Citara and Cava dell'Isola to the south, and at Chiaia and San Francesco to the north.

Near Citara are the **Gardens of Poseidon** (***t*** *081 908 7111, www.giardiniposeidon.it; open summer 8.30–7; adm*), a complex of thermal swimming pools set in a Mediterranean formal garden. More of an outdoor shopping mall, entrance to this ritzy establishment isn't cheap. Don't forget to pack your sequinned swimsuit.

On the other side of Forio, back towards Lacco Ameno on Via F. Calise 35, is **La Mortella** (***t*** *081 986 220; www.ischia.it/mortella; open Tues, Thurs and Sat–Sun April–Nov 9–7; adm*). These beautiful gardens on the hill of Zaro were designed by Russell Page for British composer William Walton, who lived on the site for many years. The gardens contain a collection of over 300 rare plant species from around the world. There is a Thai *sala* overlooking a pond of lotus flowers and a teahouse where you can listen to music by the composer himself. There is also a museum and a recital hall for concerts (check at the tourist office for a list of events).

Sant'Angelo

Continuing anticlockwise from Forio, the SS270 heads to the hill village of Panza, where there is a road leading down to Sant'Angelo, a resort on Ischia's south coast that is popular with middle-class Neapolitans. The buses to this lovely fishing port stop at the top of the hill because there isn't enough room for them to turn around in Sant'Angelo itself. The walk down to the edge of the cliff is lovely, with numerous views of the **Punta Sant'Angelo**, a small islet connected to Ischia by a narrow isthmus of sand. Only a stump remains of the Torre Sant'Angelo which once stood on top. If the wall-to-wall tourists start to get on your nerves, this is the ideal place to take to the high seas, with plenty of boats to hire in the port.

The lovely **beach of Maronti** stretches east of the village and can be reached either by taking the path or by hiring a boat. The path runs past numerous *fumaroles*, hissing and steaming like old-fashioned radiators, while the beach itself has patches of scalding hot sand where you can wrap your picnic lunch in foil and cook it. Above the beach are the hot springs of **Cavascura** (*adm*), at the mouth of an old river canyon; the sheer cliffs, the little wooden bridges and individual baths carved in the rock – each named after a mythological deity – give Cavascura a quaint old air. The Romans may have been the first to indulge in its natural hot tubs. There's also a road down to the other end of Maronti beach from the village of Barano (*see* below).

Around Monte Epomeo

From Panza, the SS270 towards Barano picturesquely winds its way around the inner valleys of **Monte Epomeo** (2,601ft) towards Barano. If you're going by bus, stop off at **Fontana**, where you can start your climb up to the old volcano (one gruelling hour) – it hasn't erupted since 1302. Mules may be hired if you're not up to the walk and there's a hermitage where you can spend the night, located in the crater itself. Watching the sun rise or set from volcanoes is always memorable, but with the entire Bay of Naples spread out below you, it is sublime.

Other villages on the slopes of the mountain include **Buonopane** ('good bread') and **Barano**, an oasis of tranquillity on exuberant Ischia, where the church of San Rocco has a characteristic campanile.

Procida

Lovely, uncomplicated and tiny, Procida is in many ways the archetypal image of all that an 'Italian island' evokes in any holiday dreamer's mind. The island is scented by groves that produce the finest lemons in Italy (the *granita* served in almost every local bar is a treat – try Bar Roma on Via Roma (***t** 081 896 7460, near the ferry port*)) – and embellished with colourful houses as original as they are beautiful. Procida was the setting for two famous love stories (*see* 'History', p.144) and, more recently, for the Oscar-winning film *Il Postino*. Most people still earn a living from the sea, as sailors or fishermen, or from carving exquisite models of historic ships. Its very proximity to the glamour, chaos and more celebrated charms of Naples, Capri and Ischia has saved it from the worst ravages of touristic excess. The pace of life is delightfully slow: when there was talk of converting the prison into a hotel, the locals shuddered. They preferred the cons to any Capri-like transformation of their idyllic life. Connected to Procida by a modern bridge is the minute islet of Vivara – officially a natural park of Naples. It teems with wild rabbits, an important ingredient in Procida's cuisine, along with the more obvious fruits of the sea.

Getting Around

There are **buses** every 20mins or so between the harbour and Chiaiolella at the other end of Procida, stopping more or less everywhere. Or you can jump on one of the colourful diesel buggies that serve as **taxis**.

Tourist Information

Marina Grande: Via Roma 92, **t** 081 810 1968, **f** 081 981 904. *Open summer 9.30–1 and 3.30–7, winter 9.30–1.* Beside the ticket office near the ferry departure point.

Where to Stay and Eat

Procida ✉ 80079

Although there are few places to stay on Procida, it's an ideal spot for relaxing in the sunshine away from the crowds. There are enough ferries not to feel isolated, but your evenings will be quiet – the nightlife popular on the other islands has yet to catch on here.

★★★**Crescenzo**, Via Marina Chiaiolella 33, **t** 081 896 7255, **f** 081 810 1260, *www.hotelcrescenzo.it* (*moderate*). Right on the harbour front and a short walk to the beach in Chiaiolella, in the south of the island, this hotel is a landmark in Procida. Its rooms are simple but pleasant, and the restaurant is worth a try even if you are not staying here, with local specialities and pizza in the evenings. Most rooms have showers and the sunroof offers a great view.

★★★**Riviera**, Via Giovanni da Procida 36, **t** 081 810 1812, **f** 081 896 7197, *www.hotelrivieraprocida.it* (*moderate*). A pretty hotel on the bus route through the centre of the island, about 10mins walk outside Chiaiolella. There are 23 rooms in a relaxed sunny environment, with very friendly owners. Half or full board only in high season. *Closed Nov–Mar.*

La Medusa, Via Roma 116, **t/f** 081 896 7481 (*very expensive*). One of several good restaurants along the port at Marina Grande. Try the house speciality, *spaghetti ai ricci di mare* (spaghetti with sea urchins) and the good local wine is literally 'on tap'. *Closed Tues except high season, Jan–Feb.*

Il Cantinone, Via Roma 55, **t/f** 081 896 8811 (*cheap*). This low-key eatery further along the Marina Grande serves pizzas, homely dishes and a great *fritto misto di pesce*. *Closed Tues except high season, Jan–Easter.*

History

Only a few kilometres from the mainland, Procida was near enough to Naples to have a minor or at least a spectator's role in many of the turbulent events that transpired there, but far enough away to stay out of trouble. Like Ischia, to which it was once connected, Procida (ancient *Prochyta* or 'deep') was inhabited in Neolithic times. The Romans used the island as a hunting reserve and there was at least an agricultural settlement there in the Dark Ages – Pope Gregory the Great wrote a letter in the 6th century praising the wine of Procida. Shortly thereafter, the first chapel of San Michele Arcangelo was erected on Punta Lingua, on the site where a statue of the saint stood; according to legend, during a pirate attack, the people prayed fervently to the statue for deliverance and the saint responded and saved his beloved Procida – at least that once.

In the 11th century, a Benedictine abbey was founded beside the chapel and the fortifications of the Terra Murata ('the walled land') were begun. These (and St Michael) proved insufficient against the ravages of Saracen pirates: first Barbarossa (1544), then Dragut (1562) and Bolla (1572). After Barbarossa burned the church, the fishermen had to donate a third of their income to reconstruct it. Pope Julius III generously decreed they could fish on Sundays and holidays as well for 10 years to make ends meet (permission was extended for 15 more years after Dragut burned the church again).

The Bourbon kings, like the Romans before them, often came to Procida to hunt. Fernando IV made the island and its town a royal domain but turned its fortress into a prison. Procida prefers to recall another event of the period: the visit in 1811–12 by the wandering French poet Alphonse Lamartine. A beautiful daughter of a fisherman fell in love with him and gave up an advantageous marriage for his sake, only to be jilted by the fickle Frenchman. Inconsolable, she died two months later, but at least she received the dubious compensation of immortality in his novel *Graziella* – a spectacular bestseller in its day. Procida, for its part, pays homage to her memory with an annual end-of-summer Miss Graziella beauty pageant.

Back in medieval times, another earlier visitor was so fond of the island that he incorporated it into his name, becoming Giovanni da Procida. Born in 1210 in Salerno, this nobleman – a good friend of Emperor Frederick 'Stupor Mundi' and his son Manfred – had a castle on the island which he often visited on tours of his domains. When Charles of Anjou, a Guelph (*see* p.273), took Naples, he confiscated all the property of the Ghibellines and Giovanni was forced to flee to Spain, where Constance (the last of the Swabians and wife of King Peter of Aragon) received him well and made him Baron of Valencia.

Giovanni had his revenge on Charles of Anjou. When the Sicilians began to chafe under the harsh rule of Charles' French barons, Giovanni acted as a middleman to assure them that should they rise up in arms, Peter of Aragon would support their cause and be their king. In the resulting uprising – the 'Sicilian Vespers' – around 8,000 Frenchmen died. Some 650 years later, the French were symbolically revenged on Giovanni: when they occupied Procida in 1806 during the Napoleonic Wars, they smashed his marble coat of arms, the last reminder of his presence on the island.

Readers of Boccaccio may recognize Giovanni's nephew, Gianni da Procida, from the Sixth Tale of the Fifth Day of the *Decameron*. Gianni so loved a girl of Ischia named Restituta that he sailed over daily to look at the walls of her house if nothing else. One foul day, a band of Sicilians pounced upon her and carried her off to Palermo, determined to give such a lovely prize to their king, Frederick of Aragon, who stowed Restituta in his garden villa, La Cuba. Gianni went in search of his sweetheart: when he finally discovered her whereabouts, he contrived to enter La Cuba to make love to her and plot an escape. The king caught them *in flagrante* and was about to burn them at the stake when a courtier recognized Gianni and informed the king he was about to execute the nephew of the man who gave him the throne of Sicily – leading to a happy ending for all concerned.

Marina Grande and Corricella

The main settlement of Procida is at the north of the island and includes the port, the high, walled district of Terra Murata and the old fishing village of Corricella.

Ships and hydrofoils call at the port of **Marina Grande**. Walk up Via Roma to Piazza Sancio Cattolico (also called Sent'Co). The church here, **Santa Maria della Pietà**

(1616), gives you a taste of Procida's delightful architecture – wide arches in random rhythms and exterior rampant stairs crisscrossing the façades, all with softly moulded lines.

North of Marina Grande is Via Annunziata, named after the **Chiesa dell'Annunziata**. The church was reconstructed in 1600 and contains a miraculous Madonna, to whom are given the many votive offerings that adorn the interior of the church. There are pretty views from here to the lighthouse and Punta Pioppeto, where people often go for a swim. Nearby is the only remaining watchtower of the three constructed in the 16th century. From **Punta Cottimo** you can see the island of Ventotene, halfway to Rome, which is part of the same volcano as Procida.

Back towards the port is **Piazza dei Martiri**, where 12 Procidanese were executed in 1799 by the Bourbons for plotting a revolt. Near the piazza is the domed 17th century **Madonna delle Grazie**, with a revered statue of the Virgin.

South of the piazza, through the Porta Mezz'Olmo, is the walled **Terra Murata Quarter**. This section of town, which occupies the highest ground on the island, was fortified as a protection against Saracen pirates and the island's inhabitants would retreat here in times of danger. The walls you can see today date from different periods – the latest portions are from 1521; the oldest parts, around the Porta, are medieval.

At the highest point of the Terra Murata, past the romantic if roofless ruins of **Santa Margherita Nuova** (*currently under restoration*), built in 1586 at the edge of the Punta dei Monaci, the **Abbey of San Michele Arcangelo** perches on a cliff edge with magnificent views. Despite its exotic, almost Saracen appearance from a distance, it wears a simple, unadorned façade. The domes are untiled – Procida receives so little rain that tiles aren't strictly necessary or at least not worth the cost. Of the original pre-16th-century structure, only part of the ceiling in the Sala del Capitolo remains. Many works of art in the three-naved church attest to the former splendour of the Benedictines; the painted wooden ceiling dates from the 17th century as do the apse paintings by Nicola Rosso, the most interesting of which shows God's aide-de-camp, Michael, and his putti swooping down to save Procida from the Turks. Pride of place goes to a splashy canvas by Neapolitan Luca Giordano.

Near the Abbey, in the Piazza d'Armi, is the Cardinal of Aragon's 1563 **Castello d'Avalos**. Bought by the Bourbons in 1744 as a royal hunting residence, it was converted into a prison in 1818 and abandoned in 1988. Around here, you can see sections of the Terra Murata walls, inside which are crammed tortuous alleyways and steep narrow houses.

In the protected cove beneath the citadel is the fishing village of **Corricella**, the oldest settlement on the island. It can only be reachd on foot via steep stone stairways that cascade down among the arches and pastel-painted houses. Some of the homes here have been extensively remodelled over the centuries, providing proof of an old island saying, that 'a house isn't only a house. A house is a story.'

Some old palaces may be seen along the escarpment overlooking Chiaia beach – including the **Palazzo Minichini** on Via Marcello Scotti, next to the fine old church of **San Tommaso d'Aquino**, and the **Casa di Graziella**.

Around Procida

The rest of the island has many little beauty spots. There are shaded walkways and narrow roads, old farmhouses and crumbling small *palazzi*, such as the Giovanni da Procida on the Via of that name. The areas around **Centane**, especially Punta Solchiaro, are especially pretty, with views over the entire east coast of the island from the belvedere. On the western coast, the long stretch of sand between Punta Serra and the peninsula of Santa Margherita Vecchia has been divided into three beaches – **Spiaggia Ciraccio**, where two Roman tombs were discovered; **Spiaggia Ciraciello**, on the other side of the pyramid-shaped rock, Il Faraglione di Procida; and, south towards the peninsula, the **Lido di Procida**. The hillock on the peninsula is capped by the ruin of the **church of Santa Margherita Vecchia**, once a Benedictine abbey but abandoned in 1586. On the other side of the hill lies the island's southern settlement, the small fishing port and beach of **Marina di Chiaiolella**, in a rounded cove that was once a volcanic crater.

From here there is a pedestrian-only bridge to the islet and nature reserve of **Vivara** (*currently closed, due to reopen 2005*), where the birds are protected these days but the rabbits are fair game. Neolithic implements discovered here (at Capitello and Punta de Mezzodi) are now in Ischia's museum. A narrow road leads through the crumbling arch of an old hunting lodge to the belvedere on the summit of Vivara, with a fine panorama of Procida and Pozzuoli on the mainland.

The Amalfi Coast

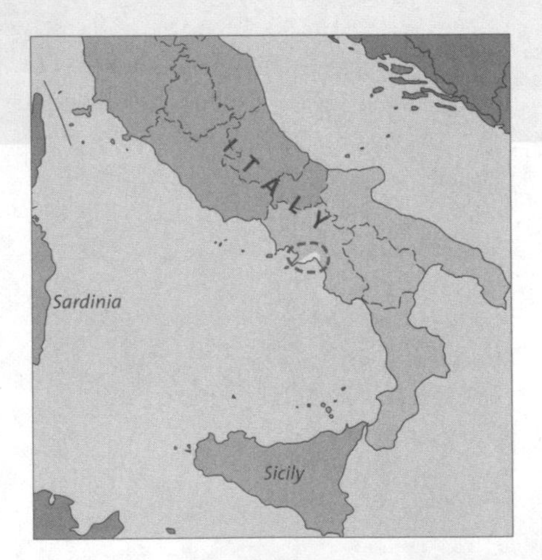

Highlights

1. The Amalfi Drive – the 'road of a thousand bends'
2. The pastel shades of Positano, Italy's most nearly vertical town
3. The 'Cloister of Paradise' in Amalfi's lovely cathedral
4. The sky-high gardens of Villa Cimbrone in Ravello

...the only delectable part of Italy,
which the inhabitants there dwelling do call the coast of Malfie,
full of towns, gardens, springs and wealthy men.
Boccaccio

Along this coast, where one mountain after another plunges sheer into the sea, there is a string of towns that not long ago were accessible only by boat. Today the Amalfi Drive, a spectacular corniche road of 'a thousand bends', covers the route; necessity makes it so narrow that every encounter with an oncoming vehicle is an adventure, but everyone except the driver will have a treat. Nature here has created an amazing

Getting Around

The SS145 coast **road** is tortuous, narrow and slow, with endless hairpins, cliff-edge sections and too much traffic. Overtaking is dangerous. Views, on the other hand, are truly impressive. Regular SITA **buses** travel between Sorrento and Salerno (about every 50mins). It takes the bus almost three hours to make the 66km one-way trip. You can also get to Positano, Amalfi and Salerno by **sea** on the Metro del Mare's MM2 service (**t** 199 446 644, *www.metrodelmare.com*; 3 trips daily). **Linee Marittime Partenopee**, **t** 081 807 1812, runs ferries from Sorrento to Positano (6 daily) and Amalfi (3 daily). A ferry called the *Faraglione* leaves Salerno's Molo Manfredi (at the western end of town) daily at 7.30am, calling at Amalfi and Positano on the way to Capri.

You can explore much of the area on **foot**.

Tourist Information

Positano: Via Saracino 4, **t** 089 875 067. *Open Nov–April 8–2, May–Oct 8–2 and 3.30–8.*

Amalfi: Via delle Repubbliche Marinare, **t/f** 089 871 107, *www.azienturismo amalfi.com*. *Open 8.30–1.30 and 3–5.15.*

Ravello: Piazza Duomo, **t** 089 857 096, **f** 089 857 977, *www.ravellotime.it*. *Open daily 9–8.*

Maiori: Corso Regina 73, **t** 089 877 452. *Open daily 9–1 nd 4–7.*

Salerno: Piazza V. Veneto, **t/f** 089 231 432, *www.salernocity.com*. Near the station: has a good hotel list for the region. *Open Mon–Sat 9–2 and 3–8.*

The *www.giracostiera.com* website has useful information on the Amalfi coast.

vertical landscape, a mix of sharp crags and deep green forests. In doing so, she inspired the Italians to add three of their most beautiful towns.

This coast, generally acclaimed as the most beautiful stretch of scenery in the entire Mediterranean, has always attracted foreigners, but only relatively recently have places like Positano become haunts for the rich, with swarms of day-trippers likely to descend at any moment. Prices are high, the traffic is terrible and there are plenty of tacky souvenir shops. But tourism will never really spoil this area – its natural beauty outshines anything humans could inflict on it. All the engineers in Italy couldn't widen the Amalfi road and the steepness of the terrain leaves no room at all for new development.

Positano

To complement the vertical landscape, here is Italy's most nearly vertical town. Positano spills down from the corniche in a waterfall of pink, cream and yellow villas. The day-trippers may walk down to the sea; only the alpinists among them make it back up (fortunately, there is a regular bus service along the one main street).

After the Second World War, Positano became a well-known hideaway for artists and writers – many of them American, following John Steinbeck's lead – and fashion was not slow to follow. Now, even though infested with coach parties, Positano reverts to the Positanesi in the off season and quietens down considerably.

Parking here, as with most of the Amalfi coast, is extremely limited and you may be forced to hand over a fat wad of euros if you bring your car. Off the main thoroughfare, the road spirals down to the town centre – avoid bringing your car this far if you can. There are usually more spaces further from the centre, and even when it looks to be a fair hike into town, steps often provide a short cut down the hillside.

Where to Stay

Positano ✉ 84017

With Positano's high-fashion status come some of the highest hotel prices in Italy. A few cheap *pensioni* can be found on Via Fornillo and other streets leading down to the beach.

*****__San Pietro__, Via Laurito 2, **t** 089 875 455, **f** 089 811 449, *www.ilsanpietro.it* (*luxury*). Many believe this intimate paradise, 1½km outside town, to be the finest resort hotel in Italy. There are 58 immaculate rooms, superb facilities including a private beach, and spectacular views around every corner. The entrance is hidden behind an old chapel – all part of the plan to protect the privacy of its celebrity clientele. *Closed Nov–Mar. Wheelchair accessible.*

*****__Le Sirenuse__, Via Cristoforo Colombo 30, **t** 089 875 066, **f** 089 811 798, *www.sirenuse.it* (*luxury*). The former home of a noble Naples family, to whom it still belongs. Everything has style, from the drawing room to the pool with mosaic tiles. It has a pool, jacuzzi and fitness area, and is close to the shops.

****__Palazzo Murat__, Via dei Mulini 23, **t** 089 875 177, **f** 089 811 419, *www.palazzomurat.it* (*luxury*). This 18th-century *palazzo* in the heart of town once belonged to Napoleon's brother-in-law, Joachim Murat, briefly king of Naples. Plenty of old-world charm, with antiques in many rooms and a beautiful courtyard shaded by lofty palm trees. *Closed Nov–Mar.*

*****__Covo dei Saraceni__, Via Regina Giovanna 5, **t** 089 875 400, **f** 089 875 878, *www.covodeisaraceni.it* (*luxury*). A comfortable hotel in a great location, at the bottom of the hill right on the harbour. The rooms are simple and spacious, with antique furniture. *Closed Nov–Mar.*

****__L'Ancora__, Via Cristoforo Colombo 36, **t** 089 875 318, **f** 089 811 784, *www.htlancora.it* (*luxury*). This small, well-run place near the water has sea views and parking. *Closed Jan–Mar.*

***__Casa Albertina__, Via Tavolozza 3, **t** 089 875 143, **f** 089 811 540, *www.casalbertina.it* (*very expensive*). A family-run place with a lovely, understated décor, great views and a rooftop restaurant. Half board only in high season.

***__California__, Via Cristoforo Colombo 141, **t** 089 875 382, **f** 089 812 154, *www.hotelcaliforniapositano.it* (*very expensive*). One of the best bargains in Positano, with 15 very pleasant rooms and a lovely terrace restaurant. Well-located and charmingly run. *Closed Nov–Mar.*

*__Maria Luisa__, Via Fornillo 42, **t/f** 089 875 023, *www.pensionemarialuisa.com* (*moderate*). A small and friendly family-run hotel. You can store your own food in their fridges and eat in a dining area underneath a huge cheeseplant.

*__Ostello Brikette__, Via G. Marconi 358, **t/f** 089 875 857, *www.brikette.com* (*moderate*). A lovely hostel facing the sea, with some private rooms.

Praiano ✉ 84010

Praiano, still a sleepy fishing village if you get off the main road, offers better value than Positano. There are some cheap old *pensioni* by the port, usually full in summer, or try:

***__Tramonto d'Oro__, Via Capriglione 119, **t** 089 874 955, **f** 089 874 670, *www.tramontodoro.it* (*very expensive*). A lovely place with tennis courts, a pool, beach access and great views. The management is helpful and the rooms are colourfully decorated.

__Continental__, Via Roma 21, **t 089 874 084, **f** 089 874 779, *www.continental-positano.it* (*moderate*). This basic but clean holiday village next to the Africana nightclub is one of the cheaper options along this stretch of coast, with wooden bungalows looking out onto the sea and a series of terraces for pitching tents. *Closed Nov–Mar.*

Conca dei Marini ✉ 84010

****__Belvedere__, Via Smeraldo 19, **t** 089 831 282, **f** 089 831 439, *www.belvederehotel.it* (*very expensive*). This airy and modern resort hotel is in a delightful setting, with terraces and expansive sea views. The pool is set into the rockface high above the waves. *Closed Nov–April.*

***__Le Terrazze__, **t** 089 831 290, **f** 089 831 296, *www.hotelleterrazze.it* (*very expensive*). A clean, reliable option right on the sea. Under the same management as Tramonto d'Oro (*see* Praiano, above).

Eating Out

Positano

Cheap places to eat are hard to find: there are some decent *pizzerias* around Via Fornillo, and some of the restaurants below, such as **Chez Black**, also provide pizzas.

La Cambusa, Piazza Vespucci 4, **t** 089 875 432 (*expensive*). In a lovely position looking out onto the beach, this Positano favourite serves excellent fresh fish and seafood. A speciality is *penne con gamberetti, rucola e pomodoro* (*penne* with prawns, rocket and fresh tomatoes). *Closed Jan.*

Buca Di Bacco, Via Rampa Teglia 4, **t** 089 875 699 (*expensive*). Across the road from La Cambusa, this is a good place to stop for a drink on the way back from the beach. The fish is always well cooked. It also has a few rooms. *Closed Oct–April.*

Chez Black, Via Brigantino 19, **t** 089 875 036 (*expensive*). As with all the places along the Spiaggia Grande, it's not what you eat that matters, but who sees you eating it. Luckily, good Neapolitan favourites like *spaghetti alle vongole* are done well in this slick and sophisticated joint by the beach, and they make pizzas, too. *Closed Jan–early Feb.*

Lo Guarracino, Via Positanesi d'America 12, **t** 089 875 794 (*expensive*). A friendly, informal *pizzeria/trattoria* in a lovely position, perched over the sea on the cliff path leading to Fornillo beach. *Closed Tues, Nov–Mar.*

O'Caporale, Via Regina Giovanna 12, **t** 089 811 188 (*moderate*). Just off the beach, this place offers simple and well-cooked seafood. The succulent swordfish and *zuppa di pesce* are especially good. *Closed Oct–Mar.*

Da Adolfo, Via Laurito, Laurito, **t** 089 875 022 (*moderate*). A delightful *trattoria* on a small beach, serving old-fashioned recipes such as *totani con patate* (squid with potatoes in oil and garlic), washed down with white wine spiked with fresh peaches. There's a free ferry service from Positano's jetty (look for boats marked 'Da Laurito'). *Closed Oct–May.*

Taverna del Leone, Via Laurito 43, Laurito, **t** 089 875 474 (*cheap*). Those with a car can try this busy *pizzeria* on the road to Amalfi, bustling with young Positanesi. The restaurant is more formal. *Closed Jan–Mar.*

Montepertuso

Il Ritrovo, Via Montepertuso 77, **t** 089 875 453, *www.ilritrovo.com* (*moderate*). A pretty *trattoria* in the hills above Positano, with tomatoes strung from beams and good local dishes: a pleasant rustic experience to escape the crowds. *Closed Jan–early Feb.*

Praiano

Petit, Via Praia 15, **t** 089 874 706 (*very expensive*). Just east of Praiano, a sharp turn down to the beach brings you to this informal eatery at the foot of Il Furore. Diners eat simple dishes such as fresh grilled fish and salad at outside tables beside gaily painted fishing boats. *Closed Jan–Mar.*

Antico Hostaria Bacco, Via G. B. Lama 9, Furore, **t** 089 830 360, **f** 089 830 352 (*expensive*). In the hills on the road to Agerola, this is a great detour if you have a car; the drive alone is spectacular. The Ferraioli family serve delicious seafood *antipasti* and pasta (try the *ferrazzuoli* with swordfish and rocket). They also offer the local white wine (*Costa d'Amalfi Furore*, on sale across the road) and have a few charming rooms with views to the sea below. *Closed 1 week in Nov.*

Trattoria San Gennaro, Via G. Capriglione 99, **t** 089 874 293, *www.ilsangennaro.it* (*moderate*). Towards the west of Praiano, this restaurant serves up huge platefuls of *antipasti*. A great place if you are on a budget or just hungry, and the meal ends with a glass of *limoncello* (bittersweet lemon liqueur) on the house. It also has some rooms for rent. *Closed Thurs, Oct–May.*

Nightlife

Africana, Via Torre a Mare 2, Praiano, **t** 089 874 042, *www.africananightclub.com*. Built into a man-made cave at sea level, you can dance with the fish as they swim in brightly lit pools beneath your feet. Watch out for the parrot! There's a boat service from Positano or you can park at the tiny bay at Furore and walk along the cliff path (about 5mins). *Closed Oct–May.*

Music on the Rocks, Grotte dell'Incanto 51, Positano, **t** 089 875 874. Cabaret entertainment a stroll left from the Spiaggia Grande. *Closed Nov–Mar.*

When you get to the bottom, there is a pebbly, grey **beach** and the town's **church**, decorated with a pretty tiled dome like so many others along this coast.

A highlight of the town's year is the spectacular **Feast of the Assumption** on 15 August – the main holiday of the summer throughout Italy – when the locals recreate the Amalfi coast's centuries-long battles with the Saracens (*see* 'Festivals', pp.56–7).

Outside Positano

Montepertuso, a village perched 3km above Positano, takes its name (which means 'hole in the mountain') from an old legend: the devil challenged the Virgin Mary to blow a hole in the mountain, saying the winner could have control of the village. The devil failed but the Virgin coolly walked through the hillside, leaving a hole still visible today. The locals re-enact the scene each 2 July with much merriment and fireworks.

On the last Saturday in August, the village stages another of Italy's best *festas*, the *Sagra del Fagiolo* – 'the Feast of the Bean'. The streets are decked out with stalls selling beans cooked in every possible way, plus a great many other home cooked dishes, and it's all washed down with local wine served from oak barrels.

From Positano, the next town east along the Amalfi Drive is **Praiano**. It could be Positano's little sister, with a similar beach and church, although it's not quite as scenic and perpendicular, and not quite as beleaguered by tourism. Her natural attractions, however, leave her ripe for creeping exploitation.

The steep, impenetrable **Furore Gorge** east of Praiano is the most impressive natural feature along the Amalfi Drive. Where the gorge meets the sea, there are a couple of tiny, isolated villages on either side, with beaches – if only you could get to them.

East of the gorge near Conca dei Marini, a lift leads down to the **Grotta Smeralda** (*open daily 9–4; adm*). The strange green light that is diffused throughout this sea-level cavern gives it its name. **Conca dei Marini** itself is another vertical village, with a not-great beach and a Norman lookout tower.

Amalfi

Sometimes history seems to be kidding us. Can it be true, can this minuscule village once have had a population of 80,000? There is no room among these jagged rocks for even a fraction of that – but then we remember that in Campania anything is possible, and we read how most of the Old Town simply slid into the sea during a storm and earthquake in 1343. Until that moment, Amalfi was a glorious place, the first Italian city to regain its balance after the Dark Ages, the first to recreate its civic pride and its mercantile daring, showing the way to Venice, Pisa and Genoa, though she kept few of the prizes for herself.

History

It is only natural that the Amalfitani would try to embroider their history a bit to match such an exquisite setting. Legends tell of a nymph named Amalphi who haunted this shore and became the lover of Hercules. As for their city's founding, they'll tell you about a party of Roman noblemen, fleeing the barbarians after the fall of the empire, who found the site a safe haven to carry on the old Roman culture. Amalfi first appears in the 6th century; by the 9th it had achieved its independence from the dukes of Naples and was probably the most important trading port of southern Italy, with a large colony of merchants at Constantinople and connections with all the Muslim lands. In 849 the chroniclers record Amalfi's fleet chasing off an Arab raid on Rome.

To begin with, the Amalfitani Republic was ruled by officers called *giudici* (judges). The year 958 brought a change in constitutions and Amalfi elected its first doge, in imitation of Venice. At about the same time, the city's merchants developed the famous *Tavola Amalfitana*, a book of maritime laws that was widely adopted around the Mediterranean. All of this came at a time for which historical records are scarce, but Amalfi's merchant adventurers must have had as romantically exciting a time as those of Venice. Their luck turned sour in the 11th century. The first disaster was a sacking by Robert Guiscard in 1073. Amalfi regained its freedom with a revolt in 1096, but the Normans of the new Kingdom of Sicily came back to stay in 1131.

Unfortunately, they proved unable to protect the town from two more terrible sackings at the hands of its arch enemy Pisa in 1135 and 1137. Today, Amalfi only gets to relive its glory days every four years, when it hosts the Pisans, Genoese and Venetians in the antique boat race of the Four Maritime Republics: the next race is in 2005.

The Town

The earthquake of 1343 completed Amalfi's decline, but what is left of the place today – with its 5,000 or so people – is beautiful almost to excess. Above the little square around the harbour, a conspicuous inscription brags: 'Judgement Day, for the Amalfitani who go to heaven, will be a day like any other day'.

The square is called **Piazza Flavio Gioia**, after Amalfi's most famous merchant adventurer (his statue looks as if he's offering you a cup of tea). He's probably another fictitious character – more Amalfitani embroidery – but they claim he invented the compass in the 12th century.

From here, an arch under the buildings leads to the centre of the town, the **Piazza del Duomo**, with a long flight of steps up to what may be the loveliest cathedral in the south of Italy (9th–12th centuries). Not even in Sicily was the Arab-Norman style carried to such a flight of fancy as in this delicate façade, with four levels of interlaced arches in stripes of different-coloured stone. Much restored a century ago, the open, lace-like arches on the porch are unique in Italy, although common enough in Muslim Spain, one of the countries with which Amalfi had regular trade relations.

The cathedral's greatest treasure is its set of bronze doors, cast with portraits of Christ, Mary, St Peter and Amalfi's patron, St Andrew. The first of such bronze doors in Italy, they were made in Constantinople in 1066 by an artist named Simon of Syria (he signed them) and commissioned by the leader of the Amalfitan colony there.

The cathedral's interior, unfortunately, was restored in the 18th-century Baroque, with plenty of frills in inlaid coloured marble. The red porphyry baptismal font in the first chapel on the left is believed to have come from the ruins of Paestum. In the crypt you

Where to Stay

Amalfi ✉ 84011

Amalfi has been a resort for much longer than Positano, and its older establishments are some of the most distinctive in the Mediterranean. Like Positano, though, prices are generally higher than average.

Luxury

★★★★★**Santa Caterina**, S. S. Amalfitana 9, **t** 089 871 012, **f** 089 871 351, *www.hotel santacaterina.it*. This converted villa just outside town has perhaps the loveliest gardens of all. It sits on a clifftop with wonderful sea views from most rooms. Its staff are courteous and discreet, and the atmosphere is cool and elegant. *Closed Jan–Feb.*

★★★★**Luna**, Via P. Comite 33, **t** 089 871 002, **f** 089 871 333, *www.lunahotel.it*. This former monastery, above the main road on Amalfi's eastern edge, was already a hotel in the days of the Grand Tour – Wagner stayed here, and they can show you the room where Ibsen wrote *A Doll's House*. The owners claim it was also a favourite of Mussolini and Bismarck. Deftly modernized, it provides comfortable rooms and attentive service.

Very Expensive

★★★★**Miramalfi**, Via Quasimodo 3, **t** 089 871 588, **f** 089 871 287, *www.miramalfi.it*. On the opposite side of town, between Positano and Amalfi, this efficient sixties-style hotel has parking, a beach and a pool on the rocks overlooking the sea.

★★★★**Cappuccini Convento**, Via Annunziatella 46, **t** 089 871 877, **f** 089 871 886, *www.hotelcappuccini.it*. A former monastery (rather than a convent) built by Emperor Frederick II in the 12th century on a hillside overlooking town. The hotel bedrooms were once monks' cells and the hotel retains the original chapel and cloister. Its colonnade bedecked with flowers offers the best view in Amalfi. Meals, like the hotel, are a treat.

Expensive

★★★**Amalfi**, Via dei Pastai 3, **t** 089 872 440, **f** 089 872 250, *www.starnet.it/hamalfi*. In the centre of town, the Amalfi is popular with package tours and is a good alternative for those without transport.

★★**Lidomare**, Largo Duchi Piccolomini 9, **t** 089 871 332, **f** 089 871 394, *www.lido mare.it*. A pleasant hotel in Piazza dei Dogi, not far from the cathedral but away from the crowds. Bright and airy rooms, a dim but cosy breakfast area and obliging staff.

★★**Sole**, Largo della Zecca 2, **t** 089 871 147, **f** 089 871 926, *www.starnet.it/hsole*. This is a cheaper option in a quiet piazza further along the Corso Roma, behind the beach front and next to the Highland Pub. It's small, clean and airy, with private parking. Book in advance.

★★**Fontana**, Piazza Duomo 7, **t** 089 871 530, *www.hotel-fontana.it*. Also near the cathedral, this hotel offers a prime location at a bargain price, with 16 clean and spacious rooms. The piazza hums until the early hours. *Closed Jan.*

Moderate

★★**Sant'Andrea**, Via Santolo Camera 1, **t** 089 871 145, **f** 089 871 023. This tiny, elaborately furnished hotel is one of a number of good-value places with views of the cathedral. Expect an effusive welcome from your obliging hostess. *Closed Nov–May.*

can see more coloured marble work and frescoes, a gift of Philip II of Spain, as well as the head of St Andrew; this relic was part of Amalfi's share of the loot in the sack of Constantinople in 1204.

One of the oldest parts of the cathedral to survive is the **Chiostro del Paradiso** (*open daily 9–6 summer, 9–1 and 3–5 winter; adm*), a whitewashed quadrangle of interlaced arches with a decidedly African air. To the side of the cloister is the **Basilica del Crocifisso**,

Eating Out

Amalfi has some fine restaurants, including those in the hotels above. The town lacks some of the pretensions of Positano but makes up for it with good, honest grub.

Very Expensive

Da Gemma, Via Fra Gerardo Sasso 9, **t** 089 871 345. One of Amalfi's oldest restaurants (since 1872), with an attractive terrace for outdoor dining and an excellent fish-based menu. Their *zuppa di pesce* is superb and try the *melanzane al cioccolato* (grilled aubergines in chocolate sauce), an unexpected but heavenly combination. *Closed Wed, mid-Jan–mid-Feb.*

La Caravella, Via Matteo Camera 12, **t** 089 871 029, *www.ristorantelacaravella.it*. Near the tunnel by the beach, this busy restaurant gives generous helpings of homemade pasta, including delicious ravioli stuffed with seafood, and a good range of homemade desserts – the tiramisu is a treat. There is an index to help you find your way round the vast wine list; around the corner, the wine cellar houses over 1,000 wines. Try the seafood-flavoured broad bean soup. *Closed Tues except high season, Nov–Dec.*

Expensive

Lo Smeraldino, Piazzale dei Protontini 1, **t** 089 871 070. Good food and bustling waiters are the order of the day in this popular eatery, on the water's edge towards the far end of the port. You'll be offered the local speciality, *scialatielli ai frutti di mare* (fresh pasta with mixed seafood) and a range of good *secondi*, most notably an excellent *fritto misto. Closed Wed; Jan–Feb.*

La Taverna del Duca, Largo Spirito Santo 26, **t** 089 872 755. Heading up the main street towards the Valley of the Mills, this is a relaxing midday stop offering pizza, pasta and traditional Amalfi cooking. Tables lie scattered around a small piazza and diners eat off handpainted plates. *Closed Thurs, Jan.*

Moderate

Da Maria, Via Lorenzo di Amalfi 14, **t** 089 871 880. If you don't want to stray far from the cathedral, this *trattoria* and *pizzeria* displays a highly embellished multilingual menu. Allow yourselves to be tempted – the waiters are cheerful and helpful, and the food better than at some of the other less expensive places. *Closed Mon, Nov.*

Cheap

Tarì, Via P. Capuano, **t** 089 871 832. This cool, welcoming *trattoria* north of the cathedral beckons in the hot and weary traveller and there are no unpleasant surprises when it is time for the bill. It's named after an old Amalfi coin. *Closed Tues.*

Il Mulino, Via delle Cartiere 36, **t** 089 872 223. Come here for a cheap meal away from the day-trippers. Head north up the hillside and you won't miss it. *Closed Mon.*

Da Barracca, Piazza dei Dogi, **t** 089 871 285. This is everything an Italian *trattoria* should be. Tables spill out on to a tranquil piazza just west of the cathedral, where diners are shielded from the midday sun by a shady awning and leafy plants. Friendly waiters proffer tasty snacks and plates of steaming pasta. *Closed Wed, mid-Jan–mid-Feb.*

San Giuseppe, Via Ruggiero II 4, **t** 089 872 640. The pizza at this family-run hostelry is sublime. It should be: the owner is a baker. Homely bowls of pasta are also available, brought to you by a trio of portly brothers, and consumed amid the noise of television and shrieking children. *Closed Thurs, Feb.*

the original cathedral. Here, among the surviving frescoes, many of the bits and pieces of old Amalfi that have endured its calamities have been assembled. There are classical sarcophagi, medieval sculptures and coats of arms. Best of all are the fragments of Cosmatesque work – brightly coloured geometric mosaics that once were parts of pulpits and pillars, a speciality of this part of Campania. Don't miss the lovely 16th-century Madonna col Bambino by the stairs down to the crypt.

From the centre of Amalfi, it's only a few minutes walk to the northern edge of the city and the narrow **Valley of the Mills**, set along a stream bed between steep cliffs. Some of the mills that made medieval Amalfi famous for paper-making are still in operation and there is a small **Paper Museum** (*t 089 830 4561, www.museo dellacarta.it; open daily 10–6; adm*) in the town. You can also see paper being made and buy paper products at Armatruda, Via Fiume, **t** 089 871 315, in central Amalfi near the museum.

One of the best ways to spend time in this area is by walking the lovely paths that navigate the steep hills into the interior of the peninsula, passing through groves of chestnut and ash. These, such as they are, were the main roads in this area in the days of the Republic.

One particularly nice one is the **Sentiero degli Dei** (Footpath of the Gods) from Agerola to Positano in the green heart of the coast, a lovely 9-kilometre walk. Another is the **Amalfi–Pontone path**, passing the ruins of the old monastery of Sant'Eustacchio. There are many other paths around Ravello and Scala; ask at the tourist offices or get the locals to point them out.

Atrani to Vietri sul Mare

Atrani

Between Amalfi and the turn-off inland to Ravello, the Amalfi Drive passes through Atrani, an old village whose **church of San Salvatore** has another tiled dome and yet another set of bronze doors from Constantinople. Inside, note the lovely Byzantine relief of a pair of peacocks (peacocks were a symbol of immortality, although it is anyone's guess why the birds are standing on a man and a rabbit). In the days of the Republic this church was called San Salvatore della Biretta and the Amalfitan doges would come here for their investiture ceremonies.

Ravello

As important as it was in its day, the Amalfitan Republic was never large. At its greatest extent, it could only claim a small part of the coast, plus Ravello and Scala in the hills. Like Amalfi, both were once much larger and richer than they are today.

Ravello enjoys a beautiful location, perched on a balcony overlooking the Amalfi coast. The sinuous climb can be made by bus or car, but parking here is a nightmare – expect to pay through the nose if you bring your car.

The village seems to have been a resort even in Roman times, for numerous remains of villas have been found. Later, as second city of the Amalfitan Republic, medieval Ravello's population reached 30,000. Today it is an example of a typically Italian phenomenon – a village of 2,000 with a first-rate cathedral.

Ravello's chief glories are its wonderful gardens, treasure houses of tropical botany. The **Villa Cimbrone** (*www.villacimbrone.it; open daily 9–one hour before sunset; adm*) was laid out by Lord Grimthorpe, the Englishman responsible for the design of Big Ben. It's priceless view over the Amalfi coast is now owned by the Swiss Vuillemier family, who also own the Hotel Palumbo (*see* 'Where to Stay', p.158). It is without doubt one of the most beautiful properties in all Italy.

Fans of Wagner will be interested to know the **Villa Rufolo** (*open daily 9–8 summer, 9–6 winter; adm*) is none other than Klingsor's magic garden. Wagner says so himself, in a note scribbled in the villa's guestbook. He came here looking for the proper setting in which to imagine the worldly, Faustian enchanter of Parsifal and his imagination was fired. The villa itself is a remarkable 11th-century pleasure palace, the temporary abode of Charles of Anjou, various Norman kings and Adrian IV, the only English pope (1154–9), who came here when fleeing a rebellion in Rome. Even in its present, half-ruined state, it is worth a visit. The villa itself houses a small collection of architectural fragments, including a Moorish cloister and two crumbling towers, one of which can still be climbed. The garden, with more fine views, is a semi-tropical paradise: in summer, it reverberates with 'sounds and sweet airs' as the setting for various open-air concerts.

The **cathedral** is named after Ravello's patron, San Pantaleone, an obscure early martyr. There is a phial of his blood in one of the side chapels and it 'boils' like the blood of San Gennaro in Naples whenever the saint is in the mood. Lately, he hasn't been, which worries the Ravellans. The cathedral has two particular treasures: a pair of bronze doors by Barisano of Trani (1179) inspired by the Greek ones at Amalfi, and an exquisite pair of marble ambones (pulpits) that rank among the outstanding examples of 12th- and 13th-century sculptural and mosaic work. The more elaborate one, its columns resting on six curious lions, dates from 1272. The sacristy contains two paintings by the southern Renaissance artist Andrea da Salerno, including an unusual subject, the *Assumption of the Magdalen*.

Downstairs there is a small **museum** (*open April–Oct daily 9.30–1 and 3–7; adm*) containing more bits of the original Cosmatesque interior and an intriguing bust of Sigilgaida Rufolo by Bartolomeo di Nicola, the sculptor of the lions' ambone. In this cathedral in 1149, the English pope, Adrian IV, crowned William the Bad King of Sicily.

You can see decorative work similar to the cathedral's at the churches of **Santa Maria a Gradello** and **San Giovanni del Toro**.

Scala

From Ravello, it is only a lovely half-hour's walk to Scala, the smallest and oldest of the three Amalfitan towns and a genteel option for the traveller seeking peace and parsimony in the refreshing mountain air. Perched on the hillside across from Ravello, this is a timeless gem of a town which offers a rural escape unfettered by the glitz of other resorts.

Scala has another interesting old **cathedral**, San Lorenzo. Inside, above the main altar, there is a 13th-century wooden crucifix. The town is also the birthplace of Gerardo da Sasso, who started out running a small hostel for pilgrims in Jerusalem and ended up founding the Knights Hospitallers or Knights of St John (1118); his family's **ruined palace** can be seen near the village. After the fall of Jerusalem, the order moved to Rhodes and subsequently Malta – today, the Sovereign Order of the Knights of Malta still share the distinctive swallow-tail cross which you can see throughout the Amalfitan towns.

Where to Stay

Ravello ✉ 84010

Hotels in Ravello have no beaches but can boast unforgettable gardens and some of the most spectacular views in the Mediterranean.

Luxury

★★★★★**Palumbo**, Via S.Giovanni del Toro 16, **t** 089 857 244, **f** 089 858 133, *www.hotelpalumbo.it*. One of Ravello's finest, with a guestbook full of famous names. The 11 rooms are decorated with antiques around an Arabic courtyard and the restaurant (also open to non-residents; booking advisable) is famous, with wine made on the premises. There's a simpler *dipendenza* (a cheaper alternative) with six rooms. Pool (shared with Hotel Giordano), transport and parking.

★★★★★**Palazzo Sasso**, Via S. Giovanni del Toro 28, **t** 089 818 181, **f** 089 858 900, *www.palazzosasso.com*. This renovated hotel in a 12th-century villa is Ravello's other top establishment. It was here that Wagner fixed on paper the vision he caught in Villa Rufolo. The plush décor, renowned restaurant and astonishing views come with friendly staff, and the hotel has won the American Five Star Diamond Award. *Closed Nov–Feb. Wheelchair accessible.*

★★★★**Villa Cimbrone**, Via Santa Chiara 26, **t** 089 857 459, **f** 089 857 777, *www.villacimbrone.it*. With the lushest gardens on the coast, this elegant old villa is a special place, perched high on the cliffs. The 10 rooms (half with sea views) are beautifully decorated and the view from the breakfast terrace is stunning. There are drawbacks: a 10-minute walk from the car park and no restaurant, but it does have a pool. *Closed Nov–April.*

★★★★**Caruso Belvedere**, Via S. Giovanni del Toro 2, **t** 089 857 111, **f** 089 857 372. An elegant old patrician villa once popular with the Bloomsbury set. Beautiful gardens and views, and excellent food. *Closed for renovation, due to reopen April 2005.*

Very Expensive

★★★★**Villa Maria**, Via Santa Chiara 2, **t** 089 857 170, **f** 089 857 071, *www.villamaria.it*. This gracious, tastefully converted villa is one of the prettiest, most welcoming places to stay in Ravello, and the choice of many celebrities. The vast suite has one of Ravello's most breathtaking terraces and the restaurant (open to non-residents) recently won an award in the prestigious *gambero rosso* scheme. Its speciality, crispy crêpes, makes a nice alternative to pasta. Guests can use the facilities at Hotel Giordano (below).

★★★**Hotel Giordano**, Via Trinità 14, **t** 089 857 170, **f** 089 857 255, *www.giordanohotel.it*. Under the same obliging ownership as the Villa Maria, and only a few minutes walk away, this comfortable hotel has a heated outdoor swimming pool and solarium. Villa Maria guests have equal access to the facilities, including parking for both hotels.

Expensive

★★**Villa Amore**, Via dei Fusco 5, **t/f** 089 857 135. For a five-star view at a third of the usual price in Ravello, try this delightful small hotel. It has 12 clean, simple rooms, a lovely terrace and a homely atmosphere not common in the larger hotels in this area.

Scala ✉ 84010

★★★**Villa Giuseppina**, Via Toricella 39, **t/f** 089 857 106 (*expensive*). This hotel in unspoilt Scala offers comfort and charm at more affordable prices. Good food and great views from the pool make this a tranquil spot to while away a few hazy summer days. *Closed Nov–Dec.*

★★★**Margherita**, Via Toricella 21, **t/f** 089 857 106, *www.lamargheritahotel.it* (*expensive*). An older-style hotel linked to Villa Giuseppina and sharing its facilities. Parking is easy and you can enjoy lovely walks down to Amalfi (although you'll probably need the bus back).

Minori ✉ 84010

The pleasant beach lidos of Minori and Maiori may be a little dull compared to Amalfi and Positano, but they can be useful bases.

★★★★**Villa Romana**, Corso Vittorio Emmanuele 90, **t** 081 877 237, **f** 089 877 302, *villaromana@libero.it* (*very expensive*). This stylish and comfortable modern hotel in the heart of the town (but not on the sea) is the best in Minori. The rooftop pool is well away from crowds and car fumes, and the rooms are clean and pleasant. Parking is difficult.

★★★**Santa Lucia**, Via Nazionale 144, **t** 089 877 142, **f** 089 853 636, *www.hotelsantalucia.it* (*expensive*). A convenient and inexpensive option on a main road near the beach and the archaeological park. Nylon furnishings will delight anyone with fond memories of the sixties. *Closed Nov–Mar*.

Maiori ✉ 84010

★★★★**Il San Pietro**, Via Nuova Chiunzi 147, **t** 089 877 220, **f** 089 877 025, *www.sanpietro.it* (*expensive*). This grey, characterless modern hotel at the far end of town is popular with Italians for its good sports facilities and family bungalows. *Closed Oct–Easter*.

★★**Baia Verde**, Via Arsenale 8, **t** 089 877 276, **f** 089 877 736 (*moderate*). Situated in a block of flats, this *pensione* has a great view from its terrace, if you can cope with the cranky lifts and noise restrictions ('no clogs!').

★★**Vittoria**, Via F. Cerasuoli 4, **t/f** 089 877 652, *www.hotel-vittoria.it* (*moderate*). One of several convenient and affordable *pensioni* near the beach. Clean but unglamorous, at the top of a modern block of flats.

Cetara ✉ 84010

★★★★**Cetus**, **t/f** 089 261388, *www.hotelcetus.com* (*expensive*). Attractively redecorated with a hint of Art Deco, its isolated position and tranquil bay make it a rising star on this coastline. Parking is available.

Vietri sul Mare ✉ 84019

★★★★★**Raito**, Via Nuova Raito 9, **t** 089 763 155, **f** 089 763 081, *www.hotelraito.com* (*expensive*). A grandiose, recently restored hotel in Raito, just outside Vietri. Smart interiors and good service make it popular for conferences.

★★★**Hotel Bristol**, Via C. Colombo 2, **t** 089 210 800, **f** 089 761 170, *www.hotelbristolvietri.com* (*moderate*). Just above the beach, this hotel is rather bland, but clean and useful for a stopover. Pool and beach.

Eating Out

Ravello ✉

Most of the best dining in Ravello is in the hotels, notably Villa Maria, Caruso and Palazzo Sasso. All three welcome non-residents.

Cumpà Cosimo, Via Roma 44–6, **t** 089 857 156 (*expensive*). Owner-cook Signora Netta Bottone is always happy to try out her English on visitors. She's something of an earth mother and swears by the fresh produce grown on the family farm in Scala. Framed recommendations from national and international newspapers line the walls, enthusing over recipes handed down by Grandma and the homely atmosphere here. A holiday high spot.

Vittoria, Via dei Rufolo 3, **t** 089 857 947 (*cheap*). This large *trattoria* off the main piazza serves delicious food at reasonable prices – a rarity in Ravello. Servings are generous; try the rich and gooey *risotto ai funghi porcini*. Head to the back for tables laid out on the shady patio. *Closed Tues*.

Scala

Zi'Ntonio, Via Torricella 39, **t** 089 857 118 (*cheap*). Serves well-cooked local dishes on a beautiful covered terrace.

Minori

Il Giardinello, Corso V. Emmanuele 17, **t** 089 877 050 (*expensive*). An elegant restaurant behind a leafy archway on a side street. The menu is varied and interesting with plenty of fish, pasta and pizza. *Closed Wed except high season, Nov*.

Maiori

Torre Normanna, Via D. Taiani 4, **t** 089 877 100 (*expensive*). As you leave Maiori, you'll see this Saracen tower jutting into the sea. Eat on the terrace (*open summer only*) – it's very noisy inside. A beautiful setting and good food at reasonable prices. *Closed Mon, Oct–Mar*.

Mammato, Via Lungomare Amendola, **t** 089 877 036 (*cheap*). There's good fresh fish at this glass-fronted restaurant, popular with beach bums and locals alike. *Closed Tues except high season*.

Vietri sul Mare

La Locanda, Corso Umberto I 52, **t** 089 761 070 (*cheap*). A mellow, candlelit atmosphere and inventive, tasty and plentiful food, served on the handpainted plates that have made the town famous. *Closed Mon*.

Above Scala, the chapel of San Pietro in **Campoleone** contains medieval carvings of St Michael and St Catherine, if you can find someone with the key.

Minori to Vietri sul Mare

Minori is a typical Costiera hill town which, despite encroaching tourism, maintains considerable charm. Its bigger sister, **Maiori**, is somewhat less enticing, mainly due to a major flood in 1954, which washed away most of the seafront. As a result, most of the buildings and hotels along the shore are now depressingly modern. **Erchie**, a tiny hamlet on the shore far below the road, seems a lovely spot – if you can figure out a way to get down to it.

East of Erchie, the real world comes back into view, with the busy port of Salerno stretching before you. Here you find the tiny old village of **Cetara**, in a sandy bay with a fine beach behind a newly constructed fishing port.

Just before Salerno, **Vietri sul Mare** is another steep and pretty town, famous throughout Italy for its beautiful majolica ware. There are ceramics shops everywhere, where you can watch craftsmen handpainting jugs, vases and tiles, and pick up souvenirs at good bargain prices.

Salerno

Anywhere else in the south of Italy, a city like Salerno would be an attraction in itself; here it gets lost among the wonders of the Campanian coast – just the big town at the end of the Amalfi drive – and few people stop for more than a brief visit. That's a shame for Salerno has its charms. Not least of these is that it is a clean and orderly place, which should endear it to people who hate Naples. It's also a town where you can rub shoulders with real Italians in the shops, restaurants and bars – a nice change from the Amalfi coast.

Salerno's setting against a backdrop of mountains is memorable, too. The Italian highway engineers, showing off as usual, have brought the highway to Salerno across a chain of viaducts, one lofty span after another, an unusual and pleasing ornament for the city; at night, the road lights hang on the slopes like strings of fairy-lights on a Christmas tree.

Salerno's ancient distinction was its medical school, the oldest and finest of medieval Europe. The school was of the greatest importance in the transmission of Greek and Muslim science to Europe (*see* **Topics**: 'The *Civitas Hippocratica*', p.24). Most of us, however, may recognize Salerno better as the site of the Allied invasion in September 1943, one of the biggest such operations of the Second World War. Seven months later, Salerno became capital of Italy, until liberation was completed.

Salerno's port is on the outskirts of town, and the shore all through the city centre is graced with a pretty park, the **Lungomare Trieste**. Parallel with it, and two streets back, the Corso Vittorio Emanuele leads into the old town. Here it changes its name to Via dei Mercanti, most colourful of Salerno's old streets. The **cathedral**, a block north on Via del Duomo, is set with its façade behind a courtyard with a central fountain and a

Where to Stay

Salerno ✉ 84100

Salerno's hotels, although fairly modest and utilitarian in general, do offer a cheaper alternative to the Amalfi coast and are also more easily accessible by car, with secure parking facilities. You could easily base yourself here and explore the towns of the Amalfi coast by bus on day trips.

Expensive

****__Jolly Hotel delle Palme__, Lungomare Trieste 1, **t** 089 225 222, **f** 089 237 571, *www.jollyhotels.it*. Pleasant, reliable and good value; a nice position on the seafront.

***__Fiorenza__, Via Trento 145, **t/f** 089 338 800, *www.hotelfiorenza.it*. 30-room hotel; clean, well-run and convenient for the beach.

Moderate

***__Plaza__, Piazza Vittorio Veneto 42, **t** 089 224 477, **f** 089 237 311, *www.plazasalerno.It*. Opposite the station with modern and comfortable rooms, this hotel is more than acceptable for an overnight stay.

***__Montestella__, Corso Vittorio Emmanuele 156, **t** 089 225 122, **f** 089 229 167, *www.hotelmontestella.it*. Another decent hotel in the pedestrian area close to the station.

__Salerno__, Via G. Vicinanza 42, **t 089 224 211, **f** 089 224 432, *www.albergosalerno.com*. Simple and comfortable, the Salerno is one of several cheaper hotels on or around the Corso Vittorio Emmanuele.

Cheap

Ostello per la Gioventu' Irno, Via Luigi Guercio 112, **t** 089 790 251, **f** 089 252 649, *youthostelsalerno@yahoo.com*. Salerno's youth hostel. *Closed daily 10.30–5; curfew 1am.*

Eating Out

Expensive

Al Cenacolo, Piazza Alfano I 4/6, **t/f** 089 238 818. Beside the cathedral, this place serves fine seafood and is recommended by locals. Booking advised. *Closed Mon, Sun eves.*

Moderate

Il Timone, Via Generale Clark 29, **t/f** 089 335 111. In Mercatello, a few kilometres east of the town centre. The speciality here is *tubetti alla pescatrice* (short pasta with a delicious fish sauce). *Closed Tues.*

Alla Brace, Lungomare Trieste 11–13, **t** 089 225 159. The usual fish dishes, a wide range of homemade desserts, plus delicious local specialities – stuffed peppers, ravioli filled with ricotta and a remarkable potato soufflé. *Closed Tues.*

Cheap

Vicolo della Neve, Vicolo della Neve 24, **t** 089 225 705. This lively restaurant in the *centro storico* is popular with local artists, whose work decorates the walls. The chef turns out local favourites such as *melanzane alla parmigiana* (aubergines with tomato, mozzarella, parmesan and basil) and the classic *pasta e fagioli*. Excellent pizza, too. *Open eves only, closed Wed.*

Da Sasa, Via degli Orti 9, **t** 089 220 330. Good cheap *trattoria*, with traditional home cooking. *Closed Fri and Sat lunch, Mon, Aug.*

Pinocchio, Lungomare Trieste 56–8, **t** 089 229 964. Great value for pizza and seafood, and popular with the locals. *Closed Fri.*

Pantaleone, Via dei Mercanti 75, **t** 089 227 825. The oldest pastry shop in town.

detached campanile – as if it were not a church at all but a mosque. The Corinthian columns around the church come from the ancient Greek city of Paestum, a short distance down the coast (*see* p.173).

Inside, the cathedral's treasures include a pair of bronze doors from Constantinople and another pair of Cosmatesque pulpits, although the biggest surprise comes with the overwhelming mosaic floor, a vast expanse of marble and polychrome tiles of Byzantine inspiration. Many of the best original details have been preserved in the adjacent **Museo del Duomo** (***t*** *089 239 126; currently closed for renovations*).

Robert the Cunning and his Blushing Bride

On the inscription across Salerno's cathedral façade, you can read how the cathedral was built by 'Duke Robert, greatest of conquerors, with his own money'. This was Robert de Hauteville, known as Robert Guiscard ('the Cunning') – one of the first and greatest of the Norman warriors who came to plunder southern Italy in the 11th century. Robert came to Italy in 1046, one of the younger brothers of the Norman family that would one day found a dynasty in Sicily. His elder brother Drogo, chief of the clan, had no lands to give him so Robert was on his own, hiring his sword out first to the Lombard Count Pandulf of Capua and later to his brothers or anyone else who could pay for it.

Contemporary accounts describe Robert as a fair-haired, blue-eyed giant. He earned his sobriquet for tricks such as the taking of Malvita, a fortified monastery in Calabria: one day, a party of unarmed Normans came up to the gate with a coffin and asked to have a funeral Mass said for one of their comrades. The monks let them in but, once inside, the coffin burst open to reveal a very live knight lying on a pile of swords. Combined with cleverness like this, Robert's formidable strength and skill in battle soon earned him an important position in the south.

In 1058 he found a fitting bride, Princess Sichelgaita of the ruling Lombard house of Salerno. Nearly as tall and as strong as Robert himself, she loved nothing better than accompanying him into battle, her long, blond hair pouring out from her helmet.

Robert's greatest exploit came in 1084, a year before his death. That year, there were two popes in Rome – one supported by the German emperor Henry and the other, Gregory VII, by Robert. When the Normans brought up a big army to force the issue, Rome resisted. Robert's men took the city and treated it to the worst sacking in its history. Gregory – the great reformer Hildebrand before becoming pope – had worked ceaselessly for decades to build the power of the papacy; now he had his victory, but the Romans hated him so thoroughly he could not stay in the city. He was forced to accompany Robert to Salerno, where he died soon after. Robert buried him in this cathedral, which he had begun, perhaps in expiation, the same year.

Salerno has a **beach**, but it's unlikely that you'll want to use it. It's littered and elbow room only in high season – there are much better beaches further south around Paestum and the Cilento coast. There's also an easy excursion up into the mountain town of **Cava de'Tirreni.** Near it there is a little-visited Benedictine monastery called **La Trinità di Cava** which has preserved a wealth of frescoes, stone carvings and Cosmati work.

Campania

11

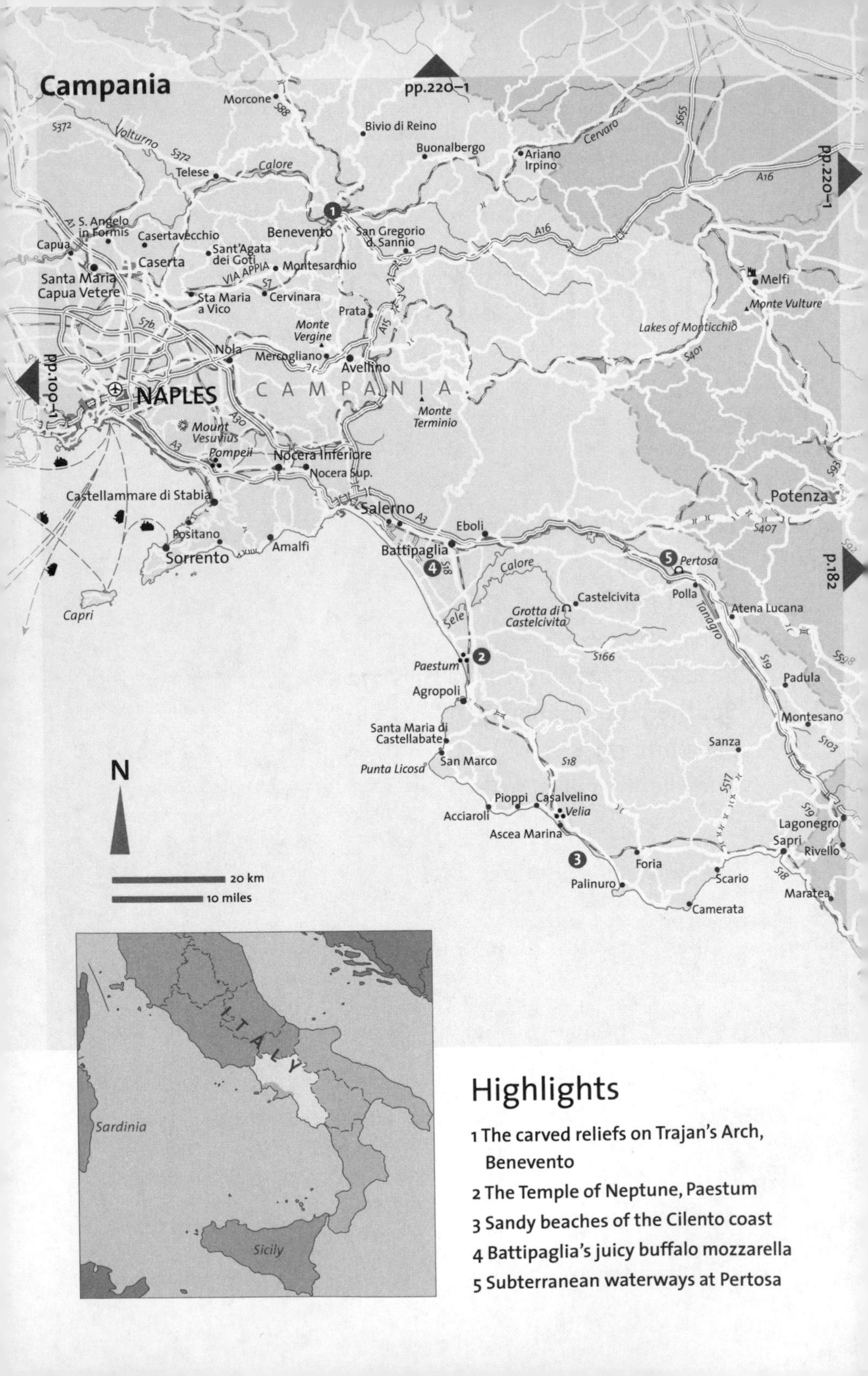

Highlights

1 The carved reliefs on Trajan's Arch, Benevento
2 The Temple of Neptune, Paestum
3 Sandy beaches of the Cilento coast
4 Battipaglia's juicy buffalo mozzarella
5 Subterranean waterways at Pertosa

There's more to this region than just the Bay of Naples. However, the bay and its many attractions draw off most of the tourists, and it's a rare soul indeed who ever makes it up to old Capua or the excellent little city of Benevento.

Quite a few do make it, however, to the gardens and palace of Caserta – Campania's second most-visited sight after Pompeii – or down to the temples of Paestum, southern Italy's finest Greek monuments.

North and East of Naples

Neapolitans call the area immediately north of Naples – around Afragola, Acerra and Secondigliano – the 'Triangle of Death'. It's an industrial wasteland of shanties and power lines ruled by the Camorra that has Italy's worst unemployment rate and some of its worst social problems.

Beyond the Triangle, however, there are a number of attractive destinations for day trips or overnight stays, including the Roman ruins at Capua, the vast palace of Caserta and the attractive town of Benevento. East of Naples, around the 'back' of Mount Vesuvius, there is mountain scenery in the Irpinia hills and the medieval pilgrimage site of Monte Vergine.

Capua

The broad garden plain that surrounds Capua has been renowned for centuries as one of the most fertile corners of Italy, although its lush landscapes have suffered a bit from creeping industrialism.

Capua itself is a double city, consisting of the 'modern' town of Capua (which was actually founded in the 9th century) and the ancient one – in Roman times, the second most important city in Italy, but deserted in the Dark Ages and now modestly reborn as Santa Maria Capua Vetere.

Capua can trace its founding back to the Oscans, blithe folk of ancient Italy who introduced farce to the theatre and who probably gave us the word *obscene*. It is believed that the Oscan farces, banned by all decent Roman emperors, created the prototypes of the *commedia dell'arte* stock characters, including Naples' favourite, Pulcinella – Punch. All that should give you some idea of the spirit of old Capua, a city best known for beautiful women and the manufacture of perfume, and as renowned for loose morals in its day as Sybaris.

Everyone but the jealous Roman historians liked to give Capua credit for defeating the great Hannibal. The Capuans had always hated those dreary, dour Romans and they eagerly took the Carthaginians' part. Hannibal's men enjoyed Capuan hospitality in the winter of 216 BC; they came out in the spring so dreamy-eyed and dissipated that they never beat the Romans again.

Of course, there was hell to pay when the Romans came back but Capua survived and even flourished for several centuries more as the greatest city of the region. Finally, though, some even worse drudges than the Romans arrived – the Arabs,

Getting Around

The interior of Campania makes up a rather large piece of territory – the three main towns are all provincial capitals. None are on the main **railway** lines, however, and you will have to scrutinize the schedules in Naples carefully to find your way around. For **Capua** take the Piedimonte Matese train from Naples to Santa Maria Capua Vetere. Trains to **Caserta** are more frequent and very convenient for the Royal Palace which is directly in front of the station. **Benevento** is on the Naples–Foggia railway line, but some Naples–Benevento trains are operated by a private railway: ask at the information booth in Naples' Stazione Centrale to make sure you buy the right ticket. The private line is faster.

Buses for Caserta, Capua, Avellino and Benevento leave Naples from Piazza Garibaldi, in front of the Stazione Centrale. **Consorzio Trasporti Pubblici**, **t** 081 700 1111, runs regular buses to **Caserta** (1hr) stopping at the station. From here, you can also take buses to Santa Maria Capua Vetere. Benevento is most easily reached by bus. The **Consorzio Trasporti Irpini**, **t** 0825 204 250, has regular services to **Avellino** (50mins) and **Benevento** (1½hrs) from Piazza Garibaldi in Naples.

In Benevento, buses to Naples and a surprising variety of other places (including one daily to Rome) leave from Piazza Pacca, on Corso Dante just west of the cathedral. There are several companies; check at the Benevento tourist office for schedules.

By far the fastest way to get to the interior of Campania is by **road**: along the A2, which passes between Caserta and Capua; the A16 Bari *autostrada*, which runs past Avellino; or the A3 *autostrada* and SS18 south to the Cilento. A slower but slightly quieter route to Caserta is along the old SS87 road. To get to it, take the Viale Maddalena to the left of Capodichino Airport, then follow the signs for Caserta. Be prepared for the upsetting sight of half-naked prostitutes lining the sides of many roads. Most of them are illegal African immigrants who do most of their business around lunchtime.

To get to Benevento by road from Naples, take the A2 north then, just south of Caserta, look for the SS265 eastwards. This joins up with the SS7 (the Via Appia) for Benevento. This road is quite slow. An alternative is to take the A16 *autostrada* to Avellino, then the SS88 north from there to Benevento.

Tourist Information

Caserta: **t** 0823 322 233. *Open 8.30–3.45*; and in the Royal Palace, **t** 0823 327 7380, *www.reggiadicaserta.org*.

Benevento: Via Nicola Sala 31, **t** 0824 319 911, **f** 0824 312 309. *Open Sun–Fri 8–2, 3–4*; and in Palazzo Bosco, Piazza Roma 11, **t** 0824 319 938, *info@eptbenevento.it*. *Open Sat 9–4*.

Avellino: Piazza Libertà, **t** 0825 74731. *Open 9–1*.

Where to Stay and Eat

Neither Capua nor Caserta makes a very attractive base for an overnight stay and they are within easy reach of Naples for a day trip. The environs of Caserta, though, do have some good restaurants.

Benevento sees few tourists and therefore accommodation is limited – one of the reasons why it is even more attractive to those chancing upon it. There are several good restaurants and prices for both food and accommodation are markedly lower than the well-visited coast and Naples. The town is an ideal base for forays into inland Campania, as well as to Caserta and Capua.

who utterly destroyed the city in about 830. The survivors refounded Capua on its new site, a few kilometres to the north.

Santa Maria Capua Vetere

At the original Capua – Santa Maria Capua Vetere – you can see the remains of the second-largest **amphitheatre** in Italy (***t*** *0823 798 864; open Tues–Sun 9–one hour before sunset; adm*), and the largest of all before Rome built its Colosseum, where Spartacus

Dining in Benevento can be interesting. It's another world from the Campanian coast, with seafood replaced on the menu by rabbit, duck, lamb and veal. Samnium, the province of which Benevento is capital, produces some good but little-known wines; ask for a bottle of stout-hearted Solopaca red to accompany your meal.

Around Caserta

Antica Hostaria Massa, Via Mazzini 55, **t** 0823 456 527, *www.ristorantemassa.it* (*expensive*). Back at Caserta itself, this is a simple and convenient place for lunch near the Reggia. They also serve pizza.

Ritrovo dei Patriarchi, Via Conte Landolfo 14, Località Sommana, **t** 0823 371 510 (*moderate*). At this restaurant just outside of Casertavecchia, you will find game in abundance, including pheasant, venison, partridge and wild boar, depending on the time of year. There are also good hearty soups and vegetable dishes. *Closed Thurs.*

Rocca di Sant'Andrea, Via Torre 8, **t** 0827 371 232 (*cheap*). This restaurant in the centre of Casertavecchia offers delicious pasta dishes and a variety of *secondi*, many of which are based on meat grilled on the open fire in front of you. There is also a good selection of homemade desserts. *Closed Mon.*

La Castellana, Via Torre 4, **t** 0823 371 230 (*cheap*). When available, you can feast on wild boar or venison at this *trattoria* near Rocca di Sant'Andrea. There is also a wonderfully innovative selection of soup and pasta openers. *Closed Thurs.*

Benevento ✉ 82100

****Gran Hotel Italiano**, Viale Principe di Napoli 137, **t** 0824 24111, **f** 0824 21758, *www.hotel-italiano.it* (*expensive*). Just a block from the Stazione Centrale, this is the best the city can offer – seventies' architecture and décor except for two amazing original prints by Piranesi. Nevertheless, the infectious enthusiasm of the owner, S. Italiano, generally high standards and a very helpful staff, along with the provincial prices, make this good value. The 20-minute walk into the historic centre is its principal drawback.

Della Corte, Piazza Piano di Corte, **t** 0824 54819 (*cheap*). It is hard to beat this *pensione* both for charm and for its location, right in the heart of the historic quarter. The rooms are clean and quiet and the proprietor has character. The hotel only has seven rooms and remains fairly undiscovered. Finding the hotel by car, if you have one, can be quite a feat; head for Corso Garibaldi, then ask.

Trattoria Nunzia, Via Annunziata 152, **t** 0824 29431 (*moderate*). Set in the pretty medieval area, and now in its third generation, this place will surprise you with specialities such as the delicious *cavatielli fagioli e cozze* (homemade pasta with beans and mussels) and the near-perfect English of Signora Nunzia's son. If you're too full to face the walk back to your hotel, they might even offer you a lift. *Closed Sun.*

Ristorante Teatro Gastronomico, Via Traiano Palazzo L. Andreotti, **t** 0824 54605 (*cheap*). This fun restaurant in the piazza in front of Trajan's Arch serves up a truly gastronomic menu of local specialities under a barrel vault painted with architectural backdrops and lined with real balconies. *Closed Mon.*

Pizzeria Rodolfo, Via Meo Martini, **t** 0824 51761 (*cheap*). Come here to enjoy what many consider to be the best pizza in Benevento.

Pizzeria Romana, Vl Spinelli 27 (*cheap*). This stand-up *tavola calda* on the corner of Corso Dante and Corso Vittorio Emmanuele, a block west of the cathedral, has an excellent selection of affordable delicacies that are also perfect for picnics.

began his gladiators' revolt in 73 BC. Few sections of the stands are still intact, but there is an underground network of tunnels and trap doors much like the Colosseum.

A short walk away, you'll find something much more interesting – perhaps the best example of a **Mithraeum** discovered anywhere in the Mediterranean (***t** 0823 798 864; guided visits by prior arrangement*). The cult of the god Mithras, imported from Persia by the legionnaires was, for a while, the most widespread of the cults that tried to fill the religious vacuum of the imperial centuries. Some scholars see in it much in common with Christianity, but the resemblance isn't readily apparent; Mithraism was an archaic, gut-level cult with mystery initiations and bull's blood. It originally took hold in the army and always remained a men-only affair, but as late as the 3rd century AD, it probably claimed more adherents than Christianity. The upper classes were never too impressed with it, which is why it eventually lost out to Christianity and why such well-executed frescoes as these are rare.

The *mithraeum* is an underground hall that was used for initiations and dominated by a large scene of Mithras – a typical Mediterranean solar hero – slaying a white bull with a serpent under its feet. The fresco representing the moon on the opposite wall is less well-preserved.

The new **Archaeological Museum of Ancient Capua** on Via Roberto D'Angio (***t** 0823 844 206; open Tues–Sun 9–7*) provides a convenient introduction to the site, complementing the more important Museo Campano in (modern) Capua. Santa Maria also has a crumbling triumphal arch and some elaborate Roman tombs, off the road to Caserta.

New Capua

The 'new' Capua has all the most interesting finds from the old town at the **Museo Provinciale Campano** on Via Principi Longobardi 1/3 (***t** 0823 961 402; open Tues–Sun 9–6; adm*) though most people make do with the new museum at Santa Maria Capua Vetere.

Just north of the town on the slopes of Mount Tifata, a site once occupied by a temple of Diana now contains the 11th-century basilica of **Sant'Angelo in Formis**. The 12th-century frescoes here are some of the best in the south, oddly archaic figures that would seem more at home in Constantinople than in Italy. There is an intense spiritual vision about these paintings – note the unearthly, unforgettable face of the enthroned St Michael above the portal. North of Capua, the last town in Campania along the Via Appia is **Sessa Aurunca**, with a Roman bridge and some other scanty ruins, as well as a 12th-century cathedral, interesting for its surviving ancient and medieval sections.

Caserta

In one shot, you can see the biggest palace in Italy and also the most wearisome. Both distinctions belong uncontestably to the **Reggia**, or Royal Palace, built here by the Bourbon King of Naples, Charles III (*Royal Apartments open Tues–Sun 9–7.30; adm*). His architect, Luigi Vanvitelli (really a Dutchman named Van Wittel) spared no expense; like the Spanish Bourbons, those of Naples were greenly jealous of Versailles and wanted to show the big Louies back home that they, too, deserved a little respect. Charles also wanted to move the royal court away from the Palazzo Reale on the waterfront in Naples, which he considered too vulnerable to a seaborne attack – the English fleet had briefly threatened it in 1742.

The Reggia, begun in 1752, has some 1,200 rooms – not much compared to the 2,800 of the Bourbon palace in Madrid, but larger than its Spanish cousin just the same (it's also larger than Versailles). The façade is 804ft across. Inside, as in Madrid, everything is tasteful, ornate and soberingly expensive; the only good touches from Vanvitelli's heavy hand are the elegant grand staircases. The Reggia was commandeered for use as Allied military headquarters in Italy in 1943: it was here that the final surrender of the German armies in Italy was accepted two years later.

It's the Reggia's magnificent **park** (*open Tues–Sun 9–one hour before sunset; adm*) that really makes the trip worthwhile. The gardens are laid out in the formal Italian-French style, along an amazingly long axis of pools and cascades climbing up to the famous **Diana fountain**, with its lifelike sculptural group of the goddess and her attendants catching Actaeon in the act. In contrast to the regimentation of the main axis, the **English garden** was the first in Italy to introduce the more romantic, less formal style of garden popular in 18th-century England. Take a picnic here if you can.

Around Caserta

The village of **San Leucio**, 3km north of Caserta, was founded by the Bourbon kings as a paternalistic Utopian experiment and for the manufacture of silk. For most of his life, Ferdinand IV personally saw to every detail of its operation, even christening the children of the workers. The successor of his Real Fabbrica is still a centre for silk.

Some 9km to the east there is the half-deserted town of **Casertavecchia**. The building of the Reggia drew most of the population down to modern Caserta, but the Old Town still has a 12th-century **cathedral** (***t*** *0823 371 318; open 3–4*) with a great octagonal *ciborium* (a type of cylindrical or prismatic dome) that is one of the glories of Arab-Norman architecture.

Benevento

In the foothills of the Apennines, Benevento is another smallish city that has often played a big role in Italian history. The town has often been shaken by earthquakes, and the city took plenty of hard shots during the battles of 1943 but there are still enough attractions around to make a stop worthwhile.

On an old tower in the town centre, the city fathers have put up maps of southern Italy that show the boundaries of the two important states of which Benevento was the capital. First, as Malies or Maloenton, it was the leading town of the Samnites, a warlike mountain people who resisted Roman imperialism for many years. The Romans were later to make a big city of it, an important stop along the Appian Way. They Latinized the name to Maleventum – 'Ill Wind' – but after the lucky defeat of Pyrrhus of Epirus here in 275 BC, they thought it might just be a Beneventum after all.

In AD 571, the city was captured by the bloodthirsty Lombards and became their capital in the south. After the Lombards of the north fell to Charlemagne, the Duchy of Benevento carried on as an independent state; at its greatest extent, under relatively enlightened princes like Arechi II (*c.* 800), it ruled almost all of southern Italy. The Normans put an end to it in the 1060s.

Coming to Benevento in the winter, you'll probably think the Romans were crazy to change the name. When people in Salerno are ready to hit the beaches, you'll find the Beneventani shivering on street corners like Muscovites in their fur caps, victims of traditionally the worst weather in southern Italy. It is often claimed this makes them more serious and introspective than people on the coast – certainly coming here from Naples seems metaphorically like a trip of a thousand miles.

The Triggio

The lower part of town, known as the 'Triggio', suffered the most during the Allied bombing. All through this quarter, you will see bits of Roman brick and medieval masonry – something ancient built into the walls of every house. There is half a Roman bridge (Ponte Leproso – 'Leper's Bridge') over the Sabato (one of Benevento's two rivers). There are ruins of the Roman baths, remains of a triumphal arch and plenty of gates and stretches of the fortified walls built by the Lombards. On Via Posillipo, a Baroque monument houses the **Bue Apis**, a sacred Egyptian bull sculpture found in Benevento's Temple of Isis.

Benevento's **cathedral**, on the main street of the Triggio, Corso Garibaldi, was almost totally destroyed by the Allies: today, only the odd 13th-century façade remains, built with bits of Roman buildings – inscriptions, reliefs, friezes and pillars – arranged every which way. In the old streets behind the cathedral, you can see a dismally kept **Roman Theatre** (*t 0824 47213; open daily 9am–one hour before sunset; adm*). It was not an amphitheatre but for classical drama – something rare this far north and an indication that, by the time the Romans conquered them, the culture of the Samnites was almost completely Hellenized. This theatre, built under Hadrian, once seated 20,000; it is now used for contemporary productions. Back past the cathedral on Corso Garibaldi, the dedicatory **obelisk** from the Isis temple stands in front of the town hall. Heading east, the little-known **Hortus Conclusus** is a small enclosed garden behind the church of S. Vincenzo, with sculptures by a local contemporary artist. Just beyond it, the **Rocca de' Rettori** is a fortress built by the popes in the 14th century; for centuries, Benevento was a papal enclave surrounded by the Kingdom of Naples. The fortress is now a part of the Museo Sannio (*see* below). Behind it there's a lovely park, the **Villa Comunale**.

Santa Sofia and the Museo Sannio

t 0824 21818; in theory open 9–1, closed Mon; adm.

Near the eastern end of Corso Garibaldi is the city's oldest church, **Santa Sofia**, built in the late 8th century. It is unusual for its plan, an irregular six-pointed star, and was built for the Lombard Prince Arechi II by an architect thoroughly grounded in the mystic geometry of the early Middle Ages. The vaulting is supported by recycled Roman columns and other columns have been hollowed out for use as holy water fonts.

The church cloister contains one of the south's most interesting provincial museums, the randomly open **Museo Sannio**. Sannio refers to the province of Samnium (*see* box, opposite), of which Benevento is the capital. The 12th-century cloister has a variety of strange twisted columns, under *pulvins* carved with monster-hunting, dancing, fantastical animals, bunnies and a camel or two. The best things are in the archaeological section: almost all the classic vases are Campanian copies of Greek ware – the production of ceramics was the engine that drove Campania Felix's economy in its glory days.

Trajan's Arch

Some people claim Benevento's triumphal arch, north of the tourist office on Via G. Manciotti, is better than Rome's. Built in AD 117, it is a serious piece of work – over 50ft of expensive Parian marble from Greece – and certainly better preserved than the ones in the capital (although it is currently clad in scaffolding). It marks the spot where the Appian Way entered Beneventum (now Via Traiana on the northern edge of the Old Town).

The skilfully carved reliefs on both faces record significant events in the career of the emperor Trajan (AD 98–117). The conqueror of Dacia (modern-day Romania) and Mesopotamia, Trajan, ranks among the greatest of the emperors and a little commemoration would not seem out of hand; nevertheless, cynics will enjoy the transparent, sometimes heavy-handed political propaganda of ornaments like this. In one of the panels, Trajan (the handsome fellow with the curly beard) is shown distributing gifts to children. In another, he presides over the *institutio alimentaria* – the Roman version of the dole.

Most of the scenes are about victories: Trajan announcing military reforms; Trajan celebrating a triumph; Jove handing Trajan one of his thunderbolts; and finally, the Apotheosis, where the late emperor is received among the gods while the goddess Roma escorts Hadrian to coronation as his divinely ordained successor.

Around Benevento: Samnium

Benevento is capital of Samnium, one of Italy's smallest provinces. The countryside, full of oak and walnut forests, is often reminiscent of Umbria. **Morcone**, to the north, has a memorable setting, draped on the curving slope of a hill like a Roman theatre. **Telese**, to

Some Samnite Curiosities

Two rooms in the museum are filled with objects from the Temple of Isis. Anyone who has read Apuleius' *The Golden Ass* will remember just how important the cult of the transcendent goddess Isis was throughout the Roman world. This Egyptian import certainly seemed to have found a home in Beneventum; nowhere in Europe has so much fine Egyptian statuary been retrieved.

The temple had imperial backing: one of the statues is of the founder, Emperor Domitian himself in Egyptian dress. Other works portray priestesses, sacred boats and sphinxes; another Apis bull and a porphyry '*cista mistica*' carved with a snake. The image of Isis is also there, formidably impressive even without a head.

Somehow this leads naturally to Benevento's more famous piece of exotica – the witches. In the days of the Lombards, women by the hundreds would dance around a sacred walnut tree on the banks of the River Sabato ('sabbath'). Even after the official conversion to Christianity in 663, the older religion persisted and Benevento is full of every sort of 'witch' story as a result. The best piece of modern sculpture in the Museo Sannio is a representation of the witches' dance.

Of course, the city has found ways to put the legend to use. In any bar in Italy, you can pick up a bottle of 'liquore Strega' (*strega* means witch) and read on the label the proud message: 'Made next to the train station in Benevento, Italy'.

the west on the road towards Lazio, lies near a small but pretty lake of the same name, with a popular spa establishment. The nearby ruins of the Samnite-Roman town of **Telesia** are remarkable for their perfectly octagonal walls with gates at the cardinal points. Further north, you will find **S.Lorenzello** – famous for its ceramic ware – which is transformed into an antiques market on the last weekend of every month.

Best of all, perhaps, is the town of **Sant'Agata dei Goti**, some kilometres north of the Via Appia between Benevento and Caserta, with its long line of buildings resembling a man-made cliff overhanging a little ravine. Sant'Agata takes its name from the Goths who founded it in the 6th century. The town was badly damaged in the 1980 earthquake, but its modest monuments, the Castello (*free*) and the 12th-century Chiesa di Santo Menna (***t*** *0823 717 159; open daily 10–1 and 3–7*) can now be visited.

East of Naples: The Irpinia Hills

South and east of Benevento there are few sights, but there is attractive mountain scenery in a region called Irpinia, which comprises most of the province of Avellino. In places, the mountains bear fine forests of oaks and chestnuts, as well as plantations of hazelnut trees. Other sections are grim and bare, a consequence of the 19th-century deforestation that devastated so much of southern Italy. Irpinia was also the region worst affected by the 1980 earthquake.

The main highway south from Caserta, circling around the north side of Vesuvius, isn't promising. **Nola**, the biggest town on the route, began life as another Oscan settlement. It had a famous early bishop, St Paulinus, a friend of St Augustine and, it is claimed, the inventor of the bell. (Bells are *campane* in Italian, from their Campanian origin.) To celebrate the anniversary of St Paulinus' return from imprisonment at the hands of the Vandals on 27 June, Nola puts on one of the most spectacular festivals in the south, the 'Dance of the Lilies' – a procession of giant, elaborately decorated wooden steeples carried by the men of the town (*see* 'Festivals', pp.56–7).

Further south, in the hills above the city of Nocera Inferiore, the ancient hamlet of **Nocera Superiore** has somehow kept intact its 4th-century church, an unusual round building with a cupola that may have been converted from a pagan sanctuary.

The road into the mountains of Irpinia begins at Nola and leads towards **Avellino**. This little provincial capital, important in Norman times, has been wrecked so many times by invaders and earthquakes that little remains to be seen. In the centre of town, the 17th-century Palazzo della Dogana has a façade of ancient statues and a big clock tower. Nearby, there is a Baroque fountain with Bellerophon dispatching the Chimæra. Archaeological finds from around Irpinia, both ancient and medieval, are kept in the modern Museo Irpino on Corso Europa.

Northwest of Avellino, **Monte Vergine** has been the most important pilgrimage site in the region since the arrival of a miraculous 'Black Madonna' in 1310 – a Byzantine icon of the Virgin, stolen from Constantinople by the Crusaders in the sack of 1204. Like others across Europe, the oxidation of its yellow paint turned it black over the centuries. Monte Vergine can be reached by a long, tortuous road or by a cable railway from the village of **Mercogliano**. The 12th-century church here, built over a sanctuary of Ceres and rebuilt many times, has two finely decorated tombs from the 1300s.

North of Avellino, separate roads lead to Taurasi, the centre of a wine region, and **Prata di Principato Ultra**, a tiny village with one of the oldest Christian monuments in the south. The Basilica dell'Annunziata was probably begun in the 3rd century; there are fragments of paintings and two small catacombs.

Eastern Irpinia is a wild, mountainous area where villages are few and far between. **Monte Terminio**, which has lately become a modest skiing area, has extensive woods and rushing mountain streams, along with plenty of pheasants, stags, boars, wild mushrooms, chestnuts and a few truffles – possibly the southernmost truffles to be found anywhere. **Sant'Angelo dei Lombardi**, further east, was an important medieval monastic centre; the earthquakes have spared bits of two simple churches from the 12th and 13th centuries.

Southern Campania

South of Salerno, the straight coastline of the Bay of Salerno cannot match the wonders of the Bay of Naples and the Amalfi coast. Most visitors head straight through to the superb ruins at Paestum, or down the A3 *autostrada* past Eboli (where Christ stopped) towards Sicily. But the Cilento region of southern Campania is well worth a stop, with an attractive coastline and a wild and scenic interior.

Paestum

t 0828 811 023; open daily 9–two hours before sunset; museum open 8.45–7.45; closed first and third Mon of each month; adm.

Paestum, at the start of the Cilento coast, is the site of the only well-preserved Greek temples north of Sicily. By the 9th century or so, this once-great city was breathing its last, a victim of economic decline and Arab raiders. As its people gradually abandoned it for safer settlements in the hills, Paestum was swallowed up by the thick forests of this subtropical corner of Italy. As usual on a Mediterranean coastal plain, when the people leave, the malaria mosquitoes take over and the anopheles mosquito, as fate would have it, can take some of the credit for preserving Paestum's ruins so well. By the Middle Ages, Paestum had become utterly uninhabitable – it meant certain death to stay there overnight – and, after a while, the city's very existence was forgotten. After being hidden away, like the Mayan temples in the Mexican jungle, for almost 1,000 years, the city was rediscovered in the 18th century; a crew of Charles III's road builders stumbled on to the huge temples in the midst of the forest. Originally *Poseidonia*, the city was founded in the 7th century BC by the Sybarites, as a station on the all-important trade route up Italy's west coast. The Romans took over in 273 BC, and the name became Latinized to Paestum. As a steadfast supporter of the Roman cause throughout the Punic Wars, Paestum was a favoured city. Famous around the Mediterranean for its flowers, especially roses, it prospered until the end of the Roman era.

Getting Around

The main **railway** line between Naples and Reggio di Calabria passes through **Paestum** and Ascea and Pisciotta on the **Cilento** coast, but only local trains call at these stops. More conveniently, there are frequent **buses** from the Piazza Concordia in Salerno (on the shore, by the Porto Turistico). These are run by several companies; some follow the coastal route, while others go through Battipaglia. Some of these go on to various resort towns on the Cilento coast. The list of towns, companies and schedules is bewildering, but fortunately, the tourist office in Salerno publishes a full list of them in the front of their annual hotel book.

There are two main **road** routes; the SS18 coast road and the A3 *autostrada* further inland (with the SS19 running alongside it through the Tanagro Valley). At Agropoli the SS267 leaves the SS18 and runs round the Cilento coast. North of Paestum there is also another turn off the SS18, the SS166 to the east – a long and winding road across the Cilento interior that eventually connects up with the A3 *autostrada*.

If you are travelling through Battipaglia, make sure you stop at one of the shops selling the locally produced buffalo mozzarella. Bite into it on the spot and let the milky juices run down your chin as the cheese melts in your mouth – you'll never taste anything like it.

Tourist Information

Paestum: in Piazza V. Veneto, **t** 089 231432. Close by the main station, it has the most complete information on transport and accommodation in Paestum and the Cilento. **AAST** has offices in Piazza Amendola, 84100, **t** 089 224 744, **f** 089 252 576, and Via Magna Grecia 155 (near the archaeological zone), **t** 0828 811 016, **f** 0828 722 322, *www.paestumtourism.it*.

Palinuro: Piazza Virgilio, **t** 0974 938 144.

Where to Stay and Eat

Most people think of Paestum as a day trip, but there are enough hotels around the site and on the nearby beaches to make overnight stays possible – and convenient if you have a car. Some of the best accommodation is at Laura beach, about 5km north of Paestum.

Hotels on the Cilento are on the whole modern and unremarkable, though there are some exceptions. ***Villaggi turistici***, of which there are dozens along the Cilento coast, offer an affordable alternative to the hotels. These are Italian-style holiday camps – but they are usually much nicer than this suggests, often with small bungalows set in well-landscaped grounds overlooking the sea, and generally with excellent sports and recreation facilities usually included in an all-in price. Look out for signs along the coast, or see the rear section of the hotel guidebook from the Salerno tourist office.

In the Cilento, most of the **restaurants** are in the hotels, and in summer, the chances are you'll have to opt for full or half board, although such arrangements are good value.

Paestum ✉ 84063

******Ariston**, Via Laura 13, **t** 0828 851 333/4, **f** 0828 851 596, *www.hotelariston.com* (*expensive*). Situated on the main road as you enter Paestum from Salerno, this modern and businesslike hotel offers large, comfortable rooms and full amenities.

******Le Palme**, Via Sterpinia 33, **t** 0828 851 025, **f** 0828 851 507, *www.lepalme.it* (*moderate*). Set back from Laura beach in Paestum, this hotel is popular with German tourists. It offers a range of good sports facilities and the private beach is a short walk away. *Closed Nov–Mar.*

Today, the forests have been cleared and the ruins of the city stand in the open on the green and quiet plain. Not only the celebrated temples have survived, but much of the 5km circuit of walls still stands to some height, along with some of the towers and gates. Most of Paestum's important buildings are grouped along an axis between the Porta Aurea and the Porta Giustizia, with the forum at its centre.

★★★Laura, Via Marittima 10, **t/f** 0828 851 068, (*moderate*). This good family hotel, just north of Le Palme, is pretty and relaxed with helpful management. It has its own private beach and 13 rooms.

★★★Villa Rita, Via Principe di Piemonte **t/f** 0828 811 081, *www.hotelvillarita.it* (*moderate*). Close to the Porta Giustizia entrance to the ruins, this modern hotel (which is under the same management as the Nettuno Restaurant) is set in attractive countryside just 1km from the sea, with a swimming pool. Convenient for an overnight visit to the temples. *Closed Nov–mid-Mar.*

Nettuno, Via Nettuno 2, **t** 0828 811 028 (*moderate*). In the archaeological zone itself, tucked into the city walls near Porta Giustizia, the excellent Nettuno has been a family run restaurant specializing in seafood for over 70 years. The wine cellar holds more than 400 labels from across Italy. *Closed Mon, mid-Jan to mid-Feb.*

Museo, **t** 0828 811 135 (*cheap*). Also in the archaeological zone, right next door to the museum, this seafood restaurant offers excellent value, with an informal dining room and outdoor terrace.

Bar Anna, **t** 0828 811 196 (*cheap*). If you are just seeking a tasty snack close to the museum, then this bar run by the kindly Signora Pia offers a good selection of cold *antipasti*, as well as the local buffalo mozzarella in a tomato salad (*insalata alla caprese*). *Closed Mon in winter.*

Santa Maria di Castellabate ✉ 84072

★★★★Castelsandra, Via Piano Melaino, **t/f** 0974 966 021 (*expensive*). Located further south, high on the point above the small towns of San Marco and Santa Maria di Castellabate, this hotel has a pretty setting and outstanding views back towards the Amalfi coast. The hotel consists of a Club Med-style complex of landscaped villas and innumerable sports facilities, as well as evening entertainment and is, unsurprisingly, popular with foreign package holiday operators.

★★★Sonia, Via Gennaro Landi 25, **t/f** 0974 961 172 (*moderate*). This authentic Cilento hotel is well-placed on the seafront, with pleasant rooms and obliging, courteous management. *Closed Nov–Mar.*

San Marco ✉ 81000

★★★★Hotel Hermitage, Via Catarozza, **t** 0974 966 618, **f** 0974 966 619, *www.hermitage.it* (*expensive*). Situated about 1km outside San Marco, the rustic façade of this pretty hotel is attractively decked out with flowers. Inside, the hotel has been completely renovated, and there's a complimentary bus service to their own beach. Traditional Cilento cooking is served in the well-situated restaurant and on the delightful open-air terrace. Half board only in high season. *Closed Nov.*

Acciaroli ✉ 84072

★★La Scogliera, **t** 0974 904 014 (*cheap*). The best of a bunch of modest hotels in the quiet village of Acciaroli. This is another 'nautical' hotel with a popular restaurant situated on the tiny harbour front.

Pioppi ✉ 84060

★★★La Vela, Via Caracciolo 96, **t** 0974 905 025, **f** 0974 905 140, *www.lavelapioppi.com* (*expensive*). For a mixture of kitsch, traditional cooking and buckets of enthusiasm, try this maritime-themed hotel a couple of kilometres beyond Acciaroli in the village of Pioppi. Portholes, ropes, rafters and boat-shaped tables complete the seafaring feel. There's an outdoor terrace hung with *pomodorini* (cherry tomatoes) and an open fire for cooking. Despite the drawbacks of a rather grubby pebble beach and a wild open sea, La Vela, is a treat for the

The two grand temples that everyone comes to see are at the southern end: the Basilica and the Temple of Neptune (*see* p.177).

To the west, some of the streets of the city have been excavated, though little is left to see. North, around the broad **Forum** – really a simple rectangular space in the manner of a Greek *agora* – are the remains of an amphitheatre, a round *bouleterion*, adventurous traveller. Half board only. *Closed Dec–Mar.*

Palinuro ✉ 84064

Towards the southern end of the Cilento coast, Ascea has a small collection of hotels around its marina, but Palinuro has developed into the region's fully fledged holiday town.

★★★★**Gabbiano**, Via Pisacane, **t** 0974 931 592, **f** 0974 931 121, *www.ilgabbianohotel.it* (*luxury*). A well-maintained and crisply furnished hotel situated on the seafront a short distance from the centre of town. The modern design incorporates a sheltered swimming pool and a fine, sandy beach. Half board only.

★★★★**King's Residence**, Via Piano Faracchio, **t** 0974 931 324, **f** 0974 931 418, *www.hotelkings.it* (*very expensive*). This hotel outside Palinuro is in a stunning setting, perched in a crow's nest position high on the cliffs and overlooking Buondormire ('Sleep Well') Bay. Every room comes with a terrace or balcony. A pathway runs down to the pretty little private beach, kitted out with a small bar for drinks and light meals. *Closed Nov–Feb.*

★★★**La Torre**, Via Porte 5, **t** 0974 931 107, **f** 0974 931 264, *www.latorre.ws* (*expensive*). Another attractive hotel, located a short distance from both the town and beach, and marred only by the rather unhelpful management. There are some apartments also available. *Closed Nov–Mar.*

★★★**Conchiglia**, Via Indipendenza 52, **t** 0974 931 018, **f** 0974 931 030, *www.hotellaconchiglia.it* (*expensive*). Like so many Cilento hotels, this place is a remnant from the 1960s. It offers 25 clean and pleasant rooms, simple hospitality and friendly management. Parking can be tricky.

Da Carmelo, just outside Palinuro, 1km along the road towards Camerota, **t** 0974 931 138 (*moderate*). At this lively *trattoria* guests dine well on dishes prepared according to traditional recipes. Seafood comes highly recommended by the throng of participating locals, and it is worth going out of your way just to savour the excellent *antipasti*. Self-catering apartments are also available above the restaurant. *Closed Wed except high season, 15 Oct–15 Nov.*

Taverna del Porto, Via Porto 50, **t** 0974 931 278 (*cheap*). Down by the harbour, this two-tiered bar/restaurant serves lunch at tables just a stone's throw from the water's edge, and dinner on the more formal upper level.

O' Guarracino, Via Porto, **t** 0974 938 309 (*cheap*). A pretty café-cum-*trattoria* with tables set out beneath a pleasantly shady canopy, also down by the harbour.

Marina di Camerota ✉ 84064

★★★★**America**, **t** 0974 932 131, **f** 0974 932 177, *www.americahotel.it* (*very expensive*). Modern, clean and acceptable, although without any particular charm, this is one of a bunch of fairly uninspiring hotels in Camerota, near the southeastern point of the Cilento. *Closed Oct–Mar.*

Da Valentone, Piazza San Domenico 3, **t** 0974 932 004 (*moderate*). Camerota's only first-class restaurant specializes in freshly caught seafood and such local specialities as *spaghetti alla valentone* (spaghetti with tuna, capers and olives). *Closed Mon.*

A Vasulata, Via S. Vito 25 (*cheap*). If you don't mind the wait, this tiny place next to the ceramics shops in Camerota Alta is a delightful spot, one of a kind that is fast disappearing in Italy. Guests eat cheek by jowl, choosing from a limited but excellent menu based on Neapolitan *cucina povera* – homemade *pizzette*, stuffed tomatoes, aubergines and all sorts of pasta. There is often a queue outside and the kitchen closes once all the food has been eaten. *Summer only; closes end of Aug.*

or council house, and other buildings. Further north is the third and smallest temple, the **Temple of Ceres**. While you are exploring Paestum, look out for the wild flowers. More than one 19th-century traveller claimed to have found descendants of Paestum's famous roses (*bifera rosaria Paestum*) growing wild, and some may still be around.

The Temple of Neptune

This is the best preserved of Paestum's two great Doric edifices and the building that is shown in all of the tourist literature. Built around 450 BC, it is about 200ft long and all of the structure survives except the roof and the internal walls. Similarities to another temple at Tarentum suggest it was dedicated to Apollo but Hera and Zeus are also possible contenders – like all of Paestum's temples, the name 'Temple of Neptune' was just a guess by the early archaeologists.

The Basilica (Temple of Hera)

A century older and a little smaller than the Temple of Neptune, the Basilica was devoted to house two cults, most probably connected with Hera, who was the tutelary goddess of the city. Because the building is missing its Doric frieze and pediment, the first archaeologists did not recognize the building as a temple: hence its name, Basilica. The aesthetic may not be quite what you would expect – the dimensions are squat and strong rather than graceful and tall. Still, this is the classic austerity of Greek architecture at its best.

There is more to it than meets the eye. If you look closely along the rows of columns, or the lines of the base, you may notice that nothing in either of them is perfectly straight The edges bulge outwards, as they do in the Parthenon and every other Greek building. This is an architectural trick called *entasis*; it creates an optical illusion, making the lines seem straight at a distance.

Greek temples like this are among the most sober and serious buildings in Western architecture, based on a simple system of perfect proportion. The unadorned form may seem austere and academic, but with a little imagination, you can picture them in their original beauty – they would have been covered in a sort of enamel made of gleaming ground marble, setting off the brilliant colours of the polychromed sculptural reliefs on the pediments and frieze.

The Museum

Paestum's museum holds most of the sculptural fragments and finds from the town. Some of the best reliefs are not from Paestum at all, but from the recently discovered **sanctuary of Hera**, a few kilometres north at the mouth of the River Sele. This temple, mentioned by many ancient writers, is said to have been founded by Jason and the Argonauts during their wanderings. From tombs excavated just outside the city come some examples of Greek fresco painting – probably the only ones in existence. Look out for the most famous fresco, *The Diver*, which you will have probably seen reproduced innumerable times elsewhere. Even though the Greeks took painting as seriously as they did sculpture, you will not find any similar surviving examples anywhere else.

Next to the museum is the 5th-century Paleo-Christian **church of SS. Annunziata**. Originally an open-plan basilica, it has been redesigned over the centuries and was finally restored to its original simplicity only a decade ago.

The Cilento

After the Bay and the Amalfi coast – two heavy courses for a holiday banquet – we can offer the Cilento peninsula as a light, refreshing dessert. The Cilento is a squarish, low massif jutting out from the coast between the Gulf of Salerno and the Gulf of Policastro, beginning just south of Paestum. Its mountain scenery may not be quite as breathtaking as the Amalfi Drive, but the Cilento makes up for it by being delightfully wild and unspoilt, and altogether one of the most beguiling out-of-the-way places to spend your time in southern Italy.

The interior of the Cilento is not traversed by any easy roads and the traveller heading south from Salerno has a choice of two routes. On the one hand, there is the long, leisurely drive along the coast, past Paestum and a number of small, casual resorts. Alternatively, you can follow the main road, the A3 *Autostrada del Sole*, inland over the mountains and around the eastern edge of the Cilento – a route of often beautiful, wild scenery along the valley of the Tanagro River.

Much of the Cilento, including the interior and the southern coast, is now part of the Cilento and Valley of Diana National Park (*www.parks.it/parco.nazionale.cilento/* and *www.pncvd.it*), which acquired UNESCO World Heritage listing in 1997.

The Cilento Coast

South of Paestum, the shore becomes jagged and mountainous, passing groves of pines alternating with rugged cliffs and pocket-sized beaches. Most of the villages along it have become quiet, cosy resorts that cater mostly to Italians.

Agropoli comes first, a noisy resort in summer with a peaceful warren of medieval streets up above the marina. Further inland, perched among the mountains, is **Perdifumo**, a sleepy village with far-reaching views over the surrounding hills to the Gulf of Salerno and the distant Amalfi coast.

Back on the coast, you come to **Santa Maria di Castellabate**, **San Marco** and **Punta Licosa**, on the westernmost point of the Cilento, named after the siren, Leucosia. Legend has it that she threw herself into the sea after her failure to entice Ulysses onto the rocks. From here, you can take a small boat out to an uninhabited islet, also called Licosa, where there are some unidentified ancient ruins. Further down the coast, **Acciaroli** and **Pioppi** are among the nicer resort towns of the Cilento.

South of the latter, and just inland from the village of Ascea Marina, you can visit the ruins of another Greek city, **Velia**. Don't expect any spectacular ruins of the order of Paestum here. Velia disappeared gradually and most of its buildings were carried off for building stone long ago. Elea, as it was known, was a colony of the Ionian city of Phocæa, and a sister city of another important Phocæan foundation – Marseille, in France. Elea was never large or important, but its name lives on gloriously in philosophy; the Elean school of philosophers produced some of the most brilliant minds of the ancient world: logical grinds like Parmenides, who proposed the first theory of atoms, and wiseacres like Zeno with his pesky paradoxes. Some of the fortifications survive, including one well-preserved gate – the Porta Rosa – and just enough of the *agora*, baths and streets to enable us to guess at how the city may have looked.

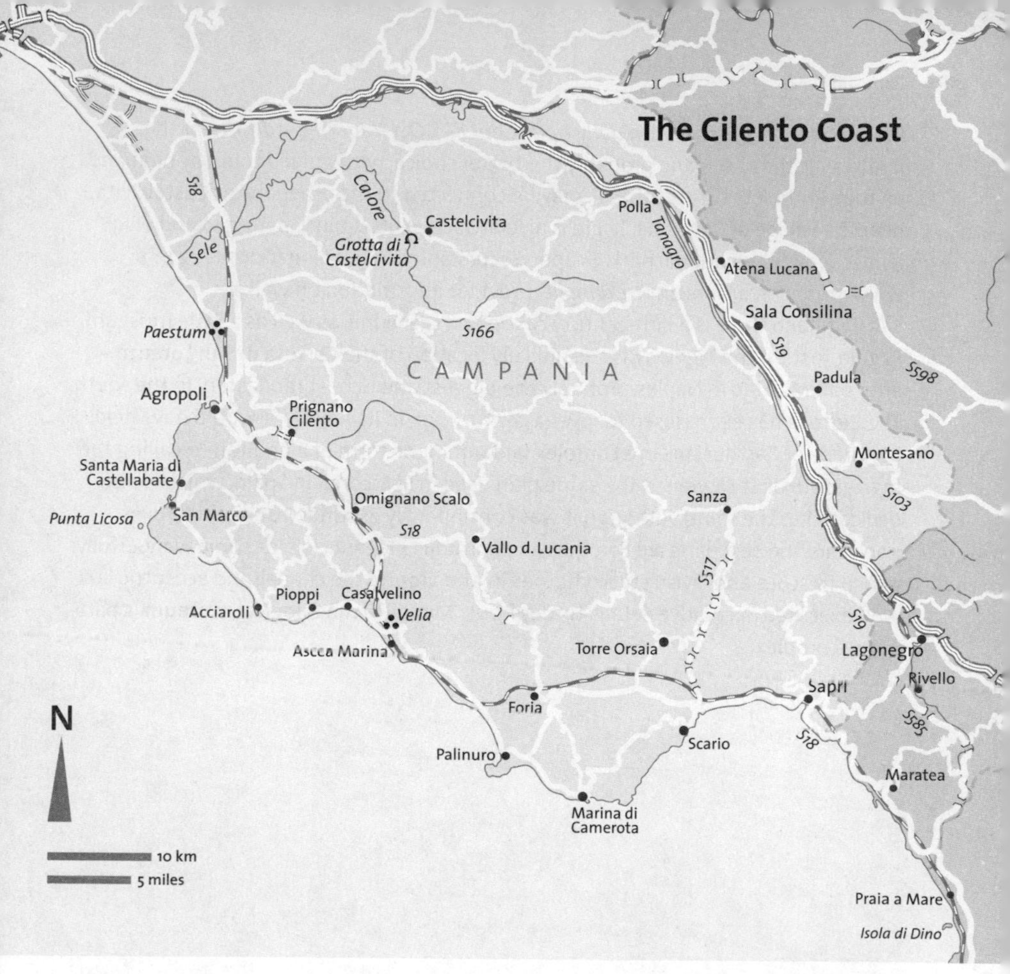

Both **Ascea Marina** and its neighbouring locality of **Casalvelino** have pretty beaches, but the best ones of all, perhaps, can be found in the rugged terrain around **Palinuro**. This town, which has a small **museum** of archaeological finds, takes its name from Aeneas' pilot Palinurus, who is supposedly buried here – Virgil made the whole story up for the *Aeneid*, but that hasn't stopped it from sticking fast in local legend. From the harbour at Palinuro, you can join a tour or hire canoes to see a series of marine caves around the headland. If the sun is at the right angle, the caves give off an eerie submarine glow, as if lit from beneath by turquoise floodlights. Beyond Palinuro, the sandy coast curves back north into the Gulf of Policastro. Here two more pleasant beach villages, **Scario** and **Sapri**, mark the southern boundary of Campania.

Inland Cilento

South from Salerno, the *autostrada* skirts the back edge of the Cilento on its way to Calabria. Christ may have stopped at **Eboli**, but there's no reason why you should – and that goes for **Battipaglia** and Polla, too – except to sample the delicious buffalo mozzarella for which Battipaglia is famous. The true delights of this region are subterranean – two first-rate caves on opposite slopes of the Monti Alburni.

Pertosa (**t** *0975 397 037; open daily April–Sept 8–7, Oct–Mar 9–4; adm*), near the highway, is the easier and probably the better choice, with guided tours by boat and on foot. Potholers suspect that it may be connected to the other one at **Castelcivita**, near the village of Controne. There is also attractive hiking in the rugged and wild landscape of the national park. Gruppo Escursionistico Trekking (**t** *0975 722 587, www.gruppoescursionisticotrekking.it*) provides information on walks.

At **Teggiano** there is a 13th-century castle and cathedral, as well as a little museum. Padula, just off the highway, is the unlikely location of the **Certosa di San Lorenzo** – after San Martino in Naples, probably the biggest and richest monastery in the south. The Certosa has been closed for over a century but, in its heyday, it would have held hundreds of Carthusians in a complex laid out in the form of a gridiron (recalling the martyrdom of St Lawrence, the same plan used in El Escorial in Spain, which is also dedicated to the saint). Although it was continuously expanded and rebuilt over 400 years, the best parts are Baroque: an enormous, elegant cloister; some wonderfully garish frescoes and lavish stucco figures in and around the chapel; and eccentric but well-executed decorative details throughout. A small **archaeological museum** is part of the complex.

Calabria and the Basilicata

12

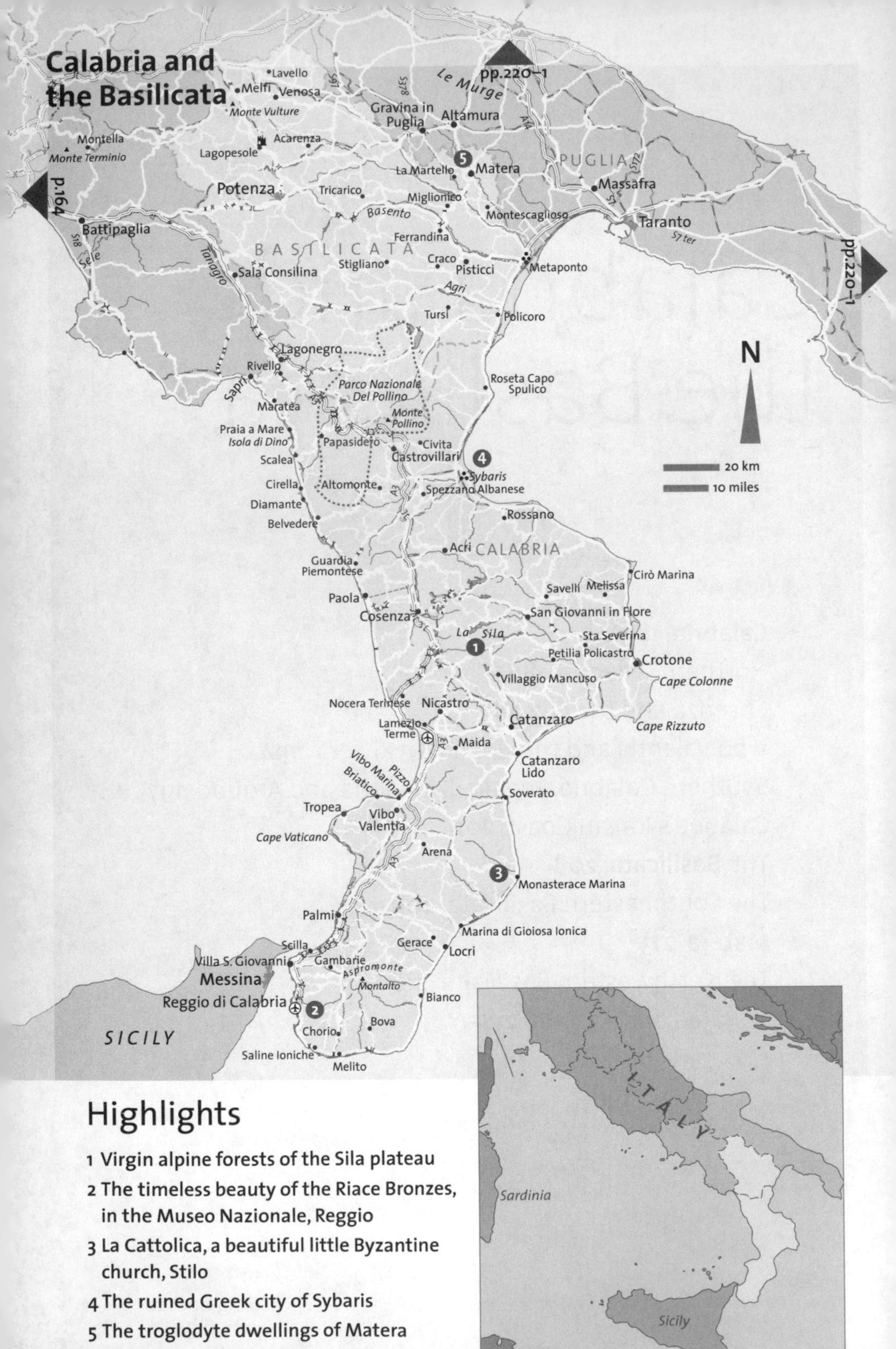

Highlights

1 Virgin alpine forests of the Sila plateau
2 The timeless beauty of the Riace Bronzes, in the Museo Nazionale, Reggio
3 La Cattolica, a beautiful little Byzantine church, Stilo
4 The ruined Greek city of Sybaris
5 The troglodyte dwellings of Matera

Italy may be a country unusually blessed by fortune, but her favours are by no means evenly spread. To balance regions like the Veneto or Campania, with their manifold delights, nature has given Italy its own empty quarter, the adjacent regions of Calabria and the Basilicata.

Calabria is the toe of the Italian boot – a gnarled, knobbly toe, amply endowed with corns and bunions and pointed accusingly at neighbouring Sicily. Almost all of it is ruggedly mountainous, leaving just enough room at the edges for the longest, broadest, emptiest beaches in Italy. It can claim four natural attractions: a scenic western coast, the beautifully forested highland regions of Aspromonte at the toe, the Sila in the centre, and Monte Pollino in the north. Most man-made attractions have been shaken to bits by earthquakes, Calabria's eternal plague and, as a result, there are plenty of ruins and ghost towns.

The Basilicata offers plenty of lonely, wild-west landscapes, some impressive castles and two increasingly popular destinations, the resort of Maratea and the strange city of Matera, where people lived in caves as recently as 50 years ago. Still known to many people by its old name of Lucania, the Basilicata takes on all comers for the title of Italy's most obscure region – or at least it did, until the furore surrounding Mel Gibson's *The Passion of The Christ* placed a spotlight on Matera, where the film was set.

Calabria

Calabria wasn't always poor. From about 750 BC, the Greeks extensively colonized southern Italy. Rhegium, today's Reggio di Calabria, came first, followed in short order by Sybaris, Croton and Locris among others. These towns, happily situated along the major trade route of the Mediterranean, rapidly became as cultured as those of Greece itself – and far wealthier. It was a brilliant hour and a brief one. After a time, blessed with a lack of external enemies, the cities of 'greater Greece' took to fighting among themselves in a series of ghastly, cruel wars over the most trivial of causes, often resulting in the total destruction of a city and the massacre of its inhabitants. Weakened by their own barbarous behaviour, the Greek cities then became pawns between Rome and Carthage in the Punic Wars; the victorious Romans took a terrible vengeance on those such as Taras (Taranto, in modern Puglia) that supported the wrong side. Roman rule meant a slow decline for the survivors, and by the 6th century, the beautiful cities of Magna Grecia were abandoned to the mosquitoes.

Don't, however, come to Calabria looking for classical ruins. The great museum at Reggio gives a hint of what these cities were but at the sites themselves almost nothing remains. Golden Sybaris has only just been found by the archaeologists, and only at Metapontum will you see so much as a few standing columns. Some may call the emptiness a monument to Greek hubris, or perhaps somehow these cities were doomed from the start. Considering Magna Grecia can be profoundly disconcerting; even in the ancient Mediterranean, it is strange and rare for so many big cities to disappear so completely.

Getting Around

Calabria's coasts are well served by **rail**; the Rome–Naples–Reggio di Calabria line runs up and down the west coast (15 trains a day), while another line hugs the Ionian coastline from Reggio to Taranto.

Reggio di Calabria has two railway stations: the Stazione Marittima, from which crossings are made to Messina in Sicily, and the Stazione Centrale. If you're just making a quick stop for the museum, the Marittima is closer.

Rail connections to the **interior** are chancy at best. A few trains go to Cosenza, but you'll usually have to change at Paola or Sibari. There are also regular buses from Paola to Cosenza. At Catanzaro it's the same; most trains stop only at Catanzaro Lido, 9km away (although there is a regular local bus to the city centre). In Cosenza, buses leave from Piazza L. Fera, at the northern end of Corso Mazzini, for Catanzaro (several daily) and points around the province, including towns in the Sila.

A pleasant way to see the **Sila** is on the old private FCL narrow-gauge railway that runs three trains each day between Cosenza and San Giovanni in Fiore. The FCL station in Cosenza is hard to find, as it is behind the now disused FS station in the town. There is another attractive local rail line around the Tropea peninsula from Pizzo to Rosarno.

Calabria has two **airports**. Lamezia-Terme, the main regional airport, is on the plain of Santa Eufemia near the SS280 Catanzaro turn-off from the SS18. It has scheduled flights to most of the major Italian cities. The airport at Reggio di Calabria, just south of the city, has regular services only to Rome and Milan.

Road routes around Calabria are simple. The SS18 hugs the west coast, the SS106 follows the east coast, and the A3 *Autostrada del Sol*e sticks to the west coast between Reggio and Cosenza, but runs inland north of Cosenza. Note that the SS18 gets crowded with Italian beachgoers in July and August.

Inland roads are winding and slow. The main roads crossing the peninsula are the scenic SS107 between Paola and Crotone via Cosenza, and the faster and shorter SS280 through Catanzaro. Fill up with petrol before venturing into the mountains.

Car and passenger ferries to Sicily leave from Villa San Giovanni – the quickest route, with the most services – and Reggio di Calabria. There are two companies: Caronte, **t** 0965 793 131, and Tourist Ferry, **t** 0965 751 413. Services are very frequent and when you arrive you'll be directed to whichever ferry is leaving next.

Nor has this corner of Italy been any more hospitable to civilization in the centuries since. Calabria, in particular, has suffered more at the hands of history than any region deserves. After the Romans and the malaria mosquito put an end to the brilliant, short-lived civilization of Magna Grecia, Calabria has endured one wrenching earthquake after another, not to mention Arab raiders, Norman bully boys, Spaniards and Bourbons, the most vicious of feudal landlords and the most backward and ignorant of monks and priests. By the 18th century, all these elements had combined to effect one of the most complete social breakdowns ever seen in modern Europe. Calabria staggered into anarchy, its mountains given over to bands of cut-throats while the country people endured almost subhuman poverty and oppression. Not surprisingly, everyone who was able to chose to emigrate; today, there are several times as many Calabresi living in the Americas as in Calabria itself.

While famine, disease and misgovernment were putting an end to old Calabria, natural disasters – such as the terrible earthquake of 1783, and the even worse one in 1908 that destroyed the city of Reggio – were erasing the last traces of it. Calabria's stage was cleared for a modest rebirth and the opportunity for it came after the Second World War, when Mr Rockefeller's DDT made the coasts habitable for the first time in over a millennium. Within a few years, a government land reform improved

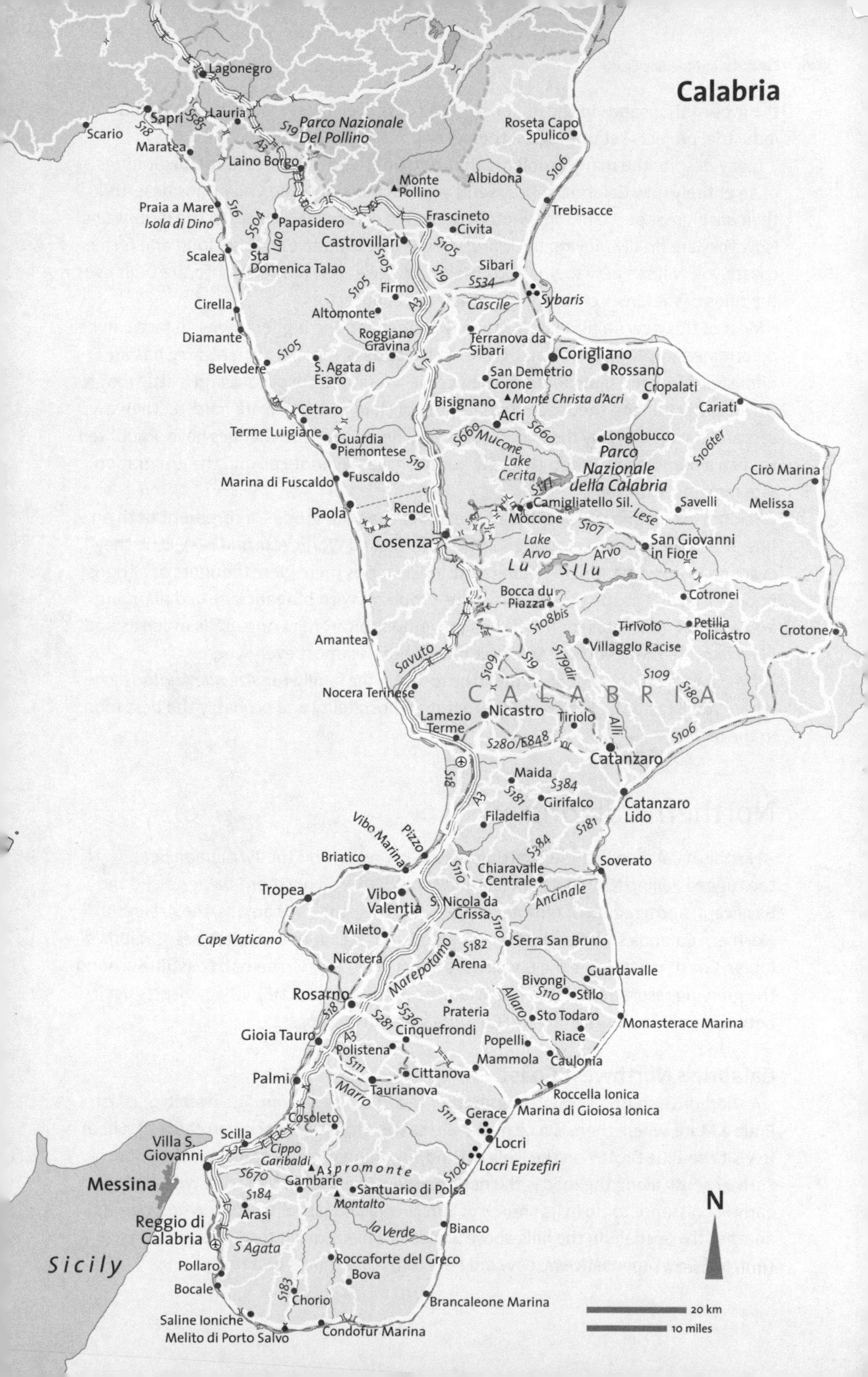
Calabria
Lagonegro
Sapri
Lauria
Scario
Parco Nazionale Del Pollino
Maratea
Laino Borgo
Monte Pollino
Roseta Capo Spulico
Albidona
Trebisacce
Praia a Mare
Isola di Dino
Papasidero
Frascineto
Civita
Castrovillari
Scalea
Sta Domenica Talao
Sibari
Sybaris
Firmo
Cascile
Cirella
Altomonte
Diamante
Roggiano Gravina
Terranova da Sibari
Belvedere
S. Agata di Esaro
Corigliano
Rossano
San Demetrio Corone
Monte Christa d'Acri
Cropalati
Bisignano
Cariati
Cetraro
Acri
Terme Luigiane
Guardia Piemontese
Mucone
Longobucco
Parco Nazionale della Calabria
Lake Cecita
Cirò Marina
Marina di Fuscaldo
Fuscaldo
Camigliatello Sil.
Savelli
Melissa
Paola
Rende
Moccone
Lese
Cosenza
Lake Arvo
Arvo
San Giovanni in Fiore
Lu Silu
Bocca du Piazza
Cotronei
Amantea
Tirivolo
Petilia Policastro
Crotone
Villagglo Racise
Savuto
Nocera Terinese
CALABRIA
Lamezio Terme
Nicastro
Tiriolo
Alli
Catanzaro
Maida
Girifalco
Catanzaro Lido
Filadelfia
Vibo Marina
Pizzo
Briatico
Soverato
Chiaravalle Centrale
Tropea
Vibo Valentia
S. Nicola da Crissa
Ancinale
Mileto
Cape Vaticano
Serra San Bruno
Nicotera
Arena
Guardavalle
Bivongi
Stilo
Marepotamo
Rosarno
Prateria
Allaro
Sto Todaro
Monasterace Marina
Cinquefrondi
Gioia Tauro
Polistena
Popelli
Riace
Mammola
Caulonia
Cittanova
Palmi
Taurianova
Marro
Roccella Ionica
Gerace
Marina di Gioiosa Ionica
Cosoleto
Scilla
Villa S. Giovanni
Locri
Cippo Garibaldi
Locri Epizefiri
Messina
Aspromonte
Gambarie
Santuario di Polsa
Arasi
Montalto
Reggio di Calabria
Bianco
S Agata
la Verde
Sicily
Roccaforte del Greco
Pollaro
Bova
Bocale
Chorio
Brancaleone Marina
Saline Ioniche
Melito di Porto Salvo
Condofur Marina
N
20 km
10 miles

the lives of thousands in the region and the *Cassa per il Mezzogiorno*'s roads and industrial projects set out to pull their economies into the 20th century.

Today, despite the many problems that remain, it's possible to see the beginnings of an entirely new Calabria. A thousand years or more ago, the Calabrians deserted their once-great port cities for wretched, though defensible, villages in the mountains. Now they are finally moving back, and everywhere around Calabria's long and fertile coasts, you will see new towns and cities. Some, like Locri or Metaponto, are built over the ruins of the Greek cities that are their direct ancestors.

Most of this new Calabria isn't much to look at yet. The bigger towns, in fact, can be determinedly ugly (like Crotone). Calabria these days, for all its rich history, has an unmistakable frontier air about it. The people are simple, suspicious and a little rough. Unlike other Italians, they seem to have lots of children. They work hard, fix their own cars and tractors, and lay their concrete everywhere. So far, the changes have amounted to such a humble revolution that few people have even noticed and the emigration rate remains enormous.

Seldom in Calabria will you see a hotel older than the 1960s – a comment both on how much the region has changed since the Second World War, and how little they ever had to do with tourism beforehand. In the 1960s there were thoughts of a tourist boom – Calabria as the new Riviera – but problems with bureaucracy, bad planning and a lack of good sites for hotels has prevented this from taking off as much as had been expected. Still, you will find acceptable hotels almost everywhere.

If you have a car, the best deals are to be found in the family-run *Aziende Agrituristiche*, where you'll taste the famed southern Italian hospitality and probably the best food in the region.

Northern Calabria

Northern Calabria includes a string of low-key resorts on the Tyrrhenian Sea, the rugged Pollino National Park (actually split between northern Calabria and the Basilicata) and a region of remote villages of Italy's ethnic Albanians, the *Arbëresh*. Northern Calabria's Ionian (east) coast is covered later in this chapter (*see* 'Calabria's Ionian Coast', p.202), as is the Basilicata's short stretch of Tyrrhenian coastline around the growing resort of Maratea (*see* 'Maratea and Around', p.218), which inserts itself between Campania's Cilento and Calabria's northwest coast.

Calabria's Northwest Coast

A short drive south of Maratea is another resort on a less dramatic stretch of coast: **Praia a Mare**, where there is a 14th-century castle. From the beach, you can rent a boat to visit the 'Blue Grotto' on the **Isola di Dino**, an uninhabited islet just off the shore. Further south along the road is the now overdeveloped **Scalea**, a resort with a good early Renaissance tomb in its church of San Nicola and bits of Byzantine frescoes in another, the Spedale. In the hills above Scalea is a place called the Mercurion, once a centre of Greek monasticism; now only the ruins of a church remain.

Where to Stay and Eat

Acquafredda ✉ 85046

****Villa del Mare, Via Nazionale 18, t 0973 878 007, f 0973 878 102, *villadelmare@tiscalinet.it*, *www.hotelvilladelmare.com* (*moderate*). Just off the SS18 and located up on the cliffs, with a lift down to its private beach, this is one of the best of the less expensive choices. *Closed Nov–Mar.*

Praia a Mare ✉ 87028

**Calabria, Via Roma 58, t 0985 72350 (*cheap*). A simple place near the sea with its own private stretch of beach. Praia is a good place to look for a cheap room, as there are at least 10 other places very similar to this one. *Closed Oct–May.*

Pan della Viene, Contrada Pan della Viene, Corso da Viscigliosa, t 0985 74190 (*cheap*). Serves a wide selection of grilled fish and dishes such as seafood served with porcini mushrooms or rocket. *Closed Tues.*

Scalea ✉ 87029

****De Rose, Corso Mediterraneo, t 0985 20273, f 0985 920 194, *www.hotelderose.it* (*very expensive*). A typical modern Mediterranean hotel, with TV in the rooms and air conditioning – both useful considerations in these parts, where it's always hot, and there can be little to do. For more traditional pastimes in this neck of the woods, the hotel also occupies the best part of Scalea's beach. *Closed Nov–Mar.*

***Talao, Corso Mediterraneo 66, t 0985 20444, f 0985 939 893 (*moderate*). You can get many of the same amenities at a slightly better rate at this hotel, which is also near the town's beaches. *Closed Nov–Mar.*

Cetraro ✉ 87022

*****Grand Hotel San Michele, t 0982 91012, f 0982 91430, *www.sanmichele.it* (*very expensive*). Here you'll find an exception to the modern hotels along this stretch of coast: this is a very pretty old villa, converted into a hotel to provide a rare island of elegance in homespun Calabria. It is near Cetraro, in a location called Bosco. The name is no deception, as there are plenty of trees around for shade, as well as a golf course, a beach and a very good restaurant that turns local specialities into gourmet treats. The delicious and distinctive house wine is made in the hotel's own vineyards. *Closed Nov–Feb, open for Christmas and New Year.*

***Park Hotel, t 0982 610 945, f 0982 610 910 (*moderate*). Although it's less grand, this is another distinctive establishment. It's not at all the usual concrete resort hotel, but a collection of attractive cottages spread out under the trees. You'll find it on the SS18 at Fuscaldo Marina, south of Cetraro. However, you have to take full board.

Viggianello ✉ 85040

Most hotels in the Pollino National Park are here, although there are a few in the villages of San Severino Lucano and Terranova del Pollino.

***Parco Hotel Pollino, Via Marcaldo 25, t/f 0973 664 018, *www.parcohtpollino.it* (*moderate*). One of the best choices in town with a pool. The hotel organizes trips into the mountains.

Castrovillari ✉ 87012

****La Locanda di Alia, Via Jetticelle 55, t/f 0981 46370, *www.alia.it* (*moderate*). It is worth stopping at Castrovillari for this surprisingly tasteful little collection of apartments set among gardens. Some of the apartments are split-level with a separate living area, and the five suites have hydromassage facilities. The hotel also contains one of Calabria's best restaurants, which serves a range of inventive seafood dishes and traditional Calabrian favourites. The menu changes daily, making the most of the best fresh ingredients. You can also sample the hotel's own wines, which are sold in their *enoteca*. *Closed Sun.*

**Skanderberg, Via Arcuri 24, Frascineto, t 0981 32117, f 0981 32818 (*cheap*). A good stopover located at nearby Frascineto, near the motorway exit.

Spezzano Albanese ✉ 87019

Most hotels here are a little outside town.

***San Francesco Terme, Loc. Bagni, t 0981 953 068, f 0981 953 251 (*moderate*). This hotel just outside of town caters mainly to spa customers.

***Due Torri, t 0981 953 613. A cheap and cheerful option on the SS19.

Piana dei Gelsi, Loc. Pantano. Run by the Rinaldi family, this *agriturismo* accommodation choice is not far from town. It will give you a taste of the *Arbërësh* hospitality and cuisine.

Further into the mountains, beyond **Papasidero**, is the **Grotta del Romito** (*tours daily 9–1 and 4–8 in summer; 9–5 in winter; adm*), which was inhabited in the early Palaeolithic period. A rock at the entrance to the cave is decorated with an unusually clear image of a bull (to be precise, the extinct Bos Primigenius), with the head of a smaller bull visible beneath. Several feet away, two tombs have been uncovered, each revealing the remains of a couple locked in an embrace. One of the pairs, thought to be 11–12,000 years old, appears to have been deformed by rickets. The position of the tomb suggests that they were given an elevated position in society as a result of their disabilities, which may have been attributed to supernatural intervention.

South of Scalea is **Cirella**; from here, you can take a boat trip to another uninhabited islet, the **Isola di Cirella**, or climb up to visit the overgrown remains of **Cirella Vecchia**, a village founded by the Greeks that survived until a French bombardment in the Napoleonic Wars; bits of a Greek mausoleum remain along with streets of half-ruined homes and churches. **Diamante** comes next, a pretty village of narrow streets, stacked on a rock above the sea. **Guardia Piemontese**, a small thermal spa on a balcony over the coast, is still partially inhabited by descendants of the Waldenses, religious dissenters from 13th-century Piedmonte and Liguria. Frederick II granted them refuge here from Church pogroms, but most of them were massacred by the Spanish in 1561.

Paola, where the road from Cosenza meets the coast, is a larger and somewhat dishevelled resort, a fitting introduction to the towns of the 'Calabrian Riviera' to the south. Above it stands the 15th-century Santuario di San Francesco di Poala dedicated to the town's most famous son, Calabria's patron saint – not the same Francis as the Saint of Assisi. The sanctuary is the object of pilgrimages from all over southern Italy, as well as the focus for the town's lavish annual *festa*, which reaches its climax on the saint's day, 4 May.

Pollino National Park

If you enjoy wild scenery, this magnificent national park, east of the A3 *autostrada* inland from Maratea, is worth a visit. This tract of high country is one of the most unspoiled natural areas of the south, and also one of the few places in southern Italy that still retains substantial areas of forest cover. The park, which was recently expanded, is now the largest national park in Italy, split between northern Calabria and the Basilicata.

The park's rugged highlands contain large stands of cuirassed pine, *Arbëresh* villages (*see* opposite) and rare animal species that have been protected by the region's inaccessibility and isolation; these include otters, grey wolves, pine martens, wildcats and golden eagles. The highest peaks are Serra Dolcedorme (7,440ft) and Monte Pollino itself (7,378ft) – the highest mountains in southern Italy except for Mount Etna in Sicily and snowcapped for much of the year. On a clear day, you can see three oceans from their summits – the Tyrrhenian, the Ionian and the distant Adriatic. Beyond the Pollino massif lies the Piani di Pollino –a beautiful alpine plateau crossed by streams, waterfalls and narrow gorges and strewn with wildflowers in summer.

If you're driving south down the A3 *autostrada*, exit at either Lauria Nord or Spezzano Terme; there are **visitor centres** in Castrovillari (*Via Mario Cappello,* **t** *0981 491 867*),

Viggianello, Mormanno and Frascineto. The Italian national parks service also has information online at *www.parks.it/parco.nazionale.pollino/* – the website includes a list of accommodation in the park and tour guides who organize hikes and excursions. Alternatively, call the **Association of Official Guides of Parco Nazionale del Pollino** (**t** *0981 33998*).

Albanian Villages

South of Monte Pollino is a once-remote mountain region with a string of Albanian villages. Albanians of the Greek Orthodox faith – called the *Arbërësh* in Calabria – came to Calabria and Sicily as refugees from the Turks in the 15th century, and today constitute one of Italy's largest ethnic minorities. They can be found all over Calabria, but particularly in the hills from Castrovillari (including the southern section of Pollino National Park) south to Acri and the northern part of The Sila plateau (*see* p.193), rather misleadingly called The Sila Greca. You'll know you've stumbled on one of their villages if you see a Byzantine-domed church or a statue of Skanderbeg, the Albanian national hero. **Castrovillari** has an Aragonese castle, a small archaeological museum and the church of Santa Maria del Castello – interesting for the odd bits of art from many centuries inside (there is a small museum in the sacristy) and for the view over the mountains. **Civita**, just to the east, has a small museum dedicated to the life and history of the Albanians in Calabria, the **Museo Etnografico Arbërësh** (*June–Sept 2–8; rest of the year on request; call* **t** *0981 73043/150*).

South of Castrovillari, tortuous mountain roads connect a string of Albanian villages. One of these, **Spezzano Albanese**, is a small spa with some accommodation. West of the *autostrada*, **Altomonte** is an unpromising village, remote even by Calabrian standards before the building of the motorway, that contains one of the most unusual churches in the south. **Santa Maria della Consolazione** is genuine 14th-century Gothic, with a big rose window. Most likely it was the work of architects from Siena. Inside, works of art include a painting by Tuscan master Simone Martini, and the fine tomb of Duke Filippo Sangineto by a follower of Tino di Camaino. Sangineto was a local boy who made good fighting for Charles of Anjou. As well as becoming a duke here, Sangineto was also Seneschal of Provence – his descendants, occupying a cultural sphere wider than most Calabrians, financed this church.

There are more Albanian villages along a difficult mountain road north of Monte Crista d'Acri. These include Santa Sofia d'Epiro, Vaccarizzo Albanese and **San Demetrio Corone**, where there has been an Albanian college since 1791. The town's 9th-century **church of Sant'Adriano** is an interesting Romanesque structure with Byzantine ornamentation and mosaic floors.

Cosenza and the Sila

Cosenza

Cosenza may not be a stellar attraction, but as cities go, it's the best Calabria can do. It has been one of Calabria's chief towns throughout most of recorded history,

Tourist Information

Cosenza: Corso Mazzini 92, **t** 0984 27485, *www.costadei.net*.

Where to Stay and Eat

Cosenza, located on the A3 *autostrada*, makes the most convenient base for a quick exploration of the Sila region. If you want to spend longer, there are hotels in a number of the villages of the Sila itself, including San Giovanni in Fiore. To the south, in the Sila Piccola, there is accommodation in Villaggio Mancuso and Tiriolo – although you could also use Catanzaro (*see* p.205) as a base for the southern Sila. To the north, near the Sila Greca, there's modest accommodation at Bocchigliero and Longobucco.

Cosenza ✉ 87100

Unfortunately, there are no hotels in the old citadel. Until they appear, the following are the best Cosenza can offer:

★★★★**Royal**, Via Molinella 24/E, **t/f** 0984 412 165, *www.hotelroyalsas.it* (*moderate*). Comfortable and reasonably priced, this is the smartest in town.

★★★**Excelsior**, Piazza Matteotti 14, **t** 0984 74383, *www.italiaabc.com/a/excelsior* (*moderate*). It has a certain grandeur on first impression, but the rooms are simple. The staff are friendly and helpful, there is parking, and some rooms overlook the colourful street painting on Corso Mazzini.

★★★**Centrale**, Via dei Tigrai 3, **t** 0984 73681, *www.hotelcentralecs.it* (*moderate*). Comfortable and well run, this is another acceptable place in the New Town for a stay of a night or two.

★★★**S. Agostino**, Via A. Modigliani 49, Rende, **t** 0984 461 782, **f** 0984 465 358 (*moderate*). In a village just north of Cosenza, this functional and clean hotel is fine for a stopover.

L'Arco Vecchio, Piazza Archi di Ciaccio 21, **t** 0984 72564 (*moderate*). In the heart of the Old Quarter, with a more sophisticated feel. *Closed Sun*.

★**Bruno**, Corso Mazzini 27, **t** 0984 73889 (*cheap*). If you are on a tight budget, this is probably Cosenza's cheapest option. It is only a short walk from the historic centre, but is very basic.

Da Giocondo, Via Piave 53, **t** 0984 29810 (*cheap*). This restaurant in the New Town will do nicely for a good meal in an informal and busy atmosphere. *Closed Sun evening*.

Bella Calabria, **t** 0984 793 531 (*cheap*). Waiters in tuxedos lend a smart feel to this place, where you eat *al fresco* at the foot of the cathedral in Piazza Duomo.

Artcafé, Piazza Duomo. After dinner in the Old Town, you can stroll across the square to this bar for a drink and some live jazz. *Closed Mon*.

San Giovanni in Fiore ✉ 87055

★★★**Dino's**, Viale della Repubblica 166, Pirainella, **t** 0984 992 090, **f** 0984 970 432, *dino@fitad.it* (*cheap*). Just outside of the village, this hotel is comfortable enough for a stopover. It also has the best restaurant in the area, specializing in local specialities such as roast kid, trout and other delights of the uplands – a great bargain.

Villaggio Mancuso ✉ 88055

★★★**Grande Albergo Parco delle Fate**, **t** 0961 922 057 (*cheap*). Set in alpine forests, this hotel allows you to see the Sila in style.

★★**Della Posta**, **t** 0961 922 033 (*cheap*). Run by the same management as the Parco delle Fate (*see* above), this is a cheaper alternative (Italians call it a *dipendenza*). It is one of a half-dozen or so modern budget options in and around the village, all of which are very similar.

Racise, Villaggio Racise, **t** 0984 922 009 (*cheap*). A pleasant campsite under the trees, located 4km to the north of Villaggio Mancuso in the village of Villaggio Racise.

Tiriolo ✉ 88056

★★**Autostello Chiarella**, Viale Mazzini 284, **t** 0961 991 005 (*cheap*). This pleasant hotel, on the main street of Tiriolo coming from the south, is another good base for the southern Sila and Sila Piccola. The hotel also has a reasonable *pizzeria*. *Closed Tues*.

★**Coniglio d'Oro**, Loc. Vaccariti, Tiriolo, **t** 0961 991 056 (*cheap*). This small, family-run place, on the main street north of the centre, is the least expensive of the village's hotels. It also has a good *pizzeria*-restaurant.

from its beginnings as the capital of the Bruttians, the aboriginal nation from whom today's Calabrians are descended. Medieval Cosenza was busy. The Arabs took it twice, Norman freebooters fought over it and at least one king of France passed through on his way to the Crusades.

Buried somewhere beneath the River Busento, which splits the city, is no less a personage than Alaric the Goth. Alaric – no drooling barbarian, but just another scheming Roman general with a Teutonic accent – came to Cosenza in 410, fresh from his sack of Rome and on his way to conquer Africa. He died of a fever here and his men temporarily diverted the Busento and buried him under it, probably along with a fair share of the Roman loot. Archaeologists are still looking for it.

Cosenza gained some unexpected notoriety in the 16th century as one of Counter-Reformation Italy's last bastions of tolerance and free thought, under the influence of the Waldenses and of an important humanist philosopher named Bernardino Telesio (1509–88), who was one of the first theorists of science. His student, the radical monk

Tommaso Campanella, became a fully fledged Utopian mystic, writing a splendidly crazy book called *The City of the Sun* and leading an astrologically ordained revolt against the Spanish in 1599. Campanella later helped defend Galileo in his Inquisition trial – by letter, since he himself spent 27 years in their jails.

Cosenza has little to show for all its history, for even in Calabria, no place is more prone to earthquakes. There have been four big ones in the last 200 years, with added destruction by Allied bombers in 1943.

Most of Cosenza's attractions are in the old citadel; there's nothing much of interest in the modern town. Just west of Cosenza, in the village of **Rende**, the **Museo Civico** (***t** 0984 443 593; open Mon, Wed and Fri 9–1, Tues and Thurs 9–1 and 3–6; adm*) has a very good collection of exhibits on every aspect of Calabrian country life and folklore.

The Old Town

The River Busento divides Cosenza neatly between the flat modern town and the old citadel on the hill. This old quarter, once almost abandoned, is being renovated with the help of EU grants. Although it feels like a building site, antique shops, trendy cafés and restaurants are popping up fast, especially around the **Piazza del Duomo** and **Corso Telesio**.

The **cathedral**, a simple Gothic structure, has survived the latest earthquakes, although it didn't back in 1184 – what we see now was rebuilt under the reign of Frederick II on the ruins of the original 7th-century basilica. Inside, lie buried one of Frederick's sons and Isabella of Aragon. Its best bits have been moved to the cloister of the **church of San Francesco d'Assisi**, down the hill on Via S. Francesco. This contains two real treasures – one is a little-known masterpiece of medieval art, a Byzantine-style relic-holder crucifix in gold and enamel, made in Sicily in the 12th century and donated by Frederick himself on the occasion of the cathedral's consecration in 1222. The other is the shiny 13th-century Byzantine icon of the Madonna del Pilerio ('the pillar's Madonna'), who was believed to have saved the city from the Bubonic Plague of 1576 and thus became patron of Cosenza.

A few blocks south of the cathedral, on Piazza XV Marzo, there is a small **Museo Civico** (***t** 0984 813 324; open daily 9–1; adm*), with paintings and archaeological finds. From there, you can also climb up to the **castle** (*open July and Aug 8am–midnight, Sept–June 8–8*). Overlooking the city, it was built by the Normans on the site of a Roman fortress, and later modified by Frederick II, the Aragonese and the Angevins. The medieval 'reception room' has delightful capitals with floral motifs carved in pink sandstone.

Across the River Busento in **Piazza Campanella**, where the Old and New Town meet, the 15th-century **San Domenico church** has a splendid façade with lacy rose window and elaborate portal. Unfortunately, the inside has been heavily Baroqued.

Sila Grande

Cosenza is the gateway to the peaceful Sila plateau. Much of the Sila is still covered with trees – beeches, oaks and *laricio* pines. In summer, you can find wild strawberries and, in winter, wolves (well, maybe) – some of Italy's last specimens hide out in the Sila's wilder corners, and there is an attempt to repopulate two small areas called the *Parco Nazionale della Calabria* (the third part of this park is on Aspromonte).

The Sila is the best place in Calabria for hiking and canoeing – from Cosenza, you can float down the River Crati all the way to the Ionian Sea. Maps and information are available from the Cosenza tourist office. Artificial lakes, built since the war as part of Calabria's hydroelectric schemes, add to the scenery, notably **Lago Arvo** and **Lago di Cecita**. Lago di Cecita borders one part of the *Parco Nazionale della Calabria*, the forested **Bosco di Gallopani**.

The biggest village, **San Giovanni in Fiore**, owes its founding to another celebrated Calabrian mystic, the 12th-century monk and devotional writer Joachim of Fiore. Emperor Henry IV granted the privileges of Joachim's new abbey in 1195, and throughout the Middle Ages, it was one of the most important communities of the south. The austere abbey complex has been restored and now contains the bizarrely titled **Demographic Museum of The Silan Economy, Labour and Social History** (*t 0984 970 059; open June–Sept Mon–Sat 8.30–6.30, Sun 9.30–12.30 and 3.30–6.30; adm*). Much of the economy, labour and history in this town has to do with handmade carpets and fabrics, a longtime speciality.

To the north of the region, down a tortuous road that resembles a pile of intestines on the map, lies remote **Longobucco**. The old centre of this medieval weaving village remains perfectly intact, with streets so narrow that Longobuccans need only lean out of their windows to shake hands with their neighbours across the street. Off the main piazza is the 'leaning tower of Longobucco', a 16th-century belltower which stands slightly askew. Behind the tower, the founding of Longobucco has been recently depicted in bronze on the doors of the Chiesa Matrice.

On the eastern edge of the Sila, the forests in many places give way to *calanchi*, weird sculpted hillsides created by deforestation and subsequent erosion. On the way to Crotone and the coast, **Santa Severina** used to be a much more important place. The village has a striking skyline, dominated by a lovely Norman castle, connected to the rest of the village by a tall bridge. Underneath is the charming 11th-century **church of Santa Filomena**, with a dainty cupola on 16 slender columns and carved floral arabesques around the windows. The cathedral was begun in Norman times, too, but it has metamorphosed into an elegant Baroque building with a façade from 1705 and a quirky rococo altar. The real surprise is found through a secret door built into the left aisle: a 7th–9th-century baptistry, one of the oldest in Italy – the Baroque refurbishers made the door invisible simply to keep the symmetry of their decoration. Like nearly all ancient baptistries, this one is octagonal, after the model of the one Constantine built at the Lateran in Rome. It is furnished with eight granite columns, a font that may be the original, and bits of frescoes.

Sila Piccola

The southern part of the Sila plateau is even wilder and more remote, and sees fewer visitors. Its main centre is **Villaggio Mancuso**, a resort surrounded by forests and embellished with wood-frame buildings and wood fences that give it a strangely

New Englandish air. Just south of the village is the Calabria National Park's Visitors' Centre, a new complex laid out with loving care by the men of the Corpo Forestale. Besides information, you can see exhibits on the flora and fauna of the Sila, a 'didactic nature path', and another one for the disabled, a herb garden and a reproduction of a *carbonaia*, an old-fashioned charcoal works.

On the southern edge of the Sila, on the road to Catanzaro, **Taverna** was the birthplace of Mattia Preti, the only notable artist to have come out of Calabria. The best work of this 17th-century follower of Caravaggio can be seen in Naples and Malta, but he left a number of paintings here; recently these have been restored and collected from the village's churches into the **Museo Civico**, in the cloister next to **San Domenico** (***t*** *0961 923 259; open Tues–Sat 9–12; adm*). **Tiriolo** is a pretty village in the southern Sila that was once famed for the costumes (which you may still see) worn by local women.

Vibo Valentia and the 'Calabrian Riviera'

The spirit of *campanilismo* (the familiar Italian vanity of local patriotism) is in the air in Italy, and not only among Umberto Bossi and the malcontents of the north. New provinces are appearing across the land; in Calabria, a little pocket along the coast from Pizzo to Nicotera has decided to secede from Reggio di Calabria and go it alone as the province of Vibo Valentia – that's VV on the car licence tags and on the signs put up everywhere by the new provincial tourist promoters, lest we fail to notice that this is a province of Vim and Vigour.

Nocera Tirinese to Vibo Valentia

Heading down the coast from Cosenza, and just a few kilometres from the main road up in the hills, is the town of **Nocera Tirinese**. It's famous for only one thing – its festival every Easter, when processions of flagellants go around the town, fervently beating themselves into a bloody mess with thorn bushes, in one of the local events that is most regularly deployed to demonstrate Calabria's distance from the modern world. If you miss it, the flagellants' paraphernalia can be seen in the village's new museum (ask at the Pro Loco). Further south again, the road descends to the plain of Santa Eufemia, one of the new agricultural areas reclaimed from the mosquito. Calabrians make good gardeners when given the chance; the orchards and nurseries that fill the plain are impressively lush. The nearby town of **Maida**, site of one of the first French defeats of the Napoleonic Wars, gave its name to London's Maida Vale.

Pizzo, a larger town on a cliff over the sea, also has its Napoleonic association. The emperor's great cavalry commander Marshal Murat, whom Bonaparte had made King of Naples, tried after Waterloo to regain his throne by beginning a new revolution in Calabria. When his boat landed here in 1815, instead of the welcome he expected, the crowd almost tore him to pieces. The Bourbons executed him a few days later in the castle built in the 1480s by Ferdinand of Aragon. By the port, there is a small **Museo del Mare** dedicated to the village's fishermen (***t*** *0963 534 903; open summer daily 8pm–midnight*). On 1 November, Pizzo's main square and surrounding

streets become a market where, amidst the modern junk, it's still possible to buy earthy terracotta pots and colourful traditional pottery and baskets.

Vibo Valentia, proud capital, has views over the coast, a 12th-century Norman castle, remains of the fortifications of the ancient Greek city of Hipponion, and a number of overwrought Baroque churches. Finds from Hipponion are on view in the **museum** in the castle (*t 0963 43350; open daily 9–8; adm*). Vibo is perched on hills like most old Calabrian towns; several kilometres below there is a growing little industrial port, **Vibo Marina**, and just west of here stands the rather romantically ruined Castello di Bivona. If you head into the hills above Vibo Valentia, there is a castle at **Arena**, served by an unusual Norman aqueduct. South of Vibo on the SS18, **Mileto** stands next to the ruins of Mileto Vecchia, destroyed in the earthquake of 1783. The extensive ruins include the cathedral and the Abbazia della Trinità, also built by the Normans.

Tropea and the 'Calabrian Riviera'

Old road maps show the road into this peninsula as a dead end, but in recent years, a good road has been built around Cape Vaticano, opening up the choicest bit of Calabria's coastline. If you come in August, expect overcrowding and inflated prices.

Tourist Information

Vibo Valentia: Galleria Vecchio, **t** 0963 42008.

Where to Stay and Eat

Vibo Valentia ✉ 89900

Miramonti, Via F. Protetti, **t** 0963 41053 (*cheap*). A simple, honest hotel, typical of the accommodation in Vibo Valentia.

Terrazzino, Largo Marinella 6, Fraz Bivona, **t** 0963 571 091 (*cheap*). Very basic *pensione* at Bivona, on the coast near the castle.

L'Approdo, Via Roma 22, **t** 0963 572 640 (*expensive*). This seafood establishment in Vibo Marina is the best restaurant in the area. Elaborate *frutti di mare antipasti*, grilled fish and swordfish *involtini* invite a worthwhile splurge.

Pizzo ✉ 88026

Casa Janca, Riviera Prangi, Loc. Marinella, **t** 0963 534 890 or **t** 0963 264 364 (*expensive*). The real reason to stop by is this *agriturismo*, a tasteful country house quirkily decorated and run with a lot of character by Rita Callipo. In summer, you will have to take full board – but you'll be grateful, since customers flock from as far as Catanzaro for glorious traditional Calabrian cooking (*moderate–cheap*). The well-travelled Rita speaks good English and loves dogs. *Closed Jan.*

***Murat**, Piazza della Repubblica 41, **t** 0963 534 201, **f** 0963 534 469 (*moderate*). A rare old establishment in the centre of the village that, although it has been somewhat modernized, still offers a pleasant stay.

Tropea/Cape Vaticano ✉ 88038

There are scores of new resort hotels east of Tropea, around Parghelia and Zambrone.

*****Baia Paraelios**, Parghelia, **t** 0963 600 300, **f** 0963 600 074, *www.baiaparaelios.it* (*very expensive*). Set on one of the prettiest parts of the coast, Baia Paraelios is a group of well-furnished cottages set on a terraced hill overlooking a beautiful beach. As with many places along this coast, you must reserve some time ahead. *Open May–Sept.*

Da Isabella, Zambrone, **t** 0963 392 891/0333 524 5467 (*moderate*). This pretty villa, set in its own lush garden, is run by Isabella Tomaschek, who speaks some English. The atmosphere is intimate, the rooms are cosy and you can start your day with an English breakfast. You'll find it up the hillside, off the coast road towards Tropea.

Vittoria, Via Stazione 16, by the station in Nicotera, **t** 0963 81358 (*moderate*). Although it's a little out of the way, this place is one of the best seafood restaurants in the region, with an outdoor dining area.

Tropea is the tourist centre – it already attracts Germans as well as Italians, but the British are starting to come, too. The town is built on a steep-sided rock overlooking some fine, long beaches. From the belvedere at the end of the main *corso*, you can see Stromboli, the volcano that spouts off every 11 minutes, as well as other Aeolian Islands, depending on how clear it is.

The Old Town is well preserved, full of contented cats, *pizza a taglio* shops and a scattering of noble palaces on the back streets that are quite elegant by Calabrian standards. The **Duomo** on the southern edge of the cliffs is an exceedingly graceful Norman work built in 1163 (but heavily restored), with blind arcades and decoration in cut stone. Inside is an icon of the Madonna – said to have been painted, like many others around the Mediterranean, by St Luke – and some other interesting medieval tombs and relics. Tropea's main square is called **Piazza Ercole**, recalling a legend that Hercules once visited; the Romans called Tropea Portus Hercules. The war memorial here was financed by the Tropeans of Montevideo, Uruguay – a reminder of how southern Italy's emigrants tended to cluster in little colonies; any town you pass through is likely to have a social club for its sons in some city of the Americas.

From Tropea's beaches, you can climb up to the ruined Benedictine monastery of **Santa Maria dell'Isola**, on an island joined to the coast by a short causeway. Around the cape itself, the road rises to more spectacular views over the Aeolians and Sicily's northern coast. As far as **Cape Vaticano**, it is lined with signs for the many holiday villages and campgrounds tucked discreetly down by the sea.

Further south, the towns along the coast are easier to reach, though less attractive. **Gioia Tauro** is a grim industrial town that squeezes out most of Calabria's olive oil. South of **Palmi** on the SS18, a new **museum** and cultural complex, the **Casa di Cultura Leonida Repaci** (*t 0966 262 248; open Tues, Wed, Fri 8–2, Mon and Thurs 8–2 and 3–6; adm*), houses among other collections the best folk museum in Calabria and a modern art gallery with works by de Chirico and other 20th-century Italian painters.

Southern Calabria: Reggio di Calabria and Around

Scilla

Scilla, at the entrance to the Straits of Messina, is a peaceful and lovely fishing town that owes its fortunes to the straits' greatest culinary treasure, the *pesce spada*. Swordfish may be tasty, but they are nobody's fools. To nab them, the Calabrians have invented one of the most peculiar styles of fishing boats you'll ever see. These delicate, insect-like craft have metal towers that can be up to 100ft in length, secured by wires and swaying precariously. One stands straight up like a mast; this is for the lookout watching for schools of fish. The other projects beyond the bow and holds a spearman who, guided by the lookout, can make the kill before the swordfish even feel the presence of the boat.

Scilla marks the spot where the mythological Scylla, a daughter of Hecate, changed into a dog-like sea monster and seized some of Odysseus' crewmen near the end of the *Odyssey*. In classical times, Scylla meant the dangerous rocks off the Calabrian side of the straits, a counterpart to the whirlpool Charybdis towards the Sicilian shore. So many earthquakes have rearranged the topography since then that nothing remains of either. Still, the narrow straits are one of the most dramatic sights in Italy, with Messina and the Monti Peloritani visible over in Sicily, neatly balancing Reggio and the jumbled peaks of Aspromonte in Calabria. Approaching Scilla from the west, the view is dominated by the town's late medieval **castle** (*open Tues–Sun 9.30–12.30 and 5.30–8.30*), which is perched high on a rock that plunges into turbulent waters at the mouth of the straits. Not far inside the straits is the port of **Villa San Giovanni**, a suburb of Reggio and today the major ferry crossing point for Sicily.

Reggio di Calabria

The last big earthquake came in 1908, which claimed the lives of 100,000 people here and in Messina across the straits. Both these cities have a remarkable will to survive, considering the damage that earthquakes have inflicted on them in the last 2,000 years. Perhaps the setting is irresistible. Fortune has favoured them unequally in the rebuilding. Although both are about the same size, Messina has made itself into

Tourist Information

Villa San Giovanni: In the Piazza Stazione.
Reggio di Calabria: Via Roma 3, **t** 0965 892 512, **f** 0965 89094. *Open Thurs–Sun and Tues 8–12, Mon and Wed 8–12 and 2–5*. Other offices at the Stazione Centrale and the airport.
Gambarie: Pzle Mangiaruca, **t** 0965 743 295.

Where to Stay and Eat

Scilla ✉ 89058

★★★**Villaggio Del Pino**, Via Boccata 11, Loc. Melia, **t** 0965 755 126, **f** 0965 755 154, *www.villaggiodelpino.it* (*moderate*). Up in the hills above the village, this is a considerably fancy option, with a pool and tennis courts. *Closed Jan–Feb. Wheelchair accessible.*

★★**Sirene**, Via Nazionale 57, **t** 0965 754 019, **f** 0965 754 121 (*cheap*). This is the only hotel in Scilla itself. It has simple, inexpensive rooms and a great position just off the beach. Book in advance.

Youth Hostel, **t** 0965 754 033 (*cheap*). Atmospherically housed in the castle, and extremely popular. *Open April–Sept only.*

Alla Pescatora, Marina di Scilla, **t** 0965 754 147 (*moderate*). Right on the beach, this place offers *al fresco* dining and a great octopus *antipasto* among other seafood specialities. *Closed Wed, Dec–Jan.*

Pizzeria S. Francesco, Via Cristoforo Colombo 29 (*cheap*). Head here for generous pizzas on the seafront. The owner seems keen to polish up her excellent English by helping you in any way she can.

Villa San Giovanni-Cannitello ✉ 89010

★★**Autostello**, **t/f** 0965 759 015 (*cheap*). A cheap and comfortable place between Scilla and Villa S. Giovanni. Be prepared for their rather indifferent approach to their guests.

Il Castello di Alta Fiumana, Loc. S. Trada, **t** 0965 759 804, **f** 0965 759 566 (*cheap*). A good eating option. The restaurant sits on a hill and has great views over the straits.

Reggio di Calabria ✉ 89100

★★★★**Excelsior**, Via Vittorio Veneto 66, **t** 0965 812 211, **f** 0965 893 084, *www.reggiocalabriahotels.it* (*luxury*). With fully air-conditioned rooms and a business feel, this is one of the poshest of the hotels around the archaeological museum in the north part of town.

★★★★**Miramare**, Via Fata Morgana 1, **t** 0965 812 444, **f** 0965 812 450, *www.reggiocalabriahotels.it* (*very expensive*). This characterful hotel on the seafront offers comfort alongside a certain old-world charm.

★★**Lido**, Via III Settembre 6, **t** 0965 25001, **f** 0965 899 393 (*expensive*). This modest hotel is well positioned, a short walk to the Museo Nazionale and the beach.

★★**Eremo**, Via Eremo Botte 12, **t** 0965 22433 (*cheap*). For a cheaper option you could check into the pleasant, plant-filled Eremo, one of the few hotels in the vicinity that has access for wheelchairs. Its only drawback is its position up the hill.

★★★**Diana**, Via Vitrioli 12, **t** 0965 891 522, **f** 0965 24061 (*cheap*). This funky but friendly hotel is just off Corso Garibaldi in a

a slick, almost beautiful town, while Reggio has chosen to remain swaddled in Calabrian humility. Its plain grid of dusty streets and low buildings was laid out after the earthquake of 1783, when the destruction was even greater than in 1908 and the city had to be rebuilt from scratch. As if earthquakes weren't enough, the Allies also did a pretty thorough job of bombing Reggio during the Second World War: it's perhaps no surprise, then, that there is little left to see of a city that began life, as Greek Rhegium, back in the 8th century BC. Bits of Greek wall and Roman baths remain, and there are some once grand 19th-century buildings along the waterfront promenade, but these are virtually the only things in the city built before 1908. Part of Reggio's shabbiness is due to the corrosive social effect of the Calabrese mafia, the *'Ndrangheta* (*see* **Topics**, 'Oil for the Madonna', p.26), which continues to have a stronger hold here even than mouldering, fascinating pre-earthquake *palazzo*.

Il Ducale, Corso Vittorio Emmanuele III 13, **t** 0965 891 520 (*expensive*). An attractive restaurant in the centre of town, beside the Museo Nazionale. Many dishes on the impressive menu are likely to be unavailable, and the food may not quite live up to the elegance of the setting, but given Reggio's shortage of restaurants, it serves well enough. *Closed May.*

Bracieria, Via Tripepi 81–3, **t** 0965 29361 (*moderate*). A wide variety of local dishes are served at this warm, cosily furnished restaurant, parallel to Corso Garibaldi in the centre of town. It comes highly recommended by locals. *Closed May.*

Il Mio Ristorante, Via Provinciale 41, Gallina, **t** 0965 682 654 (*moderate*). This is the place to come for something a bit more elegant. Just outside Reggio in the village of Gallina, it has beautiful views of the straits and serves up first-class swordfish and *aragoste*, as well as good desserts. *Closed Mon.*

Seaside Pub, Via d'Annunzio 1 (*cheap*). On a pleasant terrace overlooking the promenade and the Straits of Messina, this incongruous place serves pints of Tennants with its pizzas, as if it were some kind of exotic tonic. But it really isn't as bad as it sounds.

Villeggiante, Via Condera Vallone Mariannazzo 31, **t** 0965 25021, *www.ristorante villeggiante.it* (*cheap*). A large and popular restaurant serving traditional Calabrian cuisine. You'll find it up the hill towards Chiesa Eremo, with lovely views over the straits. *Closed Sun eve.*

Gambarie ✉ 89050

Gambarie has almost all of the hotels on Aspromonte and there isn't a lot of difference between them. Fortunately, all rooms have heating. In summer, look out for informal outdoor restaurants around town; just a few tables under the trees and good, simple food for next to nothing.

Villa Rosa, **t** 0965 740 500 (*moderate*). A wonderful place on the road to Gambarie just beyond Santo Stefano, with outdoor dining on a panoramic flower-covered terrace and delicious dishes served up by cheery staff. Try the pasta with porcini mushrooms, or something from the sizzling barbecue. The only problem is that you have to remember to ring Rosa in advance.

★★★**Centrale**, Piaza Mangeruca 22, **t** 0965 743 133, **f** 0965 743 141, *centralenel@tin.it* (*cheap*) Large and adequate, if rather characterless.

★★**Il Ritrovo**, Via Garibaldi 15, **t** 0965 743 021, **f** 0965 743 264, *ilritrovo@gambarie.com* (*cheap*). Another of the less expensive options in Gambarie.

Ristorante Nunziatina, Sant'Alessio di Aspromonte, **t** 0965 741 240 (*cheap*). This local favourite on the road up to Gambarie is typical of the summer restaurants and a stronghold of mountain cooking, with homemade Calabrian pastries for dessert.

Sapori di Calabria, **t** 0965 743 168. A very friendly delicatessen on the town's main square, where you can buy gift-wrapped porcini mushrooms or order delicious chunky sandwiches.

those that its wealthier partners in crime, the Sicilian Mafia and the Neapolitan Camorra, exert over their own respective backyards.

In recent years, however, thought and effort has gone into the development of the city centre. This is most noticeable on the seafront, where a wide and elegant promenade is under construction. The city's *lido communale* is also well designed and surprisingly clean. For a few euros, you can spend the day floating in the gentle waters of the straits; the current keeps the water clear. Reggio's daily *passeggiata*, which will soon take advantage of the new promenade, is particularly exuberant in summer, with street shows and glittering views across to Sicily. A few blocks inland there is an Aragonese castle, which is largely ignored these days, while the cathedral has been almost entirely reconstructed and contains only hints of the past.

Visions of the Straits

The opposite point seems more a tongue of land
you'd touch with a good bowshot, at the narrows.
A great wild fig, a shaggy mass of leaves,
grows on it, and Kharybdis lurks below
to swallow down the dark sea tide. Three times
From dawn to dusk she spews it up
and sucks it down again three times, a whirling
maelstrom; if you come upon her then
the god who makes the earth tremble could not save you.

***The Odyssey*, Book XII (tr. Robert Fitzgerald)**

So did Circe introduce the Straits of Messina to Odysseus? Unlike some guidebooks, we don't give out stars for memorable views, but in this case, we are tempted to make an exception. The straits may lack the postcard-photogenic qualities of, say, the Grand Canyon or Istanbul at twilight, but there is truly no other place on earth quite like it.

The Italian highway engineers have thoughtfully placed parking areas in all the choicest spots along the motorway north of Reggio di Calabria, and so many people stop to enjoy the views that they cause traffic jams in summer.

Messina and much of the Sicilian coast are visible, along with Stromboli and some of the other Aeolian Islands on a clear day – and perhaps even Mount Etna will peek

Museo Nazionale della Magna Grecia

t 0965 812 255; open Tues–Sun 9–7.30; adm.

This museum is Reggio's main attraction and houses the finest collection of Greek art between Naples and Sicily. The museum, directly north of the city centre on Corso Garibaldi, is a classic of Fascist architecture built in chunky travertine. Containing a hoard as precious as anything in Greece itself, the museum would make a trip to Reggio worthwhile just for the **Warriors of Riace**, two bronze masterpieces that rank among the greatest productions of antiquity to have come down to us. If you haven't heard of them, it is because they were only found in 1972, by divers exploring an ancient shipwreck off Riace on Calabria's Ionian coast. They are normally kept down in the basement in a room of their own, next to a big exhibition that details the tremendously complex original restoration job done in the seventies.

These fellows, both about six foot seven and quite indecently virile, may perhaps have come from a temple at Delphi. No one really knows why they were being shipped to Magna Grecia. One of them has been attributed to the great sculptor Phidias. The Warriors share the basement with a few other rare works of Greek sculpture, including the unidentified 5th-century BC subject called **the Philosopher**, as well as anchors and ship fittings, and amphorae that once held wine or oil – all recovered from the shipwreck, from mud well over a metre deep. Divers are convinced that the dangerous waters around Calabria may hold dozens of similar treasures, so some more artefacts may have found their way to the Reggio Museum by the time you

out from behind its eternal entourage of clouds. Spidery swordfish boats ply the waters below, keeping company with the busy Sicily ferries, Greek or Russian tramp steamers and every other sort of ship, passing under the two gigantic power pylons that seem to moor Sicily to the mainland – constructions as preposterous in their way as the swordfish boats.

For all that, the real wonders of the straits will never develop on your film. Nothing is left of the rock and the whirlpool, of course, but memories still continue to linger. It is as if the great sea was twisted into a knot in the middle. Everything that is eternally Mediterranean seems to live here – or at least, like Odysseus, to pass through occasionally.

If you are especially lucky, you might even be treated to an appearance of the famous 'Fata Morgana', the mirages of islands or many-towered cities that are said to loom over the Straits. The name comes from the enchantress Morgan le Fay, a figure you may recognize from Arthurian legend. Arthurian romance came to southern Italy with the Normans and rooted itself deeply in these parts; old Sicilian legends have a lot to say about King Arthur. In one of the tales, Arthur sleeps and awaits his return – not in Avalon, up in chilly England, but deep in the smoky bowels of Etna.

Roger de Hauteville himself, a close relation of William the Conqueror, is said to have seen the Fata Morgana, and his learned men interpreted the vision as a divine invitation to invade Sicily. Roger demurred, thinking it better to wait and take Sicily on his own than to do it with the aid of sorcery.

arrive. Elsewhere in the museum there are some beautiful terracotta ***ex voto* plaques** recovered from the temples of Magna Grecia. Most of these offerings are in the magical archaic Greek style. They show goddesses who had influence over death (usually Persephone) being abducted by Hades, receiving propitiatory gifts or accepting souls into the underworld. Chickens are a recurring motif; to the ancient Greeks a soul rises out of its burial urn the same way a chicken hatches from an egg.

Other works help complete the picture of life and art in Magna Grecia: Greek painted ceramics from Locris and Attica, fragments of architectural decoration from various temples (some still with bits of their original paint), records of city finances on bronze tablets, coins, some treasure recovered from tombs and a rare early Hellenistic mosaic of a dragon, actually made in Calabria. The museum also has a collection of paintings, including two works by Antonello da Messina.

Aspromonte

From Palmi as far as Locri, the interior of the peninsula seems utterly impenetrable, a wall of rough peaks looming over the narrow coastal plain. In fact, all of Italy's toe is really one great round massif called Aspromonte (literally, 'rugged mount').

The tortuous mountain roads allow few easy opportunities for climbing inland, but from the north end of Reggio, a 30km route, the SS184, will take you up to **Gambarie**, with pine forests and views over the straits to Sicily; from Reggio, take the Gallico exit on the motorway and follow the signs. In winter, Gambarie is Calabria's unlikely ski resort, with just enough snow to get by in an average year. In summer, it's a good starting-off point for walkers and there is also a **chairlift** (*daily 9–12 and 3.30–6.30; adm*) to the top of the mountain. There is little to the place but a collection of faintly alpine-looking hotels and a communications tower, but the forests around it are lovely. This area was the haunt of the chivalrous 19th-century bandit Musolino, a sort of Calabrian Robin Hood still remembered in these parts. His well-tended grave lies in the cemetery in his birthplace, **Santo Stefano**, on the way to Gambarie.

Aspromonte is a world in itself, with 22 summits and Greek-speaking villages. It has four levels of altitude, called the *piani* or *terrazze di Aspromonte*. The lowest grow the jasmine and bergamot; further up, come groves of some of the biggest olive trees you'll ever see. On top, there are still wide expanses of virgin forest, mostly beech and pine along with some white birches. Ceps (*porcini*) and other mushrooms abound; the locals put up roadside stands in the autumn and sell them by the basket. There are a number of marked hiking trails, mostly starting from Gambarie.

One popular summer excursion follows a passable road to just under the tallest summit of Aspromonte, **Montalto** (6,412ft). Look out for a small sign ('Montalto Redentore') and follow the marked route on foot to the summit. The easy 15-minute walk is rewarded, on a clear day, with incredible views that take in two seas and three volcanoes (the Aeolian islands of Stromboli and nearby Vulcano, along with Mount Etna). Seven kilometres from Montalto, the **Santuario di Polsi** is a popular pilgrimage site for the 'Madonna della Montagna'.

Like the Albanians, the Greeks of Aspromonte – called *Grecaneci* – are a Calabrian cultural minority. Scholars who have studied their language speculate that they may be descendants of the original Greek population of Magna Grecia, holding on to their cultural identity thanks to the barely accessible locations of their mountain villages. Finding these requires some effort. Most are on the southern part of Aspromonte: **Bova**, **Roccaforte del Greco** and **Chorio** are the largest. From Roccaforte, you can find another called **Galliciano**, which can only be reached by mule. Serious hikers or people equipped with mules, can also seek out the Grecaneci in **Roghudi**, east of Roccaforte, built on a nearly vertical cliff and nearly a ghost town.

Calabria's Ionian Coast

Around Italy's Toe: Reggio to Roccella Ionica

From Reggio as far as Taranto, the coasts of Calabria and later the Basilicata are one long beach – about 500km of it, broken in only a few places by mountains or patches of industry. All along this route, the pattern is the same: on the shore, there are sleepy new concrete settlements within sight of their mother towns, just a few kilometres further up in the mountains.

If you come in summer, you will find great rivers, such as the Amendola, filled not with water but with pebbles; the terrible deforestation of Calabria in the 19th century (committed mostly by northern Europeans with the assistance of corrupt Italian governments) denuded much of the interior and this has made its rivers raging torrents in the spring. Recent governments have worked sincerely to reforest vast tracts, especially on Aspromonte, but wherever you see bare rock on the mountains, there is land that can never be redeemed.

The coastal plain around Reggio is one of Italy's gardens, a panorama of lemon and orange groves. Two more exotic crops have also given some fame to the region – jasmine, which grows this well nowhere else in Italy, and bergamot, which refuses to grow nearly anywhere else. The bergamot is a small, hard, green orange, discovered and first cultivated only some 200 years ago. Now it is an indispensable ingredient in the making of the finest perfumes, and a surprisingly important source of income in this area. (It is also, of course, the stuff used to flavour Earl Grey tea.)

Many of the new villages and towns on the bottom of the Italian toe have become little resorts – two *pensioni* and a *pizzeria* on average. None is deserving of special mention, but you'll never have trouble finding clean water and a kilometre or so of empty (but usually trash-strewn) beach. South of Reggio is **Melito di Porto Salvo**, the southernmost town of mainland Italy, where Garibaldi landed in 1860. The main road into the southern Aspromonte starts from here, leading to the land of the Grecaneci, but on other roads that straggle up the massif, the main attractions are likely to be the ruins of deserted villages.

On the Ionian coast, about 3km south of **Locri**, there are fragmentary ruins of the Greek city **Epizefiri** (*open 9–one hour before sunset, closed first and third Mon of month*), consisting of a few bits of wall and bases of temples. Most of the art from Locri has been taken to Reggio and further afield (including the famous Ludovisi throne in Rome, which has been called a fake). There is just enough left in Locri to make the **Antiquarium** (***t** 0964 390 023; open daily 9–2 and 5.30–7.30 in summer, 9–2 in winter; adm*) near the sea worth a visit.

When pirates and malaria forced the Locrians to abandon their city in the 8th century, they fled to the nearby hills and founded **Gerace**. Although the population of its melancholy medieval centre today is only about 300, Gerace was an important town in the Middle Ages and has Calabria's biggest **cathedral** – an 11th-century Norman Romanesque work supported by columns from the ruins of Locri. The church contains an interesting display on the restoration and a *tesoro* with a 12th-century cross from Constantinople.

Gerace has other churches worth a look: San Francesco, a big Franciscan barn, or the small Oratorio dell'Addolorata with its ornate rococo interior. Older churches, such as Santa Cuore, show a strong Byzantine-Norman influence in their architecture.

Further inland from Gerace, **Cittanova** began as one of Italy's strange 'radial cities', a Renaissance fancy of town planning based on Campanella's mystical City of the Sun. Laid out as a new town after the earthquake of 1616, it never prospered.

North of Locri, **Marina di Gioiosa Ionica** has ruins of a small Greek theatre, while Gioiosa itself, 5km inland, can show excavations of a Roman villa with bits of mosaic. **Roccella Ionica** is an up-and-coming little town whose hill-top setting and half-ruined castle provide one of the few breaks in the beach along the coast road.

Tourist Information

Locri: Via Fiume 1, **t** 0964 29600.
Catanzaro: in Galleria Mancuso, **t** 0961 743 901.
Crotone: Via Torino 148, **t** 0962 23185.

Where to Stay and Eat

Gerace ✉ 89048

La Casa di Gianna, Via Paolo Frascà 4, **t** 0964 355 024, **f** 0964 355 081, *www.lacasadigianna.it* (*expensive*). Someone with a private 16th-century villa to spare has recently taken the initiative to convert it into this luxurious 10-roomed hotel. Hidden in a narrow medieval street, the building is constructed around an *atrium*, which bathes the upper floors in light. The bedrooms and suite are tastefully furnished, while the restaurant downstairs is cool and elegant. This is one place along the Ionian coast where you can sleep and eat in style.

A Squella, Viale della Resistenza 8, **t** 0964 356 086 (*cheap*). Just at the entrance of the town on the Locri road, this little *trattoria* serves good pizza as well as a full menu with traditional favourites like bean and chicory casserole and pasta with chick peas and hot peppers.

Marina di Gioiosa Ionica ✉ 89046

*****San Giorgio**, Via I. Maggio 3, **t/f** 0964 415 064 (*cheap*). Although none of the various tiny lidos on Calabria's Ionian shore are particularly inviting for more than a short stopover, this is one of the more pleasant spots, just north of Locri. The hotel has a nice garden, beach and pool. *Closed Oct–May.*

Bivongi ✉ 89040

La Vecchia Miniera, **t** 0964 731 869 (*moderate*). Situated just outside the village, near the Cascate del Marmarico. Try the mountain trout or pasta with stewed kid sauce. The management also organizes tours of the falls and other sites in the area. *Closed Mon.*

Stilo ✉ 89900

****San Giorgio**, Via Citarelli 8, **t/f** 0964 775 047 (*cheap*). There is just one hotel in Stilo, but

The Serre

The Serre, another range of rugged hills, lies inland from Monasterace Marina. Although lower than the Aspromonte and the Sila, the Serre's forests, medieval villages and some delightful churches make it worth a detour.

The main town of the region is **Serra San Bruno**, a pretty and refined village surrounded by forests. It grew up around the huge 11th-century Carthusian monastery, or **Certosa**, 2km outside the village. The founder of the Carthusians himself, Bruno of Cologne, lived and died here. Much of the monastery was destroyed by an earthquake in 1783, but it still has the remains of a lavish Baroque complex, a **museum** (***t** 0963 70608; open daily 9–1 and 3–8; winter Tues–Sun 9.30–1 and 3–6; adm*) and a church façade, now freestanding like a stage prop. In the village, the rococo San Biagio, or *Chiesa Matrice*, has reliefs with scenes from Bruno's life and an unusual altarpiece.

Closer to the Ionian coast, the beautiful church of **San Giovanni Theresti** (*open July–mid-Sept 5pm–sunset, mid-Sept–June Sat 10–12 and 3–5*) stands just outside the village of **Bivongi**. It's a delightful little building with blind arcading, a cupola over a drum and fake columns, all made of brick. The caretaker here is a Greek monk – the village of Bivongi invited Mount Athos to send one over to keep old memories alive.

Also near Bivongi is a beautiful and surprisingly big waterfall on the Torrente Stilo, called the **Cascate del Marmarico** (don't expect to see much water falling in summer).

it's one with an unusual degree of character: the San Giorgio occupies a former cardinal's palace and is furnished partly in period style, with a pool and a terrace with panoramic views. Full board is obligatory in August. *Closed Nov–Mar.*

Catanzaro ✉ 88100

There are a few simple hotels in Catanzaro. For food, however, there is little choice in its restaurants, with little seafood – you're really better off outside the city.

*****Grand Hotel**, Piazza Matteotti, **t** 0961 701 256, **f** 0961 741 621 (*expensive*). A modern and attractive place in the centre of town.

****Belvedere**, Via Italia 33, **t** 0961 720 591, **f** 0961 727 740 (*cheap*). A cheaper option but this is still comfortable enough.

Due Romani, Via Murano, Catanzaro Lido, off the coastal SS106, **t** 0961 32097 (*cheap*) Seafood specialities at bargain prices, and the best and most copious *griglia mista* we've ever had in Italy. *Closed Sun. evening*

La Corteccia, Via Indipendenza 30, **t** 0961 746 130 (*cheap*). This is as good a place as any to fill up on traditional cuisine.

Wine Shop, Vicolo San Rocchello (*cheap*). A rough-and-ready place with no name where you can try some powerful local specialities.

Crotone ✉ 88900

On the whole, dining along this stretch of coast is simple – little seafood shacks that only open in the summer, or small and cheap but lively *pizzerias* with a sunny little terrace.

Da Annibale, Via Duomo 35 (in Le Castella on Cape Rizzuto, not far south of Crotone), **t** 0962 795 004 (*expensive*). This is one of the few places along the Ionian coast where you can have an elaborate meal. Try the swordfish *involtini* for a rare treat.

Il Girrarosto, Via Vittorio Veneto 30, (*moderate*). You'll find this very good restaurant in the centre of Crotone, where you'd least expect it. The cook specializes in roast lamb and kid, but also really knows what to do with swordfish and other seafood. The nice terrace is a bonus.

Da Peppino, Piazza Umberto (*cheap*). This bustling *trattoria* is a simple option, serving pizza and seafood at its tables on a leafy piazza near the cathedral.

Just east of Bivongi, the Greek village of **Stilo** is famous for its 10th-century Byzantine church, **La Cattolica di Stilo**, with five small domes and remains of medieval frescoes. This church appears on almost every Calabrian tourist brochure. Back on the coast, scanty Greek and Roman ruins can be seen at **Caulonia**, where the church of San Zaccaria has a 13th-century fresco of Christ Pantocrator.

Catanzaro and Around

Down on the coast, there is little to detain you as you head north along the Gulf of Squillace to Catanzaro. At **Soverato**, a small museum contains a *pietà* and other works of the noted Renaissance sculptor from Sicily, Antonello Gagini, collected from local churches (*call the Pro Loco,* ***t*** *0867 22243, to see it*). At **Roccelletta di Borgia** there are more Roman ruins in the ancient town of Scolacium (*open daily 9–one hour before sunset*), and just south of **Catanzaro Lido**, are the imposing ruins of the 11th-century basilica Roccelletta del Vescovo di Squillace, surrounded by an olive grove.

After you have been here for a while, you will begin to understand why **Catanzaro** is the Calabrian capital. Make a wrong turn on a mountain road anywhere and Catanzaro is where you will end up. Really an overgrown mountaintop village that has straggled gradually down to the sea since the war, it is a piquant little city, the kind of place where the young men call you *capo* or *cavaliere* and ask for a light while they give you the once-over. The city park, called the Villa Trieste, has nice views and there is a **museum** of carriages (*Località Siano, in the north of the town;* **t** *0961 499 546; open Mon–Fri 9.30–11.30 and 4–6; adm*), but little else to see.

North of Catanzaro in the gulf of Taranto, the ghost cities of Magna Grecia are the only distractions along a lonely coast; after Catanzaro there is nothing to see for another 40km until **Le Castella**, where the 16th-century castle on a tiny island, accessible by a short causeway, makes a picturesque sight.

Crotone: The City of Pythagoras

Crotone, the Greek Croton, is no ghostly ruin but a dismal middle-sized industrial city. All those dams up in the Sila were built to provide electricity for the town's new chemical plants, part of a big scheme started by Mussolini in 1925. Along with Vibo Valentia, Crotone is a new provincial capital, governing a bit of the coast and an obscure inland *paese* called the Marchesato around Cutro. The new government likes to spell the name with a K, the way the Greeks did, which adds another touch of strangeness to what is already a vortex of weirdness. Crotone suffered badly from flooding in 1996 and immediately there was an outcry for an investigation. Few new cities have been so poorly planned and built, and a disaster was bound to happen.

The old Croton was often the most powerful of the Greek cities in Calabria, although it was more famous in the ancient world as the home of the philosopher Pythagoras. With his scientific discoveries, mathematical mysticism and belief in the transmigration of souls, Pythagoras cast a spell over the Greek world, and particularly over Magna Grecia. He was hardly a disinterested scholar in an ivory tower; around the middle of the 6th century BC, he seems to have led, or at least inspired, a mystic-aristocratic government in Croton based on his teachings. When a democratic revolution threw him out, he took refuge in Metapontum. Croton had a reputation for other things, too: its medical school, the success of its athletes at the Olympic games and, especially, its aggressive and unyielding attitude towards its neighbours.

Of all this, nothing is left but the **Museo Archeologico** (*Via Risorgimento 12,* **t** *0962 23082; open daily 9–8, closed first and third Mon of the month*), with a large collection of terracotta ex votos like those at Reggio. There is also the **Museo Civico** (*open Mon–Fri 9–1 and 3–7*), situated within the ramparts of the imposing 16th-century *castello* and housing a small collection of old maps and local relics. The city's **Duomo**, on Corso Vittorio Emmanuele, contains the Black Madonna of Capa Colonna, a Byzantine-style painting adorned with silver leaf. In Crotone's biggest annual festival (on the 3rd weekend of May), the icon is paraded through the town centre towards Cape Colonne, returning the following day by sea. On Cape Colonne, a promontory south of Crotone, a single standing column from a temple of Hera makes a romantic ruin. Travellers in the 1600s reported about 50 columns on the site; they must have been carted off since for building stone.

Rossano

The dry climate around **Melissa** and **Ciro**, north of Crotone, makes this Calabria's biggest and best wine-growing region. Further up, you can dip into the mountains at

Rossano, a hill town only 7km from the coast. Rossano claims to have invented licorice candy; they have been making it since 1731. The town's particular treasure, originally in the cathedral, is a beautiful 6th-century manuscript called the *Purple Codex*, believed to be the oldest illuminated gospel anywhere. It was made in Syria and almost certainly brought here by eastern monks fleeing their Muslim invaders. It can now be seen in the **Museo Diocesano** (***t*** *0983 520 282; open Mon–Fri 10–12 and 5–7, Sat–Sun 10–12*), next to the cathedral. In the cathedral itself, suffocated by the Baroque altar in the central nave, don't miss the 8th-century icon of the Madonna Achiropita: the image was believed to have painted itself, which is the meaning of the Greek name. The cathedral and many of the women in town have been named after it. Rossano is worth a look; even though many of the houses are empty, the Old Town is brightly colourful and one of the best preserved in Calabria. It's steep and complicated enough. With luck (don't ask us for directions, just keep climbing!) you will find a small Byzantine church similar to Stilo's: five-domed **San Marco**, at the highest point of the town. Further inland, between Rossano and Corigliano, you can admire the **Abbey of Pathirion** (***t*** *0984 75905*), built around 1100 in a curious combination of Arab, Byzantine and Norman styles.

Sybaris

North of Rossano, the mountains recede into the plain of Sybaris, named after the Greek city so renowned for luxurious decadence that even today it is echoed in the word 'sybarite'. Sybaris' only misfortune was to have jealous Croton for a neighbour. Croton besieged Sybaris and took it in 510 BC. After razing the city to the ground, the Crotonites diverted the River Crati over the ruins so that it could never be rebuilt. They did such a good job, in fact, that until a few years ago, modern archaeologists could not find the site; some scholars even became convinced the whole story of Sybaris was just a myth. Now that they've found it, feverish excavations are under way, and it is hoped the richest city of Magna Grecia may yield the archaeologists something worth the trouble it has caused them. So far, they have learned that the Crotonites did not do as thorough a job of destruction as had been thought. Above Sybaris proper, levels of excavation reveal ruins of Thurii, an Athenian colony and base in the Peloponnesian Wars, and a Roman town above that called Copia.

You can wander round the **excavation site** (*open Tues–Sun with or without a guide*). The tour is free and well worth the effort. Most of what you see is the Roman town of Copia, but there are a number of spots where excavations have revealed sections of Thurii, and below that, Sybaris proper. There are stables, olive presses, baths and spas, and a patrician's house with mosaics. The western flank of the site reveals the grand entrance to the Roman town and a *decumanus maximus* (main street), which has the girth of a modern motorway. One kilometre north of the excavation site, down a right turn, is a purpose-built **museum** (***t*** *0981 79391; open Tues–Sun 9–7.30; adm*). As well as ceramics, gold and silverware from the Sybaris site, there are findings from two Bronze Age settlements in the Sibari plain. Sybaris stands at the mouth of the Crati, which is now a wildlife preserve for a small colony of that increasingly rare species, the Mediterranean seal.

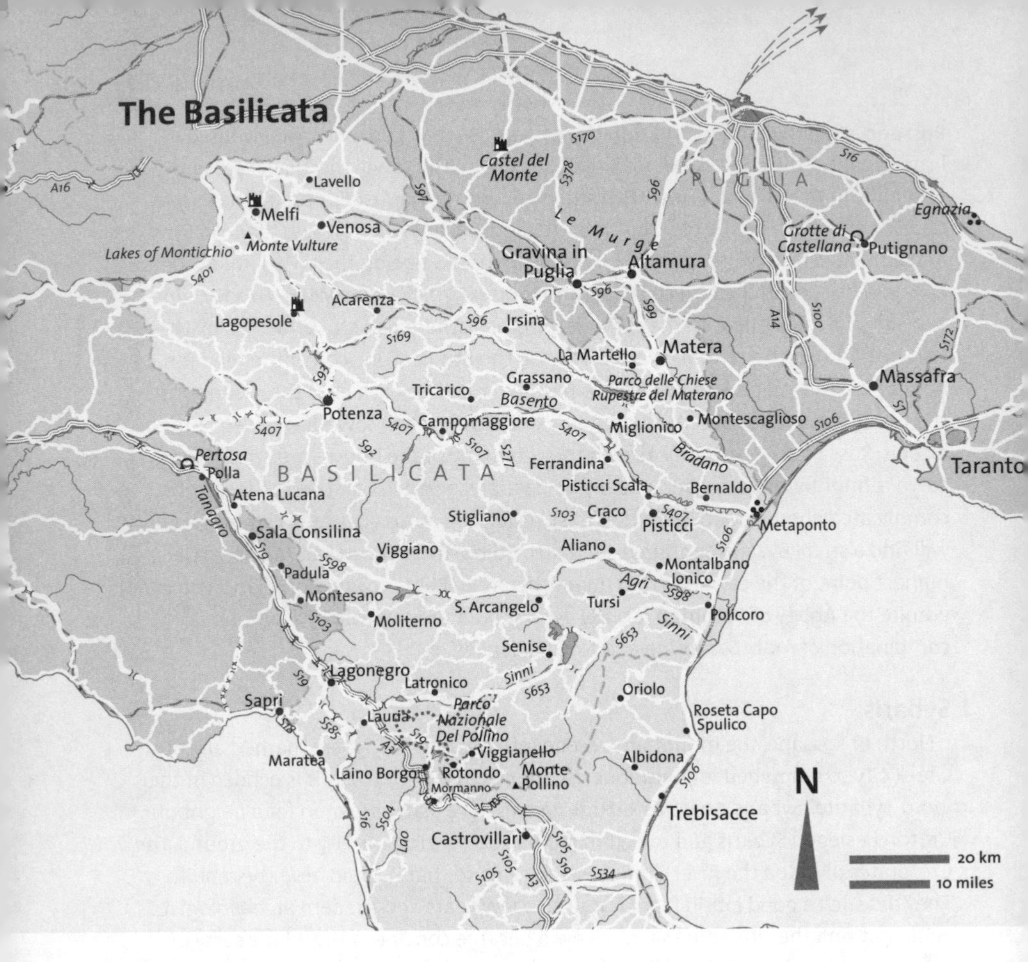

North of Sybaris, there are castles frowning down over the sea at **Roseto** and **Rocca Imperiale** (*open summer only*), the latter built by Frederick II.

The Basilicata

The Basilicata has never been one of the more welcoming regions of Italy. Divided about equally between mountains and rolling hills, the isolation of this land has usually kept it far from the major events of Italian history. The territory may be familiar if you have read Carlo Levi's *Christ Stopped at Eboli* – a novel written when the Basilicata was a national scandal, the poorest and most backward corner of all Italy. None of the famous 18th- and 19th-century travellers ever penetrated deeply into the region, and even today, it is a part of the country few foreigners ever visit. But, even though the Basilicata counts more ruined and vanished cities than live ones, things are looking up a bit. The countryside and most of the villages may seem empty but on the coast in Potenza and Matera, you will see some modest signs of prosperity.

The Southeastern Basilicata

The Basilicata's share of Pollino National Park is covered elsewhere in this chapter (*see* 'Pollino National Park' p.188). East of Monte Pollino, the southern Basilicata has a short stretch of Ionian coastline, and a little-visited interior of small villages and largely deforested hills.

Policoro

The Basilicata's share of the Ionian coast consists of the broad Piano di Metaponto, one of the largest of the new coastal agricultural regions that DDT opened up in southern Italy after the war. The new town of Policoro stands near the ancient city of Eraclea and its **Museo Nazionale della Siritide** (***t*** *0835 972 154; open daily 9–7; adm*) has a good collection of Greek vases and terracottas, as well as surprises like a little pendant of the smiling god Bes – the Phoenicians visited here, too. There are a number of moulds for terracotta *ex votos*; in all the Greek cities, the faithful would leave these in great numbers in the sanctuaries of the goddesses Demeter and Persephone. Siritide refers to this section of the coast; Taras (Taranto) and Thurii fought over it for a long time, and finally agreed to share it and co-found the city of Eraclea in 434 BC. Its scanty ruins, built on a long, narrow ridge, can be seen beyond the gardens of the museum. Two areas have been excavated, showing a long, tidy grid of streets with foundations of houses but, so far, no important temples. The **museum** has the keys to the sanctuary of Santa Maria d'Anglona at Tursi (*see* p.212).

Metaponto

North of Policoro, ancient **Metapontum** was another rich city; its prosperity was based on growing and shipping wheat. Today, its famous silver coins, always decorated with an ear of wheat, are especially prized by collectors. Even by the standards of Magna Grecia, Metapontum suffered bad luck. Among numerous sackings was one by Spartacus and his rebel army. In the Punic Wars, the city sided with Hannibal who, upon his retreat, courteously evacuated the entire population, saving them from a bloody Roman vengeance.

Modern Metaponto is, like Policoro, a brand-new town, with the disconcertingly over-planned air of an army base. Though it has more ruins to show than any of the other Calabrian sites, do not expect anything like Paestum or Pompeii. At the centre of the archaeological zone there is an **archaeological museum** (***t*** *0835 745 327; open daily 9–7 Mon 2–7; adm*). Like so many others built by the government in southern Italy, although it is fairly new it is already under serious restoration. The museum contains Greek ceramics and local Lucanian imitations, along with relics of the Oenotrians, a Lucanian tribe that inhabited the area before the Greeks arrived. The city's scanty remains, including the outlines of a horseshoe-shaped classical theatre, lie all around, encompassing a 6th-century sanctuary of Apollo Lykaios ('wolf-like Apollo') and a theatre, as well as some foundations of buildings from the Roman *castrum* that succeeded the Greek city. On the banks of the Bradano, facing the coastal SS106, stands the Temple

Getting There and Around

A **rail** line crosses the Basilicata from Battipaglia in Campania, passing through Potenza and Metaponto on its way to Taranto (6 trains a day). Another line follows the Ionian coast from Taranto to Reggio di Calabria. **Matera** is served by an FCL private rail line, with 12 trains a day from Bari – in fact, a day trip from Bari, only 46km away, may be a convenient way to see Matera. (The station is on Via Nazionale on the western edge of town.) There is also a slow FCL line between Potenza and Bari.

FCL and other companies also operate daily **bus** services from Matera's Piazza Matteotti to Ferrandina, Potenza, Naples and Metaponto.

The main **road** to the Basilicata for drivers coming from the north is the SS407 – the Taranto road – which leaves the A3 *autostrada* near Zuppino, 25km east of Eboli, and goes past Potenza and Metaponto. An interesting route to Matera is the old Roman Via Appia – now the SS7 and only a minor road for most of the stretch from Potenza.

Tourist Information

Two websites with useful information about the Basilicata are *www.regione.basilicata.it* and *www.aptbasilicata.it*.

Matera: Via de Viti de Marco 9, **t** 0835 331 983, *www.materanet.com*. *Open 9–1, closed Sun.*

Potenza: Via del Gallitello 89, **t** 0971 507 622, *infopotenza@aptbasilicata.it*.

Maratea: Piazza del Gesù 32, **t** 0973 876 908.

Where to Stay and Eat

Policoro and Metaponto ✉ 75025

★★★**Kennedy**, Viale Jonio 1, **t/f** 0835 741 960, *www.hrkennedy.it* (*moderate*). A good bargain, down by the beach at Metaponto.

★★★**Callà**, Corso Pandosia 1, **t** 0835 972 129 (*cheap*). Good-value hotel in Policoro.

★★★**Motel Due Palme**, Scanzano Ionico, **t** 0835 953 024 (*cheap*). A decent stopover on the coast just north of Policoro.

Matera ✉ 75100

★★★**Hotel Sassi**, Via San Giovanni Vecchio 89, **t** 0835 331 009, **f** 0835 333 733, *www.hotelsassi.it* (*moderate*). This restructured 18th-century complex in the heart of the *Sasso Barisano* is *the* place to stay in Matera. All 15 rooms are shaped to respect the original layout and all come with balconies overlooking the *Sassi*. Simple, tasteful décor and friendly, efficient service.

★★★**Piccolo Albergo**, Via di Sariis 11/3, **t** 0835 330 201 (*moderate*). A good option.

★★★**Italia**, Via Ridola 5, **t** 0835 333 561, *www.albergoitalia.com* (*moderate*). Quite pleasant. Some rooms have good views over the *Sassi*.

★**Roma**, Via Roma 62, **t** 0835 333 912 (*cheap*). This clean and spartan *pensione* with shared bathrooms is a good budget choice.

Il Terrazzino, Vico S. Giuseppe 7, **t** 0835 332 503 (*very expensive*). Simple but piquant Basilicatan dishes. Just off Piazza Vittorio Veneto. *Closed Tues.*

Lucana, Via Lucana 48, **t** 0835 336 117 (*moderate*). A popular *trattoria* serving a variety of local favourites. The *antipasti della casa* is a delectable meal in itself. *Closed Sun.*

Il Castello, Via Castello 1, **t** 0835 333 752 (*cheap*). Serves *orecchiette* with mushrooms and sausage, as well as good fish and meat. *Closed Wed.*

Basilico, Via San Francesco 33, **t** 0835 336 540 (*cheap*). The modern pastel décor and *cuisine soignée* seem a bit out of place in Matera, but people come here for really good pizza at reasonable prices. *Closed Fri.*

Del Corso, Via Luigi La Vista 12, **t** 0835 332 892 (*cheap*). Gorge yourself for a pittance in the company of discerning locals. *Closed Fri eve.*

Potenza ✉ 85100

Fuori le Mura, Via 4 Novembre 34, **t** 0971 25409 (*moderate*). An employee-owned restaurant, known locally for its huge choice of *antipasti* and good roast pork and lamb. *Closed Mon.*

★★**Miramonti**, Via Caserma Lucana 30, **t** 0971 22987, **f** 0971 411 623 (*cheap*). A simple budget establishment.

Lagopesole ✉ 85020

Falcon Castel, **t** 0971 86239 (*cheap*). Good-value *trattoria* below the castle. *Closed Mon.*

Melfi ✉ 85025

★★★**Due Pini**, Piazza La Stazione, **t** 0972 21031, **f** 0972 21608 (*moderate*). Just outside town at the station, this is a place for travelling salesmen, but convenient as an overnighter.

Vaddone, Corso da Sant'Abruzzese, **t** 0972 24323 (*moderate*). This family-run restaurant offers good regional cuisine washed down with local Aglianico and Vulture wines.

Il Tratturo Regio, Contrada del Casonetto, **t/f** 0972 239 295 (*cheap*). If you have a car, stay in this *azienda*, signposted on the SS road. The Imbriani family will welcome you and feed you freshly made *ricotta* and *mamma*'s home cooking.

Monticchio Laghi ✉ 85020

Il Pescatore, **t** 0972 731 036 (*cheap*). If you're visiting the Lakes of Monticchio, south of Melfi, avoid the snack bars and track down this restaurant instead; it's on the road that goes around the smaller of the two lakes. The place lacks atmosphere but the servings are lavish. *Closed Wed.*

Venosa ✉ 85029

******Orazio***, Corso Vittorio Emmanuele II 142, **t** 0972 31135, **f** 0972 35081 (*cheap*). A night in this beautifully restored *palazzo* is a real bargain. Rooms are well equipped and there is a communal terrace on the first floor with lovely views over the valley, while downstairs there's a lounge where you can watch TV or read the verses of local poet Horace.

Il Grifo, Via delle Fornaci 21, **t** 0972 35188 (*cheap*). A fine restaurant beside the castle. Try the *lagane*, they're delicious. *Closed Tues.*

Maratea ✉ 85046

*******Santavenere**, Via Santavenere, Fiumicello, **t** 0973 876 910, **f** 0973 877 654, *www.mondomaratea.it* (*luxury*). Maratea has some excellent hotels and this elegant place, 1½km north of Porto di Maratea at Fiumicello-Santavenere is the top of the tree. It is an elegantly furnished modern building in a fine setting on cliffs above the sea, with a private beach, swimming pool and tennis courts; all the rooms are air-conditioned. It also has a fine restaurant. *Wheelchair accessible.*

*****Villa degli Aranci**, Via Profiti 12, **t/f** 0973 876 344, *www.costadimaratea.com* (*expensive*). A good, cheaper hotel, near the Santavenere at Maratea-Fiumicello.

Za Mariuccia, Via Grotte 2, **t** 0973 876 163 (*expensive*). A good but pricey seafood *trattoria* in Maratea Porto, with tables overlooking the sea. The extensive menu includes excellent risottos and pasta dishes with scampi, lobster and other delights, and the very best of whatever Maratea's fishermen have come up with on that particular day. *Closed Fri lunch, Oct–Mar.*

Rovita, Via Rovita 13, **t** 0973 876 588 (*expensive*). Another of Maratea's treasures, situated up in the historic centre. The restaurant's excellent fish is matched by some equally good pasta and meat dishes. *Closed Tues, Dec–Feb.*

La Torre, Largo Immaccolata, **t** 0973 876 227 (*cheap*). This is the most popular *trattoria* in the historic centre. It is situated on the main piazza and you'll need to arrive early if you want to claim one of the tables outside.

Caffè e Dolcezze, Piazza Raglia 19. This tiny café is a great place to stop for a coffee in the Old Town. There's only one table inside, which is surrounded by a series of glass-fronted drawers packed with all kinds of sweets, liquorice and candied fruits.

Stigliano ✉ 75018

****Margariello**, Corso Umberto 55, **t** 0835 561 225 (*cheap*). You can sample the modest charms of the Margariello for a rock-bottom price, but there are only two bathrooms to share between the eight rooms.

Pisticci ✉ 75015

******Degli Argonauti**, Marina di Pisticci, **t** 0835 470 242, **f** 0835 470 240 (*very expensive*). A plush hotel centred around a lagoon-like swimming pool with 6,000 square metres for you to splash around in! It's no stopover; in the summer, a week's stay and full board are required.

Ragno Verde, Via Colombo 13, Policoro, **t** 0835 971 736. A good family *trattoria* (*cheap*). *Closed Sun.*

Ferrandina ✉ 75013

Ferrandina lies 25km south of Matera and has only one tiny *locanda*.

*****Degli Ulivi**, outside the town itself, on the SS407, **t/f** 0835 757 020 (*moderate*). It makes a pleasant stopover on the way to Taranto.

of Hera that used to be called the *Tavole Palatine* by locals – the Round Table of King Arthur. Fifteen of its columns remain.

The Interior

Heading inland 11km from Policoro, near the village of Tursi, is the sanctuary of **Santa Maria d'Anglona**. Set on an isolated hilltop with a wide view, Anglona was inhabited from the Bronze Age until about 1546, when the bishop moved down into the village. It stands above a hamlet called Troyli, recalling a local legend that Trojans once settled this place. At the top of the hill nothing is left save the impressive 11th-century church, in a style reminiscent of Pisan Romanesque and decorated with strange carved reliefs on the façade and apse, and some original frescoes inside. To get into the church, ask for the keys at the Policoro Museum.

Still further inland, in **Stigliano**, the 17th-century church of San Antonio has an odd waffle-iron rococo façade even better than the one on the Gesù Nuovo in Naples.

The wild countryside around **Aliano**, south of Stigliano, offers some of the more outlandish scenery in southern Italy. Deforestation and consequent erosion have turned parts of the area into a lunar landscape, exposing twisted rock formations called *calanchi*. Aliano is the village where Carlo Levi stayed during the time he describes in *Christ Stopped at Eboli*. The house in which he lived is at the bottom of the village and now houses a **museum** (***t*** *0835 568 074; open daily 9–1 and 4–7*) dedicated to the writer and to local folklore, customs and traditional life.

From Metaponto, the SS175 climbs from the coast towards Matera, passing through a scenic route of pines and wildflowers and the attractive whitewashed village of **Montescaglioso**. At the top of this town there is an impressive medieval monastery, the **Abbazia di Sant'Angelo**.

The Basento Valley

The valley of the Basento is one of the Basilicata's comparatively prosperous and modern regions, due largely to government industrial schemes and the discovery of some modest gas reserves. The region's main road is the SS407, which locals call the *Basentana* and which follows the river to Potenza. **Pisticci** is the largest town in the area, though by no means the most pleasant; the weirdly eroded gullies around the town make a fitting introduction to the sad landscapes you will see in much of this region. **Craco**, overlooking a steep cliff west of Pisticci, is one of the more recent of the south's many ghost towns, today almost completely abandoned after landslides made the site unsafe – a recurring problem in the region thanks to deforestation.

Ferrandina is one of the prettier villages along the Basento. Its neat rows of sun-bleached, gabled terraced houses, similar to many places in Puglia, offer an example of the Basilicata's traditional style of building. West of Ferrandina on the back roads you will see a picturesquely ruined castle on a round hill, the **Castello di Uggiano.**

From Ferrandina, the SS99 heads east towards Matera, passing **Miglionico**, where there is a mouldering castle and perhaps the best painting in the Basilicata: a glorious 18-section altarpiece by the Venetian Renaissance artist Cima del Conigliano. There's an artificial lake, **Lago di San Giuliano,** between Miglionico and Matera.

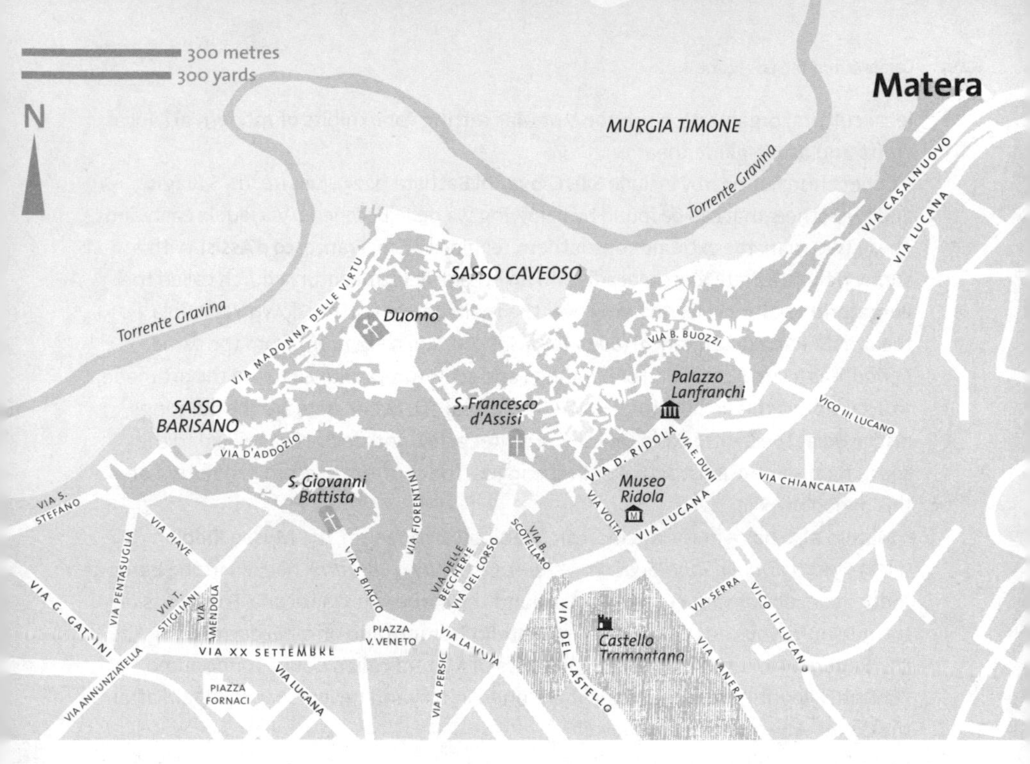

Matera

Of all the Basilicata's towns, the only one that offers a real reason for stopping is Matera, a lively provincial capital of some 55,000 people that has become famous for a kind of freak-show attraction. Matera was an inhabited town since before recorded history in these parts began and for centuries, probably millennia, its people built cave-homes and cave-churches in the easily worked tufa stone. Mel Gibson's controversial blockbuster, *The Passion of The Christ* (2004), was set in and around Matera, focusing unprecedented media attention on the baffled town.

The Town Centre

Matera never had much money, but it did have a sense of style, and whatever pennies its rulers could squeeze out of the *paisani* went into an ironically grandiose ensemble of churches and piazzas. Matera still has style, though it is subtle and you'll have to stay around awhile to see it. On a Sunday evening, when the Materesi descend to participate in one of south Italy's most enthusiastic *passeggiatas*, Matera can look very urbane.

The centre, and the most gracious square in town, is **Piazza Vittorio Veneto**. It is decorated with the smallest and most peculiar of the churches, **San Domenico**, with a shallow Byzantine-style dome, AVE MARIA spelled out in plain light bulbs across the front and a medieval rose window carved into a kind of wheel of fortune. Near this is the entrance to the recently rediscovered *hypogeum* that underlies most of the city centre. Like the 'underground cities' of Cappadocia, this is believed to have been used for storage and as a refuge in times of trouble. It is usually open; the city and a local cultural organization use the singular setting for exhibits of modern art, local crafts and avant-garde theatre.

Other churches nearby include **San Giovanni Battista** (1223), just up Via S.Biagio, and two others that can be found by following Via delle Beccherie/Via Ridola eastwards. These two mark the extremes of southern religiosity: **San Francesco d'Assisi**, with a sunny, delightful late rococo façade, and an eccentric 18th-century church called the **Purgatorio**, sporting a leering skull over the main portal. Further down Via Ridola, the ornate **Palazzo Lanfranchi** (*open Tues–Sat 9–1, Sun 9–12; adm*), from the same period, has a small collection of paintings and sculpture, a chance to see the art made to accompany this architecture. However, the real attraction here are the paintings displayed at the **Centro Carlo Levi**. Levi, a writer, artist and doctor, was exiled to the south for his anti-Fascist activities in the 1930s. The centre is a record in painting of this period of exile.

Matera also has a first-class local archaeological museum, the **Museo Ridola** (***t*** *0835 310 058; open June–Sept 9am–11pm, Oct–May 9–8; adm*), housed in the Baroque former convent of Santa Chiara, just around the corner on Via Lucana. From outside the museum, you can see the gloomy **Castello Tramontano** on a hill dominating the city. Begun by an exceptionally piggish boss of Matera called Count Tramontano ('Count Twilight'), the works were abandoned in 1515 and never taken up again after the Count was murdered in a revolt.

The Duomo

At the top of the town, perched on a narrow hill, is the 13th-century cathedral. It's a fine Puglian Romanesque building with a square campanile that can be seen all over Matera. The Duomo has quite an interior, with brilliantly carved medieval capitals, and lots of gilding and some richly decorated chapels from later centuries; one wonders what the poor children from the caves thought of it in the old days. There is also a *trompe l'œil* ceiling, noticeable if you stand at the centre of the nave. Near the entrance is a spectacular *pietra dura* altar; opposite, another altar has been removed to reveal an excellent bit of original fresco in a decidedly Byzantine style. The entire west end of the church must have been painted as a Last Judgement; only a bit of Purgatory is uncovered, along with a scene of the sea giving up its drowned souls. The main altar is a carved and polychromed Renaissance work, an introduction to the wealth of art from the same period in the two chapels to the left of it. One of these, with Botticellian frescoes of sibyls and prophets from the 1530s on its ceiling, contains a strange, folkloric carved *presepe*. From here (if the door is open) you can find your way to a tiny, older church hidden inside this one: **Santa Maria di Costantinopoli**, with a 13th-century relief over the door showing a procession with an image of the Madonna – the *Madonna della Bruna*, to be specific, who now as then gets a ride around town on a float every 2 July. A new float is made every year, covered in papier-mâché Baroque frippery, and at the end of each procession, the townspeople burn it.

A narrow opening in Piazza del Duomo leads to a street called Via del Riscatto or 'Redemption Street', where the Materese got even with Count Twilight in 1515.

The *Sassi*

Matera has chosen to preserve rather than obliterate its past poverty by turning its poorest sections, the *Sassi*, into a sort of open-air museum – one that has now made UNESCO's list of World Heritage Sites. *Sassi* are the cave neighbourhoods that line the two ravines between which Matera is built. As recently as 40 years ago, visitors reported people still living in the cave-homes in abject poverty, sharing space with pigs and chickens while their children implored outsiders not for money but for quinine.

Most of the buildings and caves in the *Sassi* are abandoned today, although some people are actually rehabilitating some of the houses – including a few trendified ones with plant-filled roof terraces. Matera and its province have benefited from the good works of the *Cassa per il Mezzogiorno* as much as any part of the south. You may think it somewhat macabre, visiting the scenes of past misery, but the *Sassi* are fascinating in their way, so don't be surprised to see tour groups being dragged through the cave-neighbourhoods' steps and winding lanes. You can get a good view over the *Sassi* from the viewpoints at the top of the town.

There are two *Sassi*, the wealthier **Sasso Barisano** north of the town centre, and the poorer **Sasso Caveoso** to the east. If you visit, before long a child or old man of the neighbourhood will come up and approach you to offer a guide service – worth the trouble and slight expense if you have the time and find the *Sassi* interesting. They know where the old churches with the Byzantine frescoes are (some as old as the 9th century) and, if you can pick out enough of their southern dialect, they have plenty of stories to tell. If you speak Italian, local guides are probably a better option than the maps and itineraries you can pick up from the tourist office – it's very easy to get lost in the *Sassi*, or to miss some of the most interesting sights, even with a map. Alternatively the very good **Tour Service Matera** (*Piazza Vittorio Veneto 42;* ***t*** *0835 334 633*), offers a wide range of tailormade guided tours.

Don't get the idea that the *Sassi* are just plain caves. They started that way, but over the centuries, they evolved into real neighbourhoods with normal-looking façades, like the cave houses of southern Spain. The predominant stone of the area is tufa, a volcanic rock that is easier to cut and shape than wood; in Matera, it was always easier to dig out a house or church than build one. Opposite the *Sassi*, along the other side of the Gravina ravine, you will see the real caves *au naturel*, many of them with traces of habitation from prehistoric times.

Two of Matera's Baroque façades can be seen in the *Sassi* themselves, set in proper piazzas among the cave homes: **Santa Maria di Idris** in the *Sasso Caveoso*, and **San Pietro Barisano** in the *Sasso Barisano*. The façades of these churches date back to the 1200s and have remains of their original frescoes.

Cave Churches

The dry, austere countryside around Matera is full of tufa quarries, caves and churches. Across the Gravina ravine from the *Sasso Caveoso* (the one south of the cathedral), the cliffs called the **Murgia Timone** hold a number of interesting cave-churches, some with elaborate fronts, even domes, cut out of the tufa, and medieval frescoes. You'll need a map and some help from the provincial tourist office, or else a guide, to find them. Among the most interesting are those of **Santa Maria della Palomba**, **La Vaglia**, the **Madonna delle Tre Porte** and **Santa Barbara**. Near Santa Maria della Palomba, you can see a functioning tufa quarry; the easily cut stone is still used for houses, although it is well-hidden under the stucco. There are more of these half-forgotten churches in parts of neighbouring Puglia, but none anywhere else in Italy. Indeed, they can only be compared to the similar Byzantine rock churches of Cappadocia in Turkey. Determined explorers can spend weeks here, seeking out the rest of the churches in the forbidding countryside around Matera. One set lies in a 20km stretch of the Gravina south of the city, the **Parco delle Chiese Rupestre del Materano**, which begins at the Murgia Timone. Another long section of this park follows the Torrente Gravina di Picciano, east of Matera around La Martella.

The Northwestern Basilicata

Western Basilicata is a province to itself, with a capital at **Potenza** – a plain, modern hilltop city regularly rattled to pieces by earthquakes. Although present on this site since it was Roman Potentia, Potenza consequently has little to show: a few medieval churches, and a small Archaeological Museum on Via Cicotto. There are mountains on all sides, with some humble skiing areas to the south.

To the east, you'll find some startling landscapes in the mountains dubbed (by some tourist official, most likely) the '**Basilicatan Dolomites**', a patch of jagged and sinister limestone peaks around the equally sombre villages of Pietrapertosa and Castelmezzano. The former has a ruined castle built by the Arabs, who were a power in this region back in the heyday of the Emirate of Bari. **Campomaggiore**, nearby, is entirely new; the original, higher up in the mountains on a dirt track, became a ghost town like Craco after a landslide in 1885. Its ruins are still visible. Route SS7, passing through Potenza, follows the course of the **Appian Way**; the road passes through **Tricarico**, a pleasant village under the round dungeon of a Norman castle.

Lagopesole's Castle

The northern end of the province, astride the important routes between Naples and Puglia, was a busy place in the Middle Ages, full of castles and fought over by Normans, Angevins and Holy Roman emperors. Frederick II, in particular, haunted these bleak hills; he spent three months here, just before moving on to Puglia, where he died of dysentery. His son Manfred spent his honeymoon here with his bride Elena of Epirus, at the well-preserved castle of Lagopesole, halfway between Potenza and Melfi. Although this castle had a military role, a strong redoubt against the frequent rebellions of the Basilicata's barons, it was largely intended as a residence. Its austere rectangularity looks strangely abstract and sophisticated, along the lines of the beautiful castle Frederick built in Prato, near Florence. Some good capitols and other sculptural details survive inside, including an image believed to be the emperor's grandfather, Frederick I Barbarossa, wearing ass's ears. The castle now hosts travelling exhibitions; it's worth taking pot luck and seeing what's on.

Acerenza

Acerenza was the Basilicata's capital when Potenza was still a mountain village. The town's impressive 10th–13th-century **cathedral** contains, along with some good Romanesque sculptural work, the drollest fraud in the Basilicata – a venerable bust believed for centuries to represent the town's patron, San Canio. Instead, the little icon has been identified as none other than that devout pagan, Emperor Julian the Apostate.

Melfi and Around

Earlier in his reign, the great Hohenstaufen spent some time at the castle at Melfi, a fortress that two centuries before was the de Hautevilles' first Italian headquarters: Robert Guiscard was crowned Duke of Puglia and Calabria here. The castle is well up to cinematic standards – none of Frederick's geomantical mysticism here; unlike Castel del Monte this one was built strictly for defence. Little remains of the original furnishings, but there is a small **archaeological museum** (*t 0972 238 726; open June–Sept 9am–11pm, Oct–May 9–7; adm*). Melfi itself is a sleepy town, with little but the castle and an 11th-century cathedral to remind it of the times when it occupied the centre stage of European politics. Several minor Church councils were held here and this was where Frederick promulgated his famous *Costitutiones Melfitanes*, perhaps the first proper written constitution in history.

Near Melfi, you can seek out two Roman bridges and also the villages of **Barile** and **Ginestra**, largely populated by Albanians. Between Melfi and Rapolla are a number of small cave-churches cut in the tufa, some with frescoes.

From Melfi's castle, the southern horizon is dominated by the ragged, menacing outline of **Monte Vulture**, a long-extinct volcano with a forest where once it had a smoking crater. Around the back side of the mountain, the Basilicata hides one of its few beauty spots, the little **Lakes of Monticchio**, with lovely woods and a funicular to the top of the mountain. Much of the mineral water you've been having with dinner across the south comes from the springs here – Gaudianello and other labels.

Venosa

East from Melfi, there is another old castle at Venosa, birthplace of the poet Horace (and also, 1,100 years later, of King Manfred, son of Frederick II). Archaeological finds are housed inside the **castle museum** (*t 0972 36 095; open June–Sept 9am–11pm, Oct–May 9–7; adm*). Venosa was Venusia back in the days when it was republican Rome's most important base in the south, and the goddess Venus must have had a sanctuary here – you can still find churches in the region dedicated to Santa Venere. Venosa's Roman past shows itself in the relief fragments built into the walls of the cathedral, last rebuilt in the 1600s, and even more in the scanty **ruins** of baths, an amphitheatre and a 5th-century basilica, just outside the town on the road to Puglia (*open daily April–Sept 9–7, rest of the year 9–one hour before sunset*).

Next to the ruins, you can visit what has survived of one of the most ambitious church-building projects ever undertaken in the south. The Benedictine **Abbazia della Trinità**, begun in the 1050s, was never completed, but it became the resting place of four of the five famous Norman brothers: William, Drogo, Robert (Guiscard) and

Humphrey de Hauteville. Their tombs are in the older, completed church, along with some very fine surviving frescoes and carved capitals. Among the heaps of stones tumbled about you may notice some Hebrew inscriptions; ancient and medieval Venosa both had important Jewish communities and some Jewish catacombs have been discovered, along with Christian ones, on the hill east of the abbey.

Maratea and Around

Squeezed between Campania's Cilento peninsula and the northwest coast of Calabria, a little corner of the Basilicata stretches out to touch the Tyrrhenian Sea. The scenery here differs little from the steep cliffs and green slopes of the Cilento; after Sapri, the SS18 becomes a spectacular and rugged corniche road, passing over cliffs covered with scrubby macchia, and soft grey beaches on hidden coves.

Maratea and the Tyrrhenian Coast

The focus of the Basilicata's Tyrrhenian coast is **Maratea**, a pretty hill village of tiny alleys and steps with more modern additions tucked between cliffs by the sea far below it. Maratea has become quite sophisticated and expensive, although the atmosphere is still pretty laid-back. As well as some of the best coastal scenery in the deep south, you can enjoy relatively uncrowded beaches and modest hotels at **Maratea Marina** (where trains on the main Rome–Reggio rail line stop), **Acquafredda** (just over the border in Calabria, *see* p.187) and several other points along the coast. The town itself lies under what must be the queerest hilltop Jesus in Italy; all marble and 66ft tall. Designed by Bruno Innocenti in 1963 at the start of Maratea's push to become a resort, from a distance it looks more like a perfume bottle with wings.

Inland from Maratea

Some of the twistiest roads in the Basilicata will take you up to the A3 *autostrada*, or to the sleepy villages of **Lagonegro**, with its Baroque churches, and **Rivello**, a charming, isolated hilltop village which, since the last earthquake, is held together by silicon glue and wooden poles. It is well worth exploring, though in its steep alleys, you'll be doing a great deal more climbing than walking.

Maratea is also a possible base for a visit to the Pollino National Park (*see* p.188).

Puglia

13

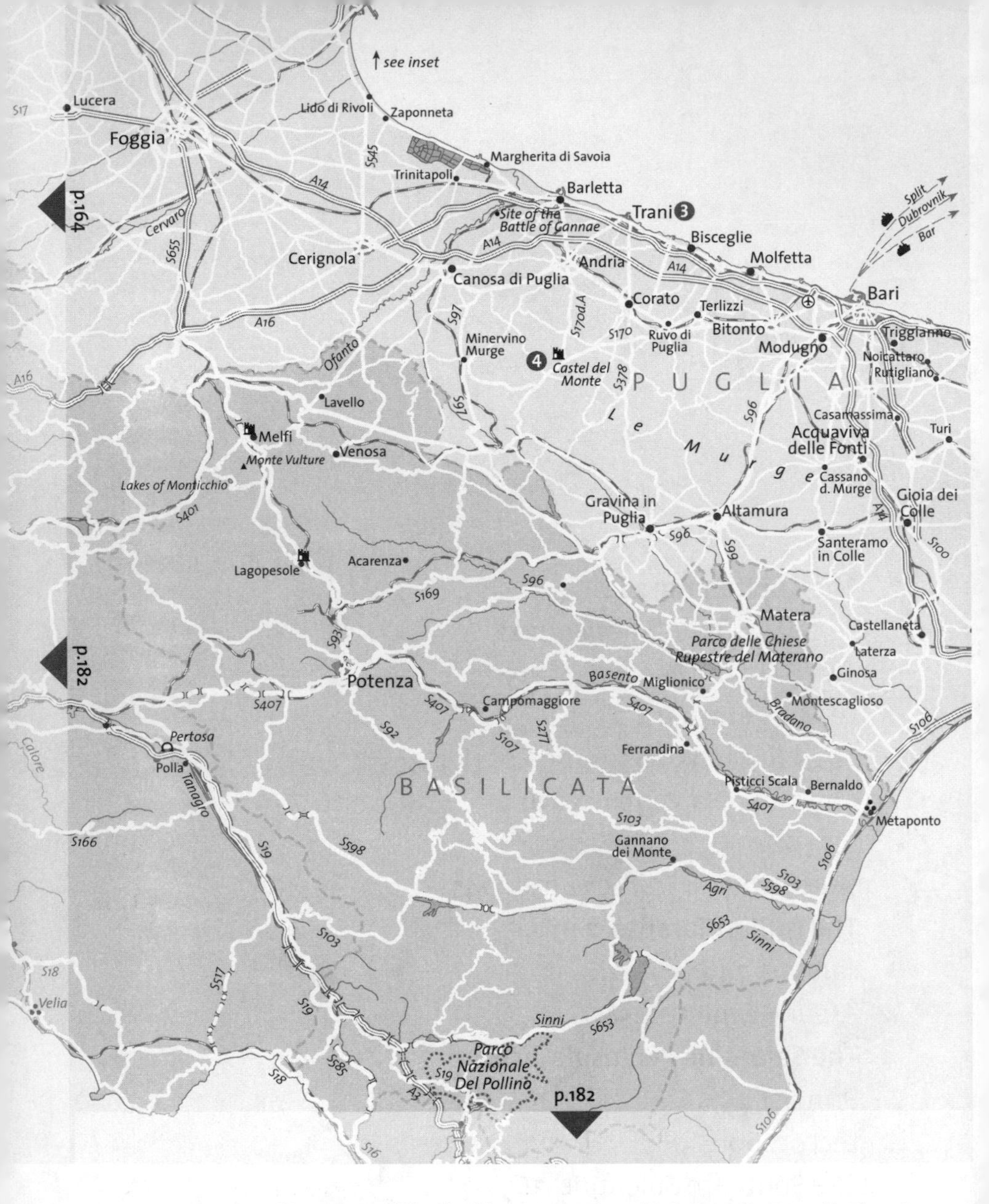

In many ways, this region will be the biggest surprise of Italy's south. From the forests and shining limestone cliffs of the beautiful Gargano peninsula in the north, through the long plain of the *Tavoliere* to the southernmost tip of Italy's heel, Puglia offers the most variety of any of the southern regions, not only in nature, but in its towns and in its art. In Puglia, you can see Byzantine art around Taranto, a score or so of Europe's finest Romanesque cathedrals, Santa Claus' tomb, the end of the Appian Way at Brindisi, Lecce – the loveliest Baroque city In the Mediterranean – and a region of buildings shaped like oil cans.

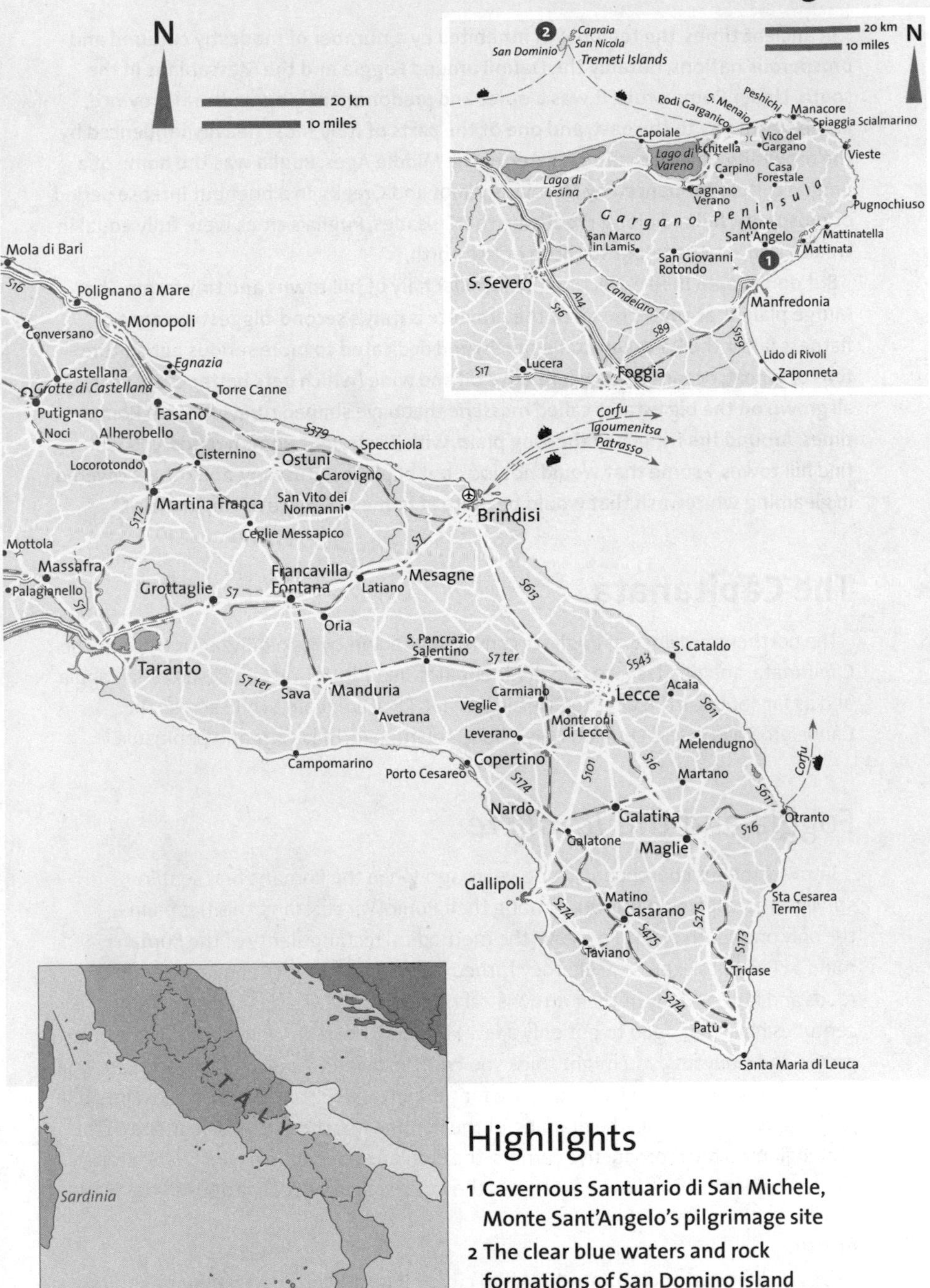

Highlights

1. Cavernous Santuario di San Michele, Monte Sant'Angelo's pilgrimage site
2. The clear blue waters and rock formations of San Domino island
3. Trani's Grand Romanesque cathedral
4. Castel del Monte's severe symmetry

In ancient times, the region was inhabited by a number of modestly cultured and prosperous nations, notably the Daunii around Foggia and the Messapians in the south. Under Roman rule, it was a quiet and predominantly agricultural province, Rome's gateway to the east, and one of the parts of Italy most heavily influenced by the proximity of Greek culture. Later, in the Middle Ages, Puglia was the home of a unique culture influenced by Normans, Arabs and Greeks. In a brief but intense period of prosperity, helped along greatly by the Crusades, Puglia's cities were fully equal in wealth and artistic talent to those of the north.

But don't come here expecting the familiar Italy of hill towns and tiny farms. The Murge plain that covers much of the province is Italy's second-biggest expanse of flatness (after the Po Valley in the north) and dedicated to more serious agriculture – tons of wheat, oceans of excellent olive oil and wine (which gets better every year), all grown on the big estates called *masserie* that have shaped rural life since Roman times. Around the fringes of the long plain, with its straight Roman roads, you will find hill towns – some that would not look out of place in Tuscany, and others covered in gleaming whitewash that would be more at home in Greece or North Africa.

The Capitanata

The northern province of Puglia is commonly known by its old Byzantine name, the Capitanata, and divides into two distinct parts. Inland, around San Severo and Foggia and as far south as the Ofanto River, is the flat *Tavoliere* plain, while across the Candelaro River is the 'spur' on Italy's boot, the rugged, hilly Gargano peninsula.

Foggia and the *Tavoliere*

Tavoliere means chessboard; 2,000 years ago, when the Romans first sent in surveyors to apportion the land among their Punic War veterans, this flat plain – the only one south of the Po – gave the methodical rectangularity of the Roman mind a chance to express itself. They turned the plain into a grid of neatly squared roads and farms. Many of their arrow-straight roads survive, and the succeeding centuries have managed to put only a few kinks into the rest. Were it not for the olive groves and vineyards, you might think you were in Iowa. But much of the *Tavoliere* was until recently too dry to be of much use for modern agriculture. One of Mussolini's big projects, as important as the draining of the Pontine marshes, has made it one of the Mezzogiorno's most productive corners: the Puglian aqueduct, carrying water from the Apennines in northern Campania, is the longest and most capacious in the world.

Foggia

Foggia, after Bari and Taranto, the third city of Puglia, was once Frederick's capital, where between campaigns he enjoyed quiet moments with his English wife, his harem, his falcons and his Muslim sorcerers. It must have been quite a place, but old Foggia has since been obliterated by two of the usual southern plagues: earthquakes have

Getting Around

Foggia's **railway** station is on Piazza Veneto, at the end of the central Viale XXIV Maggio. There are frequent trains to Bari, Naples, Bologna, Rome and Manfredonia.

Two companies operate **buses** to different points around the province: **SITA**, **t** 0881 773 425 (ticket office at Kiwi Bar, on the corner of Viale XXIV Maggio), and **HFS**, **t** free 167 296 347 (ticket office left of the station entrance). HFS also operates a private **railway** service in northern Gargano. **ATAF**, **t** 0881 770 241, and **A CAPT**, **t** 0882 641 326, run buses from the Piazza Veneto opposite the station. There are several buses a day to Monte Sant'Angelo, Vieste and Manfredonia, and Troia and Lucera.

Foggia is well connected by **road**. The A14 *autostrada* runs down the coast just to the north. It has a ring road linking all roads into town – the SS16, parallel to the A14, the SS89 for Manfredonia and the Gargano, the SS655 for the south and the SS17 to Lucera and Campobasso. For Troia, take the SS546.

Tourist Information

Foggia: Via S. E., Perrone 17, **t** 0881 723 650, *www.pugliaturismo.com*. *Open Mon–Fri 8.30–1*. Some way from the station and hard to find, upstairs in a block of flats.

Where to Stay and Eat

Foggia ✉ 71100

★★★★**Cicolella**, Viale XXIV Maggio 60, **t** 0881 566 111, **f** 0881 778 984 (*very expensive*). The best hotel in Foggia, although it's nothing exceptional. It's Victorian on the outside but remodelled within. The restaurant is one of the best in town – try the Puglian speciality *orecchiette*, the fish and the roast lamb. *Closed Sat and Sun*.

★★★**Europa**, Via Monfalcone 52, **t** 0881 721 057, **f** 0881 720 228 (*expensive*). One of the more affordable hotels near the station.

★**Venezia**, Via Piave 40, **t** 0881 770 903, **f** 0881 770 904 (*moderate*). A handy budget option, also close to the railway station.

Giordano da Pompeo, Vico al Piano 14, **t** 0881 724 640 (*moderate*). Sample seasonal and local specialities at this fine restaurant (run by the same family as the Cicolella Hotel). *Closed Sun and two weeks in Aug*.

Lucera ✉ 71036

★★**Balconata**, Viale Ferrovia 15, **t** 0881 546 725, **f** 0881 520 998 (*moderate*). One of only three hotels in Lucera and fine for a stopover.

Al Passetto, Piazza del Popolo 24, **t** 0881 542 213 (*cheap*). A fine restaurant in the town centre. *Closed Thurs*.

San Severo ✉ 71016

Just north of Foggia, **Le Arcate** is worth a stop.

★★★**Milano**, Via Teano Appulo 15, **t/f** 0882 375 643 (*moderate*). A very nice, well-appointed hotel.

Le Arcate, Piazza Cavalotti 29, **t** 0882 226 025 (*cheap*). Lighter variations on rustic cuisine, including succulent lamb and delicious desserts. *Closed 1 Jan, 15 Aug*.

levelled it on several occasions, and the French sacked it in 1528. Allied bombers finished off the remains, and the Foggia you see today is a newborn – homely and awkward as newborns are, but still somehow endearing if you come in the right frame of mind. Its citizens haven't forgotten Frederick, but these days, they seem prouder of a composer of operas named Umberto Giordano, born here in 1867. The municipal theatre is named after him and there is a big statue of him in the Piazza Giordano in the city centre, among a wonderfully eccentric set of statues representing characters from his works. Giordano's big hit was *Andrea Chenier*. Another of his works, with the intriguing title of *Fedora*, is claimed as the only opera that calls for bicycles on stage. You'll be able to see one or the other during Foggia's opera season, in the autumn.

Modern Foggia shows you broad, planned boulevards and low, earthquake-proof buildings. There's a little left of old Foggia to see, including a charming **cathedral** divided neatly in half like a layer-cake, 12th-century Romanesque on the bottom and Baroque on top. The early medieval door on the north side was only rediscovered during the Second World War, when bombs knocked down the adjacent building that was hiding it. A few twisting streets to the north, on Piazza Nigri, is Foggia's **Museo Civico** (*currently closed for restoration*), with a collection of archaeological finds and exhibits on folk life and crafts from around Puglia. The scientific section has been relocated to the **Museo di Storia Naturale** (*Via Bellavia 1;* ***t*** *0881 663 972; open summer Tues–Sat 9–1 and 5–8, Sun 9–1, winter Tues–Sat 9–1 and 4–8; adm*). The single portal with an inscription on the side of the building is the last remnant of Frederick's palace. Near the museum, on Piazza Sant'Egidio, the **Chiesa della Croce** (1693–1742) is one of Puglia's more unusual churches: an elegant Baroque gate leads to a long avenue, which passes under five domed chapels that represent stages in the passion of Christ before arriving at the church itself.

Lucera

In the 1230s Emperor Frederick II was hard-pressed. Excommunicated by his devious rival Pope Gregory IX and at war with all the Guelph (*see* p.273) towns of Italy, Frederick needed some allies he could trust. At the same time, he had a problem with brigandage in some of the predominantly Muslim mountain areas of Sicily. His solution: induce 20,000 Sicilian Arabs to move to Puglia, with land grants and promises of imperial employment and favours. The almost abandoned town of Luceria, once an important Roman colony, was the spot chosen, and before anybody knew it Frederick had conjured up an entirely Muslim metropolis 290km from Rome. The emperor felt right at home in Lucera and the new city became one of his favourite residences. Later it was the last stronghold of his son, Manfred, in the dark days after Frederick's death. Charles of Anjou took the city in 1267; attempts at forced Christianization and the introduction of settlers from Provence caused revolts among the people, which the Angevins finally settled in 1300 by butchering the lot.

Little remains of Muslim Lucera, or even of the Lucera of the French; most of the Provençals could not take the summer heat, though some of their descendants still live in the hills to the south. Still, it's a well-kept and attractive town, with an elegant centre around the simple, Gothic **cathedral** of 1300, built by Charles II directly after the massacre of the Saracens – the site probably once held the town's Great Mosque.

The cathedral does its best not to look out of place (it's the only genuine Gothic church in Puglia). Inside are some good Renaissance details, including a carved *ambo* (pulpit) and a baldachin over the baptismal font, along with big showy frescoes by Corenzio (the one who fell off his scaffolding in Naples) that no one has bothered to restore. Other monuments include the church of **San Francesco**, a typical barn-like Franciscan church built from recycled Roman ruins, as well as parts of a gate and an amphitheatre from Roman Luceria on the edge of town. Smaller fragments reside at the **Museo Civico** (*open Tues–Sat 9–1 and 4–7; adm*), just behind the cathedral.

Frederick's **castle** (*follow the signs; 2km north of the centre; open Tues–Sun 9–2 and 3–6*), one of the largest ever built in Italy, was begun in 1233, the same year as the importation of the Saracens. It is still an impressive sight, with its score of towers and walls nearly a kilometre in circumference, set on a hill looking out over Lucera and the Foggia plain. Only ruins are left of Frederick's palace inside.

Troia's Cathedral

South and west of Foggia, in the foothills of the Apennines bordering the Molise and the Basilicata, you might consider a side trip to Troia, a cosy village atop a steep hill commanding the *Tavoliere* plains. Its famous cathedral is one of the oldest and most spectacular of its kind in Puglia, and serves as an excellent introduction to the various glories of the Puglian Romanesque. Troia, once the Roman town of Aecae, was refounded in 1017 and prospered from the start. Popes held two small church councils here in the 11th and 12th centuries, and the cathedral was begun in 1093, though not finished until the time of Frederick.

Much of the inspiration for the Puglian style came from Pisa; the Pisan trademark – blind arcades decorated with circle and diamond shapes – is in evidence here. The cathedral also has the most beautiful rose window in Italy, a unique, Arab-inspired fantasy from Frederick's time. Its circle is divided into 11 sections, each with carved stone latticework in a different geometric design. This eclectic building has some other surprises, beginning with a set of bronze doors, done in the 1120s by an artist named Odisarius of Benevento, and embellished with bronze dragon door handles and incised figures of saints. Along the top of the north wall, note another Islamic contribution, intricately carved geometric arabesques that would not look out of place in the Alhambra. The cathedral has quite a bestiary carved into it and it's worth taking a closer look – besides the usual assortment of lions, you'll find all sorts of other creatures, including a mermaid and a bunny. Inside, the cathedral is dark, austere and tremendous, with a narrow nave that accentuates its great height; some of its windows are the original alabaster models, which don't let in much light. Like so many other Puglian cathedrals, it is also strangely and intentionally asymmetrical, with everything on the right side just slightly out of alignment.

Around Troia

In the pretty hills just south of Troia is **Bovino**, a resolutely medieval-looking village with a 13th-century cathedral and some Roman remains, and **Ascoli Satriano**, where a well-preserved triple-arched Roman bridge still spans the River Carapelle (*call* **t** *0885 796 450 for an appointment*). You can also make a detour to see substantial remains of the abandoned Roman town of Herdonio, near **Ordona**.

The Gargano Peninsula

The Gargano Peninsula is the only really scenic stretch of Italy's Adriatic coastline. The 'spur' of the Italian boot is, in fact, a lost chip of the Balkans, left behind when two geological plates separated to form the Adriatic Sea, several million years ago. For a long time, before silt washed down by the rivers gradually joined it to the mainland,

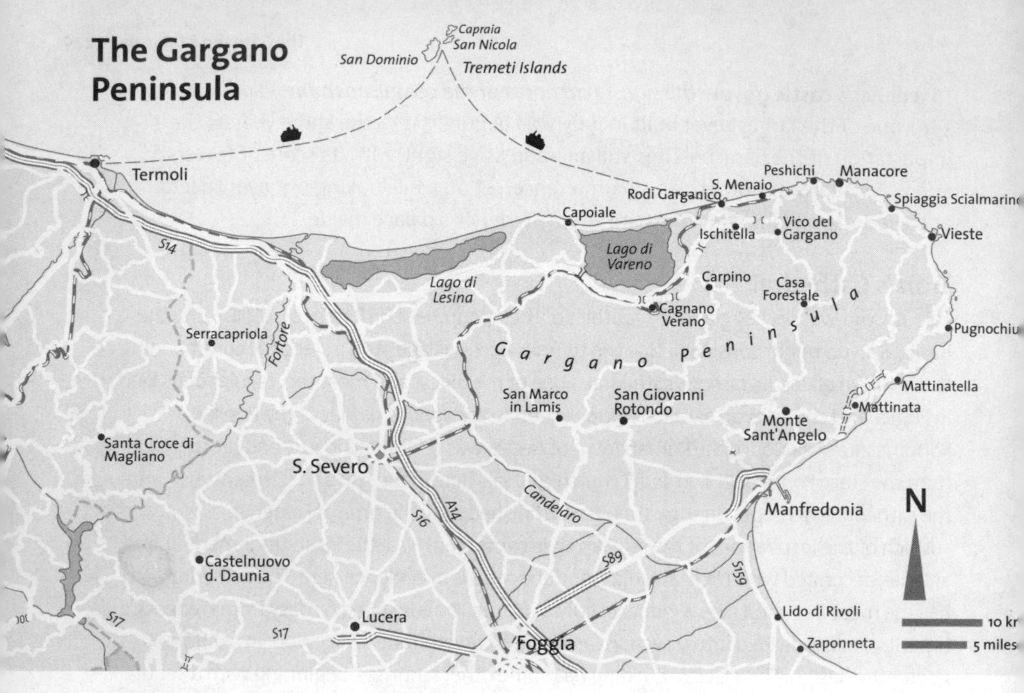

the peninsula was an island. It might as well have remained so, for the Gargano is as different from the adjacent lands in attitude as it is in its landscape.

If you are coming from the north, you will enter the Gargano by way of Lesina and the Gargano's two lakes – the **Lago di Lesina** and the **Lago di Vareno**, two large lagoons cut off from the sea by broad sand spits. From Foggia, a more logical entry point for the Gargano would be Manfredonia.

Manfredonia and Around

Manfredonia is a port town at the southern end of the peninsula with a beach and a pretty centre, once you get past its less attractive industrial outskirts. As its name implies, the town was founded by Frederick's son Manfred, and it prospered well enough until Dragut's Turkish pirates sacked and razed it in 1620. (One of the local girls ended up as the favoured wife of the sultan.) All that is left of old Manfredonia is Manfred's **castle**, rebuilt and extended by Charles of Anjou. It now contains a small **archaeological museum** (*open daily 8.30–1.30 and 3.30–7.30; closed first and last Mon of the month; adm*), where the star exhibits are the *steles* of the ancient Daunii – stones carved into warlike figures with weapons and strange military designs. Similar ones are found in Corsica, northern Tuscany and parts of southern France. The town also has a brash **cathedral**, which dates from the 17th century.

Along the Foggia road, about 2km south of the centre of Manfredonia, you can see the ruins of **Sipontum**, a Roman town that was finally abandoned to the malaria mosquitoes when Manfred moved the population to his healthier new city. The more recent town of **Siponto**, next to it, is now a popular beach resort. As evidence of how important Sipontum was in the early Middle Ages, there is the impressive 11th-century church of **Santa Maria di Siponto**, in the same style of decoration as the

Getting Around

The Gargano has a little **private railway**, called the Ferrovie del Gargano, that clatters amiably from San Severo, 30km north of Foggia, up along the western edge of the peninsula to Rodi Garganico and Peschici (about six trains a day, **t** 0882 221 415, *www.ferroviedelgargano.com* for information).

Connecting **buses** will take you from Peschici to Vieste along the coast road (SP52). Buses, run by **FG**, are less frequent between Vieste and Manfredonia and Foggia. There are several **SITA** (**t** 0881 773 425) buses a day from Manfredonia to Monte Sant'Angelo. However, getting to the Foresta Umbra and the Interior of the Gargano will be hard without a car. There is only one bus, which departs early in the morning from Monte Sant'Angelo.

There is also a regular **ferryboat** service around the peninsula from Manfredonia calling at Vieste, Peschici, Rodi Garganico and the Tremiti Islands (*mid-June–Sept*); during the rest of the year the islands are reachable only from Termoli.

Tourist Information

Manfredonia: Piazza del Popolo 11, **t** 0884 581 998. *Open Mon–Fri 8.30–1.30.*

Vieste: Corso Fazzini 28, **t** 0884 707 495. *Open Mon–Fri 8–2, Tues and Thurs also 4–7.* Also in Piazza Kennedy, **t** 0884 708 806. *Open Mon–Sat 8.30–1; also 3–9 in summer.*

Where to Stay and Eat

The Gargano has a large number of *aziende agrituristiche*. Some of these are just simple bed-and-breakfast places in the country, while others offer delicious homecooked meals at very reasonable prices.

In either case, if you have a car they make an excellent and inexpensive alternative to staying in hotels. Complete lists of *aziende* can be obtained from any tourist office. Some good hotels can also be found along the coasts around Vieste. These are usually in lovely beach spots but, again, only really convenient if you have a car.

Manfredonia ✉ 71043

Most of Manfredonia's restaurants are situated around its port, and most specialize in seafood.

★★★★**Gargano**, Viale Beccarini 2, **t** 0884 587 621, **f** 0884 586 021 (*expensive*). The best hotel in town, with a pool filled with sea water and a view from every room. Its restaurant (*expensive*) offers a range of fish preparations from soup to mixed fry. *Closed Tues and most of Nov.*

Il Baracchio, Corso Roma 38, **t** 0884 583 874 (*moderate*). You could try a meal in the cool modern surroundings of this restaurant, where the octopus salad has to be tasted to be believed. *Lunch only. Closed Thurs evening; two weeks in July.*

★**Sipontum**, Via di Vittorio 229, **t** 0884 542 916 (*cheap*). A good basic choice.

Monte Sant'Angelo ✉ 71037

Al Grottino, Corso Vittorio Emmanuele 179, **t** 0884 561 132 (*cheap*). Here you pay about €13 for a dinner worth double – roast lamb and kid, elegant *antipasti*, sweets and cheeses.

Vieste ✉ 71019

The best beach hotels here are slightly garish places – a little bit of Rimini on the Gargano. Do note though, that not all of the good restaurants in Vieste are in hotels.

★★★★**Pizzomunno**, Superiore Lungomare Enrico Mattei, **t** 0884 708 741, **f** 0884 707 325, *www.ventaglio.com* (*luxury*). Less than a kilometre south of the town centre, this gorgeous place keeps holiday-makers busy with sailing, sports, a pool, a beautiful beach and a noisy disco. *Closed Nov–April.* They also have an exceptional restaurant (*expensive*).

★**San Giorgio**, Via Madonna della Libertà 41, **t** 0884 708 618 (*expensive*). This *pensione*, in the centre of Vieste, is a good budget choice. It also has a decent restaurant, for guests only. *Full-board mandatory during Aug.*

★★★**Falcone**, Lungomare Enrico Mattei 5, **t** 0884 708 251, **f** 0884 708 252 (*moderate*). This would be the second choice in Vieste, with a private beach and resort amenities at a much better rate. *Open Mar–Sept.*

San Michele, Viale XXXIV Maggio 72, **t** 0884 708 143 (*expensive*). Many people in Vieste think this is their finest restaurant. Come here to eat fish grilled or in soups. *Closed Mon in low season; winter closure depends on business, usually Nov to Feb.*

Box 19, Via Santa Maria di Merino 13, **t** 0884 705 229 (*expensive*). You can eat seafood or grilled meats here for similar prices to those at the San Michele. *Closed Mon in low season, Nov.*

Vecchia Vieste, Via Mafrolla 32, **t** 0884 707 083 (*moderate*). A good, traditional restaurant, with friendly staff, offering seafood and specialities like *involtini alla Viestiana*. *Closed Mon; Mon–Wed from Nov–April.*

Gianpizzaiolo, Corso Madonna della Libertà 1, **t** 0884 966 363 (*cheap*). If you fancy drinking litre tankards of Nastro Azzurro with your pizza, in the cheerful and occasionally boisterous company of the local crowd, then this is the place to come.

Helvetia, Via Fontanella 2, **t** 0884 965 490 (*cheap*). This friendly *pizzeria*, with a terrace overlooking a small citrus grove, serves a wide range of snacks at lunchtime, including tasty *bruschette*.

Peschici ✉ 71010

★★★Gabbiano Beach, **t** 0884 706 376, **f** 0884 706 689 (*expensive*). Situated 7km north of Vieste on the road to Peschici, this is one of the least expensive of the good hotels along this part of the coastline. It has its own beach, a nice pool and sailing. *Closed Oct–Mar. Wheelchair accessible.*

★★Peschici, Via San Maritino 31, **t** 0884 964 195 (*cheap*). This has good views, and more facilities and services than most two-star hotels. Full-board is mandatory during August. *Closed Oct–Mar.*

Dragone, Via Duomo 8, **t** 0884 701 212 (*expensive*). Set up in a natural cave in the centre of the Old Town, this is one of Peschici's best restaurants. *Closed Tues in low season, 15 Oct–15 Mar.*

Al Castello, Piazza Castello 29, **t** 0884 964 038 (*cheap*). This hotel restaurant serves reasonable seafood and meat dishes, with tables outdoors in the pedestrian zone of the Old Quarter.

Rodi Garganico ✉ 71012

★★★Albano, Via Scalo Marittimo 33, **t** 0884 965 138, **f** 0884 965 421 (*expensive*). Another reasonably priced option below the historic centre of Rodi Garganico, with a decent if unexciting restaurant. *Wheelchair accessible.*

★Roccamare, Via Varano, **t** 0884 965 461 (*cheap*). This cheap and friendly hotel, perched on a cliff face below the centre of Rodi, is quite a special place to stay. Ask for one of the four smaller rooms that share a huge whitewashed terrace with expansive sea views.

Regina, Corso Madonna della Libera 46, **t** 0884 965 463 (*cheap*). The set menu (€15) offered by this restaurant and *birreria* is Rodi Garganico's best bargain. There's plenty to choose from, including 'Regina' *penne* with mushrooms, tomatoes, mozzarella and *pancetta*, followed by steaming mounds of fragrant *cozze* (mussels).

Tremiti Islands ✉ 71100

There isn't a lot of choice among the islands' hotels. For food, if you want to prepare a picnic for a day on the rocks, the English-speaking grocer beside the chemist (near the main square) will happily wrap up delicious slices of steaming potato pizza.

★Gabbiano, Piazza Belvedere, San Domino, **t** 0882 463 410, **f** 0882 463 428 (*very expensive*). This is a well-situated alternative where it's essential to book.

★★Al Faro, Via Cantina Sperimentale, **t** 0882 463 424 (*cheap*). If you want to stay over, it's worth booking in advance at this eight-room *pensione* near the central square on San Domino. The rooms are rather cramped but its restaurant is excellent value for money. Half board is obligatory, but that is no hardship; the restaurant offers good home cooking influenced by the food traditions of the San Nicola monastery, all washed down with some delicious quality wines. You even get to choose your own fish direct from the fridge. *Closed Oct–Easter.*

cathedral at Troia but built on a square, Byzantine-Greek plan. It is built over a much earlier underground Christian building, from around the 5th century. An even better 11th-century church survives 9km further along the road to Foggia: **San Leonardo**, with finely sculpted portals and a small dome.

Monte Sant'Angelo

(*see* **Topics**: 'The Lady and the Dragon', p.23)

Tourists who come to the Gargano for the beaches probably never notice, but this peninsula is holy ground, as it has probably been since the time of the ancient Daunii. Sanctuaries, ancient and modern, are scattered everywhere. There are many stories of apparitions of saints and angels, and only 25 years ago, a holy man who lived at San Giovanni Rotondo received the stigmata.

The centre of all this, for the last 1,000 years at least, has been Monte Sant'Angelo, one of the most important pilgrimage towns in Italy (and thus well served by public transport from Manfredonia). Before Christianity, the cavern now dedicated to Saint Michael was the site of a dream oracle; a 5th-century bishop of Sipontum had a vision of the archangel, who left his red cloak as a token and commanded that the sanctuary be converted to Christian worship. Soon Monte Sant'Angelo was attracting pilgrims from all over Europe. Among the pilgrims were the first Normans, in the 9th century. They returned home with tales of a rich and fascinatingly civilized Puglia – a place they suspected just might be a pushover for mounted, heavily armoured knights. The first Norman adventurers were not slow in taking up the challenge. All the other sites dedicated to St Michael around the coasts of Europe – including, of course, Mont St Michel in Normandy – are the spiritual descendants of this one, founded as the cult of St Michael spread across Christendom in the Middle Ages.

That Monte Sant'Angelo is a special place becomes evident even before you arrive. The trip up from Manfredonia passes through an uncanny landscape: chalky cliffs dotted with caves, ancient agricultural terraces and a strange clarity in the light and air. The road climbs so quickly that you seem to be looking straight down into Manfredonia, even though it is 14km away.

The *Junno*

After much twisting and grinding of gears, you arrive at the quiet, whitewashed city, a maze of steps and tunnels. The medieval centre of town, known as the *Junno*, is one of the most beautiful old quarters in southern Italy, a nonchalant harmony of colour and form that only a few coastal towns in Puglia can achieve.

Inside the *Junno*, next to the half-ruined church of **San Pietro**, is a 12th-century work called the **tomb of Rotari** (*open April–Sept 8.30–12.15 and 2.30–7.30, Oct–Mar 8.30–12.15 and 2.30–4.30; adm*). The idea that this was the tomb of 'Rotarus', a Lombard chief, stems from a misreading of one of the inscriptions. It is now believed this was originally intended to be a baptistry – a very large and unusual baptistry. If so, it is hard to make out the original intention, since much of it has been swallowed up by the surrounding buildings. Some of the sculpted detail is extremely odd indeed; note the figures of a woman suckling a serpent – or dragon.

More intimate scenes of ladies and dragons await next door, in an incredible relief over the entrance to **Santa Maria Maggiore**, completed in 1198. Inside this lovely church are two odd domes, very like the *trulli* of Alberobello (*see* p.246), plus a dignified fresco of St Michael in Byzantine court dress and tantalizing fragments of other Byzantine paintings from the 13th–14th centuries. The town also has a small museum of the folk arts and culture of the Gargano, the **Museo Tancredi** (*open daily summer 9–1 and 5–7, winter 9–1 and 3–5; adm*). At the top of the town, there is a ruined Norman **castle**, rebuilt by the Aragonese kings but left alone since.

The Santuario di San Michele

Open July–Sept daily 7.30–12.30 and 2.30–5.

Behind an eight-sided tower built by Charles of Anjou, which reproduces the proportions (on one level) and much of the decoration of Frederick's Castel del Monte (*see* p.237), is the Santuario di San Michele. The exterior of the sanctuary seems to be a normal church with a Gothic porch and portals (mostly built in the 19th century; see if you can guess which of the two identical portals is the original 12th-century work). Above the doors is a Latin inscription meaning: 'Terrible is this place; this is the house of God and the Gate of Heaven'. Inside, instead of the expected church, there is a long series of steps leading down to a cavern, passing a beautiful pair of bronze doors made in Constantinople in 1076, perhaps by the same artists who did the ones at Amalfi's cathedral (*see* p.153). Most of the scenes are difficult to make out in the darkness, but Jacob's ladder and the expulsion from Eden stand out clearly. Down in the cave it is chilly and dark; in the old days, pilgrims would come down on their knees, shuffling through the puddles to kiss the image of the archangel. The grotto is laid out like a small chapel. There are plenty of bits of medieval sculptural work around, but the best is a wonderful crazy-medieval bishop's chair from the 12th century.

The town records give us an almost endless list of celebrity pilgrims: a dozen popes, King Ferdinand of Spain, four Holy Roman emperors, Saints Bernard, Thomas Aquinas, Catherine of Siena, and so on – even St Francis, and they can show you the mark he made on the cavern wall.

Behind the altar, you can see the little well that made this a holy site in the first place. Long before there was a St Michael, indigenous religions of Europe had a great interest in springs and underground streams – some scholars believe the idea of dragons began with a primeval fascination with buried streams and accompanying lines of telluric forces beneath the earth's surface; the sleepless 'eye' of the dragon is the fountain, where these forces come to the surface. In the icons of Monte Sant'Angelo, as well as in the endless souvenir figurines hawked outside the sanctuary, Michael is shown dispatching Lucifer in the form of a dragon.

The Gargano's Interior

From the back of Monte Sant'Angelo, a narrow road leads into the heart of the Gargano. The road forks: head right for the **Foresta Umbra** ('Forest of Shadows') – a thick, primeval forest of beeches, oaks and pines similar to those that covered most of Puglia in the

Middle Ages. A visitors' centre run by the Corpo Forestale, past the turning for Vico del Gargano on the SS528, will help you learn more about it. The forest can also be reached from Vieste (*see* below).

Alternatively, take the left fork for **San Giovanni Rotondo**, a little town on the slopes of Monte Calvo. The strange round temple that gives the town its name was believed, like the tomb of Rotari (*see* p.229), to have been a baptistry. Next door is a 16th-century monastery that for more than 50 years was home to Padre Pio de Pietralcina. This simple priest not only received the stigmata – the bleeding wounds of Christ – on his hands, feet and side, but was also said to have the ability to appear before cardinals in Rome while his body was sleeping back in the Gargano. After a long period of suspicion, the Church finally canonized Padre Pio in 2002.

Padre Pio's presence made the town a popular pilgrimage destination, and before he died in 1968, he was able to attract enough donations to build a large modern hospital, the first in the Gargano. If you've been around the south much, you're bound to know what he looked like by now – only the Virgin Mary herself gets her picture in more bars, petrol stations and hotels. You can visit the **sanctuary of Santa Maria della Grazia** and Padre Pio's cell as well as the new pilgrims' church, the **Chiesa di San Pio**. Even before the canonization, Padre Pio's grave was attracting so many pilgrims that a new building was needed. Completed by the renowned architect Renzo Piano in 2004, this one is drawing some architectural pilgrims too. It's an impressive space, an immense dome supported by soaring, slender stone arches, and filled with light by a transparent façade. There is room for over 7,000 pilgrims, and 30,000 more on the new piazza outside. Some critics find the church austere; Piano himself said that the greatest challenge in the design was creating such a huge space without monumentality – something the modest Padre Pio would never have approved.

West of San Giovanni – and another old stop on the pilgrimage route to Monte Sant'Angelo – the town of **San Marco in Lamis** is another monastic centre. The present, huge Franciscan house dates from the 16th century.

Vieste and the Coast

Enough of the holy Gargano. Once past Monte Sacro on the coast north of Monte Sant'Angelo, you are in the holiday Gargano – an exceptionally lovely coastline of limestone cliffs, clean blue sea and good beaches decorated with old watchtowers, or stumps and columns of rock and other curious formations. **Vieste**, at the tip of the peninsula, is in the middle of it, a lively and beautiful white town on white cliffs surrounded by beaches. Within the last 10 years, Vieste has become the major resort of the southern Adriatic, and boutiques and restaurants crowd the town centre.

On Via Duomo near the old town centre is the Chianca Amara or 'bitter stone', where it is believed 5,000 of the town's people were beheaded by the Turks when they sacked Vieste in 1554. Nearby are the 11th-century cathedral, with 18th-century additions and, beyond that, another castle built by Frederick II, with fine views over the town and the Grotta Sfondata ('bottomless lagoon'), one of a few marine grottos and lagoons accessible by boat tour from Vieste. There is also a peculiar early Christian *hypogeum* (burial cave) on the coast, at the site of a long-disappeared town called Merinum.

The best parts of the coast are to the south of Vieste: beautiful coves like **Cala San Felice**, with a little beach and a natural arch in the cliffs, and **Cala Sanguinaria**. A bit further south at **Acqua della Rosa**, when conditions are just right, the reflection from the limestone cliffs gives the water near the shore a rosy tint.

Most of the tourist sprawl, with kilometres of beaches and campsites, extends to the north of Vieste. Near the road inland for Monte Sant'Angelo, **Mattinata** is one of the more eccentric examples of Puglian vernacular architecture, a gleaming white village of rectangular houses stacked in tidy rows like sugar cubes.

On the Gargano's northern coast, **Peschici** and **Rodi Garganico** are two other pretty fishing villages that are now fast-developing resorts and particularly crowded in August. The Old Quarter of Peschici, on a hilltop above the sandy bay, is a maze of narrow streets and Arabesque whitewashed houses, many of which have now been converted into boutiques for tourists. Rodi is a more down-to-earth place, Greek in origin and now the capital of the Gargano's citrus production. The wide sandy beach that stretches away to the west of Rodi remains relatively uncrowded and makes a good spot for a swim or a stroll.

The Tremiti Islands

In winter this minuscule archipelago, 40km from the coast, has a population of about 50. August, however, finds it crawling with the 100,000 holiday-makers who annually spill over from the resorts of the Gargano. The striking beauty of this tiny archipelago is its main attraction – the bluest waters in the Adriatic and pale calcareous cliffs much like the Gargano mainland (there's only one beach). If you can avoid coming in July or August, the Tremitis can be a perfect spot to let your watch run down.

San Domino and San Nicola are the two main islands. The other two islands are uninhabited. **Pianosa** is low and flat and used by fishermen and Balkan smugglers on overnight trips; **Capraia** is an island of rabbits with an enormous natural arch and a lovely cave known as the **Grottone**, almost 100ft high at its mouth.

The islands enter the history books first as a place of exile – Augustus' daughter and Charlemagne's troublesome Italian father-in-law were both confined here – or as a monkish retreat. Later the Tremitis were ruled by abbots; in 1010, Benedictines from Montecassino founded an abbey on San Nicola. They became wealthy with treasures deposited by mainlanders fearful of the Normans, until in 1236, the Inquisition dissolved the abbey and grabbed the booty. The Cistercians who followed lasted until the 1350s, when pirates tricked them into believing their captain was dead and desired a Christian burial. The Cistercians complied, but during the night, the captain rose from the grave and let his men in at the gate to massacre the monks. In 1412 yet another order, the Lateranesi, was sent by Pope Gregory XII to restore the monastery. The Bourbons of Naples claimed the islands in 1737, ending monastic rule and creating yet another island penal colony.

San Domino

San Domino, largest and most luxuriant of the Tremitis, was indefensible and thus uninhabited for most of its history. Its marvellous coastline of cliffs and jutting rocks, penetrated by grottoes, is easy to explore in a day either by boat or on foot. Tourist facilities are concentrated around the beach, **Cala delle Arene**. From here, you can walk to the **Capella del Romito** at the island's highest point – all of 380ft.

Along the coast are the violet-coloured **Grotta delle Viole**, the **Grotta delle Murene**, where sea eels breed, and the Punta del Diavolo. The most spectacular feature of the island – the 246ft crag known as the **Ripa dei Falconi**, where falcons were bred in the days of chivalry, and the **Grotta del Bue Marino** beneath it – may seem familiar if you've seen *The Guns of Navarone*. Over 150ft long, the cave is the largest on San Domino; if you go by boat, take a torch to see the rock formations.

San Nicola

Nearby San Nicola is dominated by its fortress-monastery. Boats call under its main gate where an inscription reads *Conteret et Confringet* ('Crush and Kill') – referring to the rights granted to the abbot by Pope Paul III to torture and kill heretics. Principal sights within the walls include the ancient church of **Santa Maria a Mare** (1045), with mosaic fragments and a large, celebrated icon of Christ as well as its old cloister; a fine cistern; and the grand **Dormitorio Nuovo**, built by the Lateranesi.

Le Murge

South of the *Tavoliere* plain, Le Murge is a long region of rolling hills and farmland that stretches down to Brindisi. The region contains a number of cathedral towns and old ports and, south of Bari, the enchanting *trulli* country. Further west, towards the Basilicata, the terrain rises to bare, sparsely inhabited hills.

The Gargano to Bari: The Coast

The coastal road passes through a string of attractive medieval port towns, each with its contribution to Puglian Romanesque in the shape of grand old cathedrals. Each, that is, except **Margherita di Savoia**, the first town south of the Gargano, a funky urban smudge surrounded by salt pans and one of the main centres for salt production in Italy since Roman times. No one seems to remember what the old name was, but they changed it a century ago to honour the formidable wife of King Umberto I. Today it is the best place to inspect a modern Puglian architectural fancy – houses entirely covered in colourful, patterned bathroom tiles.

Barletta

Barletta, the next town south, is also one of the largest. Though quite a prosperous place these days, Barletta has sadly neglected its historical centre. If you pass it by, however, you will miss a unique and astounding sight. On Corso Vittorio Emmanuele, beside the church of San Sepolcro, stands the largest surviving ancient bronze statue, locally known as the **Colosso**. To come upon this 20ft figure in the middle of a busy city street, wearing an imperial scowl and a pose of conquest, with a cross and a sphere in his hands, is like lapsing into a dream. Scholars have debated for centuries who it

Getting Around

Two different **railways** serve this area. All the coastal towns from Barletta to Monopoli are on the main FS east-coast route, while from Barletta there is an FS branch line to the south with infrequent services to Spinazzola and Altamura. And one of the three private lines that operate from Bari, the Ferrovia Bari-Nord, runs a frequent service through inland towns such as Andria, Ruvo and Bitonto.

There are reasonably regular **buses** on the coast road and inland from Barletta or Bari. The hardest place to reach without a car is Castel del Monte; call the guides at the castle or the tourist office in Andria (**t** 0883 592 283) for the times of the scarce bus service.

The straight Roman **roads** of Puglia's flat plain are faster than the mountain roads elsewhere in the south. The main road is the A14 *autostrada*. Near Canosa di Puglia, this is joined by the A16 *autostrada* from Naples and the west coast. Two other roads – the SS16 along the coast and the SS98 through Andria and the inland towns – run roughly parallel with the A14 into Bari. If you are driving to Castel del Monte from Bari, turn off the SS98 onto the SS170 just west of Ruvo di Puglia. For Altamura and the Murge, take the SS96 south from Bari.

Tourist Information

Barletta: Corso Garibaldi 208, **t** 0883 531 555. *Open Mon–Fri 8–2, Tues and Thurs also 4–7.*

Trani: Piazza Trieste 10, **t** 0883 585 530. *Open Mon–Sat 8.30–1.30, Tues and Thurs also 3–6.*

Where to Stay and Eat

Barletta ✉ 70051

Barletta can be a discouraging place to spend a night, but if you insist, try these:

Antica Cucina, on Via Milano near the station, **t** 0883 521 718 (*expensive*). Has light, tasty fish dishes and good desserts. *Closed Sun eve and Mon, July.*

********Artù****, Piazza Castello 67, **t** 0883 332 121 **f** 0883 332 214 (*moderate*). Situated between the castle and the cathedral, this will do.

Trani ✉ 70059

There are several cute restaurants around the harbour, if a little touristy and overpriced.

******Royal**, Via De Robertis 29, **t** 0883 588 777 **f** 0883 582 224 (*expensive*). Quiet rooms, all renovated in the original Liberty décor. *Wheelchair accessible.*

Padri Bernabiti, on Piazza Tiepolo, **t** 0883 481 180 (*expensive*). Offers basic, clean rooms with great views. Book ahead. *Reception closed 1–5; curfew 1am.*

Torrente Antico, Via Fusco 3, **t** 0883 487 911 (*expensive*). Uses local produce, both fish and meat, in interesting ways and has a fine list of the best Puglian wines. *Closed Sun eves, Mon, last two weeks in July.*

La Nicchia, Corso Imbriani 22, **t** 0883 482 020 (*moderate*). The best-value place for fish and shellfish. *Closed Thurs and Sun eve.*

Molfetta ✉ 70056

*****Garden**, Via Provinciale per Terlizzi, **t** 080 334 1722, **f** 080 334 9291 (*moderate*). Good-value modern hotel with own tennis courts.

Bufi, Via Vittorio Emmanuele 15, **t** 080 397 1597 (*moderate*). Has a spectacular wine cellar, and presents old, and in many cases, almost forgotten, recipes in innovative ways. *Closed Sun evening, Mon, last two weeks in Jan, one week in Aug.*

Bistrot, Via Dante 33, **t** 080 397 5812 (*moderate*). This is another adventurous but cheaper restaurant, especially for fish. *Closed Wed, Sun eves, and middle two weeks of Aug.*

Andria ✉ 70031

La Fenice, Via Firenze 35, **t** 0883 550 260 (*expensive*). Excellent, though overpriced, 'The Phoenix' has a choice of three tempting *menu degustazione*, based on fish, meat and traditional dishes. *Closed Mon, Sun eve, Aug.*

Gravina in Puglia ✉ 70024

Madonna della Stella, Via Madonna della Stella, **t** 080 325 6383 (*moderate*). Local fare at this panoramic restaurant. *Closed Tues and Feb.*

Osteria, Piazza Pellicciari 4, **t** 080 326 1872 (*cheap*). Serves a Puglian/Emilian mix of specialities such as *cavatelli ai legumi* and pumpkin or walnut ravioli. *Closed Sun eve, Mon and last two weeks of Aug.*

might be. It's obviously a late Roman emperor and the guesses have included Valentinian, Heraclius and Marcian. The last is most probable, and especially intriguing, since the triumphal column of Marcian (a useless emperor with no real successes to commemorate) still stands in Istanbul, and the statue of the emperor that once stood on top of it was probably carried away by the Venetians after the sack of Constantinople in 1204. A ship of booty from the sack foundered off Barletta's coast and the Colosso washed up on a nearby beach. The superstitious citizens let it stay there for decades before they got up the nerve to bring it to the city. The figure is surpassingly strange, a monument to the onset of the Dark Ages; the costume the emperor wears is only a pale memory of the dress of Marcus Aurelius or Hadrian, with a pair of barbaric-looking leather boots instead of imperial buskins.

San Sepolcro, finished in the 13th century, is interesting in its own right. Above the plain French Gothic vaulting there is an octagonal dome, recalling the Holy Sepulchre in Jerusalem. Corso Garibaldi leads from here to the heart of old Barletta and the 12th-century **cathedral**. Look on the left-hand wall, between the façade and the campanile, and you will see a cornice supported by 13 strange figures. If you are clever and have a good eye, you may make out the letters on them that make an acrostic of *Richardus Rex I* – Richard the Lionheart, who contributed to the embellishment of the cathedral on his way to the Crusades.

The nearby 13th-century church of **Sant'Andrea** has another fine façade, the main portal of which (from 1240) was the work of Dalmatian sculptor Simon di Ragusa. The Third Crusade was launched from Barletta's often-rebuilt **Castello** (***t*** *0883 578 613; open Tues–Sun 9–1 and 3–7; adm*), in a great council of Frederick and his knights. The polygonal bastions you see were added in the 1530s. Apart from a collection of antiques, coins and armour, the castle also houses the **Pinacoteca Giuseppe de Nittis**, which has in its collection the only surviving statue of Frederick II – a little the worse for wear, poor fellow – as well as a large collection of works by the local Impressionist-influenced painter Giuseppe de Nittis (1846–84). The admission ticket to the castle will also get you into the **Cantina della Disfida** in Via Cialdini, where in 1503, after much drinking, 13 'Italian' knights challenged 13 French knights to a duel for control of the besieged town. The Italians won and Barletta's siege was lifted. The event is re-enacted in one of Puglia's largest pageants on the second weekend in September.

Site of the Battle of Cannae

On the banks of the River Ofanto, between Barletta and Canosa di Puglia (on the SS93), you can visit the site of the Battle of Cannae. Here, in 216 BC, Hannibal trapped and annihilated four Roman legions in one of the most famous battles of Italian history. Military strategists still study the Carthaginians' brilliant ambush, the last serious defeat Rome was to suffer for centuries.

At the time, Hannibal and his elephants had already been in Italy for two years. Cannae was the opportunity he was waiting for and historians are puzzled why he didn't immediately follow it up with a march on Rome – probably it was due to a lack of siege equipment. The chance was missed. Hannibal spent another eight years campaigning fruitlessly in Italy, while the Romans locked themselves up in their towns and sent their armies off to conquer Spain and North Africa. Cannae taught the Romans to be careful and it could be said Hannibal's victory meant the defeat not of Rome, but of Carthage. A small museum contains archaeological finds.

Trani

Trani is a faded old port that still has a large and prosperous fishing fleet. It was an important merchant town in the early Middle Ages – it once fought a war with Venice and its merchant captains created perhaps the first code of laws of the sea since ancient times. The town's famous **cathedral** (*open Mon–Sat 8–12.30 and 4–8; use side entrance*) stands in an open piazza on the edge of the sea. It's another excellent work of the Puglian Romanesque and a monument to the age of the Crusades. At the centre of the façade is another pair of 12th-century bronze doors, much like the ones in many other cities of the south. These are special, though, since the artist who did them and several others in the town is a native, Barisano of Trani.

This cathedral is in fact three buildings stacked on the same site; the lower church, called **Santa Maria della Scala**, is really the earlier, Byzantine cathedral. Below that is the **Crypt of San Leucio**, an unusual early Christian church or catacomb with solid marble columns and bits of medieval frescoes.

A short walk west of the cathedral along the seafront stands the newly restored **Castello Svevo** (***t*** *0883 506 603; open daily 8–7.30; adm*), another of Frederick II's symmetrical fortresses. Guides offer uninspiring tours of the parts of the castle that are open to the public. The castle also houses regular exhibitions of local art.

Other notable buildings in Trani include the **Ognissanti** (*usually closed*), a typical church of the 12th-century Knights Templar; the **Palazzo Cacetta**, a rare example of late Gothic architecture in southern Italy from the 1450s; and two small churches that were once synagogues, **Santa Maria Scuolanove** and **Sant'Anna**, converted after the Spaniards expelled Trani's long-established Jewish community in the 16th century.

Trani to Bari

Bisceglie has another good Romanesque cathedral. Further south is **Molfetta**, a city known for drugs and gangsters. Molfetta has a cathedral like Trani's on the harbour's edge, the Duomo Vecchio. Its plan, subtly asymmetrical like that of Troia, has a wide nave covered by three domes, the central one elliptical. The west front is almost blank, while the back side has elaborate carved decoration and a door leading to the apse.

Molfetta also has another cathedral, the Baroque Duomo Nuovo, from 1785.

Canosa to Bari: Inland

Canosa di Puglia

Canosa isn't much today but, in Roman times, it was one of the most important towns in the region. The reminders of its former status include three large tombs on the edge of town, excavated in 1843, and a collection of archaeological relics in the **Museo Civico** (***t*** *0883 616 867; open Mar–Oct Tues–Sat 9–1 and 4–6, Nov–Feb and hols 8–2*).

The town's undistinguished five-domed **cathedral** has in its courtyard the tomb of Bohemund – a striking marble chapel with a small cupola (octagonal, of course) that holds the remains of the doughty Crusader. Bohemund, who died in 1111, was the son of Robert Guiscard. Renowned for valour and chivalry, he seized the main chance when the First Crusade was being preached, and ended up Prince of Antioch. The most remarkable feature of his tomb is the pair of bronze doors, signed by an artist named Roger of Melfi. The one on the left, inscribed with geometrical arabesques, is a single slab of bronze. Inside the cathedral, notice the early medieval bishop's chair, resting on two weary-looking stone elephants. If the cathedral is closed, you can at least see the tomb from the adjacent town park. On the outskirts of Canosa, there are the remains of a 6th-century church, the **Basilica San Leucio**, and a small museum.

Andria

This large, thriving market centre is another city associated with Frederick and has an inscription from the emperor on its St Andrea's Gate, honouring it for its loyalty. Two of Frederick's wives, Yolande of Jerusalem and Isabella of England, daughter of King John, are buried in the crypt of Andria's **cathedral**. Other churches worth a look include the 13th-century **Sant'Agostino**, built by the Teutonic Order, of all people, and the 16th-century **Santa Maria dei Miracoli**, restored in the Baroque.

Castel del Monte

t 0883 569 848; open daily Mar–Sept 10–7.30, Oct–Feb 10–6.30; adm.

In Enna, the 'navel of Sicily', Emperor Frederick built a mysterious, octagonal tower at the highest point of the town. In Puglia, this most esoteric of emperors erected an equally puzzling palace. It, too, is a perfect octagon – if you have been travelling through the region, you may have noticed that nearly every town has at least one eight-sided tower, bastion or campanile, and that Frederick was usually behind them. Castel di Santa Maria del Monte, to give it its original title, was begun by Frederick in the 1240s on a high hill overlooking the plain, south of the town of Andria.

At each of the eight corners of Castel del Monte is a slender octagonal tower. The 80ft tall building has only two storeys; each has eight rooms, almost all interconnected and each facing the octagonal courtyard. The historians sometimes try to explain the castle as one of Frederick's hunting lodges. This won't do; the rooms each have only one relatively small window, and in spite of the wealth of sculpted stone the castle once had, it would have seemed more like a prison than a forest retreat – in fact the emperor's grandsons, the heirs of his son Manfred, were later imprisoned here for 30 years. Neither is it a fortification; there are no ramparts, no slits for archers, and not even a defensible gate. Some writers have suggested that Frederick had an artistic monument in mind. The entrance to the castle, the so-called 'triumphal arch', is a unique work for the 13th century: an elegant classical portal that prefigures the Renaissance. Inside, every room was decorated with columns, friezes and reliefs in Greek marble, porphyry and other precious stones. Almost all of these have disappeared, vandalized by the Angevins and the noblemen who owned the castle over the last five centuries. The delicately carved

Gothic double windows survive, one to each room, along with a few other bits of the original decoration: grotesques at the points of the vaulting in some rooms, elegant conical fireplaces, capitals (some Corinthian, some in the Egyptian order) and, in two of the corner towers, corbels under the arches carved into peculiar faces and figures.

At Castel del Monte, the things you can't see are the most interesting. This is nothing less than the Great Pyramid of Italy and the secrets Frederick built into it have for centuries attracted the attention of cranks and serious scholars alike. The guides here are full of opinions. One suggests that the castle was built for meetings of a secret society – and considering the atmosphere of eclectic mysticism that surrounded the emperor and his court, this seems entirely possible. Whole books have been written about the measurements and proportions of the castle, finding endless repetitions of the Golden Section, its square and cubic roots, relations to the movements of the planets and the stars, the angles and proportions of the Pythagorean five-pointed star, and so on.

Idiosyncrasies in the design are as interesting. For all its octagonal rigour, the castle is full of teasing quirks. Looking from the courtyard along the eight walls, there are two large windows, two doors and two balconies, studiously arranged to avoid any pattern or symmetry. Some of the windows seem centrally placed from one side, but several feet off-centre from the other: intentional, but impossible to explain.

The relation of the castle to the ancient surveying of the Puglian plain is a fascinating possibility. Frederick's tower in Sicily has been found to be the centre of an enormous rectilinear network of alignments uniting scores of ancient temples, towers and cities in straight lines that run the length and breadth of the island. The tower is believed to be built on the site of some forgotten holy place; the alignments and the vast geometrical temple they form probably predate even the Greeks. No one has yet suggested that Castel del Monte replaced any ancient site, but the particular care of Puglia's ancient surveyors, and the arrangement of the region's holy places, sanctuaries and Frederick's castles, suggest that something similarly strange may be hidden here. The wildest theory so far claims that the castle marks the intersection of the two greatest alignments of them all: lying exactly halfway between the Great Pyramid and Stonehenge, and halfway between Jerusalem and Mont Saint Michel.

Ruvo di Puglia

In this corner of Bari province, there are altogether eight noteworthy cathedrals on a narrow strip of land only some 64km long. They are the only real monuments – nothing has been built ambitiously and well around here since the 14th century – and they stand as the best evidence of Puglia's greatest period of culture and prosperity. One of the best cathedrals in Puglia is at Ruvo di Puglia, an ancient settlement that was famous in classical times for pottery – reproducing Greek urns at a lower price, above all between the 5th and the 3rd centuries BC when the trade was at its height. A large collection can be seen at the **Museo Jatta** (*Piazza Bovio, **t** 0808 12848; open daily 8.30–1.30, Fri–Sat also 2.30–7.30*).

The cathedral is a tall, almost Gothic work, with a richly decorated façade that incorporates a fine rose window. The little arches along the sides of the building are decorated with figures of pagan gods, copied from pieces of ancient Ruvo's pottery.

Bitonto

Bitonto is the market town for the vast olive groves of Le Murge – it calls itself the 'City of Olives' and there seem to be barrels of them just about everywhere. To find the cathedral, wind your way through the labyrinthine centre where cars cannot fit. Fortunately, the town has put up maps at the entrances to help you find your way around.

Bitonto's **cathedral** is considered by many to be the classic of Puglian Romanesque. Here the best features of the exterior are the side galleries and carvings of fantastical animals and scriptural scenes over the three front portals (note the Three Kings on the lintel of the main portal, amidst mermaids, cockatrices and elephants) and on the apse, with cartoon-like lions and griffins. Inside, there is a famous pulpit of 1226 displaying a fierce-looking eagle; on one side, a curious, primitive relief shows Emperor Frederick, Isabella of England and their family.

Another church worth seeking out in Bitonto is the 1670 **Purgatorio**, a bit of pious Baroque perversity of the sort common in southern towns. Here the façade shows a skeleton with a sundial halo, plenty of tortured souls, and crowned and mitred skulls.

Altamura

Le Murge's western borders are a slightly elevated jumble of plain and rolling hills. It isn't the prettiest part of Puglia – in some parts, the deforested hills have severe erosion problems, making for landscapes as empty and eerie as anything in the Basilicata. Here the most important town, Altamura, can seem like an oasis in midsummer.

Altamura was founded by Frederick on the site of an abandoned ancient city. For centuries, it was a town of some distinction, even having its own university. This advanced outlook led Altamura to support the French and the short-lived Parthenopean Republic during the Napoleonic Wars. As a result, a mob led by a cardinal and egged on by monks (called the Army of the Holy Faith) sacked and burned the city in 1799.

The university never recovered but Altamura still has a beautiful **cathedral**, begun by Frederick in 1232. Heavy damage from an earthquake in 1316 accounts for the departures from the Puglian norm; the building retains its exceptional rose window and portal but the twin towers above were added during the Renaissance. For some reason, in the course of doing so, they turned the cathedral backwards – the old portal and rose window were carefully taken apart and placed where the apse used to be. On the façade, note the wonderful portal of the Last Supper, along with the other excellent, well-preserved details: the relief of the Three Kings on the right, a delicate rose window, and a later addition, the arms of Charles V, above it.

The recently reopened **Museo Archeologico** (*Via Santeramo 88; open daily 8.30–1.30 and 2.30–7.30*), houses one of Italy's most interesting collections, with first-rate finds related to the people of the Murge from prehistoric times to the Middle Ages. Nearby, the little church of **San Nicola** has an unusual portal of 1576 with abstract, almost primitive scenes of Noah, the life of Christ, and Adam and Eve. Across from the church stands a giant, fading outdoor fresco of St Christopher. (This saint was always painted large because in popular legends, St Christopher was a giant, and also so that you wouldn't miss him – it was good luck to see this saint before going on a trip.)

Gravina in Puglia

Gravina in Puglia, on the road towards Potenza, has yet another **cathedral**, but it is only a dull 15th-century replacement for the Norman original. Gravina does have other charms, though. The town is set above a steep ravine lined with caves, where the inhabitants took refuge from pirates and barbarians during the Dark Ages.

One of the town's churches, **San Michele dei Grotti**, is a cave, too (*contact the Cooperative Benedetto XIII*, **t** *0338 567 8017, inside the cathedral, for free tours in English of San Michele and other cave-churches; donations appreciated*), with a heap of human bones believed to be those of victims of Arab pirates during the 8th century.

Other churches show somewhat eccentric versions of Renaissance styles, notably the **Madonna delle Grazie** near the railway station. On Piazza Santomasi there is a **museum** (*open Mon–Sat 9–1 and 4–7, Sun 9.30–1.30*), containing a full-size reconstruction of another ancient cave-church,with fragments of Byzantine frescoes, as well as a more conventional collection of musty archaeological discoveries.

Bari

Somehow Bari should be a more interesting place. The second city of the peninsula Mezzogiorno is a bustling town full of sailors and fishermen, and can also boast a university and a long heritage of cultural distinction. Yet Bari will be a disappointment if you come here expecting Mediterranean charm and medieval romance. If, on the other hand, you'd like to see a southern city that has come close to catching up with the rest of Italy economically, Bari will be just the place. It has oil refineries, a busy port and a new suburban business centre of glass skyscrapers called the Baricentro. The newer districts, with their smart shops and numb boulevards jammed with noisy traffic, exhibit a thoroughly northern glitter, and the good burghers who stroll down the Corso Cavour for their evening *passeggiata* are among the most overdressed in Italy. Bari has also become one of the Italian cities most often visited by international rock music tours.

Be warned, though – and you probably will be – that the city has one of the highest street-crime rates in the country, so take care and try to avoid carrying with you anything of particular value, including cameras, above all in the Old Town and at night.

History: The Town That Stole Santa Claus

Bari can trace its history back to before the Romans, but it only began to make a name for itself in the 10th century. As an important trading city and seat of the nominally independent Byzantine governor, Bari was sometimes a rival of Venice, though more often its ally. Robert Guiscard and his Normans, who took the city in 1071, favoured Bari and helped it become the leading town of Puglia. In 1087, a fleet of Barese merchantmen in Antioch got word that some of their Venetian counterparts were planning a little raid on Myra, on what is now the southern coast of Turkey. Their intention was to pinch the mortal remains of St Nicholas, Myra's 4th-century bishop, canonized for his generosity and good deeds. Relic-stealing was a cultural imperative for medieval Italians, and the

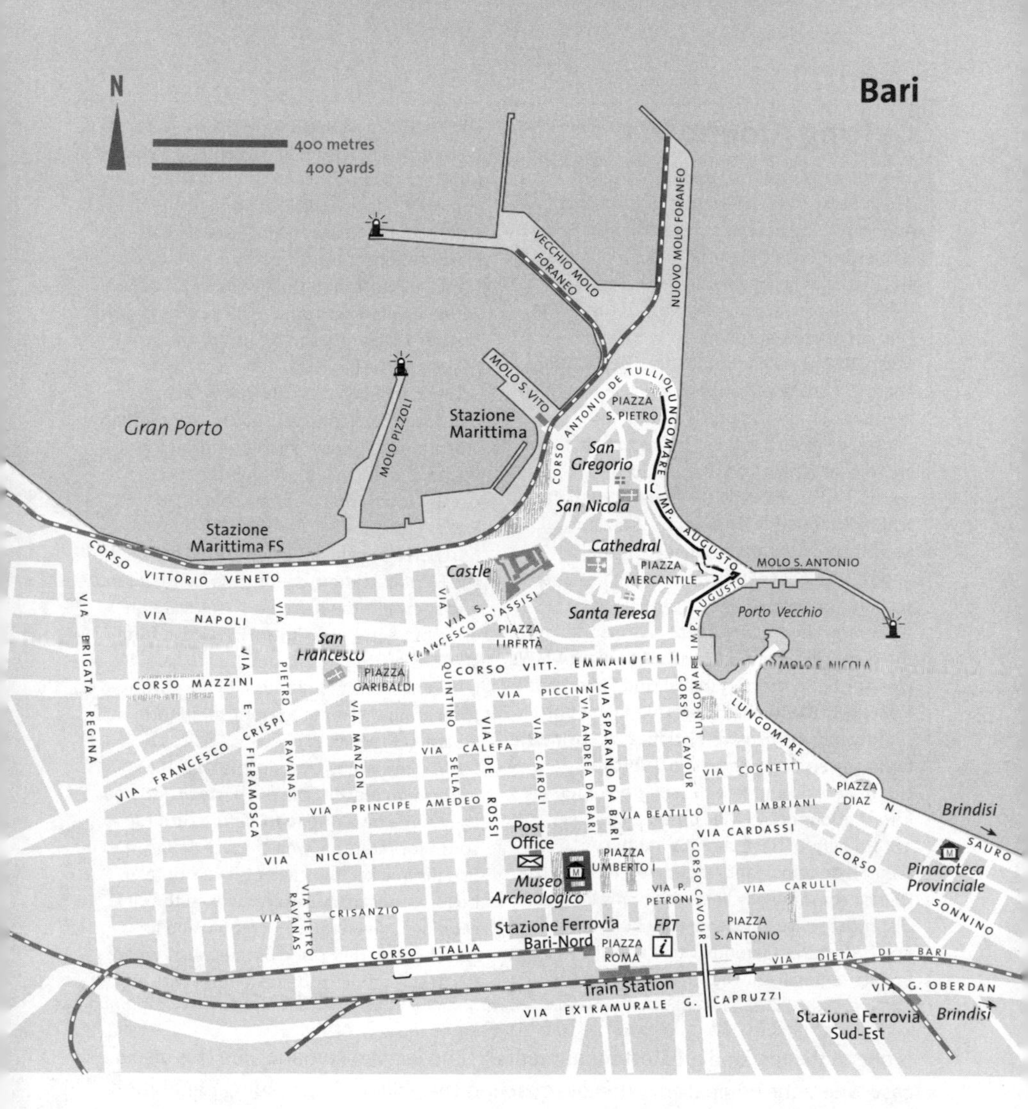

Barese sneaked in by night and beat the Venetians to their prey – something that did not happen often in those days.

The Greek Christians of Myra were disgusted by the whole affair but the Baresi had them outmatched, and so St Nicholas went west (his sarcophagus was too heavy to move, and so you can still see it today in the museum at Antalya, Turkey). Every year on 8 May, the Baresi celebrate their cleverness with a procession of boats in the harbour, and an ancient icon of the saint is held up to receive the homage of the crowds on shore, recreating the scene of Nicholas' arrival 900 years ago.

Basilica di San Nicola

To provide a fitting home for such an important saint, Bari almost immediately began to construct the Basilica di San Nicola at the centre of the Old Town. Even though this

Getting Around

Bari is a compact city, and once there it doesn't take long to see the sights on foot. And that is the best way to see them; this isn't Naples, but both the traffic and parking are still predictably horrible.

Bari's **airport**, about 9km west of the city at Palese, has regular connections to Rome, Milan, Turin, Pisa and some other destinations. There is a bus to the airport which leaves from the central train station.

If you discover a sudden desire to bolt, there are regular **ferries** from Bari to Corfu, Greece (Igoumenitsa and Patras), Albania, Croatia and Turkey. All ferries leave from the Stazione Marittima on the Mole San Vito, at the opposite end of the city from the main FS rail station (connected by bus 20).

Car ferry services to Greece are operated by the Ventouris line, c/o **Agenzia P. Lorusso**, Via Piccinni, **t** 080 521 7643 (daily), and **Superfast**, **t** 080 528 2828, whose ferries are faster but slightly more expensive. **Adriatica**, Via Liside 4, **t** 080 553 1555, runs ferries to Dubrovnik (*summer only*) and to Montenegro. For ferry information try CTS, Via Fornari 7, **t** 080 521 3244, a helpful travel agent's in town.

Bari is an important junction on the main FS east coast **railway** line, with many long-distance services, and there is a busy branch line from Bari to Taranto. There are also three private regional railways that run from the city. The **Ferrovia Sud-Est** (FSE), **t** 080 542 6552, runs a line from Bari's central FS station (on Piazza Aldo Moro) to Lecce, Taranto (in competition with the FS) and towns in the *trulli* country. Nearby is the **Ferrovia Bari-Nord** station, **t** 080 521 3577, with frequent trains to Andria and the towns en route; while **Ferrovie Calabro-Lucane** (FCL), **t** 080 572 5229, on Corso Italia, goes to Altamura and to Matera in the Basilicata.

There are long-distance **bus** services from Bari to Rome, Naples and other major Italian cities, most of which also leave from the Piazza Aldo Moro, although bus services to coastal towns north of Bari operate from Piazza Eroi del Mare (on the east side of the port). **SITA** buses (Largo Sorrentino behind the FS train station) connect Bari with inland and southern towns, while the private rail lines' bus services (**FCL** and **FSE**) leave from stations on Corso Italia and Largo Ciaia respectively. Bright orange city buses run from around 5.30am to 11pm; main terminus Piazza Aldo Moro.

If you're coming by **road**, the A14 *autostrada* reaches the outskirts of Bari near the town's own ring road, before turning south for Taranto. Given the size of Bari, it's usually quicker and easier to walk or take buses rather than use a car within the city. Moreover, given the city's reputation for street crime, this is one of the places where it's best for drivers to find a hotel with a

is one of the first and greatest monuments of the Puglian Romanesque, it is also a case where the original ambition overreached the ability of succeeding generations to finish the job. The two big towers remain unfinished and much of the decorative scheme was abandoned, giving the church a dowdy, barn-like appearance. Still, this is the first of the great Puglian churches, the place where the style was first translated from Norman French to southern Italian. Inside, the only surprise is the **tomb of Bona Sforza**, Queen of Poland and Duchess of Bari. The daughter of a 16th-century Duke of Milan, she inherited Bari on her mother's side and as a teenager was packed off to marry Sigismund, one of Poland's greatest kings. She survived him, and had a brief but eventful career as a dowager queen before retiring to sunny Puglia in her last years. Near the main altar, note the wonderful 11th-century **bishop's throne**, one of the greatest works of medieval sculpture in Puglia. Its legs, carved into the figures of men groaning as if they were supporting some unbearable burden, must have been a good joke on any fat bishop over the centuries.

lock-up garage and leave their car there. Above all, do not leave any valuables on view in a car.

Tourist Information

Bari: Piazza Aldo Moro 33/A, **t** 080 524 2361, situated to the right of the FS station. *Open Tues and Thurs 8.30–1.30 and 4–5.30; Mon, Wed and Fri 8.30–1.30.*

Where to Stay

Bari ✉ 70100

Bari makes the most convenient base for seeing the whole region, but be careful; the city is a major business centre, and full of bad hotels at outrageous prices.

****Villa Romanazzi Carducci**, Via Capruzzi 326, **t** 080 542 7400, **f** 080 556 0297 (*luxury*). This is one up-market hotel in Bari that is not a total rip-off. It has ample, comfortable rooms facing a (rather spartan) garden. *Wheelchair accessible.*

***Albergo Moderno**, Via Crisanzio 60, **t** 080 521 3313, **f** 080 521 4718 (*moderate*). At a third the price of the Villa Romanazzi, this hotel is quite pleasant.

***Costa**, Via Crisanzio 12, **t** 080 521 9015, **f** 080 521 0006 (*moderate*). Unremarkable but pleasant hotel at quite reasonable prices.

Albergo Giulia, **t** 080 521 6630, **f** 080 521 8271 (*moderate*). In the same building as the Costa, and one of the best budget choices.

Eating Out

Bari is famous for fish and, as with all the smaller towns around it, still sends its own fishing fleet out each morning.

Murat de l'Hotel Palace, Via Lombardi 13, **t** 080 521 6551 (*expensive*). The adventurous should try this highly rated restaurant devoted to innovative Italian cuisine. *Closed Sun and two weeks in Aug.*

Al Pescatore, Via Federico II di Svevia 6, **t** 080 523 7039 (*expensive*). Come here for excellent grilled fish in informal surroundings. *Closed Jan 1–15.*

Taverna Verde, Largo Adua 19, **t** 080 554 0870 (*cheap*). A few steps down the road, this is a popular place for fish and beer. *Closed Sun, Aug, and 24 Dec–6 Jan.*

Terranima, Via Putignani 213, **t** 080 521 9725 (*cheap*). Arguably the best *trattoria* in town, the short daily menu here features very solid dishes served in a pretty ambience. *Closed Sun evening July and Aug.*

Enzo e Ciro, Via Imbriani 79, **t** 080 554 1535 (*cheap*). The place to come if you're after a good pizza. *Eve only, closed Mon.*

Down in the crypt, you can pay your respects to St Nicholas. There will nearly always be somebody down there, praying or conducting a service; Nicholas' tomb has always been one of the south's most popular places of pilgrimage, as much for Orthodox Christians from abroad as for Italian Catholics. Most of the visitors today are local, but an Orthodox chapel has been added to accommodate pilgrims from Greece, and before 1917, the tomb was much visited by Russian Orthodox believers (and now may well be again). The church is also home to a centre for ecumenical studies, as the Baresi try to make amends after nine centuries. One of Nicholas' tricks is to exude gallons of a brownish liquid the faithful call *manna*, to which all sorts of miracles are attributed; half the families in this part of Puglia have a phial of it for good luck. The saint's reputation for helpfulness is certainly still current. Until a recent remodelling, the walls of the crypt were covered with supplications, written in ballpoint pen, along the lines of 'Dear San Nicola, please let me be married to Alfredo...'

Around the Old Town

South of San Nicola is the **cathedral** (*open 8.30–1 and 5–7 but closed at time of writing*), which is difficult to distinguish from San Nicola, although it was begun almost a century later. The plan is the same, as is the general feeling of austerity broken by small areas of richly detailed carving around some of the doors and windows. Unlike San Nicola, the cathedral still has its original beam ceiling, interrupted only by an octagonal cupola and much more suited to its Romanesque plainness. Two unusual features of the church are the stone baldachin over the main altar and the *trullo*, the large round building adjacent to the north wall that once served as the baptistry.

Old Bari, as we have said, is a bit drab for a medieval historic centre. There is a reason for this, in that Bari has had more than its share of trouble. The Normans levelled it once after a revolt. A plague in the 1650s wiped out most of the population, and the port area was heavily bombed in the Second World War. As a result, old Bari in some parts has the air of a new town. But although the buildings in the old centre may be all rebuilt or restored, at least the labyrinthine old street plan survives – it's famous, in fact, for being one of the easiest places in all Italy to get lost.

There will be no trouble, however, finding the **castle** (*open daily 9–1 and 3.30–6.30; adm*), just across the Piazza Odegitria from the cathedral. The Normans began it, Frederick II completed it, and later centuries added the polygonal bastions to deflect cannonballs. Inside, some sculpted reliefs and windows survive from Frederick's time, along with bits of sculpture and architectural fragments from all over Puglia. Excavations are currently under way in the castle grounds; apparently the centre of Roman Bari lies directly underneath.

Modern Bari

On your way up towards the railway station, you will be crossing the Corso Vittorio Emmanuele – site of both the city hall and Bari's famous fish market, and also the boundary between the old city and the new. When Bari's fortunes began to revive at the beginning of the 19th century, Joachim Murat's Napoleonic government laid out this broad rectilinear extension to the city. It has the plan of an old Greek or Roman town, only with wider streets, and it fits Bari well. Many streets have a view to the sea. Via Sparano di Bari and Corso Cavour are the choicest shopping streets.

Bari's two main museums are in the New Town. The **Pinacoteca Provinciale** (***t*** *0805 412 421; open Tues–Sat 9–1 and 4–7, Sun 9–1; adm*) is in the Palazzo della Provincia on Lungomare Nazario Saura, and has a good selection of south Italian art. Few Neapolitans are represented, although there is a genuine Neapolitan *presepio* (crib).

The **Museo Archeologico** (*closed at time of writing*) occupies a corner of Bari University's sprawling, crowded palace on the Piazza Umberto I, near the railway station. As is usual in southern museums, the star exhibits are classical ceramics: there are painted vases from Attica, including one very beautiful figure of the Birth of Helen from Leda's egg, and also several Puglian copies, some as good as the best of the Greek work. Much of the rest of the collection is devoted to the pre-Greek Neolithic cultures of Puglia.

South of Bari: *Trulli* Country

Southeast of Bari is a small but attractive region of little towns in an extraordinary, unique man-made landscape. It's given its character by one of the oldest forms of building in Italy still in regular use – the strange, whitewashed, dome-roofed houses known as *trulli*. The towns and villages in this district are among the most beautiful in southern Italy. In each of them, white arches and steps climb the hillsides, sometimes punctuated by *trulli* and topped with surprisingly grand Baroque churches.

Castellana Grotte

t 080 499 8211; open April–Oct daily 8.30–1 and 2–7; Nov–Mar daily 9.30–12.30 and 3–4; tours hourly (lasting about 1hr 45mins); adm.

The people around the Castellana Grotte never tire of bragging that their famous cave is the most beautiful in Italy. They may be right: the deepest section of the grotto tour, called the *Caverna Bianca*, is a glistening wonderland hung with thousands of bright glassy stalactites.

Like much of Puglia, this region is what the geologists call karst topography, built mostly of easily dissolving limestone. The territory is laced with every sort of cave, accompanied by such phenomena as streams and rivers that disappear into the ground, only to pop back up to the surface a few miles away.

Around Fasano

In the Middle Ages, the more inviting of the region's caves filled up with Greek Basilian monks. Following their burrowing instinct as they did in Asia Minor and elsewhere, the Greek hermits turned dozens of caves into hidden sanctuaries and chapels. You can see some of these caves along the ravines near the town of **Fasano**, where they are called *laure*; four can be sought out near Fasano's rail station. (There are more around Taranto and outside the town of San Vito dei Normanni, south of Ostuni.)

Also near Fasano, just off the Ostuni road in the village of **Montalbano**, you can visit what may be the most impressive dolmen in the south. Puglia's earliest cultures were not often great builders but they could be counted among the most sophisticated of all the Mediterranean Neolithic peoples. Much of their geometric pottery, which you can see scattered among Puglia's museums, is distinctively beautiful. This *dolmen*, a chamber formed by one huge slab of rock propped horizontally over two others, has acquired an odd local nickname: the Tavola Palatine (Table of the Knights) – the Round Table of King Arthur.

On the coast near Fasano is a small resort, **Torre Canne**. North of that, straddling the coastal road in an isolated setting, are the ruins of the Messapian-Roman town of **Egnazia**. The site is worth a brief visit, if only to admire the stupendous polychromatic mosaics with geometrical patterns and wild beasts, housed in the small **museum** (***t*** *080 482 9056; open 8.30–sunset; adm*). The museum also contains some Messapian artefacts, pottery and architectural fragments.

Getting Around

One of the best ways to see this area is on the Ferrovia Sud-Est **rail** line between Bari and Taranto or Lecce, which stops at Putignano, Alberobello, Locorotondo and Martina Franca, where the Lecce and Taranto lines divide. The FSE also operates **bus** services to the area from Taranto and Bari. The most attractive **road** route through the district is the SS172 – to get onto it from Bari, take the main Taranto road (SS100) south to Casamassima (about 20km) and turn left on to the SS172.

Tourist Information

Ostuni: Corso Giuseppe Mazzini 6, **t** 0831 301 268. Located in the Old Town in the summer. *Open summer Mon–Fri 8.30–1.30 and 5–8.30, winter 3.30–6.30.*

Martina Franca: Piazza Roma 37, **t** 080 480 5702. *Open Mon–Fri 9–1 and 5–7.30, Sat 9–1.*

Fasano: Piazza Ciaia 10, **t** 080 441 3086. *Open Mon–Sat 8–2 and 4–8.*

Where to Stay and Eat

There are dozens of privately owned *trulli* whose owners rent them out to visitors as part of the local *agriturismo* programme. Ostuni and its stretch of coast is also well equipped with hotels.

Castellana Grotte ✉ 70013

Fontanina, **t** 080 496 8010 (*moderate*). Another welcoming restaurant that serves generous portions of traditional food. On the *strada provinciale* towards Alberobello. *Closed Mon.*

Taverna degli Artisti, Via Matarrese 23, **t** 080 486 8234 (*cheap*). Try the *cannelloni*, the lamb or the sweet *torcini* at this friendly establishment. *Closed Thurs, Dec.*

Savelletri di Fasano ✉ 72010

*******Masseria San Domenico**, Strada Litoranea 379, **t** 080 482 7769, **f** 080 482 7978, *www.masseriasandomenico* (*luxury*). Recently opened, and not far from Egnazia, this is one of the most relaxing and luxurious hotels in Puglia. The renovated buildings of an old manor house, set amidst olive groves, look out onto a beautiful swimming pool in the shape of a natural lake and filled with filtered sea water.

Alberobello ✉ 70011

Because the *trullo* towns are easy to reach by rail from Bari or Taranto, few people stay over. But Alberobello's unaffected hospitality makes it one of the most pleasant bases imaginable, and there is a wide choice of both hotels and restaurants.

*******Hotel dei Trulli**, Via Cadore 32, **t** 080 432 3555, **f** 080 432 3560, *www.hoteldeitrulli.it* (*very expensive*). This group of *trulli* cottages, set in a garden, comes at the top of the list. Each cottage has its own patio and is beautifully furnished. There is also a pool and a fair restaurant. *Wheelchair accessible.*

Il Poeta Contadino, Via Indipendenza 21, **t** 080 432 1917 (*very expensive*).

Alberobello

The Valle d'Itria, between the towns of Putignano and Martina Franca, is the best place to see *trulli* (*see* box, p.248). Alberobello, the *trulli* capital, has over 1,000 of them – and nearly as many souvenir stands and craft shops. Although it's undeniably touristy, Alberobello is the best base for visiting the *trulli* country, a gracious and lovely white village, one where people never seem to lose their surprise that people would come all the way from Rome, let alone other countries, to visit them.

Modern (although not-too-modern) Alberobello stands on top of a hill. Here you can find the **Sovrano**, once the headquarters of a group of *carbonari* (secret progressive political societies of the early 19th century) and now home to a church group.

'The Peasant Poet' is another one of Puglia's fine 'creative' restaurants. The atmosphere is soothing and sophisticated, and both the food and wine are among the best you'll find anywhere. *Closed Mon, 3 weeks in Jan.*

Trullo d'Oro, Via Cavallotti 27, **t** 080 432 3909 (*expensive–moderate*). Good, sophisticated cuisine. You could try the Puglian-style *spiedini*. *Closed Mon, Sun evening and 3 weeks in Jan.*

Cucina dei Trulli, Piazza Ferdinando IV 30, **t** 080 432 1511 (*cheap*). This is a family-run restaurant that has been in business for more than a century as part of the budget hotel Lanzillotta, and serves excellent home cooking. *Closed over Christmas.*

Locorotondo ✉ 70010

This village is the centre of Puglia's most famous wine region and, for dinner, a bottle of Locorotondo wine is mandatory: it's a pale, dry white, much more delicate than most of the strong Puglian wines.

Centro Storico, Via Eroi di Dogali 6, **t** 080 431 5473 (*cheap*). The owner's love of food is obvious in the care taken with the cooking and presentation at this intimate *trattoria. Closed Wed, 2 week in Mar.*

Casa Mia, Via Cisternino, **t** 080 431 1218 (*cheap*). They'll be happy to slip you a bottle of Locorotondo with the stuffed peppers or *coniglio al forno* at this fine establishment, 2km towards Ostuni. *Closed Tues.*

Martina Franca ✉ 74015

★★★**Dell'Erba**, Via dei Cedri 1, **t** 080 430 1055, **f** 080 430 1639 (*expensive*). This place has a garden, a pool and child-minding facilities, as well as an excellent restaurant. *Wheelchair accessible.*

Ostuni ✉ 72017

★★**Tre Torri**, Corso Vittorio Emmanuele 298, **t** 0831 331 114 (*cheap*). A pleasant hotel that is fine for a short stay.

Rosa Marina ✉ 72017

★★★★**Hotel Rosa Marina**, on the SS379 north of Ostuni, **t** 0831 350 411, **f** 0831 350 412 (*luxury*). Along the shoreline, the sharp, modern design of this hotel stands out from the crowd. It's a comfortable place, too, with a pool, private beach and all the amenities.

Ceglie Messapico ✉ 72013

Al Fornello da Ricci, Contrada Montevicoli, **t** 0831 377 104 (*expensive*). This is one of the very finest restaurants in Puglia – an absolute must for foodies interested in Puglian cuisine. *Closed Mon eve, Tues, three weeks in Sept and 10 days in Feb.*

La Taverna dei Dominicani, Via Dante 15, **t** 0831 384 910 (*moderate*). Sophisticated cuisine in a restored pilgrims' hostel.

Messapica, Piazza del Plebescito 17, **t** 0831 388 318 (*cheap*). This *trattoria* offers typical home cooking. *Closed Mon.*

★★**Tre Trulli**, Str Montevicoli 115, **t** 0831 381 312 (*cheap*) A simple budget option.

The well-signposted **Zona dei *Trulli*** lies on the opposite slope and consists of two adjacent neighbourhoods called the Rione Monti and the Ala Piccola, where most of the hobbit-houses now house shops or restaurants. Here also the modern church of Sant'Antonio has been built *trullo*-fashion. There is a small **museum** next door.

Locorotondo

Trulli look pretty out in the countryside, too, and particularly so around Locorotondo, a town on a hill with views all around the Itria Valley. Locorotondo itself is stunning, a gleaming white town topped not with *trulli*, but tidy rows of distinctive gables. The street plan, from which the town takes its name, is neatly circular, built around an

The Love of *Trulli*

It takes you by surprise. Turning a corner of the road or passing the crest of one of the low hills of the Murge, all at once you meet a kind of landscape you have never seen before. Low stone walls neatly partition the countryside, around acres of vines propped up on arbours, covering the ground like low, flat roofs. The houses are the strange part, smooth whitewashed structures in a bewildering variety of shapes and forms, each crowned with one or more tall, conical stone roofs. These are the *trulli* and, when there are enough of them in one place, they make a picture that might be at home in Africa, or in a fairy tale, but certainly nowhere else in Italy.

The *trulli* are still built these days; the dome is easier to raise than it looks and the form is adaptable to everything from tool sheds to petrol stations. It is anybody's guess as to their origins; some scholars have mentioned the Saracens, others, less probably, the Mycenaean Greeks. None of the *trulli* you see today are more than a century or two old. They are exotically beautiful, but if the form has any other advantage, it would be that the domes give warmer air a chance to rise, making the houses cooler in the broiling Puglian summers. Beyond that modest contribution, there is no real reason for building *trulli* – only that they are an inseparable part of the lives of the people who live in this part of Puglia. There is no special name for the area around Alberobello where most of the *trulli* are concentrated; people simply call it the '*trulli* district'.

Trulli are built of limestone, with thick, whitewashed walls and only a few tiny windows. The domes are limestone, too, a single row of narrow slates wound in a gradually decreasing spiral up to the top. Most have some sort of decoration at the point, and a few of the older ones are embellished with some traditional but obscure symbols, painted like Indian tepees. *Trulli* seem only to come in one size; when a *trullo*-dweller needs more room, he simply has another unit added. In this way, some of the fancier *trullo* palaces come to resemble small castles – Loire châteaux for hobbits. Grandest of all is the one on Piazza Sacramento in Alberobello – the only specimen with a second floor; they call it the Sovrano, the Supreme *Trullo*.

ancient **well** dedicated to St George. Nearby, at the top of the town, the pretty church of **Santa Maria Grecia** has a carved altarpiece, bits of frescoes and valley views.

For a more heady diversion, pay a visit to the **Cantina del Locorotondo** (*Via Madonna della Catena 99*, **t** *080 431 1644, www.locorotondodoc.com*), a modern winery that produces some of the best vintages in southern Italy. Ask for Oronzo Mastro, who is passionate about his wine and will be more than happy to give you a tour in perfect English. He'll lead you around the various chambers packed with gleaming vats that churn out some 10 million bottles a year – then crack open a few bottles for you to taste. If you haven't yet seen inside a *trullo*, the Cantina has one of its own, too.

Martina Franca

The highest town in Puglia (although that's not particularly high) is a lovely Baroque town with a garland of monuments including the old **Palazzo Ducale**, a number of other palaces and a **cathedral** at the top, which towers over the city like a castle. For a short period each year, in July and August, Martina Franca becomes an important point on the Puglian cultural map when it hosts the **Valle d'Itria Festival** (*t 080 480 5100*) – an international music festival that attracts opera, classical and jazz performers from around the world. (You can also get information on tickets and performances from the tourist office, *see* p.246).

Ostuni

Ostuni is one of the loveliest towns in the region – indeed, in Puglia – with an ornate 16th-century cathedral and a handful of other Renaissance and Baroque confections standing out among its white streets, and even a Neapolitan-style *guglia* (spire).

The **Chiesa delle Monachelle** (*t 0831 336 383; open daily 8.30–1 and 5–7; Tues and Thurs only in winter; adm*) contains the **Museo delle Civiltá Preclassiche della Murgia Meridionale**, a permanent display on prehistoric society and agriculture in this part of southern Italy. This used to be home to the town's archaeological highlight – namely Delia, the well-preserved skeleton of a pregnant young woman found in a crouched position, her skull decorated with coloured beads and stones for burial during a religious ceremony. You will now find her in the new **Parco Archeologico e Naturale di Arignano**.

The evening *passeggiata* in Ostuni goes on until well past midnight, and souvenir shops, restaurants and pizzerias stay open late. Ostuni also has the advantage of being near the sea, at the centre of a strip of modest but peaceful resorts that line the coast between Monopoli and Brindisi.

The Gulf of Taranto

Nestling in the underbelly of Puglia, where the Ionian coast curves round into the Basilicata, the Gulf of Taranto centres around the town of the same name, one of the main industrial centres in the south.

Taranto

Perhaps unique among cities, Taranto has two seas all to itself. Its harbour consists of two large lagoons, the **Mare Grande**, separated from the Ionian Sea by sand bars and a tiny archipelago called the Isole Cheradi (one of which is big enough to hold a farm), and the **Mare Piccolo**. The city is on a narrow strip of land between them, broken into three pieces by a pair of narrow channels. The western section, around the railway station, is almost entirely filled up with Italy's biggest steel plant, which was begun as the showpiece project of the *Cassa per il Mezzogiorno* in the early fifties. This gargantuan complex provides an unexpected and memorable sight if you enter the city by night.

According to legend, Taranto was founded by Taras, a son of Poseidon who came riding into the harbour on the back of a dolphin. According to historians, however, it was merely a band of Spartans, shipped here in 708 BC to found a colony. They chose a good spot. It's probably the best Italian harbour and the only good one on the Ionian Sea. Not surprisingly, the new town of Taras did well. Until the Romans cut it down to size, Taras was the metropolis of Magna Grecia, a town feared in war but more renowned in philosophy.

Taras, now Taranto, is still an interesting place, with an exotic old quarter, a good museum and maybe the best seafood in southern Italy. It wears a decidedly north Italian air – this is the one city in the Mezzogiorno where things work, and where not quite all the public's money goes down the drain. Nevertheless, the best part of the story is all in the past.

History

With its harbour and the help of a little Spartan know-how on the battlefield, Taras had little trouble acquiring both wealth and political power. By the 4th century BC, the population had reached 300,000. In its balmiest days, Taras' prosperity depended on an unusual variety of luxury goods. Its oysters were a highly prized delicacy, as far away as Rome. Another shellfish, the murex, provided the purple dye – really a deep scarlet – used for the robes of Roman emperors and every other style-conscious ruler across the Mediterranean. This imperial purple, the most expensive commodity in the ancient world, was obtained by allowing masses of murex to rot in the sun – an enormous heap of the shells, with perhaps the molluscs that coloured Caesar's cloak somewhere near the bottom, was mentioned by travellers only a century ago.

For a similarly high price, the Tarantines would have been happy to provide you with the cloth, too. Their sheep were known for the softest and best wool available, and Tarantine shepherds actually put coats on their flocks to keep it nice.

If contemporary historians are to be believed, Taras managed to avoid most of the terrible intercity conflicts of Magna Grecia simply by being much larger and more powerful than its neighbours. It was spared civil troubles by a sound constitution, with a mix of aristocratic and democratic elements. Pythagoras spent part of his life in Taras, an exile from his native Croton, and he helped to set a philosophical tone for the city's affairs. The height of Taras' glory was perhaps the long period of rule under a Pythagorean mathematician and philosopher named Archytas (*c.* 400 BC), a paragon of wisdom and virtue in the ancient world. Plato himself came to visit Archytas, though he never mentions Taras in his writings.

When Taras and Rome went to war in 282 BC, they did so as equals. Taras called in Pyrrhus of Epirus as an ally, but after 10 years of inconclusive Pyrrhic victories, the Romans gained the upper hand and put an end to Taras' independence. Rome graciously refrained from razing the city to the ground after Taras helped Hannibal in the second Punic War but the Tarantines still felt the iron grip of the victors, and their city quickly dwindled both in wealth and importance.

Yet of all the Greek cities of the south, Taras, along with Reggio, proved to be the best survivor. Throughout the Dark Ages, the city never quite disappeared, and by the time of the Crusades, it was an important port once more.

The modern city, italianized to Taranto, substantially industrialized and a major base for the Italian navy, has known little of philosophers or well-dressed sheep, but still manages to send its fame around the world in other ways. The city gave its name to the country quick-dance called the *tarantella*, and also to the *tarantula*.

Getting There and Around

Taranto has two **railway** lines, but both use the central station at the far western end of town – between the Old Town and the steel mills – on Piazzale Duca d'Aosta. Regular **FS** trains leave for Lecce, Brindisi, Bari and further north, as well as for the horrible endless trip around the Ionian Sea to Reggio di Calabria. On one or another of the FS lines, you can get to Massafra, Castellaneta, Grottaglie or Manduria. Local trains run by **FSE** (Ferrovie Sud-Est), **t** 099 471 5901, operated from one side of the station, will take you to Locorotondo, Martina Franca and Alberobello.

FSE also operates a large proportion of the province's **bus** services: there are several a day for Alberobello, Bari or Lecce, leaving from Piazza Castello, while their buses for Ostuni and Manduria leave from Via di Palma.

SITA buses to Matera also leave from Piazza Castello, and there are daily buses to Naples run by the **Miccolis** company from the train station. Buses to Metaponto leave from Piazza Castello.

The A14 *autostrada* comes to an end just north of Taranto and all major **roads** from the north meet up with an outer ring road through the west of the city, part of the Via Appia (SS7) bound for Brindisi. The only trunk route that involves crossing to the older, southern part of Taranto is the SS7ter, for Lecce.

Tourist Information

Taranto: Corso Umberto I 113, **t** 099 453 2392.
Open Mon–Fri 9–1 and 4.30–6.30, Sat 9–12.

Where to Stay and Eat

Taranto ✉ 74100

Most of the better hotels are inconveniently located on the far eastern edge of town. The real bargains are scattered around the Old Town, in the picturesque environs of the fish market. This is also the best place to head for dinner; right across the street there are a number of places you can feast on the fruits of the sea and rub elbows with half of Taranto at the same time. All of these places offer the local speciality: mussels or *cozze* (also called *mitili*).

There are also many good and inexpensive places to eat in the new city:

★★★**Plaza**, Via d'Aquino 46, facing Piazza Archita, **t** 099 459 0775, **f** 099 459 0675, *www.hotelplazataranto.com* (*expensive*). A well-run spot in the centre. Most of the rooms have a balcony over the square.

Le Vecchie Cantine, Via Girasoli 23, Lama **t** 099 777 2589 (*expensive*). This sophisticated place is one of the best, as well as one of the newest, places to eat. The menu changes daily but is always focused on fish. *Eve only except Sun and hols, closed Jan and Wed in winter.*

★★**Sorrentino**, Piazza Fontana 7, **t** 099 470 7456 (*moderate*). This clean and shipshape place, near the fish market, is one of the best of the budget choices.

Al Gambero, Via Litoranea Salentina, **t** 099 731 9971 (*moderate*). For something with a touch of elegance, Al Gambero has earned a high reputation for creative dishes involving nearly all the fantastic array of marine delicacies the Ionian Sea has to offer.

Vecchia Taranto, Piazzetta Sant'Eligio 12, **t** 099 470 9000 (*moderate*). A new, high-quality restaurant. *Closed Mon.*

Da Mimmo, Via Giovinazzi 18, **t** 099 459 3733 (*cheap*). Another good seafood restaurant; the dishes available may include roast squid and *tubettini alle cozze*. *Closed Wed and two weeks in Aug.*

Ristorante Basile, Via Pitagora 76, **t** 099 452 6240 (*cheap*). Across from the main city park, this place is perhaps even better. Excellent dinners are served here at rock-bottom prices. *Closed Sat, Christmas and mid-Aug.*

Castellaneta Marina ✉ 74011

★★★★**Golf Hotel**, Località Riva dei Tessali, **t** 099 843 9251, **f** 099 843 9255 (*very expensive*). A resort complex of cottages on the coast north of Taranto. Set in a grove near the links – not much of a course, really, but a full 18 holes, and a genuine novelty in these parts. Half board obligatory.

Before you change your travel plans, there are no large hairy poisonous spiders in Puglia, just a few innocent little brown ones. Their bite isn't really that bad, but a little notoriety still clings to them, thanks to the religious pathology of the southern Italians. Throughout antiquity and the Middle Ages, various dancing cults were popular around the Mediterranean. Everything from the worship of Dionysus to the medieval Dance of Death touched this region, and when the Catholic Church began to frown on such carryings on, the urge took strange forms. People bitten by spiders became convinced they would die, and that their only salvation was to dance the venom out of their system – dance until they dropped, in fact. Sometimes they would dance for four days or more, while musicians played for them and their friends sought to discover the magic colour – the 'colour' of that particular spider – that would calm the stricken dancer. *Tarantism*, as 19th-century psychologists came to call it, is rarely seen anywhere in the south these days – and for that matter neither is the *tarantella*, a popular style of music that took its name from this bit of folklore and was in vogue at the beginning of the 19th century.

The Città Vecchia

Directly below the station along the Via Duca d'Aosta, a bridge takes you over to the Old Town, a nearly rectangular island that is only four blocks wide, but still does its best to make you lose your way. The ancient Tarantines, lacking any sort of hill, made the island their acropolis – though in those days, it was still attached to the mainland. Most of the temples were here, along with a famous gold-plated bronze statue of Zeus that was the second-largest piece of sculpture in the classical world, surpassed only by the Colossus of Rhodes.

Today, all that remains of ancient Taras are some columns from a **Temple of Poseidon**. They have been re-erected in the main square next to Taranto's **castello**, built in the 1480s by King Ferdinand of Spain and now the navy headquarters. From the square, a **swinging bridge**, something rare in Italy, connects the Old Town with the new. The Mare Piccolo, besides being an enormous oyster and mussel farm for the fishermen of Taranto, is also the home of one of Italy's two main naval bases. Very early in the morning, when the bridge is open, you may see big warships waiting their turn with little fishing boats to squeeze their way through the narrow channel.

Follow the fishermen home and you'll end up in the **fish market** on Via Cariati, near the docks at the opposite end of the Città Vecchia. In sometimes slick and up-to-date Italy, this is one place where you can truly believe you are in the Mediterranean: a wet and mildly grubby quay awash with the sounds and smells of the sea, where tired fishermen appear each morning at dawn to have coffee, sort out the catch and bang the life out of octopi on the stones. Of course, there are plenty of cats around. True 'aristocats' they are, too, the descendants of the first cats of Europe; ancient historians record how the ancient Tarantines imported them from Egypt.

From the fish market, pick your way a short distance across the Città Vecchia to the **cathedral**, built in the 11th century and rebuilt in a hotchpotch of different styles. Most of the last, florid Baroque remodelling has been cleared away, saving only a curious coffered ceiling with two golden statues suspended from it. Roman columns and capitals support the arches and there is a good medieval baptismal font under a baldachin. Some bits of mosaic survive on the floor, which must originally have been similar to the one in Otranto; one of the figures still visible is a centaur blowing a horn. Taranto's cathedral is dedicated to St Cataldus, a Munster Irishman who did good works here on his way to the Crusades. You can see his tomb down in the crypt, as well as the chapel dedicated to him upstairs, the ornate **18th-century Cappellone**, with fantastical (and fantastically expensive) decoration in *pietra dura* – vases of flowers cut out of stone. From outside the cathedral, you can get some idea of its original appearance on the north side, with Norman blind arches and a small cupola on a drum of columns, similar to some of the Byzantine churches in Calabria.

The rest of the Città Vecchia is residential and ancient, a series of parallel alleys and stairways connecting the Mare Grande and Mare Piccolo sides. The area was down at heel and half-forgotten for a long time, but with Taranto's new-found prosperity, the city is putting a good deal of money into housing rehabilitation and restoring old palaces and other monuments, a process that is finally making a difference.

The New Town

As in Bari, crossing over from the sleepy Old Town into the hyperactive new centre is a startling contrast. But Taranto has no need to envy Bari these days; its New Town is surprisingly bright, busy and sprawling, with as many grey-suited businessmen as blue-clad sailors. As in Bari, the showcase of the New Town is the **Lungomare**, built over an embankment over the Mare Grande. Also like Bari, this leads to a Fascist-era civic centre, including a striking **Palazzo del Governo** from the twenties. Taranto has some good modern buildings, too, including the witty, postmodernist **Monte dei Paschi** bank offices on Via d'Aquino, built in 1992 to look as if they are falling down.

Museo Nazionale

Piazza Archita (Corso Umberto I 41), two streets west of the swinging bridge; t 099 453 2112. At the time of writing, the collections were at the Palazzo Pantaleo, Corso Vittorio Emmanuele in the Old Town during renovation; open daily 8.30–7.30.

It's worth stopping in Taranto just to visit this museum, which rivals those in Naples and Reggio di Calabria for its collection of treasures from Magna Grecia. And, with building activity going full blast around Taranto, new discoveries are being made all the time. There are some fine pieces of sculpture from temples and funeral sites, including the well-preserved 6th-century BC tomb of an athlete, a head of Aphrodite and several other works attributed to the school of Praxiteles, and also a wonderful bronze of the god Poseidon in the angular, half-oriental Archaic style, not to mention curiosities like a monkey-headed statue of the Egyptian god Thoth.

The museum has what is believed to be the largest collection of Greek **terracotta figures** in the world. They are fascinating in their thousands, the middle-class *objets d'art* of antiquity. The older ones are more consciously religious images of Dionysus, Demeter or Persephone, which served the same purpose as the crucifix on the wall of a modern Italian family. Later examples give every evidence of creeping secularism.

The subjects range from ladies at their toilette to grotesque theatre masks, comic dancers and figures from mythological stories. A few are copies of famous monuments; one figurine reproduces a statue of Nike, or Victory, erected in Taras after one of Pyrrhus' defeats of the Romans – and later moved to the Roman forum after the war went the other way.

Among the fragments from Taras' buildings there is an entire wall of leering Medusas, protection against the evil eye – as much a preoccupation among the ancient Greeks as it is with southern Italians today. As well as large collections of delicate, exquisite jewellery, glass trinkets, cosmetic cases, mirrors and coins (many minted with the city's own symbol of Taras riding his dolphin), there is also an important selection of **Greek ceramics**. The vases include fine examples of the earlier, less common black figurework, and are admirably laid out according to motifs – such as funerals, war and athletics – near a case full of such odd finds as javelin points and a genuine ancient discus; on the vases and accompanying explanations, you can learn anything you ever wanted to know about the ancient Greek games. The vases are particularly fascinating to see, with their figures of humans and gods fighting, taking part in sports or revelling. In one room, a rare evocation of Magna Grecia at play is provided by scenes on vases of Athene and contending athletes.

Around Taranto

Massafra and Around

West of Taranto, toward Matera, you can visit one of the most unusual towns of Puglia. **Massafra**, even more than Matera, was a city of troglodytes and monks. A steep ravine called the Gravina di San Marco cuts the city in two; the ravine and the surrounding valleys are lined with **caves**. Many were expanded into *laure* (cave-chapels) by Greek monks in the early Middle Ages. Between the caves and the old church crypts, it has been estimated that there are over 100 medieval frescoes in, around and under Massafra – including some of considerable artistic merit.

One of the best is a beautiful Byzantine Virgin called **La Vergine della Scala**, in a sanctuary of the same name in Massafra's Old Town, reached from Via del Santuario by a long naïf-Baroque set of stairs. The Madonna is shown receiving the homage of two kneeling deer, the subject of an old legend. Next to the sanctuary, there are some 13th-century paintings in the **Cripta della Bona Nova**.

Apart from these well-visited examples, you'll have to rely on the locals' considerable goodwill towards strangers to find the rest of the caves, crypts and frescoes. None of the sites is well marked. At the bottom of the ravine is the **Farmacia del Mago Greguro**, a now rather neglected complex of caves that it is believed were once used by monks to store and prepare medicinal herbs.

Other cave-churches and frescoes can be seen at Mottola, Palagianello and Ginosa, built like Massafra over a ravine full of caves. **Laterza**, perched on the edge of a dramatic 650ft-deep gorge near the border with the Basilicata, has about 180 caves and *laure*, of which some 30 can be visited. **Castellaneta** also has a ravine – the steepest and wildest of them all – and some cave-churches, but this town prefers to be known as the birthplace, in 1895, of Rudolph Valentino. There's a life-size ceramic statue of the old matinée idol in the main square, dressed as the Sheikh of Arabia.

Grottaglie

Just 15 minutes by train to the east of Taranto, Grottaglie is the ceramics capital of southeast Italy. The town's potters continue to produce plates, vases and pots in enormous quantities – attracting throngs of visitors on summer weekends, eager to buy their traditional (and sometimes more modern) styles. Grottaglie boasts an unbroken tradition of working in ceramics since at least the Middle Ages, and the thousands of plates and vases stacked on the pavements and rooftops make an arresting sight.

As well as producing copies of ancient Greek wine bottles and amphorae (all glazed with flowers and abstract patterns), the town still makes the huge plates that were traditionally used for communal eating on the threshing-room floor during harvests. The giant vases that now make good plant pots or umbrella stands were originally intended to hold soaking laundry before wash day. Grottaglie pottery is found on sale all over Italy, but at its source it is available at almost half the price – a great bargain, especially if you're travelling by car.

Terracotta (production of which is centred around Bari) and ceramics have been two of the main products of Puglia since the days of the ancient Greeks. The museums of southern Italy contain thousands of terracotta *ex voto* plaques with images of gods that were left as religious offerings at a temple (usually those dedicated to Demeter or Persephone). The region's pots may today be put to different uses to those for which they were originally designed but their forms and shapes remain much as they have always been.

Francavilla Fontana and the Specchia Miano

Further along the road and rail line towards Brindisi is the town of **Francavilla Fontana**, which takes its title of 'free town' from a favour granted by King Ferdinand IV. The town boasts several 14th–18th-century palaces, including a small one that once belonged to the 18th-century Bourbon kings, as a reminder of its days as a feudal stronghold.

On the road from Francavilla to Ceglie Messapico is the 30ft-high tower known as the **Specchia Miano**. This is the easiest to track down of three *specchie* – conical stepped towers – in this area. They were built by the ancient Messapians (*see* Oria, p.256) and get their name from the Latin *speculum*, which means mirror, but no one really knows what they are or what purpose they served. Many *specchie* are found on high land, and it is possible that they were used for some sort of long distance signalling.

To find the Specchia Miano, take the right turn (if coming from Francavilla) by the petrol station 3km south of Ceglie (there's a *trullo* on the corner). Then turn right again, directly after you cross the railroad tracks. Take the next dirt track on the left, and follow it to a paved road, where a yellow sign directs you the rest of the way.

It's worth the trip. You're back in *trullo* fairyland here, a green rolling landscape covered in wildflowers where everything is on a tiny scale: tiny farms and tiny *trulli* farmsteads on every side (although most of their owners now live in the towns and only use them for summer houses; the electricity cables seem rather strange and incongruous). Behind one of these *trullo* stands the Specchia Miano, an irregular, much-eroded terraced heap of small stones. Climb it, and you'll notice that part of the tower seems collapsed, as if there had been a chamber inside. From the top, you can clearly see the hill top centres of Oria and Ceglie. The *specchia* seems to be exactly on a line between them, and in the distance, you can see parts of an old track that follows the line.

Oria

Oria is believed to have been the capital city of the ancient Messapians, a quietly civilized people who suffered many indignities at the hands of the Greek colonists and finally succumbed to the allure of classical culture. Ceglie Messapico, south of Ostuni, was another of their cities, although the *specchie* (*see* above) are the Messapians' most noteworthy surviving monuments. Like Siena and so many other Italian cities, Oria is divided into legally chartered communities, each with its special festival, colours and symbols. These *contrade* may date back to the tribes of pre-Roman times.

Oria is a lovely town with brightly coloured tile domes over its churches and many of its original old gates. Frederick II built a strong **castle** (***t*** *083 184 5025; open daily summer 9.30–12.30 and 5–8, weekends 9–12, winter 9.30–12.30 and 3.30–6.30; adm; free guided tours in English*) for the town in 1227–33. With its three tall round towers, it now resembles a toy fortress. It's one of the few such castles you can visit, and the town has assembled a collection of antiquities and bric-a-brac in the museum inside.

In the Middle Ages, Oria had an important Jewish community; the **ghetto** and its buildings are still intact.

Manduria

Manduria was another Messapian city, mentioned in the histories as fighting continuous wars with the Greeks of Taras. The ruins of its **fortifications** can still be seen – three concentric circuits of which the outermost is 5km around – along with caves, **necropoli** and a famous **well** mentioned in Pliny's *Natural History*. To find the well, turn right in front of the church of the Capuccini on Via Sant'Antonio.

Old Manduria is a somewhat gloomy place, an effect that is only heightened by its ensemble of mouldering Baroque churches and palaces, and especially by the paving stones of black volcanic basalt, similar to those found in some towns in Sicily. Like Oria, Manduria is one of the towns where the streets and some of the buildings of the old Jewish **ghetto** still survive. The new city has an interesting **cathedral**, with a beautifully carved Renaissance rose window and portals.

The Salentine Peninsula

Puglia's extreme south contains dowdy Brindisi, lovely Lecce, some flat but unusual countryside, the sun-bleached and sea-washed old towns of Gallipoli and Otranto, and lots of caves and Neolithic remains. Its coastline, while not as ruggedly beautiful as that of the Gargano, does have its charms, not least of which is that it is relatively uncrowded. Few foreign tourists make their way to this distant Land's End, although it teems with Italians in August. If you are beachcombing or backpacking and can resist the temptation presented by the ferries to Greece, this might be a perfect place to spend a lazy week or so.

Brindisi

The word *brindisi* in Italian means 'to toast'. It's just a coincidence; the town's name comes from the original Greek colony of Brentesion, and it isn't likely that anyone has lately proposed any toasts to this grey and dusty port. Brindisi today is what it was in Roman times: the gangplank to the boat for Greece. On the Viale Regina Margherita, right of the port, a small piazza at the top of a formal stairway holds a magnificent **Roman column**, once topped by the statue of an emperor, that marked the end of the Appian Way. For six centuries, all of Rome's trade with the

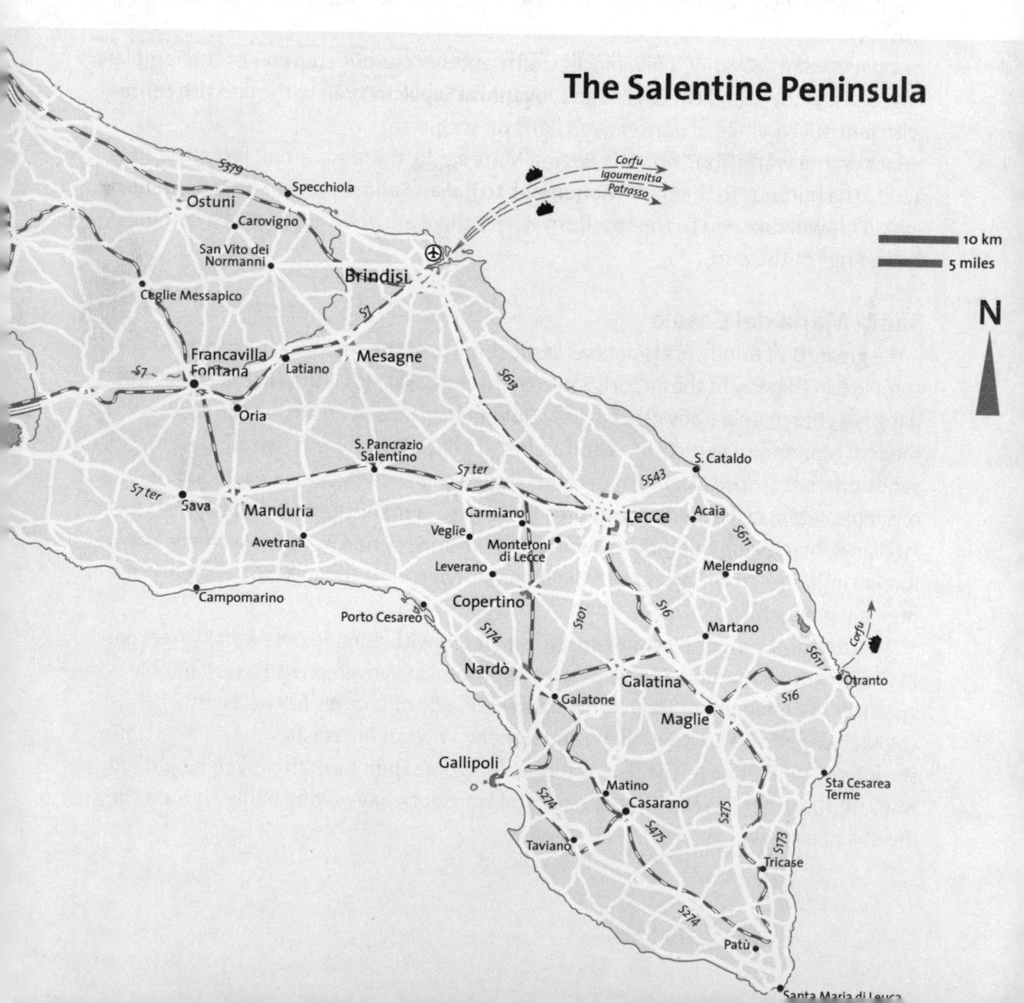

East, all its legions heading toward new conquests and all its trains of triumphant or beaten emperors and generals passed through Brundisium. Later, from the 11th century on, the city was one of the most important Crusader ports. A memory of this survives, too; if you enter the city from the north or west, you will pass the **Tancredi Fountain**, an Arab-inspired work built by the Norman chief, Tancred. Here the Christian knights watered their horses before setting out for the Holy Land.

As a city where people have always been more concerned with coming and going than settling down, Brindisi has not saved up a great store of monuments and art. Travel agents and shipping offices are more in evidence than anything else, helping expedite the hordes of tourists flowing to and from Patras, Corfu and Igoumenitsa. If you're staying, there are a few things to look at.

Alongside the 12th-century **cathedral**, rebuilt in warmed-over Baroque, there is a small exotic-looking portico with striped pointed arches; this is all that remains of the **Temple**, headquarters church of the Knights Templar, and closely related to the Temple in London. Nearby, a small collection of ancient Puglian relics has been assembled at the **Museo Archeologico** (***t*** *0831 221 401; open daily 9–1, Tues also 4–6.30, closed Sat and Sun in winter*).

Down Via San Giovanni, a few blocks south, another curious souvenir of the Templars has survived: the round church of **San Giovanni al Sepolcro**, built in the late 11th century, with fanciful carvings of dancers and lions on the portal.

Back on the waterfront, on Viale Regina Margherita, there is a small ferry that runs across the harbour to the 150ft **Monument to Italian Sailors**, erected by Mussolini in 1933. A lift will take you to the top, from where there are good views of the comings and goings of the port.

Santa Maria del Casale

The greatest of Brindisi's attractions lies just north of the city, near the sports complex on the way to the airport. Santa Maria del Casale (to visit ring the bell at the gate) is a church unlike any other in Italy. Built in the 1320s in an austere, almost modern economy of vertical lines and arches, the **façade** is done in two shades of sandstone, not striped as in so many other Italian churches, but shaped into a variety of simple, exquisite patterns. The church makes use of many of the features of Puglian Romanesque, but defies classification into any period or style. Neither is any foreign influence from Saracens or Greeks readily apparent. Santa Maria is a work of pure imagination.

The **interior**, a simple, barn-like space, is painted with equally noteworthy frescoes in the Byzantine manner. The wall over the entrance is covered with a remarkable visionary Last Judgement by an artist named Rinaldo of Taranto, full of brightly coloured angels and apostles, saints and sinners; a river of fire washes the damned into the inferno while, above, the fish of the sea disgorge their human prey to be judged. Many of the other frescoes, in the nave and transepts, have faded badly, though they are still of interest.

Getting There and Around

Brindisi's Casale **Airport** is 4km north of the city and has regular flights to Rome, Milan and Verona. There is a frequent bus service that runs between the airport and the main FS rail station in the city centre.

Brindisi is the most important Italian port for **ferries** to Greece. It has daily connections almost year-round to Corfu, Igoumenitsa and Patras, with several a day in the busy summer season. All ferries leave from the Stazione Marittima in the centre of the port. The EPT office has up-to-date schedules and prices. That may not be much help in summer – although the boats run frequently they can be crowded, and it's a good idea in July and August to book before you arrive in Brindisi.

If you do need to buy a boat ticket here, avoid the ticket touts clustered around the train station and the Stazione Marittima. Even the enormous number of agencies in Brindisi offering ferry tickets are notoriously unreliable; it is always advisable to buy tickets from the boat companies or approved agents.

The two most established ferry companies and their main agents in Brindisi are **Adria Shipping SRL**, Corso Garibaldi 112, **t** 0831 523 825, and **HML Ferries**, Corso Garibaldi 8, **t** 0831 528 531. The most reliable agents are **UTAC Viaggi**, Via Santa Lucia 11, **t** 0831 524 921, *www.utacviaggi.it*, and **Grecian Travel**, Corso Garibaldi 79, near the harbour, **t** 0831 568 333.

Between June and September ferries also operate between the port of Otranto and Corfu and Igoumenitsa. They are faster than many Brindisi boats, but more expensive.

Buses from Brindisi to all nearby towns and provincial cities leave from the Viale Porta Pia. **Marozzi**, **t** 0831 521 684, and **Miccolis**, **t** 0831 560 678, operate several buses daily to Rome and Naples respectively, from Lungomare Regina Margherita near the tourist office.

By **road**, the Via Appia (roughly following the modern SS7) reaches its end in Brindisi, as it has done for over 2,000 years. Traffic leaving the port can be very slow in summer, so it is often best to get away from the city along the SS16 to San Vito dei Normanni in the *trulli* country, or along the coast road.

Tourist Information

Brindisi: Piazza Dionisio, off Lungomare Regina Margherita, **t** 0831 523 072. *Open Mon–Fri 8.30–1 and 4–8, Sat 8.30–1.*

Where to Stay and Eat

Brindisi ✉ 72100

Brindisi's hotel-keepers, accustomed to folks staying just overnight while waiting for the boat to Greece, have not been inspired to exert themselves, and there are no really outstanding places in the city.

If you are waiting for a train or ferry, there are any number of passable *pizzerias* and *trattorias* along the Corso Umberto and Corso Garibaldi where you'll find cheap, filling food.

****__Internazionale__, Lungomare Regina Margherita 23, **t** 0831 523 473 (*very expensive*). An older hotel, though well kept and probably the best in Brindisi. Expect grandmotherly furnishings, and maybe you'll get a room with a marble fireplace. It's very convenient for the ferry docks. *Wheelchair accessible.*

***__Barsotti__, Via Cavour 1, **t** 0831 560 877 (*expensive*). A plain, acceptable place near the train station.

Youth Hostel, Via Brandi 2, **t** 0831 413 123, *hostelbrindisi@hotmail.com* (*cheap*). You'll find it 2km to the west of the city centre.

La Lanterna, Via G. Tarantini 14, **t** 0831 564 026 (*expensive*). Behind the Appian Way column in Brindisi, you'll find the city's most elegant restaurant. It mixes traditional and new ways of serving meat, seafood and pasta. *Closed Sun, Aug 10–30.*

Trattoria Pantagruele, Via Salita di Ripalta 1–3, **t** 0831 560 605 (*expensive*). Here you'll find something simpler, but still good. Try to save yourself for the delicious homemade desserts. *Closed Sat lunch and Sun, two weeks in Aug.*

Carovigno ✉ 72012

Giàsotto l'Arco, Corso Vittorio Emmanuele 71, **t** 0831 996 286 (*expensive*). An interesting, traditional restaurant 30km north of Brindisi. Try to book the table on the balcony if you can. *Closed Mon and Sun evenings.*

Lecce

You have to come a long way – to the furthest corner of Puglia and the last city in this book – to find the most beautiful town in southern Italy. Unfortunately for Lecce, its pretty streets and Baroque monuments are currently being drowned in traffic that is worse than Naples'. A distinguished but sleepy university town only a decade ago, Lecce has been transformed almost out of recognition by modern times and a modicum of prosperity. Nevertheless, it is worth a visit. Its history and its tastes have given it a fate and a look different to any other Italian town, and Lecce is the capital of southern Baroque – not the chilly, pompous Baroque of Rome, but a sunny, frivolous style Lecce created on its own.

History

Lecce started as a Messapian town and flourished as the Roman Lupiae, but really only came into its own during the Middle Ages as the centre of a semi-independent county comprising most of the Salentine peninsula. The last Norman king, Tancred, was Count of Lecce, and he favoured the city, founding SS.Nicolò e Cataldo. This is one of the few buildings left from the Middle Ages, but only because Lecce, uniquely among Puglian cities, was prosperous enough to replace them in later centuries when styles changed.

Lecce enjoyed royal favour under the Spaniards in the 16th century and, with its location near the front lines of the continual wars between Habsburg and Turk, Lecce often found itself the centre of attention even though it was not a port. Somehow, during the Spanish centuries, while every other southern city except the royal seat of Naples was in serious decline, Lecce enjoyed a golden age. In these centuries, the city attained distinction in literature and the arts, giving rise to such nicknames as 'The Athens of Puglia'. Lecce also found the wealth to rebuild itself, and the town took the form we see today with the construction of dozens of palaces, churches and public buildings in the city's own distinctive style.

Even though Lecce did well under the Spaniards and Bourbons, its citizens did not seem to enjoy being ruled by them. On the contrary, perhaps more than any other city in Italy, Lecce's resistance to the new order manifested itself in four serious revolts. First, in 1648, came a popular revolution coinciding with Masaniello's revolt in Naples. Like that uprising, it was bloodily repressed by Spanish troops. A second rebellion, in 1734, almost succeeded; the rebels were tricked into submitting by the Bourbons, who offered them reforms that were later withdrawn. In the wake of the French revolution, another revolt occurred and the last came in 1848. The Leccesi also worked hard for the unification of Italy and contributed both men and ideas to the fight.

Piazza Sant'Oronzio

A Baroque city was conceived as a sort of theatre set, with its squares as stages on which decorous gentlemen could promenade. An odd chance has given Lecce's main piazza something even better – a genuine arena right in the middle. In 1901, much to the surprise of the Leccese, workmen digging the basement for a new bank

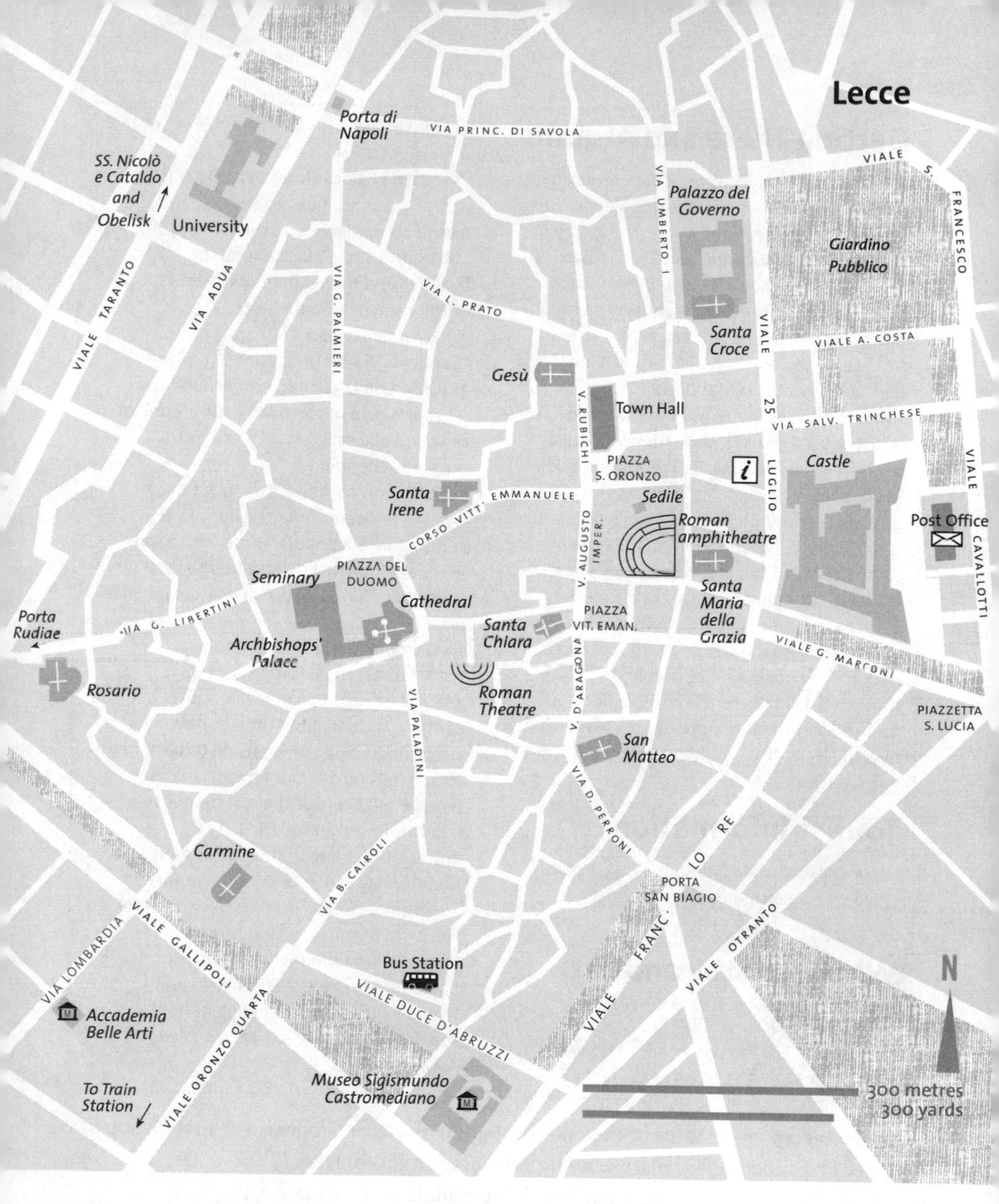

building discovered a **Roman amphitheatre**, with seats for some 15,000, directly under the city centre. In the thirties, the half that lay under the piazza was excavated; occasionally the city uses it for concerts and shows. Only the lower half of the grandstand has survived. The stones of the top levels were probably carted away for other buildings long ago, allowing the rest to become gradually buried and forgotten.

In Brindisi, by the column that marked the end of the Appian Way, there is an empty pedestal of a vanished second column. Lightning toppled that one in 1528, and the Brindisians let it lie until 1661, when the city of Lecce bought it and moved it here,

Getting There and Around

Lecce, despite its location, is well served by **rail**; the city is a terminus for long sleeper runs across Italy via Rome and Milan. These trains also pass through Brindisi, and both towns also have frequent trains heading for Bari or Taranto. In addition, there is always the tired but game **FSE**, **t** 0832 668 233, with services from Lecce to Otranto, Gallipoli and Nardo, Bari, and Taranto via Manduria.

In Lecce, **buses** to towns in the Salentine, run by **STP**, **t** 0832 302 873, leave from Via Adua near the old western walls. **FSE**, Via Torre del Parco, near Porta Napoli, **t** 0832 347 634, connects Lecce with Taranto, from where you can reach other destinations in the region.A company called **Salento in Bus**, *www.salentonline.it*, has regular services between the main towns south of Lecce. It also lays on guided tours of the peninsula. Tickets can be bought from newsagents, bars and tobacconists in the centre of Lecce (look out for the 'SalentoInBus' signs); buses leave from nine different stops round town.

Tourist Information

Lecce: Corso Vittorio Emmanuele 43, **t** 0832 248 092. *Open Mon–Fri 9–1 and 5–7.*

Where to Stay and Eat

Lecce ✉ 73100

Hotels are like the town: quiet, tasteful, restrained. Many of Lecce's restaurants specialize in fish – it's an inland town but the sea is not far away.

*****Patria Palace Hotel**, Piazzetta Riccardi 13, **t** 0832 245 111, **f** 0832 245 002, *www.patriapalacelecce.com* (*luxury*). This comfortable place has all the facilities and many rooms with views of the church of Santa Croce. *Wheelchair accessible.*

Cappello, Via Montegrappa 4, **t** 0832 308 881, **f** 0832 301 535, *hcappello@tin.it* (*cheap*). South of the town centre – one of only two places to stay if you want anything cheaper.

Gino e Gianni, Via Adriatica Km 2, **t** 0832 399 210 (*moderate*). A little out of the centre, this is a popular place with a long list of seafood dishes prepared to local traditions. *Closed Wed, first week in Jan, two weeks in Aug.*

Villa Giovanni Camillo Della Monica, Via S. S. Giacomo e Filippo 40, **t** 0832 458 432 (*cheap*). In a renovated 16th-century *palazzo* along the run-down Via Giacomo e Filippo, this fine restaurant in a marbled courtyard is an oasis of old-world elegance; but the real treat is the beautifully presented food. Try the entrecôte steak with fresh asparagus and Chardonnay sauce, or bream wrapped in aubergine. *Closed Tues, 1–20 Nov and two weeks in July.*

Casareccia, Via Colonnello Archimede Costadura 19, **t** 0832 245 178 (*cheap*). Friendly *trattoria* with excellent home cooking. *Closed Sun eve, Mon and end Aug–early Sept.*

attaching a copper statue of their patron, Sant'Oronzio, or Orontius, the first bishop of Lecce and supposedly a martyr during the persecutions of Nero.

What appears to be a small pavilion in the middle of the square is the **Sedile**, an elegant early masterpiece of the Leccese style (1596) that once served as the town hall. The lovely portico, now glassed in, houses meetings and official functions. Around the square, the church of **Santa Maria della Grazia** is one of its few Baroque buildings that has survived. Much of the rest dates from the Fascist era. Behind Santa Maria is Lecce's **castle**, built by Emperor Charles V, and used to host conferences and exhibitions.

Whenever you see a digital clock, you can thank (or curse) Lecce. A local boy invented them in the twenties, and one of his original models used to stand in this piazza near the Sedile. It must have finally broken, for the city has done away with it.

North of Piazza Sant'Oronzio

The most outrageous Baroque of all awaits along Via Umberto I. **Santa Croce** (*open daily 8–1 and 5–8*) was begun in 1549 but not completed until 1680, giving Lecce's Baroque berserkers a chance at the façade. The original lower half of it was done mainly in a sober Renaissance style: the portal and everything above, however, is a fond fancy of Zimbalo and his colleague Cesare Penna. Among the florid cake-icing decoration, the rose window stands out, made of concentric choirs of tiny angels. Look carefully at the figures on the corbels supporting the second level. Among various cartoon monsters can be made out Romulus' and Remus' she-wolf, a few dragons, a Turk, an African and an equally exotic German. Santa Croce's interior is one of Lecce's best, with beautiful altars in the transept chapels by Penna and Antonio Zimbalo.

Giuseppe Zimbalo designed the **Palazzo del Governo** next door, once a monastery. Behind Santa Croce, the pretty **Giardino Pubblico** marks old Lecce's eastern edge.

South of Piazza Sant'Oronzio

Via Augusto Imperatore (Augustus was in Lecce when he got the news of Julius Caesar's assassination) passes another Baroque church, **Santa Chiara**, and a Salesian convent with a skull and crossbones over the portal – the ultimate Spanish touch. Even better, in a small garden opposite the church there is the most preposterous statue of **Vittorio Emmanuele** in all Italy, surpassing even the bronze colossus on the Altar of the Nation in Rome. This Vittorio is smaller, but the comical contrast between his ponderous moustache and his jaunty stance leaves him looking half like a pirate, half like the leader of a firemen's band. Behind Santa Chiara, in the back streets off Via Paladini, there is a small but well-preserved **Roman theatre**. Finds from the excavation site are displayed in the adjacent **museum** (*open daily 10.30–12.30; adm*).

The next Baroque church is **San Matteo** (1700), one of the last and architecturally the most adventurous of the lot, with an elliptical nave and a complex façade that is convex on the lower level and concave above. Continue straight down Via Perroni and you will come to one of Lecce's fine Baroque town gates, the **Porta San Biagio**.

To prove that this city's curiosities are not all Baroque, we can offer the Neoclassical **War Memorial**, across Piazza Roma near the gate, and off to its right a block of **mansions**, built around the turn of the last century, in a style that imitates the Alhambra in Spain, complete with pointed arches, minarets and Koranic inscriptions.

Just south of the bus station, the **Museo Sigismundo Castromediano** is Lecce's city museum. The founder of this collection was a duke and famous local patriot who fought against the Bourbons and earned long spells in the Neapolitan dungeons. His prison memoirs shocked Europe in the 1850s and moved William Gladstone to a few rousing anti-Bourbon speeches. Duke Sigismundo would no doubt be happy if he could see how his little collection has become the basis of one of the best-arranged and most modern museums in Italy. A corkscrew-shaped ramp through its middle makes it accessible to wheelchair users, and virtually all the exhibits are clearly labelled. The most prized works are some excellent Puglian and Greek vases from all over the

Salentine, although there is also a good collection of medieval art and architectural fragments and a small picture gallery.

Piazza del Duomo

Leaving Piazza Sant'Oronzio by Corso Vittorio Emmanuele, you pass the church of **Santa Irene**, a relatively modest Baroque church of the 1720s, with a splendid statue of the saint above the main portal. If you're not careful, you may miss the little alley off to the left that leads to the **Piazza del Duomo**, one of the finest Baroque architectural groups anywhere, and, as with many of Lecce's historic buildings, recently restored. It was the plan of the designers to keep this square cut off from the life of the city, making it a sort of tranquil stone park; the alley off Corso Vittorio Emmanuele is the only entrance. The kids of the neighbourhood appreciate the plan more than anyone and the piazza has become the most popular football venue in town – one where you can't break any windows or lose the ball.

The **cathedral** (1659–70) is one of the finest works of Giuseppe Zimbalo. To make the building stand out in the L-shaped medieval piazza, the architect gave it two façades: one on the west front and a second, more gloriously ornate one facing the open end of the piazza. The angular, unusually tall **campanile** (240ft), with its simple lines and baby obelisks, echoes the Herreran style of imperial Spain. If you can find someone to let you in, the long climb is worth the trouble, with an exceptional view over the city and most of the Salentine; on a clear day, you can even see Albania.

Adjoining the cathedral are the complementary façades of the **Archbishops' Palace** and the **Seminary**, the latter the work of Giuseppe Cino, a pupil of Zimbalo.

North and West of Piazza del Duomo

Via Libertini passes several good churches, including the unique Rosario (1691–1728), also known as **San Giovanni Battista**, the last and most unusual work of Giuseppe Zimbalo. Just beyond it, the street leaves the city through the **Porta Rudiae**, the most elaborate of the city's gates, bearing yet another statue of Sant'Oronzio. Leading away to the right from here, Via Adua follows the northwestern face of this diamond-shaped city, passing the **University** (the Università Salentina) and some remains of the walls Charles V rebuilt to keep out Turkish corsairs. Further up, at the next gate, the **Porta di Napoli**, you don't need to read Latin to recognize more of Charles' work in the **triumphal arch**, erected in 1548. Most destructive and least modest of monarchs, Charles erected such monuments around the Mediterranean, often after unsuccessful revolts, to remind the people who was boss. This one, featuring crowned screaming eagles and a huge Spanish coat of arms, is a grim reminder of the militaristic, almost totalitarian government with which the Habsburgs tried to conquer Europe. From here broad Via Palmieri leads back toward the cathedral, passing the delightful **Piazzetta Ignazio Falconieri**, which faces a palace decorated with whimsical caryatids and corbels in a style that approaches Art Nouveau.

In a little park in front of the Porta di Napoli, there is an attractive monument to the less grisly, though thoroughly useless King Ferdinand I, called the **Obelisk**. From here,

Leccese Baroque

One critic has called Baroque the 'most expensive style of architecture ever invented'. Considering all the hours of skilled labour it took to carve all those curlicues and rosettes, it's hard to argue. Lecce, like southern Sicily, some parts of Spain, and Malta – all places where southern Baroque styles were well developed – was fortunate to have an inexhaustible supply of a perfect stone. Pietra di Lecce is a kind of sandstone of a warm golden hue, possessing the additional virtues of being extremely easy to carve and becoming hard as granite after a few years in the weather. Almost all of Lecce is built of it, giving the city the appearance of one great, delicately crafted architectural ensemble.

The artists and architects who made Lecce's buildings were almost all local talent, most notably Antonio and Giuseppe Zimbalo, who between them designed many of Lecce's finest buildings in the mid-17th century and carried the style to its wildest extremes. Leccese Baroque does not involve any new forms or structural innovations; the ground plans of the Zimbalos' buildings are more typical of late-Renaissance Italy. The difference is in the decoration, with an emphasis on vertical lines and planes of rusticated stonework, broken by patches of the most intricate and fanciful stonecarving Baroque ever knew. These churches and palaces, along with the hundreds of complementary little details that adorn almost every street – fountains, gates, balconies and monuments – combine to form an elegant and refined cityscape that paradoxically seems all gravity and restraint. Leccese Baroque owes more than a little to Spanish influences, and the city itself still has an air of Spanish reserve about it. As a king of Spain once described a similar Baroque city – Valetta, in Malta – Lecce is a 'town built for gentlemen'.

a road off to the right leads to the city cemetery, home to a tribe of contented cats who pass in and out through a quite elegant 19th-century neoclassical gate. Next to it stands the church of **SS. Nicolò e Cataldo** (*open daily 9–12, also June–Aug Mon–Sat 5–7; earlier afternoon hours the rest of the year*), founded in 1180 by Count Tancred. The façade is typical Baroque, but if you look carefully you will notice that the portal and rose window are much older. Behind the 18th-century front hides one of the best Puglian Romanesque churches, and one of the only medieval monuments to survive in Lecce. The nave and the dome are unusually lofty with a strong Arab-Norman look about them. The carvings on the side portal and elsewhere are especially good, with a discipline and tidiness that is unusual for medieval sculpture. To see them, enter the cemetery (on the left side of the church) and ask for Don Oronzo Marzo.

The Southern Salentine

Italy's furthest southeastern corner is one of the quieter parts of the country. It offers a low, rocky coastline rather like that of the Gargano without the mountains, a number of towns embellished in the Leccese Baroque style, and a lonely beach or two. One of the most noticeable features of the countryside – and this is true for all of the Salentine peninsula – is the eccentricity of the rural architecture. There aren't many modern *trulli* here but you'll find a few of their ancient predecessors, low-domed houses of unknown age, in addition to little houses with flat roofs curled up at the corners, some recent artistic do-it-yourself experiments in cinder-block and many tiny pink Baroque palaces, sitting like jewel-boxes in a prairie landscape of olive trees, tobacco and wildflowers.

The towns here show an almost African austerity, except perhaps **Nardò**, decorated with a lovely square called the Piazza Salandra, in which there is a *guglia* (spire) as frilly as those in Naples; on the same square San Domenico sports a wild, Leccese-style façade. Nardò's much-rebuilt 11th-century cathedral retains some medieval frescoes. Near the town walls on Via Giuseppe Galliano is a strange, unexplained circular temple called the **Osanna**, built in 1603.

Among the other interesting towns and villages around Lecce are **Acaia**, with a romantically ruined Renaissance castle, and **Calimera**, one of the centres of Puglia's tiny Greek community – oddly enough, the town's name means 'good morning' in Greek. Few people anywhere in Puglia still speak Greek, though their thick dialect has led many writers into thinking so. Any Greeks left are more likely to be descendants of 16th-century refugees from Albania than survivors of Magna Grecia.

Nearby **Copertino**, in the early 17th century, was the home of the original flying monk. St Joseph of Copertino, a carpenter's son born in a stable, was a simple fellow, if his many biographers are to be believed, but he got himself canonized for his nearly effortless talent for levitating. Thousands saw him do it, including a king of Poland, the Pope's emissaries and a Protestant German duke, who immediately converted. Joseph's heart is buried under the altar of the little church named after him. The town also has a large Angevin castle.

Galatina

Situated smack in the middle of the Salentine, Galatina is a rambling old town that makes a sort of a living from wine. Its fanciest church is **SS. Pietro e Paolo**, on the main square, with a grand Leccese-style façade outside and clouds of gloom inside. But the real reason for stopping is one of the Mezzogiorno's most unusual artistic treasures, in the Franciscan church of **Santa Caterina**. In 1389, Pope Boniface IX charged the Franciscans with the task of 'Latinizing' the Salentine; even at this late date, most of the peninsula was still strongly Greek in language and religion. They built this church for their convent and made terrible nuisances of themselves by proselytizing the population, but it was left to their French patroness, Marie d'Enghien de Brienne, to pay for the frescoes that would provide the artistic side of the Church's propaganda. Marie was the wife of Raimondello Orsini del Balzo, the most powerful lord in the Salentine (whose tomb can be seen here), although after his death she married Ladislas of Durazzo and became Queen of Naples. No one knows the names of Marie's artists, but most likely they were southerners who had been up north to see the revolutionary new style of painting that was taking shape in Tuscany. The result is a strange marriage of influences – a little Giotto, a little Byzantium. Whoever they were, they had talent and covered the walls of Santa Caterina with an acre or two of scenes that, were it not for their intense southern expressiveness (emphasized by the night-time backgrounds of many of the frescoes), would look perfectly at home in Florence or Assisi.

Tourist Information

Otranto: Piazza Castello, **t** 0836 801 436. *Open 9–1.30, also 4–9 in May–Sept.*

Santa Cesarea Terme: Via Roma 209, **t** 0836 944 043. *Open Mon–Sat 8–2.*

Where to Stay and Eat

Otranto ✉ 73028

There are several modern and pleasant hotels:

★★★**Albania**, Via S. Francesco di Paola 10, **t** 0836 801 877 (*expensive*). A pleasant place. *Wheelchair accessible.*

★★**Miramare**, Viale Lungomare 55, **t** 0836 801 023, **f** 0836 801 024 (*expensive*). Another newish hotel, near the beaches. *Wheelchair accessible.*

Da Sergio, Corso Garibaldi 9, **t** 0836 801 408 (*expensive*). Otranto's best restaurant, even though the Sergio of the title prides himself on having a local clientele and is inclined to be patronizing to foreigners. His father is a fisherman, and the restaurant has good fish. *Closed Wed, Jan and Feb.*

Gallipoli ✉ 73014

Most accommodation is along the outlying beaches. There are some fine modern resort hotels at Baia Verde, on the Via Litoranea to S. Maria di Leuca.

★★★★**Costa Brada**, **t** 0833 202 551, **f** 0833 202 555, *www.grandhotelcostabrada.it* (*expensive*). One of several modern resort hotels, with a good restaurant. Half board obligatory. *Wheelchair accessible.*

★★★**Le Sirenuse**, **t** 0833 202 536, **f** 0833 202 539, *info@attiliocaroli.it* (*expensive*). A typical white Mediterranean palace, also housing a good restaurant. Half board is obligatory.

★★★**Al Pescatore**, Riviera Colombo 39, **t/f** 0833 263 656 (*moderate*). This is the place to stay in the Old Town. Its 16 rooms are set round a pleasant courtyard, while its seafront restaurant draws in the crowds every night.

Il Capriccio, Viale Bovio 14, **t** 0833 261 545 (*expensive*). You can choose from a great variety of seafood dishes here, as well as the local speciality, *orecchiette alla Gallipolina*. *Closed Mon, two weeks in Nov.*

Rossini, Via Lamarmora 25, **t** 0833 573 009 (*expensive*). A fish restaurant with a terrace, along the coastal road towards Porto Cesareo. Specialities include a rich risotto or *gnocchi con crema di gamberetti e rucola*. *Closed Mon.*

Scoglio delle Sirene, Riv. N. Sauro 83, **t** 0833 261 091 (*moderate*). A cheerful seafood *trattoria* overlooking the beach in the Old Town. This is a quiet alternative to the popular string of restaurants behind the castle, where you often have to queue for a table.

Fico d'India, beside the crumbling Torre Uluzzi, north of S. Caterina (*cheap*). A roadside bar which does simple food well: *panini*, salads, and dreamy fruit salad with yoghurt, honey and cinnamon. They stay open late and are a popular venue for live 'world' music.

The first bay, by the entrance, has scenes from the Apocalypse; the second, Genesis; the third, the life of Christ; and the fourth, by the main altar, the life of St Catherine. Some of the best work, though, is in the shadows of the right aisle, a brilliant and eccentric life of Mary. Bring a torch. The grand decorative scheme was never finished; perhaps Marie lost interest when she went to Naples. Consequently, some of the frescoes here are still in the cartoon state (*sinopie* in Italian) and you can see only the artist's sketch of a planned fresco on the bare walls of the church.

Otranto

Readers of Gothic novels might choose to leave Otranto out of their itineraries, but there's no reason to be afraid. Horace Walpole, when he was writing his *Castle of Otranto*, knew nothing about the place; he merely picked the name off a map. There really is a **castle** (***t*** *0805 286 260; open Tues–Sun 9–1 and 4–7*), built by the

Otranto's Mosaic

The best reason for visiting Otranto is the cathedral, begun in the 11th century by the Normans, and the only one in the south to have conserved an entire medieval mosaic pavement. H.V. Morton wrote that coming here felt like 'walking on the Bayeux tapestry'. The vigorous, primitive figures are the work of a priest named Pantaleone, from about 1165. Pantaleone is a Greek name – or Puglian Greek – and we might expect the work of a 12th-century Pantaleone to show some Byzantine influence. Instead what we get is Germanic fancy and anarchy, as if the Norman conquerors had taken pains to make the Italians draw badly, the way they liked it: the pavement really is closer to the Bayeux tapestry than anything in southern Italy.

Whatever the sources of Pantaleone's inspiration, his art is a subtle one, making good use of a limited palette of reds and browns to make a unified composition against the cream-coloured *tesserae* of the background. Three great trees stand at the centre of his composition, supporting small encircled images that encompass all creation: scriptural scenes, fantastic animals, heroes, symbols of the months and seasons. These are 'trees of life', a common motif in early Christian and Islamic art, as well as in Middle Eastern and Germanic mythology – and therefore a perfect symbol for the syncretic, tolerant world of southern Italy under the Normans. All the myriad figures in the mosaic above are connected to their branches, as if to demonstrate the interconnectedness of nature. The trees have a common root, balanced on the backs of two strong elephants; below the one on the right you can see where the artist Pantaleone signed his name in mosaic.

If you look carefully, you can find Alexander the Great (lower right, below Noah's Ark) and King Arthur, *Re Artû*, above the 12 circles with scenes of the *Labours of the Months*, each pictured with its astrological sign. These will teach you a farmer's year, still the same in Puglia and different to anything known in Britain or America: *January, Capricorn*: a man warming himself by the fire.

Aragonese in the 1490s, which in Walpole's times was probably already largely in ruins. It has recently been thoroughly restored and is now used as a meeting point for cultural events. Today Otranto (with the stress on the first syllable, as for most Puglian towns), is an austere and arch-Mediterranean town draped over bare hills, one probably most familiar to outsiders as a better option than Brindisi for ferries to Greece.

Although originally a Messapian settlement, the city first appears in history as Greek Hydruntion, conquered and probably resettled by Taras, and its proud citizens still refer to themselves as *Idruntini*. It rivalled Brindisi as Rome's window on the east, and re-emerged in the 11th century as one of the leading Crusader ports.

Otranto's finest hour came in 1480, during Naples' wars with the Turks and their Venetian allies. According to a delicately embroidered legend, Turkish pirates sacked the city, killing some 12,000 or so and massacring the 800 survivors when they refused to forsake Christianity. The last victim, according to the legend, was the executioner, who declared himself a Christian after witnessing the steadfast faith of the *Idruntini*. The place hasn't

February, Aquarius: a man pouring his water into the pot of a woman who is making *porchetta* (roast pork), just as country women do today.
March, Pisces: a man cleaning his feet (there can't be much to do in March).
April, Aries: a shepherd taking the flocks to summer pasture.
May, Taurus: a woman in costume for the summer festival.
June, Gemini: the grain harvest.
July, Cancer: threshing the grain.
August, Leo: the wine harvest.
September, Virgo: stamping the grapes.
October, Libra: ploughing for next year's crop.
November, Scorpio (as a lizard): woodcutting.
December, Sagittarius: with his arrows, helping the men out with a boar hunt.

The strangest parts are in the choir, which common folk would probably not often see: above the tree of life lies an utterly incomprehensible composition of 16 rings, some with Latin or Arabic inscriptions, enclosing Adam and Eve and fantastical beasts. At the top are King Solomon and the mystic Mermaid (the same one pictured at Monte Sant'Angelo and so many other places in Puglia – *see* **Topics**: 'The Lady and the Dragon', p.23) surrounded by another inscription in Arabic.

Beyond this ensemble, in the apse, the composition dissolves into total anarchy; among the scenes here are Samson and the lion, a King of Nineveh, a serpent crushing a reindeer, prophets and men fishing.

With so much on the floor to wonder at, it's easy to miss the other attractions: a beautiful wooden coffered ceiling and some fine Renaissance carved detail on the pillars and side portal, all done around 1480. The cathedral crypt seems a church in itself, and a museum of columns and capitals; classical Corinthian, Byzantine and medieval among others. Some frescoes can be seen, including a 12th-century Madonna and an exquisite early Renaissance relief of two angels at the rear.

been the same since; only recently, thanks to the tourist ferry business, has Otranto begun to regain some of the importance it had in the Middle Ages.

Across the street from the **cathedral** (*see* box, above), note the plaque on the town hall. It commemorates two local boys who died at Adowa in the unsuccessful campaign to subjugate Ethiopia in 1898. Only Italians could come up with the ironic inscription describing the soldiers as *vittime del dovere*, 'victims of duty'. Not far away in the Old Town, **San Pietro** is the city's oldest church (*key at 1 Piazza del Popolo*); like its Byzantine predecessor it is oriented towards Jerusalem. Another ancient church, now in ruins, can be seen just behind San Pietro, built into the city wall.

Back by the port the town **park** on the seafront is the centre of what action there is in Otranto. In summer, a shuttle bus from here takes visitors around the beaches and to the small wooded lakes up in the hills. For Neolithic fans, a map in the park points you to the local **dolmens** and other monuments – the area around Otranto, especially around the neighbouring villages of **Giurdignano** and **Bagnolo**, probably has a denser population of these than any place in Italy.

Land's End

Along the Adriatic coast south of Otranto, the road passes through some of Puglia's prettiest scenery: limestone cliffs like those of the Gargano, and maquis that seems to be in bloom all the time. There are also plenty of caves, many of which show evidence of Stone Age habitation or later religious uses. The **Grotta Zinzulusa**, hung with stalactites, is probably the best one to visit. Just to the north is a thermal spa, **Santa Cesarea Terme**, built on an old Neo-Moorish bathhouse.

The Salentine's southern tip, not surprisingly, is called **Land's End** – *Finibus Terrae*. The spot is marked by the church of **Santa Maria di Leuca**, built over the ruins of a temple of Minerva that must have been a familiar landmark to all ancient mariners. The church's altar stone fulfilled the same purpose in the original temple. As at the Land's Ends of Celtic Europe, this corner of the Salentine has a few standing stones and *dolmens* left from the days of the Messapians or earlier. The most important Neolithic monument is the **Centopietre** – 'Hundred Stones' – near the village of **Patù**; it is a small temple of two aisles divided by columns, with flat stone slabs for a roof.

Gallipoli

Gallipoli, along with its namesake on the Hellespont, was once thought of highly by somebody; the name comes from the Greek *kalli polis*, or 'beautiful city'. The name still fits. Whitewashed and resolutely cheerful, the Old Quarter still has a Greek air about it, with houses scoured by the sea air and fishermen folding their nets in the port. Children bounce around the narrow steets while their mothers boil *orecchiete* with the doors and windows wide open, stopping now and then to stand in the doorway and talk to the neighbours across the way.

The oldest part of town, once an island, is now bound to the mainland by a short causeway. At the landward end stands the **nymphaion**, a trough-like fountain that is decorated with classical fragments: caryatids and badly faded mythological reliefs. Across the causeway, the huge **castle** with squat rounded bastions dates back in part to the Byzantines. Lately the town has put it to use as an open-air cinema. Just up the *corso*, there is a Baroque **cathedral** that would look right at home in Lecce; behind the well-frosted façade, though, is a light and airy interior – quite shipshape, as churches in old port towns often seem to be.

Gallipoli has the best sort of **museum** (*open mid-June–mid-Sept Mon–Sat 9.30–12.30 and 5–8, mid-Sept–mid-June 9–1 and 4–7*), on Via De Pace – nothing pretentious, nothing even labelled, but good fun, in a big atrium lined with dusty bookshelves and full of cutlasses, whalebones, old cannonballs, coins, amphorae, an arrow from Tierra del Fuego and even a crocodile skeleton.

Elsewhere around old Gallipoli, you will find a couple of old olive presses, still ready for use and, by the beach on the back side of town, the delightful little church of **Santa Maria della Purità**, with a floor of painted ceramic tiles and almost naïve paintings of Judith and Holofernes, and Moses parting the waters.

Further Reading

General and Travel

Cerio, Edwin, *The Masque of Capri* (Thomas Nelson, 1957). A lively account of the magic island, its history and the many odd characters who have washed up on its shore.

Douglas, Norman, *Old Calabria* (Phoenix, 2001). Reprint of a 1915 travel classic.

Gissing, George, *By the Ionian Sea: Notes of a Ramble in Southern Italy* (Lost and Found Series, Signal Books, 2004) A VIctorian novelist slogs through the Mezzogiorno in the 1890's.

Morton, H. V., *A Traveller in Southern Italy* (Methuen, 2002). Another readable and delightful travel classic from the 60's.

History

Acton, Harold, *The Bourbons of Naples* (Prion, 1998). Bourbon nostalgia, in an-depth study of Naples' last kings.

Behan, Tom, *See Naples and Die* (IB Tauris, 2002). A thorough account of the Camorra that names names; the roots go deeper than you think.

Brown, Gordon, *The Norman Conquest of Southern Italy and Sicily* (McFarland, 2003).

Ginsborg, Paul, *A History of Contemporary Italy: Society and Politics 1943–1988* (Penguin, 1990). A good modern account of national events since the fall of Mussolini, with many insights on the south.

Hamilton, Lady Emma, *Memoirs of Emma, Lady Hamilton: The Friend of Lord Nelson, and the Court of Naples* (University Press of the Pacific, 2001).

Lewis, Norman, *Naples '44* (William Collins, 1978) First-rate writing, and an unforgettable, horrific vision of the beginning of the Allied occupation by a British intelligence officer who was there.

Loud, Graham, *The Age of Robert Guiscard* (Medieval World Series, Longman, 2000). Tells the story of Guiscard's remarkable career, and gives the context of the Norman takeover and the new world it created.

Lumley, Robert (ed.), *The New History of the Italian South: Mezzogiorno Revisited* (University of Exeter Press, 1997). A collection of essays with new interpretations of the south's curious destiny and how it came to be.

Rea, Ermanno, *A Mystery in Naples* (Guernica Editions 2003) A compelling account of the turbulent and squalid Neapolitan political scene of the 50's and 60's.

Art and Literature

Gotze, Heinz, *Castel del Monte: Geometric Marvel of the Middle Ages* (Prestel, 1998). An exploration of Frederick II's architectural masterpiece and its cultural influences.

Leach, Eleanor Winsor, *The Social Life of Painting in Ancient Rome and on the Bay of Naples* (Cambridge University Press, 2004). A view of daily life and social relations in the ancient world through its art.

Levi, Carlo, *Christ Stopped at Eboli* (Penguin, 2000). Disturbing post-war account of the author's time in the Basilicata.

Food

Amandonico, Nikko, *La Pizza: The True Story From Naples* (Mitchell Beazley Food Series, 2004). The spirit of Naples evoked through its food, with some good recipes.

Glossary

acroterion: decorative protrusion on the rooftop of an Etruscan, Greek or Roman temple. At the corners of the roof they are called *antefixes*.

ambones: twin pulpits (singular: ambo), often elaborately decorated.

ambulatory: an aisle around the apse of a church.

atrium: entrance court of a Roman house or early church.

badia: an abbey or abbey church; also known as *abbazia*.

baldacchino: baldachin, a columned stone canopy above the altar of a church.

basilica: a rectangular building, usually divided into three aisles by rows of columns; Roman Christians adapted it for their early churches.

borgo: from the Saxon burh of S. Spirito in Rome, a suburb or village.

Bucchero ware: black, delicately thin Etruscan ceramics, usually incised or painted.

Calvary chapels: a series of outdoor chapels, usually on a hillside, that commemorate the stages of the Passion of Christ.

campanile: a bell tower.

campanilismo: local patriotism; the Italians' own word for their historic tendency to be more faithful to their home towns than to the abstract idea of 'Italy'.

campo santo: a cemetery.

cardo: the transverse street of a Roman castrum-shaped (q.v.) city.

carroccio: a wagon carrying the banners of a medieval city and an altar; it served as the rallying point in battles.

cartoon: the preliminary sketch for a fresco or tapestry.

caryatid: supporting pillar or column carved into a standing female form; male versions are called *telamones*.

castrum: a Roman military camp, always neatly rectangular, with straight streets and gates at the cardinal points. Later the Romans founded or refounded cities in this form, hundreds of which survive today (Aosta, Florence, Brescia, Ascoli Piceno and Ancona are clear examples).

cavea: the semi-circle of seats in a classical theatre.

Cenacolo: fresco of the Last Supper, often on the wall of a monastery refectory.

chiaroscuro: the arrangement or treatment of light and dark areas in a painting.

ciborium: a tabernacle; the word is often used for large, freestanding tabernacles, or in the sense of a *baldacchino* (q.v.).

comune: commune, or commonwealth, referring to the governments of the free cities of the Middle Ages. Today it denotes any local government, down to the smallest village.

condottiere: the leader of a band of mercenaries in late medieval and Renaissance times.

confraternity: a religious lay brotherhood, often serving as a neighbourhood mutual aid and burial society, or following some specific charitable work.

contrapposto: the dramatic but rather unnatural twist in a statue, especially in a Mannerist or Baroque work, derived from Hellenistic and Roman art.

convento: a convent or monastery.

Cosmati work (or *Cosmatesque*): referring to a distinctive style of inlaid marble or enamel chips used in architectural decoration (pavements, pulpits, paschal candlesticks, etc.) in medieval Italy. The Cosmati family of Rome were its greatest practitioners.

cupola: a dome.

decumanus: street of a Roman castrum-shaped (q.v.) city that runs parallel to the longer axis; the central, main avenue is called the *decumanus major*.

Dodecapolis: the federation of the 12 largest and strongest Etruscan city-states.

duomo: cathedral.

ex voto: an offering (such as a terracotta figurine, painting, medallion, silver bauble, or whatever) made in thanksgiving to a god or Christian saint; the practice has always been present in Italy.

forum: the central square of a Roman town, with its most important temples and public buildings. It means 'outside'; the original Roman Forum was outside the city walls.

fresco: wall painting, the most important Italian medium of art since Etruscan times. It isn't easy; first the artist draws the *sinopia* (q.v.) on the wall. This is covered with plaster, but only a little at a time, as the paint must be on the plaster before it dries.

Ghibellines (*see* Guelphs): one of the two great medieval parties, supporters of the Holy Roman emperors.

gonfalon: the banner of a medieval free city; the *gonfaloniere*, or flag-bearer, was often the most important public official.

graffito: originally, the incised decoration on buildings, walls, etc.; only lately has it come to mean casually scribbled messages in public places.

Greek cross: in the floor plans of churches, a cross with equal arms. The more familiar plan, with one arm extended to form a nave, is called a Latin Cross.

grisaille: painting or fresco in monochrome.

grotesques: carved or painted faces used in Etruscan and later Roman decoration; Raphael and other artists rediscovered them in the 'grotto' of Nero's Golden House in Rome.

Guelphs (*see* Ghibellines): the other great political faction of medieval Italy, supporters of the Pope.

intarsia: decorative inlaid wood or marble.

loggia: an open-sided gallery or arcade.

lunette: semicircular space on a wall, above a door or under vaulting, either filled by a window or a mural painting.

matroneum: the elevated women's gallery around the nave of an early church, a custom adopted from the Byzantines in the 6th and 7th centuries.

narthex: the enclosed porch of a church.

palazzo: not just a palace, but any large, important building (though the word comes from the Imperial *palatium* on Rome's Palatine Hill).

Pantocrator: Christ 'ruler of all', a common subject for apse paintings and mosaics in areas influenced by Byzantine art.

pieve: a parish church.

pluteo: screen, usually of marble, between two columns, often highly decorated.

podestà: in medieval cities, an official sent by the Holy Roman emperors to take charge; their power, or lack of it, depended on the strength of the *comune*.

predella: smaller paintings on panels below the main subject of a painted altarpiece.

presepe: a Christmas crib.

putti: flocks of plaster cherubs with rosy cheeks and bums that infested much of Italy in the Baroque era.

quattrocento: the 1400s – the Italian way of referring to centuries (*duecento, trecento, quattrocento, cinquecento*, etc.).

sbandieratore: flag-thrower in medieval costume at an Italian festival; also called an *alfiere*.

sinopia: the layout of a fresco (q.v.), etched by the artist on the wall before the plaster is applied. Often these are works of art in their own right.

stele: a vertical funeral stone.

stigmata: a miraculous simulation of the bleeding wounds of Christ, appearing in holy men like St Francis in the 12th century, and Padre Pio of Puglia in our own time.

telamon: *see* caryatid.

thermae: Roman baths.

tondo: round relief, painting or terracotta.

transenna: marble screen separating the altar area from the rest of an early Christian church.

triptych: a painting, especially an altarpiece, in three sections.

trompe l'œil: art that uses perspective effects to deceive the eye – for example, to create the illusion of depth on a flat surface, or to make columns and arches painted on a wall seem real.

tympanum: the semicircular space, often bearing a painting or relief, above the portal of a church.

voussoir: one of the stones of an arch.

Language

The fathers of modern Italian were Dante, Manzoni and television. Each played its part in creating a national language from an infinity of regional and local dialects. The Florentine Dante was the first to write in the vernacular, while Manzoni's revolutionary novel, *I Promessi Sposi*, heightened national consciousness by using an everyday language all could understand in the 19th century.

Television in the last few decades has performed an even more spectacular linguistic unification; although many Italians still speak a dialect at home, school and work, their TV idols insist on proper Italian.

Italians are not especially apt at learning other languages. English lessons, however, have been the rage for years, and at most hotels and restaurants there will be someone who speaks some English. In small towns and other out-of-the-way places, finding an Anglophone may prove more difficult. The words and phrases below should help you out in most situations, but the ideal way to come to Italy is with some Italian under your belt. Your visit will be richer, and you're much more likely to make some Italian friends.

Pronunciation

Italian words are pronounced phonetically. Every vowel and consonant except 'h' is sounded. Consonants are the same as in English, with the following exceptions.

The *c*, when followed by an 'e' or 'i', is pronounced like the English 'ch' (*cinque* thus becomes cheen-quay). Italian *g* is also soft before 'i' or 'e' as in *gira*, or jee-rah. *Z* is pronounced like 'ts'.

The consonants *sc* before the vowels 'i' or 'e' become like the English 'sh, as in sci, pronounced 'shee'. The combination *ch* is pronouced like a 'k', as in *Chianti*, 'kee-an-tee'. The combination *gn is pronounced* as 'nya' (thus *bagno* is pronounced ban-yo). The combination *gli* is pronounced like the middle of the word million (so *Castiglione* is pronounced Ca-steel-yoh-nay).

Vowels are pronounced as follows: *A* is as in English *father*. *E* when unstressed is said like 'a' in *fate* (as in *mele*); when stressed, it can be the same or like the 'e' in *pet* (*bello*). *I* is like the 'i' in *machine*. *O*, like 'e', has two sounds, 'o' as in *hope* when unstressed (*tacchino*), and usually 'o' as in *rock* when stressed (*morte*). *U* is pronounced like the 'u' in *June*.

The stress usually (but not always) falls on the penultimate syllable. Accents indicate if it falls elsewhere (as in *città*). Also note that in the big northern cities, the informal way of addressing someone as you, *tu*, is widely used; the more formal *lei* or *voi* is commonly used in provincial districts, *voi* more in the south.

Useful Words and Phrases

yes/no/maybe *sì/no/forse*
I don't know *Non (lo) so*
I don't understand (Italian) *Non capisco (l'italiano)*
Does someone here speak English? *C'è qualcuno qui che parla inglese?*
Speak slowly *Parla lentamente*
Could you assist me? *Potrebbe aiutarmi?*
Help! *Aiuto!*
Please *Per favore*
Thank you (very much) *Grazie (molte/mille)*
You're welcome *Prego*
It doesn't matter *Non importa*
All right *Va bene*
Excuse me/I'm sorry *Permesso/Mi scusi/Mi dispiace*
Be careful! *Attenzione!/Attento!*
Nothing *Niente*
It is urgent! *È urgente!*
How are you? *Come sta?*
Well, and you? *Bene, e Lei?/e tu?*
What is your name? *Come si chiama?/Come ti chiami*
Hello *Salve or ciao (both informal)*

Good morning *Buongiorno (formal hello)*
Good afternoon, evening *Buonasera*
Good night *Buonanotte*
Goodbye *Arrivederla (formal), Arrivederci/Ciao, (informal)*
What do you call this in Italian? *Come si chiama questo in italiano?*
What?/Who?/Where? *Che?/Chi?/Dove?*
When?/Why? *Quando?/Perché?*
How? *Come?*
How much (does it cost?) *Quanto (costa)?*
I am lost *Mi sono perso*
I am hungry/thirsty/sleepy *Ho fame/sete/sonno*
I am sorry *Mi dispiace*
I am tired *Sono stanco*
I feel unwell *Mi sento male*
Leave me alone *Lusciami in pace*
good/bad *buono/cattivo*
well/badly *bene/male*
hot/cold *caldo/freddo*
slow/fast *lento/rapido*
up/down *su/giù*
big/small *grande/piccolo*
here/there *qui/lì*

Days

Monday *lunedì*
Tuesday *martedì*
Wednesday *mercoledì*
Thursday *giovedì*
Friday *venerdì*
Saturday *sabato*
Sunday *domenica*
holidays *festivi*
weekdays *feriali*

Numbers

one *uno/una*
two/three/four *due/tre/quattro*
five/six/seven *cinque/sei/sette*
eight/nine/ten *otto/nove/dieci*
eleven/twelve *undici/dodici*
thirteen/fourteen *tredici/quattordici*
fifteen/sixteen *quindici/sedici*
seventeen/eighteen *diciassette/diciotto*
nineteen *diciannove*
twenty *venti*
twenty-one/twenty-two *ventuno/ventidue*
thirty *trenta*
forty *quaranta*
fifty *cinquanta*
sixty *sessanta*
seventy *settanta*
eighty *ottanta*
ninety *novanta*
one hundred *cento*
one hundred and one *centouno*
two hundred *duecento*
one thousand *mille*
two thousand *duemila*
one million *un milione*

Time

What time is it? *Che ore sono?*
day/week *giorno/settimana*
month *mese*
morning/afternoon *mattina/pomeriggio*
evening *sera*
yesterday *ieri*
today *oggi*
tomorrow *domani*
soon *fra poco*
later *dopo/più tardi*
It is too early/late *È troppo presto/tardi*

Public Transport

airport *aeroporto*
bus stop *fermata*
bus/coach *autobus*
railway station *stazione ferroviaria*
train *treno*
platform *binario*
taxi *tassì/taxi*
ticket *biglietto*
customs *dogana*
seat (reserved) *posto (prenotato)*

Travel Directions

One (two) ticket(s) to xxx, please *Un biglietto (due biglietti) per xxx, per favore*
one way *semplice/andata*
return *andata e ritorno*
first/second class *prima/seconda classe*
I want to go to... *Desidero andare a...*
How can I get to...? *Come posso andare a...?*
Do you stop at...? *Si ferma a...?*
Where is...? *Dov'è...?*

How far is it to...? *Quanto è lontano...?*
What is the name of this station? *Come si chiama questa stazione?*
When does the next ... leave? *Quando parte il prossimo...?*
From where does it leave? *Da dove parte?*
How much is the fare? *Quant'è il biglietto?*
Have a good trip! *Buon viaggio!*

Driving

near/far *vicino/lontano*
left/right *sinistra/destra*
straight ahead *sempre dritto*
forwards/backwards *avanti/indietro*
north/south *nord/sud*
east *est/oriente*
west *ovest/occidente*
crossroads *bivio*
street/road *strada/via*
square *piazza*
car hire *autonoleggio*
motorbike/scooter/moped *motocicletta/vespa/motorino*
bicycle *bicicletta*
petrol/diesel *benzina/gasolio*
garage *garage*
This doesn't work *Questo non funziona*
mechanic *meccanico*
map/town plan *carta/pianta*
Where is the road to...? *Dov'è la strada per...?*
breakdown *guasto*
driving licence *patente di guida*
driver *guidatore*
speed *velocità*
danger *pericolo*
parking *parcheggio*
no parking *sosta vietata*
narrow *stretto*
bridge *ponte*
toll *pedaggio*
slow down *rallentare*

Shopping, Services, Sightseeing

I would like... *Vorrei...*
Where is/are...? *Dov'è/Dove sono...?*
How much is it? *Quanto costa?*
open/closed *aperto/chiuso*
cheap/expensive *a buon prezzo/caro*
bank *banca*
beach *spiaggia*
bed *letto*
church *chiesa*
entrance/exit *ingresso/uscita*
hospital *ospedale*
money *soldi*
newspaper *giornale*
pharmacy *farmacia*
police station *commissariato*
policeman *poliziotto*
post office *ufficio postale*
sea *mare*
shop *negozio*
room *camera*
tobacco shop *tabaccaio*
WC *toilette/bagno/servizi*
men *signori/uomini*
women *signore/donne*

Useful Hotel Vocabulary

I'd like a double room please *Vorrei una camera doppia (matrimoniale), per favore*
I'd like a single room please *Vorrei una camera singola, per favore*
with/without bath *con/senza bagno*
for two nights *per due notti*
We are leaving tomorrow morning *Partiamo domani mattina*
May I see the room, please? *Posso vedere la camera, per cortesia?*
Is there a room with a balcony? *C'è una camera con balcone?*
There isn't (aren't) any hot water, soap, *Manca/Mancano acqua calda, sapone,*
...light, toilet paper, towels *...luce, carta igienica, asciugamani*
May I pay by credit card? *Posso pagare con carta di credito?*
May I see another room please? *Per favore, potrei vedere un'altra camera?*
Fine, I'll take it *Bene, la prendo*
Is breakfast included? *E' compresa la prima colazione?*
What time do you serve breakfast? *A che ora è la colazione?*
How do I get to the town centre? *Come posso raggiungere il centro città?*

Index

Main page references are in **bold**. Page references to maps are in *italics*.

Bay of Naples & Southern Italy touring atlas

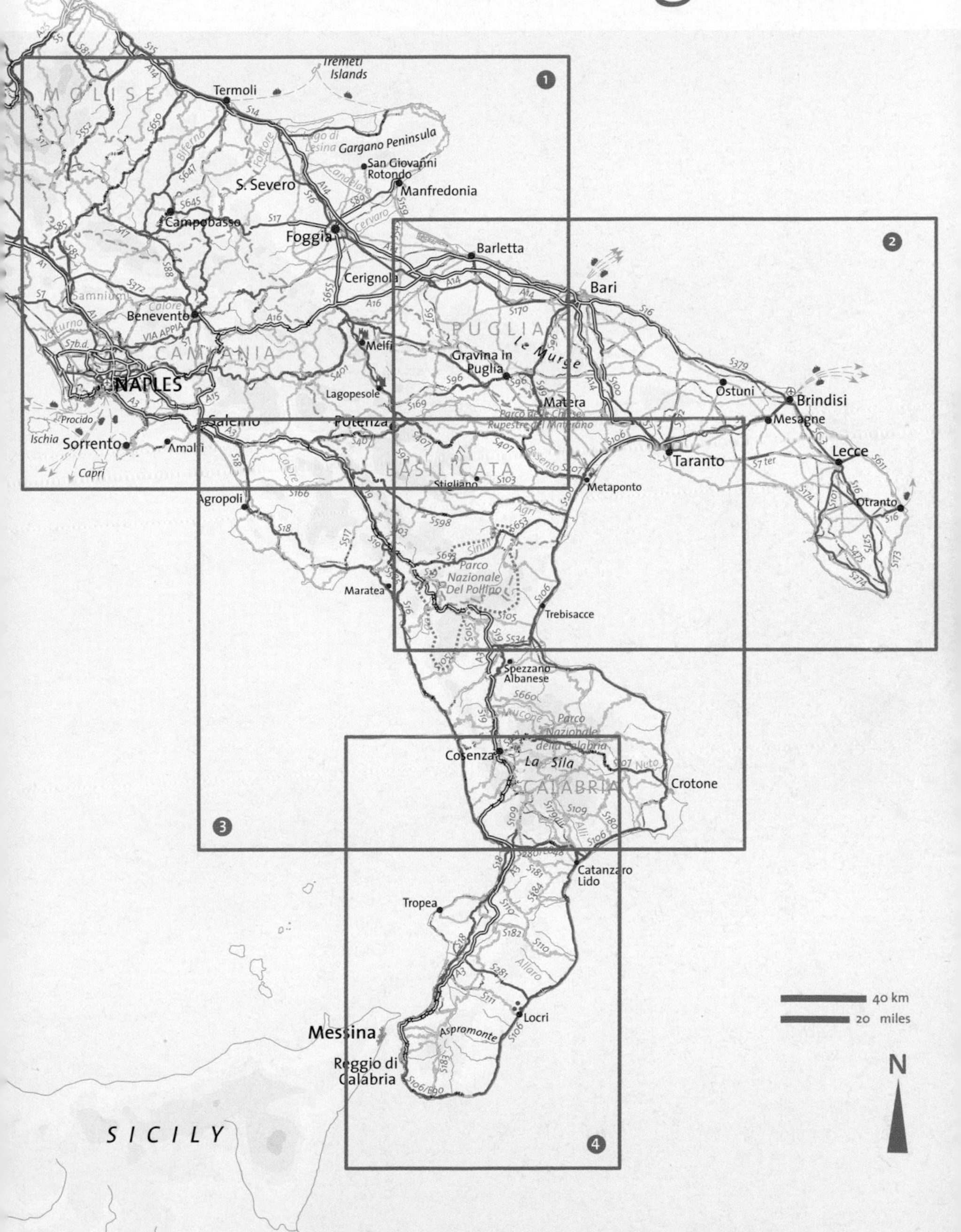

Vasto
Sulmona
Termoli
MOLISE
Larino
Serracapriola
Santa Croce di Magliano
Isernia
Castelnuovo d. Daunia
Campobasso
Cantalupo nel Sanno
Lucera
Troia
Piedimonte Matese
Morcone
Volturno
Guardia Sanframondi
Bivio di Reino
Buonalbergo
Ariano Irpino
Sessa Aurunca
Samnium
Telese
Calore
Pignataro Magg.
Caiazzo
Frasso Telesino
Cautano
Benevento
S. Angelo in Formis
Limatola
Casertavecchia
Capua
S. Agata de' Goti
San Gregorio d. Sannio
Grottaminada
Santa Maria Capua Vettere
Caserta
Airola
Montesarchio
Maddaloni
VIA APPIA
Marcianise
Sta Maria a Vico
Cervinara
Prata
CAMPANIA
Cicciano
Baiano
Monte Vergine
Mercogliano
Atripalda
Marigliano
Nola
Avellino
Lago d'Averno
Cumae
Pozzuoli
Solfatara
NAPLES
Montella
Monte Nuovo
Lago de Fusaro
Agnano
Mount Vesuvius
Solofra
Monte Terminio
Porto Vecchio
Baia
Bacoli
Herculaneum
Ercolano
Palau
Capo Miseno
Pompeii
Nocera Inferiore
Torre Annunziata
Nocera Sup.
Ischia Porto
Procida
Forio
Ischia
Ischia Ponte
Montecorvino
Castellammare di Stabia
Cava de'Tirreni
Campagna
Salerno
Camaldoli
Vico Equense
Monte Faito
Minori
Maiori
Scala
Vietri sul Mare
Fuorni
Amalfi
Ravello
Cetara
Pontecagnano
Eboli
Sorrento
Positano
Atrani
Conca del Marini
Battipaglia
Massa Lubrense
Furore Gorge
Grotto Smeralda
Calore
Cagliari
Palermo
I. Stromboli
Anacapri
Monte Solaro
Capri Town
Marina Piccola
Capri
Castelcivita
Grotta di Castelcivita
Sele
A1
A3
A14
A15
A16
A30
S7
S7b
S7b.d.
S17
S18
S372
S552
S650
S647
S645
S81
S85
S87
S88
Biferno
Fortore

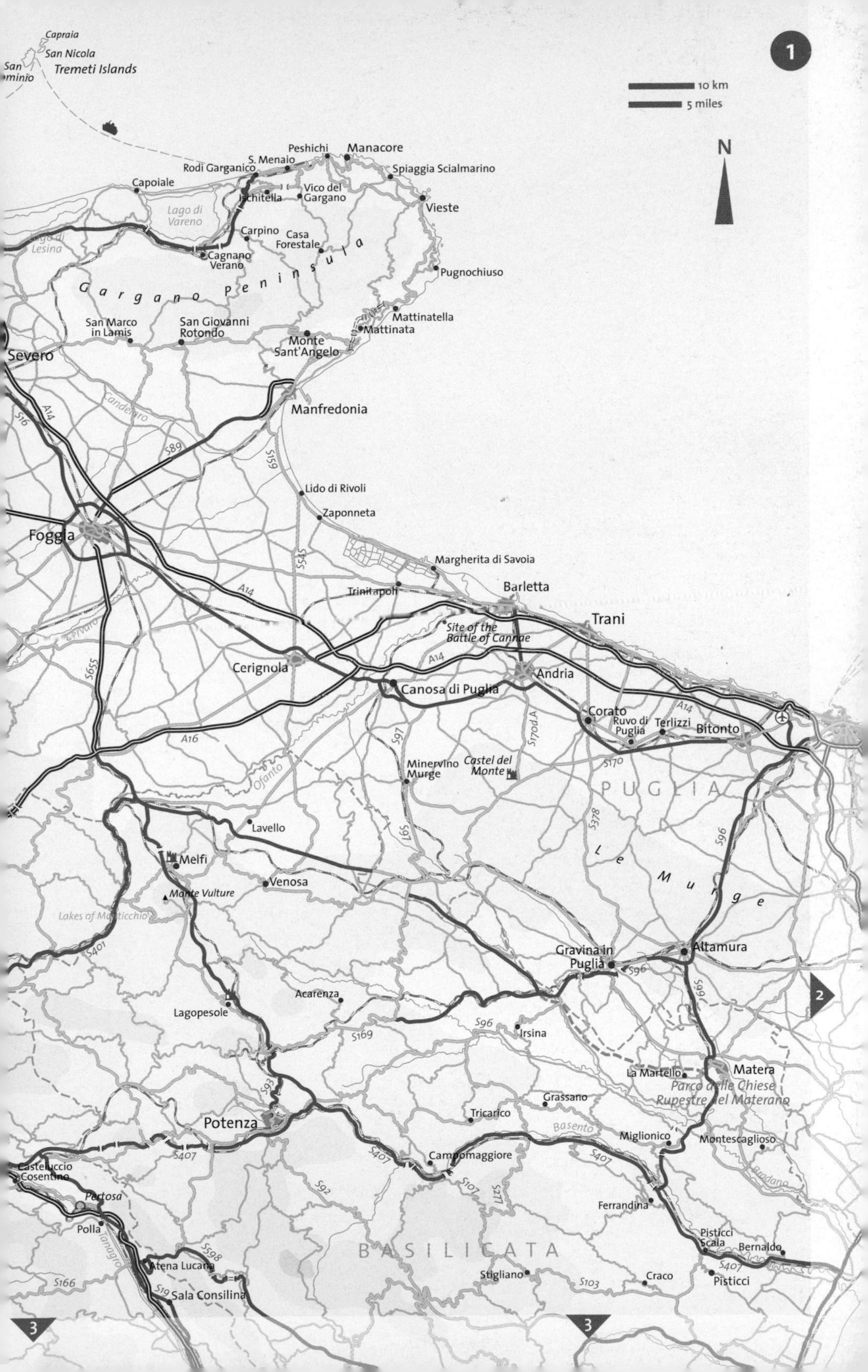

1

10 km
5 miles
N

Capraia
San Nicola
San Domino
Tremeti Islands

Peshichi
Manacore
S. Menaio
Rodi Garganico
Spiaggia Scialmarino
Capoiale
Ischitella
Vico del Gargano
Vieste
Lago di Vareno
Carpino
Casa Forestale
Lago di Lesina
Cagnano Verano
Pugnochiuso
Gargano Peninsula
Mattinatella
Mattinata
San Marco in Lamis
San Giovanni Rotondo
Monte Sant'Angelo
Severo
Manfredonia
Candelaro
A14
S16
S89
S159
Lido di Rivoli
Zaponneta
Foggia
S545
Margherita di Savoia
Trinitapoli
Barletta
A14
Trani
Site of the Battle of Cannae
Cervaro
S655
Cerignola
A14
Andria
Canosa di Puglia
Corato
A14
Ruvo di Puglia
Terlizzi
Bitonto
S97
S170d.A
A16
S170
Minervino Murge
Castel del Monte
Ofanto
PUGLIA
S378
Lavello
S97
S96
Melfi
Le Murge
Venosa
Monte Vulture
Lakes of Monticchio
S401
Gravina in Puglia
S96
Altamura
S655
2
Acarenza
Lagopesole
S96
Irsina
S169
La Martella
Matera
Parco delle Chiese Rupestre del Materano
S93
Grassano
Tricarico
Potenza
Basento
Miglionico
Montescaglioso
S407
S407
Campomaggiore
S407
Castelluccio Cosentino
Bradano
Pertosa
S92
S107
S277
Ferrandina
Polla
Tanagro
Pisticci Scala
Bernaldo
BASILICATA
S598
Atena Lucana
S407
Stigliano
Craco
Pisticci
S166
S103
S19
Sala Consilina
3
3

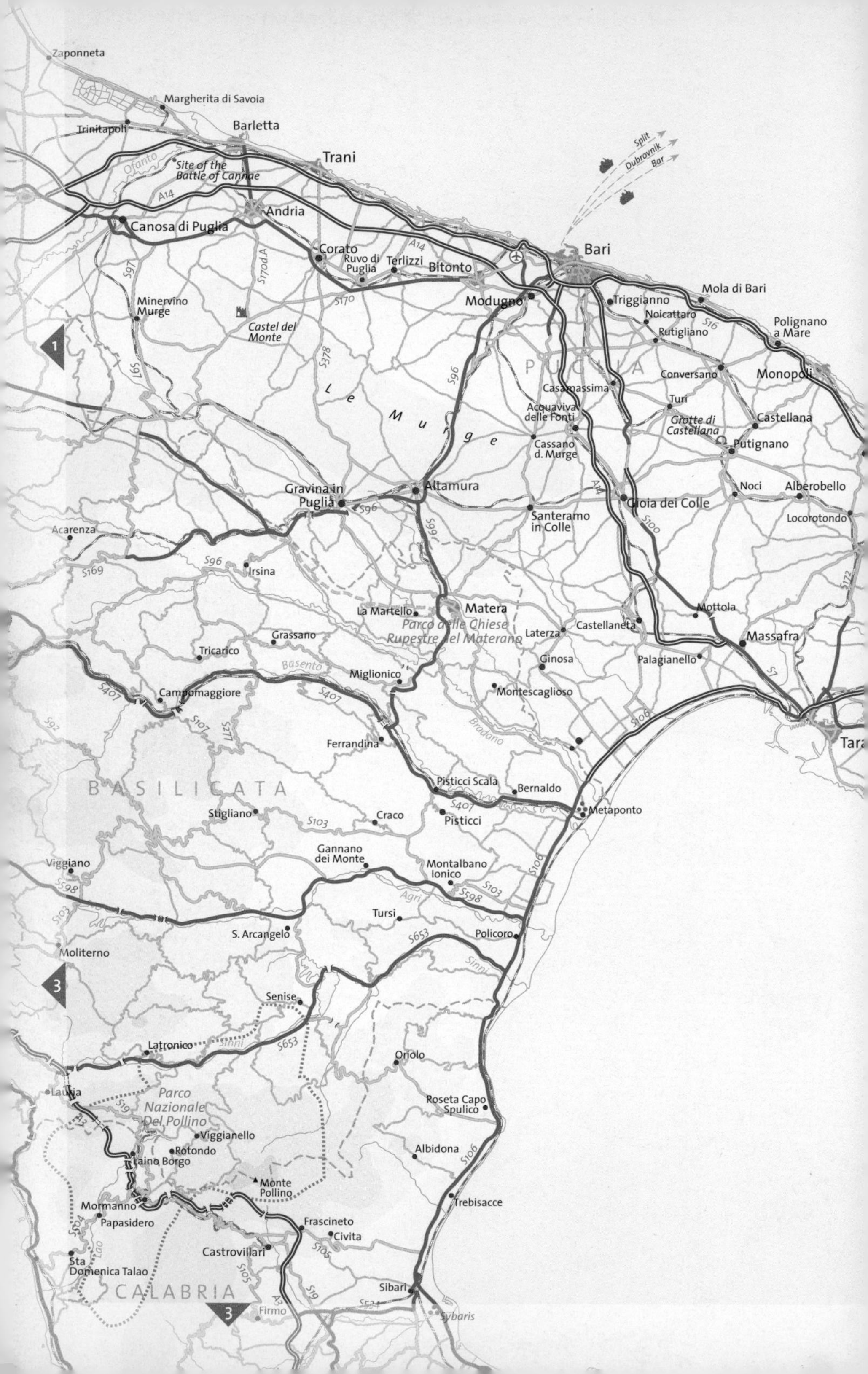

Zaponneta
Margherita di Savoia
Trinitapoli
Barletta
Split
Dubrovnik
Bar
Trani
Ofanto
Site of the Battle of Cannae
A14
Andria
Canosa di Puglia
Corato
Ruvo di Puglia
Terlizzi
Bitonto
Bari
Modugno
S97
S170d.A
S170
Minervino Murge
Castel del Monte
Triggianno
Mola di Bari
Noicattaro
Rutigliano
S16
Polignano a Mare
1
S378
S96
P U G L I A
Conversano
Monopoli
Casamassima
Le Murge
Turi
Acquaviva delle Fonti
Grotte di Castellana
Castellana
Cassano d. Murge
Putignano
Gravina in Puglia
Altamura
A14
Noci
Alberobello
Gioia dei Colle
Santeramo in Colle
Locorotondo
S96
S99
S100
Acarenza
S169
Irsina
S172
La Martello
Matera
Mottola
Parco delle Chiese Rupestre del Materano
Castellaneta
Laterza
Massafra
Grassano
Tricarico
Ginosa
Palagianello
Basento
Miglionico
S7
S407
Campomaggiore
Montescaglioso
S106
S107
S277
Bradano
S92
Ferrandina
Tara
B A S I L I C A T A
Pisticci Scala
Bernaldo
S407
Metaponto
Stigliano
Craco
Pisticci
S103
Gannano dei Monte
Montalbano Ionico
Viggiano
S106
S598
S103
Agri
S598
S103
Tursi
S. Arcangelo
S653
Policoro
Moliterno
Sinni
3
Senise
Latronico
Sinni
S653
Oriolo
Lauria
Parco Nazionale Del Pollino
Roseta Capo Spulico
S19
A3
Viggianello
Rotondo
Albidona
Laino Borgo
S106
Monte Pollino
Trebisacce
Mormanno
S504
Papasidero
Frascineto
Civita
Castrovillari
S105
Lao
Sta Domenica Talao
S105
C A L A B R I A
S19
A3
Sibari
S534
3
Firmo
Sybaris

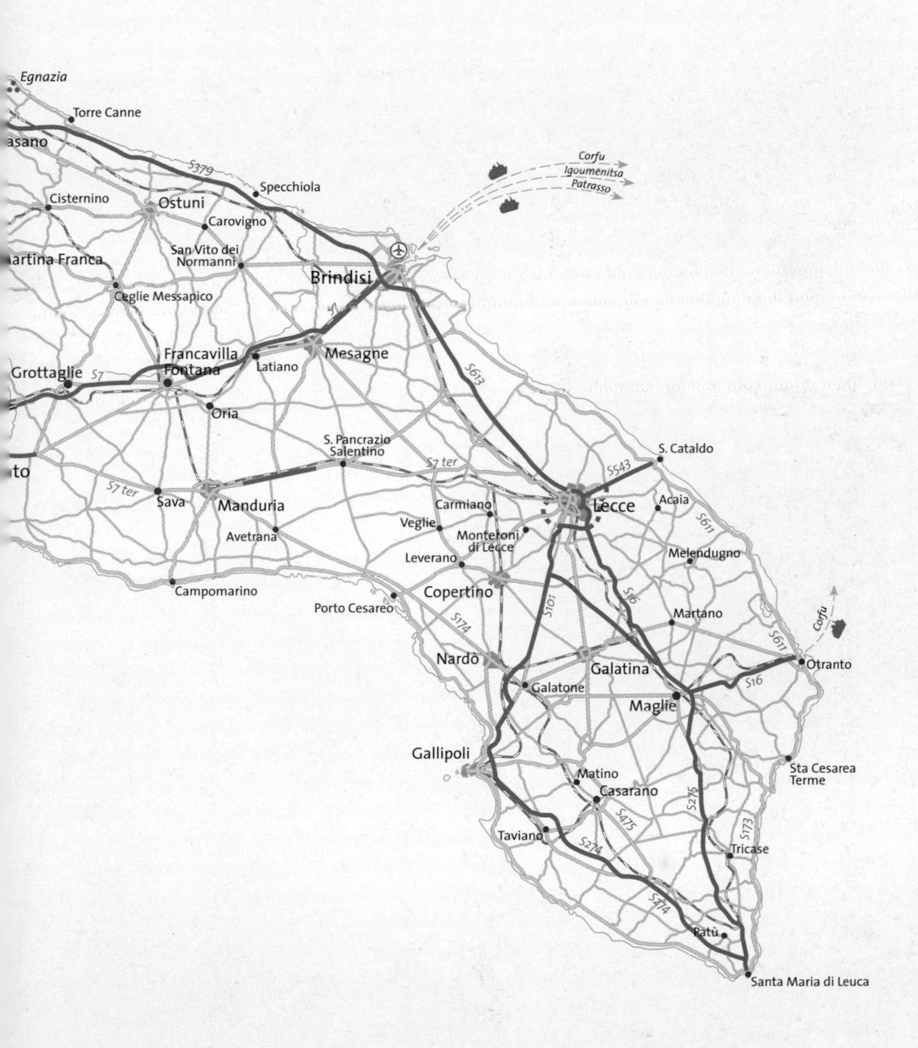

10 km
5 miles
N
Egnazia
Torre Canne
asano
S379
Specchiola
Cisternino
Ostuni
Carovigno
San Vito dei Normanni
artina Franca
Brindisi
Corfu
Igoumenitsa
Patrasso
Ceglie Messapico
Francavilla Fontana
Latiano
Mesagne
Grottaglie
S7
Oria
S613
S. Pancrazio Salentino
S7 ter
S. Cataldo
S543
nto
S7 ter
Sava
Manduria
Carmiano
Lecce
Acaia
Veglie
Monteroni di Lecce
Avetrana
S611
Leverano
Melendugno
Campomarino
Copertino
Porto Cesareo
S101
S16
Martano
S174
Corfu
S611
Nardò
Galatina
Otranto
Galatone
S16
Maglie
Gallipoli
Sta Cesarea Terme
Matino
Casarano
S275
S475
S173
Taviano
S274
Tricase
S274
Patù
Santa Maria di Leuca

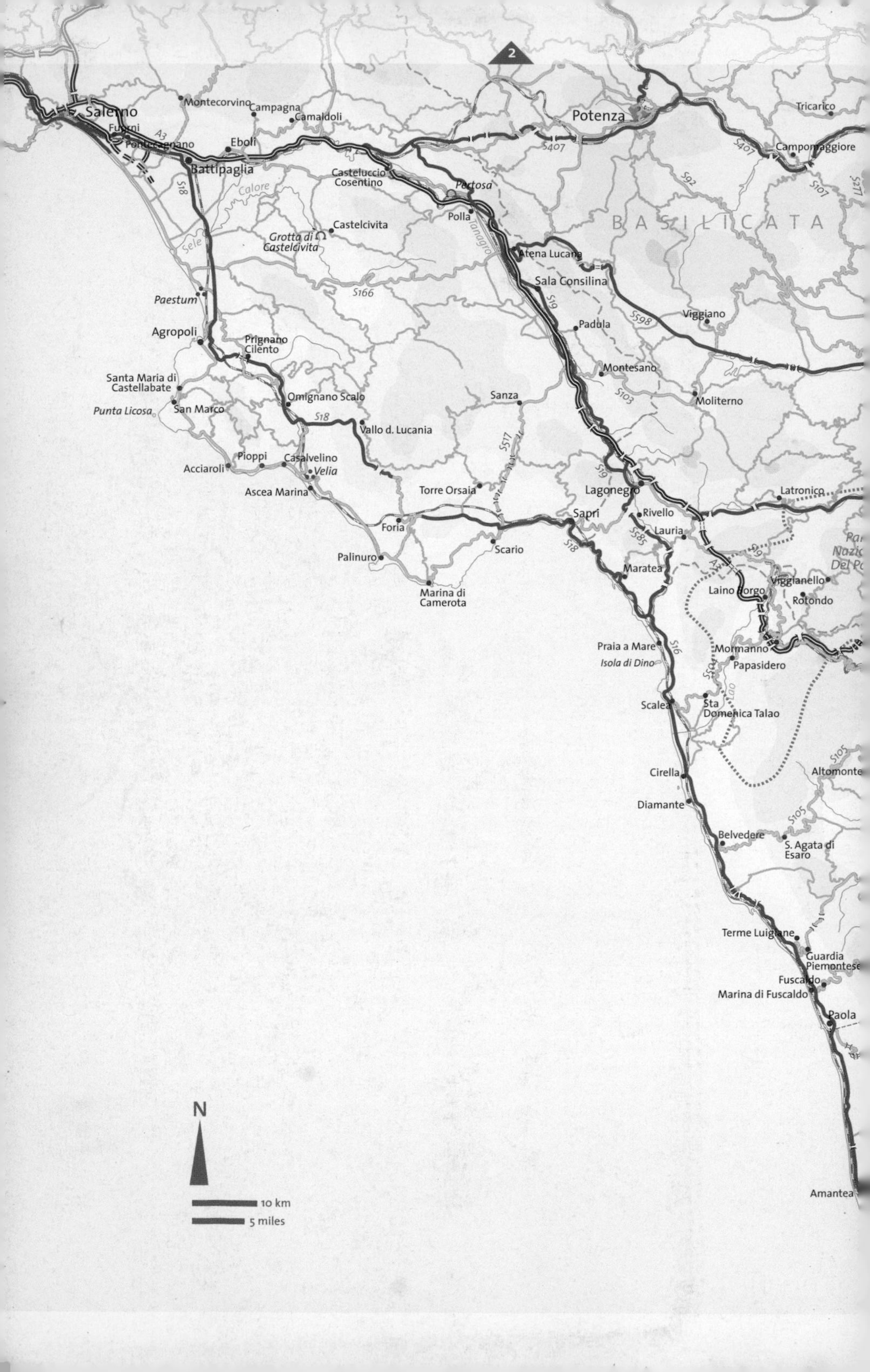
2
Salerno
Montecorvino
Campagna
Camaldoli
Potenza
Tricarico
Fuorni
Pontecagnano
A3
Eboli
Battipaglia
S407
Campomaggiore
S92
S107
Castelluccio
Cosentino
Pertosa
Polla
Calore
S18
BASILICATA
Castelcivita
Grotta di
Castelcivita
Tanagro
Sele
Atena Lucana
Sala Consilina
S166
S19
Paestum
Viggiano
S598
Padula
Agropoli
Prignano
Cilento
Montesano
Santa Maria di
Castellabate
Moliterno
Omignano Scalo
S103
Sanza
Punta Licosa
San Marco
S18
Vallo d. Lucania
S517
Pioppi
Casalvelino
Acciaroli
Velia
S19
Ascea Marina
Torre Orsaia
Lagonegro
Latronico
Sapri
Rivello
Foria
Lauria
S585
Scario
S18
Palinuro
Maratea
Marina di
Camerota
Laino Borgo
Viggianello
Rotondo
Praia a Mare
S18
Mormanno
Isola di Dino
Papasidero
Lao
Scalea
Sta
Domenica Talao
S105
Altomonte
Cirella
Diamante
S105
Belvedere
S. Agata di
Esaro
Terme Luigiane
Guardia
Piemontese
Fuscaldo
Marina di Fuscaldo
Paola
N
10 km
5 miles
Amantea

3
2
Grassano
Basento
Miglionico
Ginosa
Palagianello
Massafra
Grottaglie
Francavilla Fontana
Oria
Montescaglioso
S407
Ferrandina
S106
S7
S172
Taranto
Sava
S7 ter
Manduria
Pisticci Scala
Bernaldo
Stigliano
S103
Craco
Pisticci
Metaponto
Campomarino
Gannano dei Monte
Montalbano Ionico
Agri
S598
Tursi
S. Arcangelo
Policoro
S653
Sinni
Senise
Oriolo
Roseta Capo Spulico
Albidona
Monte Pollino
Trebisacce
Frascineto
Civita
S105
Castrovillari
S19
Sibari
Firmo
A3
S534
Sybaris
Spezzano Albanese
Terranova da Sibari
Roggiano Gravina
Corigliano
Rossano
San Demetrio Corone
Cropalati
Monte Christa d'Acri
Cariati
Bisignano
Acri
CALABRIA
Crucoli Torretta
S660
Mucone
Longobucco
S106ter
Parco Nazionale della Calabria
Lake Cecita
Cirò Marina
S177
Camigliatello Sil.
Lese
Savelli
Moccone
S107
Melissa
Torre Melissa
Rende
Strongoli
Marina di Strongoli
Cosenza
Lake Arvo
Arvo
San Giovanni in Flore
La Sila
Neto
Cotronei
Sta Severina
Bocca du Piazza
S108bis
Petilia Policastro
Crotone
Tirivolo
Villaggio Racise
Villaggio Mancuso
S179dir
Savuto
Cape Colonne
Cutro
S109
S180
Nocera Terinese
Isola di Capo Rizzuto
Alli
Nicastro
Lamezio Terme
Tiriolo
4
Catanzaro
S280/E848
Cape Rizzuto

4

3

10 km
5 miles
N

Paola
Rende
Cosenza
Moccone
Savelli
Lese
S107
Lake Arvo
Arvo
San Giovanni in Flore
La Sila
Parco Nazionale della Calabria
Cotronei
S108bis
Bocca du Piazza
Petilia Policastro
Tirivolo
Villaggio Racise
Villaggio Mancuso
S179dir
Amantea
Savuto
Nocera Terinese
S109
S19
S180
Alli
Nicastro
Lamezio Terme
Tiriolo
Catanzaro
S106
S280/E848
S18
A3
Maida
S181
S384
Girifalco
Catanzaro Lido
Filadelfia
CALABRIA
Pizzo
Briatico
Vibo Marina
Soverato
Chiaravalle Centrale
Tropea
Vibo Valentia
S. Nicola da Crissa
S110
Cape Vaticano
Mileto
S182
Serra San Bruno
Nicotera
Arena
Mareptamo
Guardavalle
Bivongi
Stilo
Rosarno
S536
Prateria
Sto Todaro
Riace
Monasterace Marina
S281
Gioia Tauro
Cinquefrondi
Polistena
Popelli
Allaro
Caulonia
S111
Cittanova
Mammola
Palmi
Taurianova
Marro
Roccella Ionica
Marina di Gioiosa Ionica
Oppido Mamertina
Gerace
Cosoleto
Scilla
S. Eufemia d'Aspromonte
Locri
Villa S. Giovanni
S670
Cippo Garibaldi
Locri Epizefiri
Aspromonte
Messina
S184
Gambarie
Santuario di Polsa
Santo Stefano
Montalto
Arasi
Reggio di Calabria
S Agata
La Verde
Bianco
Roccaforte del Greco
Pollaro
Bova
Bocale
S183
Chorio
Amendolea
Brancaleone Marina
S106/E90
Saline Ioniche
Melito di Porto Salvo
Condofuri Marina
Stracia